Securitisation

Securitisation

Edited by:

David C. Bonsall   MA, LLM (Cantab)

Partner, Freshfields

Butterworths
London, Boston, Dublin, Edinburgh, Hato Rey,
Kuala Lumpur, Singapore, Sydney, Toronto, Wellington
1990

United Kingdom	Butterworth & Co (Publishers) Ltd, 88 Kingsway, London WC2B 6AB and 4 Hill Street, EDINBURGH EH2 3JZ
Australia	Butterworths Pty Ltd, SYDNEY, MELBOURNE, BRISBANE, ADELAIDE, PERTH, CANBERRA and HOBART
Canada	Butterworths Canada Ltd, TORONTO and VANCOUVER
Ireland	Butterworth (Ireland) Ltd, DUBLIN
Malaysia	Malayan Law Journal Sdn Bhd, KUALA LUMPUR
New Zealand	Butterworths of New Zealand Ltd, WELLINGTON and AUCKLAND
Puerto Rico	Equity de Puerto Rico, Inc, HATO REY
Singapore	Malayan Law Journal Pte Ltd, SINGAPORE
USA	Butterworth Legal Publishers, AUSTIN, Texas; BOSTON, Massachusetts; CLEARWATER, Florida (D & S Publishers); ORFORD, New Hampshire (Equity Publishing); ST PAUL, Minnesota; and SEATTLE, Washington

A CIP Catalogue record for this book is available from the British Library.

ISBN 0 406 11722 5

Printed by Mackays of Chatham PLC, Chatham, Kent

Preface

Securitisation appears to be the latest in a long line of inventions spawned by the decade of the eighties. Will it just be a passing phase to be remembered with fondness by investment bankers and lawyers or is it here to stay as a worthwhile technique meeting a genuine need in the financial markets? I and many others believe the latter is, and will continue to be, true. Securitisation is not a gimmick—rather, it is a financial tool which can lead to greater efficiency and better management of risk without compromising other desirable commercial objectives.

As the pace of the financial markets continually quickens and the regulatory constraints on lenders increase, it will become more important for all users of the financial markets to have a clear understanding of their short and long term objectives and the tools available to help achieve them. It is likely that securitisation will develop in different ways in different countries. The experience of the United States has not been merely duplicated in the United Kingdom. Similarly, France and other countries such as Australia are devising their own format to meet specific economic needs. Nevertheless, while individual countries, industries and issuers will all have different objectives and concerns and different means of meeting them according to their own regulatory and economic environment, universal lessons and principles can be drawn from the experiences of those who have so far used this tool of securitisation.

This book has been written by actual practitioners in the market who have had to grapple with the problems and devise products which are acceptable to investors and issuers. Most of the authors have seen how securitisation operates in the United Kingdom where the assets securitised to date have been residential mortgages. Unlike the United States, there is no government sponsored system for securitisation and no new legislation has been passed (as in France) to assist the process. In a sense, therefore, the United Kingdom has seen a 'purer' form of securitisation. In the space of less than three years securities totalling more than £6 billion have been issued. Various issuing structures have been used and a range of new mortgage products has been devised to meet the changing needs of borrowers. The market is mature and developing. The lessons learned in the United Kingdom from these transactions should be relevant in many other jurisdictions even where the legal and regulatory systems are different.

Many people (including potential investors) who have heard of securitisation but not experienced it are put off by its complexity. Undoubtedly the transactions are complicated and demanding but the objective of this book is to remove some of the mystery from the process. It has been written with the aim of providing a better understanding of what securitisation can provide and what it means on a practical basis. The book commences with an overview of the development of securitisation to date. An analysis of legal and tax aspects follows to enable readers to understand the manner in which legal theory and commercial objectives can be reconciled. Three chapters then discuss, from the perspective of different types of lenders, how securitisation can help. After a review by a merchant banker of the market, the rating agencies explain their approach to asset-backed debt. An insurance company and a professional trustee then explain their separate views of securitisation, followed by a discussion of various current issues which are being hotly debated in the United Kingdom. The accounting treatment of securitisation is then analysed before the securitisation of non-mortgage assets is discussed. The penultimate chapter considers securitisation in France and its new legal regime before the final chapter discusses the pressures and trends which are likely to develop in international financial markets in the coming months and years. The appendices contain a summary of all public UK transactions to date, the Bank of England's paper on loan transfers and securitisation (reproduced with their kind permission) and the Statement of Practice on transfers of mortgages issued by the United Kingdom Department of Environment (reproduced with their kind permission).

I hope this book will be of value to current and future practitioners and investors in the financial markets, to observers of these markets and, particularly, to those who are considering securitisation but who want a better understanding of what it will involve.

I would like to express my gratitude to all the contributors who have so willingly given their time—I hope that they will regard the final product as a worthwhile justification of their efforts. I must also thank the publishers for their enthusiasm, realism and patience in the preparation of this work.

David C. Bonsall
December 1989

Contributors

Kenneth Cox

Ken Cox is a Director of Baring Brothers & Co Limited. He has been in banking for over 20 years in a variety of capacities spanning the lending, capital markets and corporate finance areas both domestically and internationally. He has been committed to securitisation for over four years in what he describes as a love/hate relationship but which he will still admit on occasion to being one of the most stimulating and interesting challenges he has had to date.

He hopes to retire before the final maturity date of his first securitisation.

David Bonsall

David Bonsall is a partner in Freshfields, one of the largest London law firms. After graduate and post-graduate law degrees at Cambridge University, he joined Freshfields in 1979 and became a partner in 1987.

He has been involved in a wide range of corporate finance and capital markets transactions, both domestic and international. In the last five years he has gained particular experience in securitisations and structured financings, advising both issuers and lead managers. He has written several articles on securitisation and has spoken at many conferences in London and New York.

He is married to a solicitor and they have one daughter. His other interests include golf, skiing, travel and music.

Ben Staveley

Ben Staveley joined Freshfields as an articled clerk in 1979 and has been working in the Freshfields tax department since 1980. He became a partner in 1987 and since then has concentrated to some extent on capital markets work.

He has a Master of Arts degree in law from Cambridge University and is an Associate of The Institute of Taxation.

Robert Weir

Robert Weir, 41, is Executive Director and Head of Trading and Treasury Operations of Household Mortgage Corporation PLC.

Prior to joining HMC he was Group Treasurer of Debenhams PLC, and Managing Director of Welbeck Treasury Services. He has also worked for Peat Marwick Mitchell & Co.

He is a Fellow of the Institute of Chartered Accountants and a member of the Association of Corporate Treasurers.

Bruce Gaitskell

Bruce Gaitskell, 35, is currently Chief Executive of Mortgages PLC and a Director of CIBC Mortgages PLC (both subsidiaries of Canadian Imperial Bank of Commerce), where he is responsible for capital markets and strategic planning.

Previously, he was Controller—Securitisation for The National Home Loans Corporation PLC where he was responsible for the UK's first rated mortgage-backed security and first senior/subordinate structure.

At CIBC he project managed the first mortgage-backed ECP transaction in the UK and is currently working on the securitisation of other types of asset. He is also engaged in securitisation consultancy in the UK and overseas.

Robert Neill

Robert Neill is the Managing Director of Leamington Spa Building Society. He originally joined the Society in 1977 as Computer Manager, moving into general management in 1983. He was appointed Chief Executive in 1986 and Managing Director in 1987.

He has previously worked for Burroughs Machines as an Account Manager, and Courtaulds as a research chemist.

He has a Bachelor of Science degree in chemistry from University College, London.

His hobbies include bridge and chess.

Paul Orchart

Paul Orchart is a Director of S. G. Warburg & Co Ltd, specialising in UK corporate finance both in the banking and capital markets. He joined Warburg in 1985 and has tended to specialise in asset-backed financing, particularly in the area of mortgages, whilst retaining certain responsibilities for business development with a variety of UK companies.

Prior to joining Warburg, he worked at Chemical Bank, Northern Trust and Midland Montagu. Apart from working in the UK, he spent periods of time in New York and Chicago, working principally with multi-national companies.

He has a Master of Arts degree in geography from Cambridge University.

Lionel Marsland-Shaw

Lionel Marsland-Shaw joined the London office of Standard & Poor's Corporation in 1987 and is directly involved in the rating of international asset-backed financings.

Prior to joining Standard & Poor's Corporation he spent over 16 years in various roles in the banking and financial sector, concentrating on credit analysis, including both corporate and consumer finance, syndicated credits and leasing.

Donald Selzer

Donald Selzer is an Assistant Vice President with Moody's Investors Service Ltd's Structured Finance Group (London). He is in charge of the analysis of UK mortgage- and asset-backed transactions, and is also involved in the analysis of structured transactions originated in other European countries.

His previous experience includes the analysis of collateralised mortgage obligations and US 'whole loan' residential mortgage pass-throughs.

Stephen Haines

Stephen Haines is currently with Commercial Union, having a corporate finance role in Commercial Union Wholesale Funding Limited.

Prior to joining Commercial Union he has worked for Morgan Grenfell, and for Chase Manhattan Bank as a product specialist in corporate trust.

He has Master of Arts degrees in political science from the University of Freiburg im Breisgau, and in theology from Cambridge University.

Tony Buckland and Julie Craik

Tony Buckland is the Managing Director of Bankers Trustee Co Limited.

Julie Craik is an Associate Director of Bankers Trustee Co Limited and Product Manager of asset-backed trustee products.

Bankers Trustee Co Limited is part of Bankers Trust Company.

Nigel Terrington

Nigel Terrington, 30, has been with the National Home Loans Group since September 1987.

He was recently appointed Group Treasurer and is responsible for all funding, both off- and on-balance sheet, relationship management and risk management. He is also a Director of National Mortgage Bank PLC. Prior to this position, Nigel was Divisional Director, Structured Financing, with responsibility for the structuring and execution of all off-balance sheet transactions and their on-going management, together with the acquisition of asset-backed portfolios from third parties.

Prior to joining NHL, he spent five years with Union Bank of Switzerland, London Branch, where he was responsible for the financial services sector.

Nigel is an Associate of the Chartered Institute of Bankers.

Michael Wildig

Michael Wildig, an economics graduate and Chartered Accountant, is a partner in the Financial Markets Group of Arthur Andersen & Co in London.

He leads the London Office Securitisation Group and is a member of Arthur Andersen & Co's worldwide financial services team providing advice to major clients on the significant global changes that are taking place in the financial markets.

He speaks and writes regularly on financial industry topics.

Joseph Smallman

Joseph D. Smallman is currently the Executive Manager of Asset-backed Securitisation for the Australia and New Zealand Banking Group and is a leading authority on securitisation.

He started his career 12 years ago with Century 21 Aid Realty structuring specialised financing for real estate acquisition. Subsequently, he formed Mortgage Brokers Incorporated which established a secondary owner-originated mortgage market. In 1987 he commenced an in-depth study at the London School of Economics on the complexities of global securitisation, which resulted in him becoming the first recipient of the Postgraduate Studentship in Business Administration.

Mr Smallman has acted as a consultant to a wide range of organisations, including some of the major investment banks. In addition to his consulting, he has lectured extensively on securitisation, his most recent lecture series being given at Cambridge University.

Michael Selby

Dr Michael J. P. Selby is currently Reader in Accounting and Finance at the London School of Economics.

Since the mid-sixties he has worked primarily as a management consultant in most aspects of financial analysis and corporate planning, in both the public and private sectors. In addition to his industrial career, he has held academic positions in Europe, Australia and the United States.

His prime research and teaching activities lie in the fields of contingent claims analysis and risk management. In particular, the development, pricing and hedging of financial instruments employing options and futures, as well as the development of management information systems for the purpose of managing overall risk positions.

He has published widely in the field of finance and is an Associate Editor of 'Mathematical Finance'.

Michel Quéré

Michel Quéré, Conseil Juridique, is a partner in Freshfields' Paris office. He has particular experience in corporate finance and international financing. He is also experienced in company law, new financial instruments, international leasing transactions, contract and mining law.

He is the author of various articles on international leasing and in the fields of capital markets and take-over bids and acquisitions of companies in France.

He has a Bachelor of Arts degree in law from the University of Kent at Canterbury and a Maitrise en Droit from Universite de Paris XI.

John Van Deventer

John Van Deventer is an Executive Director of Goldman Sachs International Limited. He has been with Goldman Sachs since 1986.

Prior to joining Goldman Sachs, he was an attorney with a practice in the corporate, securities and tax areas.

He is a graduate of Yale University and holds a Juris Doctor degree from the University of Virginia.

Contents

Chapter 1

Introduction and Overview

Kenneth Cox
Baring Brothers & Co Limited

At the end of a decade which has seen the introduction of some remarkable new techniques in the world's financial markets and even more remarkable 'jargon' used to describe the more visible transactions, it is somewhat surprising that the word 'securitisation' does not yet feature in any of the recognised dictionaries of the English language. Or is it so surprising? After all, what is securitisation? To the reader who has read more than one of the small number of books that have been published to date on the subject, there might seem to be a certain amount of confusion as to the real meaning. And what is new anyway about asset-backed financings when history records that the Prussians were issuing mortgage-backed bonds over two centuries ago?

The casual user of the word often has in mind some form of asset refinancing, probably in order to achieve matched funding of the asset to maturity and off-balance sheet treatment for the asset under current accounting rules. To the investor it spells both opportunity and difficulty: opportunity through the ability to invest in an attractive and different instrument or range of instruments but difficulty in dealing with an inevitably more complicated structure with perhaps less certainty of cash flow than conventional securities. Professional advisors will tell you exactly what the true definition really is from which you will rapidly discern that, of course, it is exactly the very thing that is needed for your business!

To some extent, each is right. But what does it mean to the man in the street—to the individual who has, to date in the United Kingdom, been responsible for shouldering the burden of most of the debt which the financial markets have used as a guinea pig for their financial engineering skills? Nothing!

That is hardly surprising, of course, since there is an aura of mystery and technical complexity surrounding securitisation that can be quite daunting even to the most experienced treasurer or financier. Yet a careful review of any specific transaction will reveal a perfectly logical approach to minimising the individual risks associated with that transaction in order to protect issuer and investor alike. Some financial journalists and others with a peripheral knowledge of securitisation have raised concerns that the impact on the individual will be negative. To date in the United Kingdom these doubts have mainly been raised in relation to the transfer of mortgage obligations to unknown third parties.

In my view, these concerns are almost entirely baseless and stem largely from an inherent mistrust of the financial community's intentions and a lack of understanding of the detailed workings of particular schemes. If anything, the situation is the reverse. As the reader will see from other chapters in this book, the process of securitisation calls for a rigorous examination of all parts of the business which is the subject of securitisation. In the course of that examination, it is generally found that improvements can and must be made to a significant number of procedures which benefit not only the 'securitiser' but also (although perhaps less obviously) the individual borrower. After all, is the implementation of a strict arrears policy that bad? I suspect that, if we were to apply to our private financial affairs the principles which we rigorously adhere to on a daily basis in our capacity as financial advisors or practitioners, we could only agree that it is not!

But I digress. This book is intended to provide a comprehensive introduction to, and review of, securitisation in the United Kingdom, its development, the current situation and possible future applications. Any introduction should set the scene for what follows and in order to do that we must first settle on a definition for securitisation and then examine briefly the events in the United States which led to the emergence of this product in the United Kingdom.

The authors of the various chapters of this book would probably agree on a basic definition of securitisation as the process under which pools of individual loans or receivables are packaged, underwritten and distributed to investors in the form of securities. These securities are collateralised by the assets themselves and/or the cashflows arising therefrom which represent the primary source of repayment to the investor. This is the definition which we will be using throughout the book. Many of the techniques which have been developed in the course of securitisation (such as credit enhancement) lend themselves to similar transactions where pools of loans are packaged and sold or transferred to other purchasers but without the use of securities and intermediaries to underwrite them. Such transactions would not fall within this definition of the word since they do not create marketable or transferable securities. Nevertheless, many practitioners would take the view that the effect of such schemes is often the same for the purchaser and the vendor as a true securitisation and frequently, therefore, such schemes may be referred to as securitisation arrangements.

Having defined securitisation, the next most frequently asked question is 'What led to the sudden development of this new securitisation market?' Not unnaturally, most of us would respond that it was due to a number of different factors. That is true to some extent but there is one single reason why it suddenly became possible—the desktop computer. For the first time significant computing power was made available to the financial engineers working in investment and merchant banks and in their clients' finance departments. Most importantly, it was made available to them in a form which was readily usable and could be accessed at their convenience. It was no longer a case of having to ask the data processing department to write a program which then had to be run on the mainframe at a convenient early hour of the morning after the previous day's batch run had been finally completed. It was available on the spot and it was cheap, so that all of the young mathematicians could have their own machine. Huge leaps in the scope and volume of numerical analysis were made possible as bigger and faster machines were made available.

The financial markets had, therefore, been provided with an enormous technological advance in terms of the ability to analyse and structure highly sophisticated and sensitive transactions thus underpinning the flow of new ideas. The market's development, however, cannot be attributed solely to the infamous personal computer. That certainly made it possible, but there were other driving forces at play which led to the growth of the market. These were most apparent in the United States during the 1970s and early 1980s and led to the development of financial techniques which have subsequently been adopted world-wide. It is worth examining briefly, therefore, the events in the United States which led up to this sudden surge of activity.

The first modern securitisations were carried out in the early 1970s when the United States Government National Mortgage Association (GNMA or 'Ginnie Mae') began to issue mortgage pass-through certificates. Other agencies such as the Federal Home Loan Mortgage Corporation (FHLMC or 'Freddie Mac') and the Federal National Mortgage Association (FNMA or 'Fannie Mae') promptly followed suit and the United States market developed rapidly thereafter beyond agency-related transactions into the private sector. The existence of these government agencies empowered to insure loans made by private lenders and to guarantee principal and interest on securities issued by other lenders simplified the whole process of structuring suitable securities backed by pools of mortgages. At the same time, the process of packaging and selling mortgage loans provided significant benefits to the mortgage originators themselves.

The United States markets had been inefficient for a long time in two specific areas. First, partly because of interstate banking regulation, there had long been a mis-match between the demand for mortgage loans (typically strongest in the southern and western states) and the supply of funding which historically had lain with the east coast banks and financial institutions. Simply stated, a bank is not allowed by law to lend money outside its own state boundaries even though there may be compelling reasons to do so. However, securitisation was to provide a very lasting solution to this economic (and legal) conundrum and enabled originators and investors to operate on a national basis. The second problem inherent in the mortgage lending process was the interest rate mis-match between the traditional fixed rate at which mortgage loans were made and the floating rate at which many of the lending institutions were raising funds. As money market rates throughout the world were beginning to demonstrate the kind of short-term volatility which we all have come to accept, the mortgage providers found themselves sitting very uncomfortably on previously unimaginable risks. Through the process of securitisation, their funding arrangements were matched more precisely to the terms of the mortgage loans. Securitisation in the United States had, therefore, begun to demonstrate its value to the financial institutions in the mortgage markets and has since grown into the $681 billion mortgage-backed securities market (as at 31 December 1987) with an annual new issue volume of approximately $100 billion. It is currently estimated that approximately 37% of the total United States residential mortgage market is securitised.

Securitisation brings with it other significant benefits to both the originator of the loans and the purchaser of the securities. Typically in any securitisation, the seller seeks not only to match-fund as closely as possible the asset being securitised, but also as part of the overall process will seek to obtain off-balance sheet status for the assets under the relevant accounting rules. For the seller this enables a reduction in the capital originally required to support the assets whilst they remain on the balance sheet and consequently provides the ability to write a greater volume of new business against the same level of capital employed. The accounting benefits will be immediately apparent with the ability to reduce and improve the balance sheet significantly, enhance return on capital and improve profitability from fee income generated through the off-balance sheet earnings.

The purchaser of the securitised asset also benefits in various ways. Instead perhaps of investing in corporate securities which carry with them a wide range of risks, the investor's risk is largely isolated to the performance of the assets within the particular pool backing the security. For the first time it has become possible to tailor-make portfolios of assets with particular characteristics to suit the needs of the investor, be they credit, rate or maturity-related.

Did this process help the individual whose loan was being securitised? The answer in the United States at first was probably not, although it enabled more institutions to offer more loans than they would otherwise have been able to undertake. It certainly helped an industry, part of which was suffering significant structural problems, to survive and recover. Perhaps more interestingly, however, over the longer term it has resulted in a cheaper cost to the individual borrower which some United States observers have quantified as a saving of approximately 100 basis points per annum in the cost of a fixed rate mortgage (measured as a spread over the yield on the appropriate United States Treasury bond during the last ten years). At the same time, there has been a dramatic increase in the variety and flexibility of mortgage products available to the man in the street.

The market in the United States has moved on since the early days of residential mortgage securitisation. Commercial mortgages, credit cards, auto and truck receivables, lease receivables, healthcare and other trade receivables and even yacht loans have all been securitised. In early 1988 the first stock and bond-backed financings emerged with collateral backing from pools of corporate and utility debt instruments and common stock. 1988 also saw the first securitisation of 'junk bonds' and even the first securitisation of a problem loan (Grant Street National Bank in liquidation). In total during 1988, some $40 billion of non-mortgage assets have been securitised.

Of course, a number of further factors combined to enable securitisation to flourish in the United States. First and foremost, the sheer scale of the marketplace, both in terms of assets potentially available for securitisation and the debt securities markets, meant that there would be a plentiful supply of products for all parties from which to recoup the relatively expensive product and market development. We have already mentioned a few of the specific economic incentives, but it must be borne in mind that these events were taking place within a highly regulated, although free, marketplace. There was, therefore, plenty of scope for imaginative solutions to the many regulatory hurdles which had to be overcome. The existence and wide acceptance of an established rating agency function, which quickly adopted these new financial instruments, enabled a broad understanding of critical benchmarks and speedy acceptance of rated securities by investors.

The regulators themselves have watched the explosion of asset-backed securities in the United States with some caution. There is an obvious risk in any financial engineering that if it is poorly executed, the very risks which it was designed to protect the investor from will, in fact, be magnified. Furthermore, if securitisation is seen to be the way forward for institutions which are already suffering from capital adequacy problems, once again the situation may be compounded as attention is diverted from the root problem of the institution. The example of Equity Programs Investment Co's (EPIC) mortgage-backed securities failure in 1985, largely as a result of poor initial underwriting procedures and an over-dependence on a single credit enhancement provider, has resulted in regulators, rating agents and participants in the United States focusing on the risks even more closely.

But let us now turn away from the United States and examine events in the United Kingdom where the market characteristics are inherently different from those in the United States.

The key practitioners of the art in the United States, the New York investment banks, and Salomon Brothers in particular, were anxious to repeat elsewhere their successes in the domestic United States markets and looked hard at other markets to identify those with the potential for securitisation. The United Kingdom mortgage market was an obvious choice. For years, it had been operated as a cosy cartel by the building societies with their roots deeply embedded in their history as mutual institutions. They typically funded themselves short-term through the retail markets where there had been little competition and lent on a long-term floating rate basis. The mortgage market itself was large and extremely stable with a superb arrears and default record. In 1980, the United Kingdom housing stock was estimated at £501 billion and the volume of mortgages £52 billion, approximately 10% of the mortgageable value. The British public seemed to have embraced home ownership as a key ingredient of their newly found wealth. Although small by American standards, there was plenty to go for. The United Kingdom was just beginning to reap the financial rewards of Thatcherism in the early 1980s, exchange control was a thing of the past and 'Big Bang' in the City of London had yet to come. These were the first signs that, on a long-term basis, the cost of retail funding and wholesale funding had begun to converge. The seeds were there for a revolution in the mortgage industry.

Others had spotted the opportunities too. The United Kingdom clearing banks, who had been lending against property for some time, stepped up their efforts to win not only the retail deposit base, but also the mortgage business traditionally held by the building societies and embarked on ambitious lending programmes. Foreign banks too, led in the main by a few United States banks hungry to expand their customer base in the United Kingdom, set up mortgage lending operations. After all, where else could loan spreads well in excess of 1 % be earned with the cast iron security of United Kingdom residential property? Memories of the 1973/1974 property crisis had long gone.

It was to these banking institutions that Salomon and others took their ideas on securitisation. At first the discussions were vague and confusing, on both sides. The techniques used in the United States did not appear to work as well in the United Kingdom. The regulatory environment was distinctly different and the floating rate structure of the mortgages led to a whole host of other problems. Nevertheless, the first stirrings of interest began in 1983/1984 which were to result in a single securitisation in 1985.

Suddenly a clutch of new private mortgage companies (the 'new lenders') emerged. The National Home Loans Corporation plc was formed with ambitious plans and was the first mortgage company to seek a public listing on the London Stock Exchange. Whether out of frustration with the speed of events in the United Kingdom or out of desire to reap more of the rewards, time alone will tell, Salomon set up their own wholly-owned mortgage company, The Mortgage Corporation, to take advantage of the opportunities offered by wholesale funding and securitisation. At the same time Kleinwort Benson, an early and enthusiastic convert to this future technological revolution, was instrumental in setting up the Mortgage Funding Corporation, itself organised utilising a (then) revolutionary off-balance sheet structure. Household Mortgage Corporation and First Mortgage Securities, both 'new lenders' with significant institutional backing, began operations.

The first public issue of mortgage-backed securities in the UK, a £50 million floating rate note issue, was launched in January 1985 by a vehicle company called Mortgage Intermediary Note Issuer (No 1)—Amsterdam BV ('MINI') formed to fund mortgages originated by Bank of America. At the time, the financial and investing community had other things on their plate and although the issue caught the eye of a number of interested parties, its relative complexity and small size meant that it was largely ignored. Bank of America itself was in the throes of a greater series of problems and, shortly after the issue, it was to sell its mortgage business. Like Chemical Bank which was to follow in Bank of America's footsteps, it had spent a great deal of money, time and effort, overcoming many of the obstacles to securitisation, only to find itself unable to reap the rewards.

Other mortgage lenders who might have been in a position to follow Bank of America did not. It was thus left to the new lenders, led by National Home Loans ('NHL'), to pick up the threads over two years later with what is widely acknowledged to be the issue which led the way to the market developing into the £9 billion market which it is today. The Mortgage Corporation and Household Mortgage Corporation ('HMC'), fellow new lenders, swiftly followed NHL with issues and others have not been slow to respond to the opportunities offered by this new market and a number of mortgage lending arms of foreign banks and two of the UK clearing banks have joined the ranks of issuers.

The bulk of the securities issued before the end of December 1989, some 39 issues totalling a new issue volume of £6.45 billion, have been long-term public floating rate notes ('FRNs') with final maturities of between 27 and 35 years and carrying a variety of spreads over three month sterling LIBOR. A further £200 million of fixed rate paper has been issued by HMC and it is estimated that approximately £2.4 billion represents private placements and US dollar denominated commercial paper. The Mortgage Corporation dominates the ranking of issues by volume, at the time of writing, having issued £2,575 million of securities through 14 transactions. Appendix 1 on page 304 contains a complete list of public issues up to and including December 1989.

Initially, most of the paper was placed with banks who saw the FRNs as a lucrative, secure and transferable alternative to their traditional investments. Certainly, when compared with other instruments in the market, and considering their high rating (AA or AAA) and level of collateral, they were priced very generously indeed to compensate for the perceived lack of liquidity in the market and relative complexity. The investor base has broadened significantly from the early days. There is now wide placement amongst the domestic UK institutional and corporate marketplace and offshore institutions too have contributed extensively to both primary and secondary market investment demand.

Other techniques have been used since the earliest days of pool insurance, still part of the staple diet. HMC and NHL, in particular, have developed the senior/junior market and there is now a healthy, if specialised, appetite for subordinated mortgage-backed securities. As mentioned earlier, HMC was the first to tap the fixed rate sterling markets through a sophisticated structure that provides the issuer with the opportunity to take advantage of particularly attractive swap opportunities to raise funds at levels well below those offered elsewhere. National Home Loans has, amongst other innovative financings, turned to the offshore markets and has established a United States domestic commercial paper programme ultimately backed by UK mortgages—a financing opportunity unheard of a few years ago.

The sterling markets as a whole welcomed the introduction of this new form of security. The level of liquidity in the United Kingdom life and pension funds during 1988, at around £20 billion, stood at historic high levels both in percentage and absolute terms with early expectation that these levels would continue well into the 1990s. The Bank of England is expected to operate a large purchase programme in the gilts market as up to £10 billion of government stock will need to be retired in order to maintain a neutral funding position. These two factors alone will have a significant impact on the volume of net new funds requiring investment and investment managers will be keen to take advantage of new instruments and opportunities, particularly in the fixed rate market. In the FRN markets, the announcement of the Basle Agreement on the weighting of mortgage-backed securities followed by the Bank of England's adoption of the 50% weighting gave the sector as a whole an unexpected fillip in November 1988. The Chancellor's removal in the March 1989 Budget of the capital gains tax benefits accorded to mortgage-backed securities as a result of their non-corporate bond status had little to no impact on a market which has begun to demonstrate its increasing maturity and resilience.

The Bank of England's recent relaxation of its 'five year rule' on the issuance of sterling securities coupled with the changes to the criteria for the issue of sterling commercial paper should encourage the issue of short-dated mortgage-backed paper. With plenty of liquidity at both the short and very long ends of the maturity spectrum it is only to be expected that we will see the development of sterling 'slow pay/fast pay' issues during 1990. NHL has already raised £225 million through an innovative four-tranche issue taking advantage of this new opportunity.

Liquidity for the investor is a much discussed issue. Initially there was only a limited amount of secondary market trading capability but as skills and understanding developed in line with the growing volume of issues, more market-makers have emerged and there is now a viable secondary market with several of the leading specialist houses making prices in all of the tradeable issues to date. Screen-based prices are posted on a daily basis and weekly price reporting under AIBD rules has been undertaken for over a year by Barings amongst others. The market has demonstrated on more than one occasion its ability to absorb investor sales of sizeable mortgage-backed FRN portfolios without any discernable effect on price levels.

All of this innovation has, however, come from the new lenders and a few of their banking competitors. What have the building societies been doing during all of this time? Only one, the relatively unknown Leamington Spa Building Society, 22nd by asset ranking and not in the mainstream of society lending, has entered into the foray. It established an off-balance sheet mortgage warehouse entirely wholesale funded through a US dollar-denominated Euro-commercial paper programme secured against mortgage assets. To date no other society has established a securitisation programme, although a number are believed to be actively developing their capabilities.

What is behind this lack of activity on the part of the traditional lenders? There are several reasons, but I would venture to suggest that the root cause is the legislative environment under which societies have historically operated. For many years the building society movement has operated under very restrictive legislation which was drawn up in another era. The legislators have made some remarkable changes in the last three years to allow societies to compete on a more level playing field, but it has inevitably been a process of catching up on, rather than seizing, an initiative. As a result, and as you will read in later chapters of this book, significant changes to systems, personnel and infrastructure will be required throughout the building society movement before advantage can truly be taken of securitisation.

Nobody could have foreseen quite what would take place in mid-1988 either. Following the Chancellor's handouts in the Spring 1988 Budget, the housing market roared ahead. The August changes to MIRAS compounded the problem as buyers rushed to purchase houses prior to the deadline. When the crunch came it was hard! House sales and mortgage business almost stopped dead in their tracks as interest rates leapt to 13% with further rises to 15% to follow. Suddenly, the outlook was unclear. The wholesale funding advantage which the new lenders had held for so long disappeared equally as quickly as the mortgage business when LIBOR rates led the way up. For the first time in many years the building societies found themselves with a significant competitive rate advantage through their retail funding sources. Societies seized the initiative and throughout 1989 engaged in fierce competition with the new entrants to the market on mortgage rates.

These events have had a significant impact on the securitisation market. With the lack of new mortgage business came a sharp decline in the asset levels available for securitisation. The number of new issues tailed off sharply throughout the last quarter of 1988 and into 1989.

At the time of writing, the securitisation market is finely poised. Whilst the long-term expectations of all participants, investors, arrangers and issuers remain high, the short-term impact of a poor mortgage market has been to delay the growth of securitisation. Nevertheless, there are all the signs that momentum will be regained as soon as confidence is restored in the housing market. It is estimated that during 1988, approximately 8.25% of new mortgage loans were securitised. With a housing stock of approximately £1,100 billion and mortgage loan balances as at June 1989 of £237 billion (now well in excess of the rapidly contracting gilt market) there is plenty of scope for securitisation to play a bigger role in the future. Amongst new issuers of mortgage-backed securities during 1990, insurance companies have the greatest potential, whilst the rest of the decade will probably belong to the building societies and banks as they begin to embrace these new techniques and recover ground lost to their competitors in the late 1980s.

The question of regulation must be highlighted since it has had a considerable impact on the way in which the securitisation market has developed in the United Kingdom and the structures adopted for individual issues. The Bank of England has played a leading role in publishing guidelines for banking institutions in its 'Loan Transfers and Securitisation' Notice of February 1989 (see Appendix 2 on page 312) which clarified the key criteria which the Bank viewed as critical in order to obtain off-balance sheet status for the securitised assets. The Bank has also been instrumental in moves to promote harmonisation of the regulatory environment within the United Kingdom and, indeed, throughout Europe and to this end has held detailed discussions with a large number of market participants and fellow regulators. The Building Societies Commission has reacted swiftly to the myriad of changes demanded by a rapidly changing marketplace and through a series of Prudential Notes and Statutory Orders empowered building societies to participate in the marketplace as both issuers and investors. With the emergence of the insurance companies as a major force in the mortgage market, the Department of Trade and Industry has played a bigger part and the accounting profession has not been silent with the issue of the Accounting Standards Committee exposure draft (ED42) entitled 'Accounting for Special Purpose Transactions'. ED42 has now been in existence for over 12 months and has given rise to considerable discussion and, perhaps, delay but it now seems some helpful amendments and interpretations may be obtained that should assist mortgage companies in proceeding with off-balance sheet securitisation. Finally, the Department of the Environment has espoused the rights of the individual and, through the mechanism of the Secondary Mortgage Market Working Group, has published a code of conduct (see Appendix 3 on page 326) to which it is hoped most mortgage originators will subscribe.

It is often argued that market developments in the field of securitisation have preceded supervisory techniques and accountancy practice and have crystallised interpretation of certain aspects of law. Perhaps we have been fortunate to date in the United Kingdom in being able to draw from the United States' experience and at all levels continual dialogue has been taking place which has the benefit of ensuring long-term stability in the marketplace. With the advent of 1992 rapidly approaching, other regulators such as the Bank for International Settlements and the European Commission have played a key role in establishing a common ground for the treatment of securitised assets throughout the European Economic Community.

And what of other assets? A great deal has been talked about the opportunities for following the United States' experience, but to date there is little tangible evidence that there is a sustainable demand from issuers in the short term. Following the considerable publicity afforded to the development of techniques for securitising commercial property through the mechanisms of 'SPOTs', 'SAPCOs' and 'PINCs' the securities envisaged have largely failed to materialise although a few individual transactions have been completed mainly in the private placement market. The first public transaction, for Billingsgate City Securities plc, was the securitisation of a City of London office property arranged by Barings and Goldman Sachs. At the time of writing, the Billingsgate transaction is the lone SAPCO but the securities are to be called early and the scheme wound up. Work on further development of a trust-based market for SPOTs has been suspended pending a change in the government's attitude regarding tax transparency for such vehicles and efforts to launch public issues of PINCs have been temporarily abandoned. Whilst the state of the property market has been partly responsible for the lack of progress in securitising single commercial properties, the unavailability of simple, tax efficient, structures has proved a formidable impediment.

There were early efforts to securitise ECGD assets through the Credit for Exports vehicle which Morgan Grenfell established in 1984. That was followed by a financing for the Guaranteed Export Finance Corporation by Lloyds Merchant Bank in 1987. However, at the end of July 1989, GEFCO launched a highly successful £250 million long-dated sterling issue fully guaranteed by HM government through ECGD which, whilst by no means a securitisation exercise, was welcomed warmly by the market as a potentially new and growing source of prime long-dated paper and it would appear that subsequent ECGD financings will follow this route.

A handful of small leasing transactions have also been completed on a private placement basis. That is not to say that we do not expect securitisation of other assets to follow that of mortgages. With the widening of experience and the installation of new systems we would expect the banks and building societies to apply the same techniques to consumer lending as they begin to manage their balance sheets more aggressively. It will be more difficult, however, to bring the same economies of scale to apply as existed in the mortgage market. Even the casual observer cannot fail to notice that the residential mortgage market in the United Kingdom is estimated to be some 18 times the size of the credit card receivables market and 52 times as large as the car loan market—a very different state of affairs from the United States and Continental Europe. Certainly, the relaxation by the Bank of England of the five year rule on sterling borrowing should help the development of short-term instruments more suited to these assets.

With the advent of a truly European financial marketplace, if not by 1992, then by the mid 1990s, securitisation will receive another boost from the ability to structure cross-border, cross-currency financings. As financial institutions increasingly adopt a European business base and the development of genuinely homogenous pools of assets based in more than one country becomes more than a dream, the real challenge will be to develop securities capable of mixing assets from different jurisdictions. It is likely that, only then, will economies of scale emerge large enough to tempt key sectors of the marketplace to securitise.

Certainly, much will also depend on other sectors of the capital markets such as currency swaps but the attraction of major pools of retail demand for securities in Europe or the widespread use of a common European currency such as the ECU will act as a major spur to development. Although there have been mortgage-backed securities in existence for many years in certain European countries, these are not 'securitised' transactions as we know them.

At the moment, therefore, the United Kingdom is at the forefront, not only from a financial market perspective, but also from the product supply viewpoint. Whether the United Kingdom will manage to hold on to its lead remains to be seen as emerging technologies and capabilities in Europe begin to compete. To date France is the only country to have begun to develop its own capabilities which, during 1989, resulted in the first European automobile loans transaction and the first securitisation of stockbroker loans using the new French law. An Italian private placement of automobile loans has also been seen. These developments, which are outlined elsewhere in this book, will be keenly watched by United Kingdom practitioners.

We asked ourselves at the outset whether securitisation brings any benefit to the individual. In the case of the United Kingdom mortgage industry it can be demonstrated that this is unequivocally true. Since the advent of the 'new lenders' and the associated technology required for the administration of securitised pools of mortgages, there has been a revolution in the entire mortgage industry. It will be argued, no doubt, that many of these events would have occurred in any event and that competition has merely advanced the process. It is more than that however. The process of securitisation brings with it the need to examine every facet of the business to establish its cost, its sophistication and its reliability. In the course of that process it has been found that the introduction of technology coupled with the use of the most sophisticated financial techniques has led to the development of a more focused approach to business strategy and a considerably sharpened decision-making process. This has led the way not only to lowering the cost of the mortgage itself, but also widening the variety of the products on offer and tailor-making them to suit the needs of a changing marketplace.

It is often said that there is nothing new in the world. Undoubtedly building societies have been offering 'low start', 'deferred interest' and 'fixed rate' mortgages for years. However, I would venture to suggest that their infrastructure and systems did not provide adequate resources to analyse such products in the context of the market opportunity presented nor did they adjust product ranges and pricing to suit market conditions and funding opportunities. With increasing pressure on all lenders from 'Big Bang' in the mortgage markets, the acquisition of these skills will become even more important and ultimately will sustain and improve the level of benefit enjoyed by the individual borrower.

Securitisation brings with it many hidden benefits in terms of management information. These should not be under-estimated. It brings with it a degree of commitment to systems, resources and level of staff knowledge and expertise which will take a practitioner into the highest levels of financial engineering currently practised in this country. Although not to be entered into lightly, the benefits of the disciplines required will be very significant and long lasting to the organisation as a whole, its personnel and customer base.

Perhaps after publication of this book someone will include securitisation in their dictionary!

Chapter 2

Legal Aspects and Considerations

David Bonsall
Freshfields

This chapter will address the main legal aspects and considerations which need to be borne in mind in any securitisation. These legal matters will often determine the structure and details of a transaction and are an integral part of the planning and execution of any successful deal of this type. I shall inevitably focus mainly on mortgage securitisations although many of the principles are similarly applicable to securitisations of non-mortgage assets.

OUTLINE OF A TYPICAL STRUCTURE

The diagram (on page 14) illustrates the typical structure of a transaction involving an issue of securities in the Euromarkets backed by mortgages over property in England and Wales.

As can be seen from the diagram, a mortgage lender or originator with a substantial pool of mortgage receivables transfers or sells the portfolio of mortgages (and any collateral security) to a special purpose issuing vehicle ('SPV'). The SPV is established separately from the originator and it issues notes to investors. The proceeds of the issue are used by the vehicle to pay the originator the purchase price for the portfolio. The investors are collectively represented by a trustee which holds the various types of security interest or charge on behalf of the investors. As security for the payments of principal and interest on the notes, the SPV charges to the trustee its entitlement to all moneys derived from the portfolio of mortgages (and any collateral security) and any other credit support or liquidity support which is included in the structure.

In order to cover the possibility that the mortgage portfolio will generate insufficient income to fund payments of note interest when due (for example, as a result of borrowers falling into arrears), some form of liquidity support is provided, usually by a credit facility from a third party lender. To guard against credit losses where the vehicle would be exposed to a failure to recover

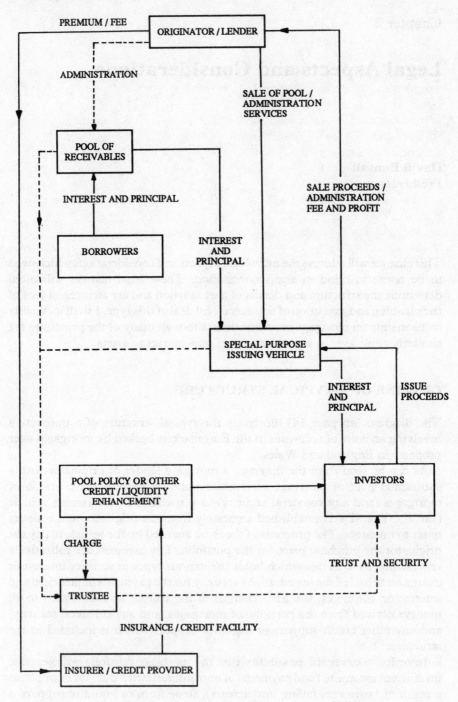

the full amount of expenses, interest and principal owing under the mortgage, some form of credit support is required. This is often provided by a pool insurance policy. Subject to a fixed limit, this policy is available to meet an ultimate loss after enforcement of a mortgage and collateral security which would otherwise result in the vehicle having insufficient principal to repay the notes. The originator will pay the relevant premium or fee for these protections at the beginning of the transaction. An alternative form of liquidity and credit support (not shown in the diagram) is provided by the issue of junior or subordinated notes by the SPV, payments of interest and principal on which rank behind payments on the senior notes.

The originator will usually be appointed to administer the mortgage portfolio on behalf of the issuer and continue to conduct the relationship with borrowers in return for a fee. The transaction will also be structured so that any profit remaining in the vehicle after paying the investors will be passed back to the originator.

In order to attract the widest range of investors, the securities are often independently rated by Standard & Poor's Corporation or Moody's Investors Service Inc and the securities are usually listed on a public stock exchange such as London or Luxembourg.

There can, inevitably, be many variations on the above structure and some of these are discussed in other chapters of the book. However, for present purposes, the typical structure should serve as a useful reference point for the analysis of the legal aspects involved in a securitisation.

NATURE OF THE ASSETS TO BE SECURITISED

In any securitisation it is critical for all those involved to have a clear understanding of the legal and commercial nature of the assets being securitised. Let us first focus on the residential mortgages themselves.

When we speak of a mortgage, what we really mean is a loan to an individual borrower secured by a charge over the freehold or leasehold property where the borrower lives. The terms of the loan and the security granted by the borrower (the mortgagor) to the lender (the mortgagee) are often contained in more than one document. The main document will be the mortgage deed which will incorporate the mortgage conditions and the mortgage offer. The mortgage conditions can vary considerably from lender to lender although the conditions used by any one lender are often in its standard form. The standard conditions are usually only changed from year to year or even less frequently while the mortgage offer will set out the specific terms applicable to the individual borrower. The mortgage documentation for most lenders will not have been drafted with securitisation specifically in mind. Even if it has been, the need to amend the basic terms to accommodate new mortgage products and new techniques and securitisation structures will inevitably mean that much of this documentation will lag behind developments in the market. It is essential that, as soon as a securitisation is contemplated, the underlying mortgage documentation is reviewed closely to identify what problems may come up and what solutions may be available. Inadequate mortgage documents can seriously delay or, indeed, prevent a transaction taking place until a new portfolio of loans based on proper documents has been originated. Less serious flaws may nevertheless result in costly solutions for the originator. For example, if the mortgage conditions do not permit an assignment of the mortgage by the originator without the borrower's specific consent, this must be obtained before the transfer to the SPV. Sending individual notices to some 5,000 borrowers who may be involved in a £200 million transaction is administratively burdensome and expensive and it will inevitably take some time before all the replies are received.

A further and more important example is the need for the interest rate setting mechanism in the mortgage conditions to permit complete flexibility. It is a requirement of the rating agencies that the issuer and the trustee are the persons empowered to set the mortgage interest rate, although it will be usual for this power to be delegated to the originator as administrator of the issuer's business and assets. It is critical that the mortgage rate can be increased as and when necessary to increase the income receivable by the issuer to a level sufficient to pay interest on the notes and meet the ongoing expenses of the transaction—whether and, if so, when this can be done depends entirely on the powers set out in the mortgage documents. If, for example, the mortgage conditions provide that the rate of interest shall be 1% above the base rate from time to time of the originator or a third party, it will not be possible to change the rate on the securitised mortgages independently. The rating agencies will rightly insist on this risk to the issuer being covered by a greater injection of initial capital or the provision of some form of liquidity facility or additional reserves which are dedicated for this purpose. The originator is likely to bear the cost of these additional protections.

TYPE OF MORTGAGE

There are many different types of mortgage product available, not all of which are suitable for securitisation. The particular characteristics of each of these mortgages would need to be examined, both in the legal and the commercial context, to enable appropriate modification to the typical structure to be determined. The vast majority of mortgages in the United Kingdom, which have been ideally suited to securitisation, are endowment mortgages, where the borrower only pays interest during the term of the mortgage, the principal typically being paid from the proceeds of an endowment life assurance policy which forms part of the collateral security for the mortgage debt.

Pension or personal equity plan linked mortgages have also been securitised even though the lender in this case does not have the benefit of any security interest in the pension or personal equity plan and there is no guarantee (except on death) that the borrower will have the necessary funds to repay the mortgage principal at the end of the term. With the decline in the housing market at the end of 1988 and throughout 1989, new mortgage products which effectively subsidise the interest cost for the borrower for a period have proliferated. The effect of including low start, fixed rate and stabilised rate mortgages in securitisation pools has led to noteholders effectively pre-funding the cost of these arrangements until they revert to standard variable rate mortgages.

It has not always been appreciated that these new mortgage products can give rise to legal as well as commercial risks for the originator and the SPV. The mechanism whereby the borrowers are subsidised is typically through the making of further advances on a monthly basis. There are four main areas which need to be considered—the obtaining of effective security for the further advances through the same first legal charge over the property as secured the original mortgage debt, the capital implications, the effect on the borrower's ability to obtain tax relief at source under the MIRAS system and the implications of the Consumer Credit Act 1974.

When a borrower requests a lender to make him a further advance, the mortgagee will normally make various enquiries to ascertain that commercially the borrower can support the increased debt and legally the security for the further advance is equally as good as for the original debt. This would entail making searches at the appropriate registries to ensure that no second charge had been created over the property in favour of another lender behind which the original mortgagee would rank for the further advance. Ideally, the mortgagee would like to leapfrog any intervening lender by 'tacking' the further advance onto the original debt secured by the first legal charge. Under the Law of Property Act 1925 (dealing with unregistered land) and the Land Registration Act 1925 (dealing with registered land) tacking will only be permitted where the further advance was made pursuant to an obligation to make the further advance.

In the case of a normal discretionary further advance the absence of such an obligation on the lender is not a problem—the lender makes enquiries and, if he discovers a second charge, he refuses to make the advance without the second chargee postponing his security. The position is different with these new mortgage products. While the mortgage conditions will normally contain the relevant obligation, the borrower may be in breach of one or more of his covenants. In such a case, the lender's obligation no longer exists and the benefit of tacking will not be available but the further advance will nevertheless be made because the mortgagee will usually be unaware of the breach. The mortgagee may also be unaware of any intervening 'equities' or third party rights, such as rights of occupation of a spouse or child who was, say, 16 when the mortgage was advanced but has now become 18 and is still living in the secured property. It will not be practical for any mortgage lender to make constant enquiries of borrowers to ascertain whether there has been full observance of the (non-payment) covenants or any change in the borrowers' personal circumstances so these legal risks have to be assumed in the structure and appropriate commercial safeguards provided.

The transfer of a mortgage by the originator to the SPV will not normally relieve the originator of any continuing obligations it has to the borrower. In most cases no such obligations exist but, in the case of low start and stabilised rate mortgages, further advances are required to be made. If the originator is a bank or building society subject to the capital requirements of the Bank of England or the Building Societies Commission, the treatment by those authorities of the transaction for capital purposes will be critical to its commercial success. The requirements of these authorities for off-balance sheet treatment are discussed more fully in other chapters. In this context it is sufficient to note that the residual obligation of the originator to make further advances of a known amount may have adverse capital consequences unless the borrower specifically releases the originator from the obligation in return for a corresponding obligation from the SPV or other arrangements are made which effectively eliminate any continuing risk to the originator.

Under the Mortgage Interest Relief at Source (MIRAS) system, borrowers obtain tax relief by making net payments to mortgage lenders who recover the deducted amounts from the Inland Revenue. This is commercially desirable for all concerned. The ability of a borrower to take advantage of MIRAS depends on the loan being for a qualifying purpose and tax relief is only given for the interest paid on principal of up to £30,000. Some mortgage lenders operate their administrative systems for further advances on low start or stabilised rate mortgages by allowing the borrower to pay a reduced amount. Under current Inland Revenue practice this treatment would take the loan out of MIRAS and the borrower would cease to be entitled to tax relief which is, obviously, commercially undesirable. If, however, the mortgagee requires the borrower to pay the full amount of interest at the unsubsidised rate and immediately credits the borrower with an amount equal to the subsidy, MIRAS will continue to operate. The application of MIRAS to these new mortgage products is being reviewed by the Inland Revenue and more flexibility may be available in the future.

The Consumer Credit Act does not normally apply to loans above a certain limit, currently £15,000. Very few mortgage loans will be initially below that figure and the requirements of the Act regarding the conduct of regulated loan business and the format and content of the documentation and publicity material will not apply. However, the monthly further advances of subsidised interest will all be comparatively small and could be regulated by the Act. If the Act's detailed requirements apply but are not complied with, the loan would be unenforceable without an order of the court. It is therefore critical to examine the particular circumstances of the originator and the SPV to determine whether any of the complicated exemptions in the Act are available. While it is normally thought unlikely that a court would relieve a borrower of his obligation to repay the loan merely because of a technical breach of the regulations, it is obviously undesirable to have to go to court and suffer the delays which would be involved.

The four difficulties outlined above which apply to some of the new mortgage products illustrate the degree of attention to detail which is a critical element of securitisations and indicate the care with which commercially desirable means of generating assets need to be reconciled with the securitisation structure which will ultimately be supported by those assets.

OTHER CONSIDERATIONS

The mortgage loans will, of course, be secured on the borrower's property. This property may be either unregistered land or registered land. It may be a freehold or leasehold interest and it may be a house or a flat or other type of dwelling. The lending criteria which are applied when the originator is advancing the loans initially will all need to be carefully reviewed as these will determine, in large measure, the likelihood that payments of interest and principal will be made in full and on time. They will certainly be closely checked by the rating agencies against their benchmarks for the ideal mortgage pool for securitisation issues. Chapter 8 describes their approach more fully.

It is, of course, important to understand the limitations to which the mortgagee will be subject if a borrower defaults in payment of the moneys due under the mortgage. While the mortgage will invariably allow the mortgagee a power of sale, this cannot, in fact, be exercised until certain events have occurred and, commercially, the best price is likely to be realised only if the property is sold with vacant possession. The mortgagee cannot, however, evict the borrower from his house just because there has been a default—an application must first be made to the court for an order for vacant possession. The court will usually allow the borrower a reasonable period of time, according to his particular circumstances, to pay the outstanding amounts but will not relieve the borrower of his liability. Nevertheless, it is unlikely in practice that a mortgagee would be able to put the property up for sale in less than nine months after the default occurred. Whether the proceeds of sale (net of expenses) will cover all the moneys owed to the mortgagee is obviously uncertain and the mortgagee will aim to protect itself against ultimate credit loss by insurance in appropriate cases. These insurances form part of the collateral security for the mortgage debt which is also assigned to the SPV.

COLLATERAL SECURITY

As has been mentioned in the case of endowment policies, the borrower will have assigned to the mortgagee the benefit of an endowment life assurance policy which is guaranteed, on the borrower's death, to repay the principal advanced and is expected to produce, at the end of the mortgage term, an amount sufficient to redeem the mortgage in full. If there is a default, the mortgagee can surrender the policy, the value of which will depend upon the premiums which have been paid so far and the bonuses which have been added, this value obviously increasing the longer the policy is outstanding before surrender.

The benefit of these policies is obviously a significant commercial element in the security for the transaction (even though they are often not accorded much importance by the rating agencies). As a prudent business matter the originator should obviously have as full details as possible of the policies, eg their numbers and the details of the insurance company providers, which support the particular loan. It is often difficult to gather this information quickly for the purposes of a transaction and prudent administrative practices early on can significantly reduce the overall burden.

The role of insurance companies in securitisations is discussed in more detail in Chapter 9, but one particular problem for life companies which are mortgage lenders is worth mentioning here. Many such companies issue the endowment policies to their borrowers and purport to take a charge over the benefit of those policies as security for the mortgage debt. Following the decision in *Re Charge Card Services Ltd* (1986), it is arguable that the life companies cannot, as a matter of law, create a charge over the benefit of the endowment policy. Instead, the mortgagee has probably created for itself a right to set off the payment it would make (in its capacity as endowment policy provider) against the payment owed by the borrower to it under the mortgage. It is unlikely that the benefit of such a set off could be transferred to the SPV. While the life company originator may be able to guarantee proper payment under the policies, it may not wish to do so for capital adequacy reasons.

A mortgagee will typically have the benefit of other forms of insurance protection and these will also form part of the collateral security which will be transferred to the SPV. These will include various types of contingency insurances, buildings insurance taken out in conjunction with the borrower if the property is damaged or destroyed and mortgage indemnity cover if the loan to value ratio exceeds a certain figure. The terms on which these insurances have been provided, the basis on which claims can be made and other relevant details must all be examined carefully, not least because they will be reflected in the warranties required from the originator and in the description of the security in the prospectus.

Last, but not least, the mortgagee is entitled to sue the borrower on his personal covenant to pay. While this right is obviously not capable of being given any identifiable commercial value it nevertheless forms part of the rights of a mortgagee which are transferred to the SPV. This is in contrast to the position, for example, in the United States where the borrower has no personal liability and is perhaps, therefore, more likely to abandon his home to the mortgagee and travel elsewhere in the knowledge that he cannot be pursued for his failure to meet his obligations.

NON-MORTGAGE ASSETS

There are those who say that any asset which has a cash flow can be securitised. The experience of, and potential for, securitising non-mortgage assets is discussed more fully in Chapter 13. Again, the legal nature of the assets must be analysed as well as the commercial aspects. The particular nature of the receivables in question will dictate to some extent the predictability and certainty of the payments. In most cases the loans will be unsecured personal loans, eg credit card receivables, or not represent loans at all but rental for the use of an asset, eg a car, where the residual value of the asset if it had to be seized and sold is likely to be much less than the initial purchase price. It is also more likely that the continuing relationship between the debtor and the creditor would give rise to rights of set off or counterclaim where, for example, the lessee complained that the car was always breaking down. Where consumers are concerned, the Consumer Credit Act, the Unfair Contract Terms Act, the Sale of Goods Act and the Supply of Goods and Services Act are just four examples of statutes which could interfere with the relationship between payor and payee and make the receivable less certain or valuable.

THE SPECIAL PURPOSE ISSUING VEHICLE (SPV)

In many financing transactions it is attractive to locate the issuer in a tax haven so that the profit arising from the transaction is appropriately sheltered. In the securitisation of non-mortgage assets, this may be possible provided that the flow of the receivables can be made to the SPV without withholdings or deductions. It is obviously imperative that the issuer's cash flow matches its obligations. However, in a mortgage securitisation in the United Kingdom, it is not possible to establish the SPV offshore. As noted above, mortgage originators will not wish to upset their borrowers by a transaction which removes from them the ability to take advantage of MIRAS. The MIRAS scheme only operates in favour of 'qualifying lenders' which are, in practice, usually taxable in the United Kingdom. Unless the SPV falls within a category of persons such as authorised institutions under the Banking Act 1987, the SPV must be designated as a qualifying lender by means of a statutory instrument. A formal application has to be sent to the Inland Revenue and, if this is approved, the company will be prescribed in the next statutory instrument. However, it is worth noting that these only occur twice each year, that the Inland Revenue are unwilling to allow large numbers of these companies to be held 'in stock' and a change of control of such a company requires specific Inland Revenue approval. All of these steps can take time and must be appropriately factored into the timetable and planning for a securitisation.

It is worth noting at this stage why an SPV needs to be used at all. After all, building societies have themselves issued hundreds of millions of pounds of floating rate notes in the Euromarkets. However, these have not been securitisations as such because they have been unsecured issues and have depended upon the market's credit assessment of the building society rather than of the portfolio of mortgage loans supporting the particular issue. There are two overriding reasons why special purpose companies have been established as the issuers in these arrangements—balance sheet considerations and security.

It would be virtually impossible, in the United Kingdom at any rate, for the balance sheet of the issuer not to reflect the debt undertaken. Thus, the mere fact that the debt was matched by an appropriate pool of assets in the issuer would not enable the debt to be left off the balance sheet. A true and fair view of the company's position would not be shown as required by s 236 of the Companies Act 1985. Secondly, it would be very difficult to isolate the particular mortgage assets within the company itself so that claims by other creditors would not adversely affect the security for the noteholders of the particular issue. If, for example, the mortgage originator was put into liquidation because of a failure to meet obligations under a syndicated loan, how would the liquidator treat the assets subject to the charge for the noteholders? Technical and practical problems abound. It is almost inevitable that while the complexities were being resolved, payments to noteholders would not be made in full or on time, which is obviously a necessary ingredient in the rating for the notes. Given the almost unavoidable difficulties, it has been the invariable practice that a special purpose vehicle has been established to which the relevant assets are transferred and which can be viewed in isolation from the mortgage originator. There are, in any case, many difficult insolvency related issues which need to be addressed (see 'Insolvency Considerations' below) without adding to them.

OWNERSHIP OF THE SPV

Ideally, a mortgage originator securitising its assets would wish to be able to have control over the SPV but not have it consolidated on its balance sheet for accounting or regulatory purposes. This is not universally the case—HMC, for example, uses wholly-owned subsidiaries for its securitisation issues but, for most of the other major players in the market, off-balance sheet treatment has been critical. Whether it can be achieved will depend upon satisfying a combination of legal requirements (in the Companies Acts), accounting practice and, if the originator is a bank or building society, regulatory requirements. The detailed guidance from the Bank of England in its Notice dated February 1989 entitled 'Loan Transfers and Securitisation', the prudential guidelines laid down by the Building Societies Commission (see, for example, Prudential Note 1988/2) and the initial views of the accounting profession (currently embodied in exposure draft 42 published in March 1988, which has been seriously overtaken by events) are all discussed in more detail in subsequent chapters.

Until the Companies Act 1989 became law recently, off-balance sheet vehicles were established in a way which took advantage of the different requirements in the Companies Act 1985 for consolidation in group accounts and in tax legislation for treatment as part of the same tax group as the originator for corporation tax and stamp duty purposes (albeit not for value added tax purposes). The structures used involved complex share capitals and strange dividend rights designed to enable profit extraction. The position now is that accounts drawn up for any accounting reference period commencing after 23 December 1989 will have to consolidate 'subsidiary undertakings' as defined in the Companies Act 1989. This means not only that the corporate structures which have been much used in the past will no longer work, but the companies still in existence which meet the new definition of subsidiary undertaking will have to be consolidated for the first time in the originator's group accounts. This may come as a nasty shock to several originators to the extent that these deals remain outstanding.

However, all is not lost. While the Secretary of State has reserved the ability to change, by statutory instrument, the definition of subsidiary undertaking to catch new schemes, it is still possible to create off-balance sheet corporate structures which meet the legal, accounting and regulatory requirements. A holding company is established with the entire share capital being held by trustees on discretionary trusts for charitable purposes. The holding company will own the entire share capital of one or more subsidiaries which can be used as the issuers in securitisations or other financing transactions. This is often referred to as the orphan structure. It is common to insert an intermediate holding company above the SPV and below the ultimate holding company as this can assist with the profit extraction methods which are discussed further below. The holding company and any intermediate holding company do not need to be highly capitalised and they can be private companies. However, the SPV will need to be a public company with a minimum paid up share capital of £12,500. This is because a private company is not permitted by the Companies Act 1985 to agree to allot its debentures with a view to them being offered for sale to the public—this would occur when it signs the subscription agreement with the managers of the issue. The funding of the SPV is provided principally by retained earnings and subordinated loans from third parties and/or the originator—these are also discussed in more detail in other chapters.

OFFICERS OF THE SPV

In the old off-balance sheet structures it was common for the originator/administrator to appoint two directors to the board of the SPV with friendly shareholders or third parties providing the other two directors, but the voting power of the originator's appointees outweighed that of the third party appointees. This device will no longer work and one requirement of the Bank of England is that the board of the SPV must be independent of the administrator, although the administrator may appoint one director. The need to have genuinely independent directors is likely to be of practical importance especially as more attention is being focused on the personal liability of directors in certain circumstances. They will usually be personally liable to investors if the information in the offering circular proves to be untrue or misleading and the effects of *Re Produce Marketing Ltd* (1989) continue to be widely felt. In that case, two directors were found personally liable to contribute to the assets of an insolvent company where they had allowed the company to continue trading wrongfully when they knew or ought to have concluded that there was no reasonable prospect that the company would avoid going into insolvent liquidation. Section 214 of the Insolvency Act 1986 has been shown to have teeth and the section could apply if the issuer's financial position deteriorated, for example through a combination of borrower defaults, decline in property values and an unwillingness to raise the mortgage rate, so that the SPV becomes unable to meet its debts as they fall due.

The secretary of the SPV is likely to be an employee of the originator/ administrator. This is not likely to jeopardise the off-balance sheet position but it is worth remembering that, under s 286 of the Companies Act 1985, the secretary of a public company must have certain qualifications (being, for example, a solicitor, barrister or chartered accountant) or have appropriately relevant experience.

OTHER CONSIDERATIONS

The SPV will need to be registered under the Data Protection Act 1984. This is because it will make use of the data on the mortgagors kept by the originator on its computer systems. Access to the computerised records of the originator is a crucial element in the proper security for the noteholders. If the originator becomes insolvent or ceases business, it is essential that the trustee for the noteholders can either itself or through a substitute administrator ensure that appropriate steps can be taken to enable administration of the portfolio to continue. Registration under the Act is not onerous but it is often a detail which is left to the last minute. A failure to register when required to do so is a criminal offence and can lead to the imposition of significant fines. There has recently been a hardening of approach by the Data Protection Registrar which should not be ignored.

The SPV will also need a licence under the Consumer Credit Act 1974. Some of the potential difficulties raised by this Act have already been noted in the context of new mortgage products. Obtaining the licence is relatively simple and is usually done as a matter of course. However, having the licence will not necessarily mean that the detailed requirements noted above no longer apply to the particular circumstances.

TRANSFERRING ASSETS TO THE SPV AND TAKING SECURITY OVER THOSE ASSETS

Once the nature of the assets underlying the transaction and the structure of the SPV have been determined, the assets must be transferred to the SPV in a manner which is legally effective and commercially practical. The SPV must also be able to give good security to the trustee for the noteholders.

A. Transfer of assets

1. METHOD OF TRANSFER AND TYPES OF ASSETS

The mortgage pool is transferred to the issuer at a price equal to the principal sums outstanding under the mortgages, ie there is no overcollateralisation in the sense that the originator has to dedicate assets to the issue without receiving any value for them. The mortgage pool will usually consist of mortgages of both registered and unregistered land. The transfer may be effected at law or in equity.

(a) Legal assignment of mortgages by originator to issuer

This involves a legal transfer by deed in respect of unregistered land and a transfer in land registry form, which is then registered at HM Land Registry, in the case of registered land. Notice of the transfer is given to the borrower.

Section 114 of the Law of Property Act 1925 states that, unless a contrary intention is expressed, a transfer of a mortgage by deed will operate (inter alia) to transfer the right to recover and give receipts for the mortgage moneys, the benefit of all securities for the mortgage moneys, and the right to exercise all the powers of the mortgagee. Accordingly, it is not strictly necessary even to specify that the collateral security of the life policy is also being assigned. However, in practice, all of the elements of the security package given by the borrower will be specified in the transfer to the issuer, so that they are not overlooked when the sub-charge to the trustee (or agent for syndicate banks in a private passthrough structure) is being drafted.

The issuer will take the security subject to any equities arising between the borrower and the originator prior to notice of the transfer to the issuer being given to the borrower, and the issuer will be bound by the actual state of accounts between the borrower and the originator. The giving of notice, therefore, crystallises the position.

A further reason for requiring notice is that s 136 of the Law of Property Act 1925 requires a legal assignment of a debt to be perfected by notice in writing to the debtor (ie, in this case, the borrower). There is an argument that despite the provisions of s 114 of the Law of Property Act 1925 notice is required to be given to the borrower under s 136 to transfer the debt. However, the wording of s 114 is quite clear and on the basis of this wording the argument does not appear correct. If notice is not given, the borrower will still be entitled to redeem by paying the originator, so it is clearly in the trustee's (or agent's) interests that notice be given. In practice, for so long as the originator remains agent of the issuer and the trustee to administer the mortgages, the borrower will still repay capital to the originator in its different capacity as administrator.

In its Notice on 'Loan Transfers and Securitisation' the Bank of England identified a number of risks for both the originator and the issuer in the case of assignments where no notice is given to the borrower (described by the Bank as 'silent assignments'). As already mentioned, if no notice is given to a borrower further equities and, in particular, rights of set-off may arise between the borrower and the originator. Amounts owed by the originator might be set-off against, and therefore reduce, the amount owed by the borrower under the receivable. This has not been of much real concern to date (except as noted earlier in the context of new mortgage products involving an obligation to make further advances) as most securitisations have been made by specialist mortgage lenders which do not carry on a retail banking business. If, however, the originator is a retail bank or building society with which borrowers hold current or deposit accounts or if non-mortgage assets (such as lease or trade receivables) are involved, the question will have far greater practical relevance. It should be noted, in any event, that notification to borrowers can only prevent future set-offs arising. It will not affect rights of set-off existing at the time of notification.

The Statement of Practice of the Secondary Mortgage Market Working Group also addressed the question of notification to borrowers. The Statement is not legally binding on mortgage lenders operating in the United Kingdom market. However, institutions which adopt the statement undertake to obtain the consent of borrowers before transferring their mortgages. The Statement identifies two forms of consent which are acceptable (depending upon the type of securitisation structure being utilised):

(i) the general consent—where, at the time the mortgage is created, the borrower consents to a transfer of that mortgage; and

(ii) the specific consent—obtained from the borrower at the time of transfer of his mortgage to a vehicle company.

In broad terms the Statement of Practice permits a transfer to proceed with a general consent where the originator continues to be responsible for decisions on key matters, for example, operating the arrears procedures or setting the interest rate (or if the issuer has undertaken that its policy in exercising a discretion in the setting of interest rates or handling arrears will be identical to that of the originator). Specific consent will be required in other cases, which can obviously be impractical and administratively expensive to obtain.

(b) Equitable assignment of mortgages by originator to issuer

An equitable assignment of the mortgage pool can be effected by:

(i) agreement to assign or transfer with power of attorney from the originator in favour of the issuer to enable him to perfect a legal transfer;

(ii) declaration of trust by the originator in favour of the issuer with power of attorney by the originator to the issuer to enable him to perfect a legal transfer;

(iii) the originator handing over to the issuer executed but undated assignments in legal form with a power of attorney to complete them;

(iv) handing over executed and dated assignments but without giving notice and without registration. In registered land this route should be effective as the Land Registration Act provides that a charge of registered land, until registration is completed, takes effect in equity only. However, in the case of unregistered land, it is arguable that this method actually creates a legal assignment because s 114 of the Law of Property Act 1925 applies.

(c) Advantages and disadvantages of legal and equitable assignments

It might be thought that the technical distinction between legal and equitable assignments is one to keep the lawyers amused on dark winter nights but has no real importance to their clients. Not so. The main disadvantage of an equitable assignment (other than the question of priority which is examined later) is that the originator remains the lender of record and so must be joined in any action relating to the relevant mortgage. This could be awkward if the originator was unco-operative or even insolvent although in such a case the irrevocable power of attorney should enable the necessary steps to be taken.

The major disadvantage of a legal assignment is the increased administrative burden (to effect registration of transfers of the mortgages) and increased costs (including HM Land Registry fees) associated with effecting such registration. It is frequently the case that substitutions and discretionary further advances can be made by the originator on behalf of the issuer using the moneys received from early redemptions by mortgagors in the securitised pool. These steps extend the average life of the notes. However, each dealing with a mortgage of property which is registered land will incur a cost (currently of £5). If, say, 4,000 mortgages of registered land are securitised in a £200 million issue, it will cost £20,000 to register the transfer to the issuer and the charge to the trustee, a further £20,000 on redemption and perhaps £10,000 more when mortgages are substituted or further advances made.

The trustee (and the rating agencies) will wish to ensure that the best security possible is achieved. Given the difficulties caused by insisting on a full legal assignment, an equitable assignment is now usually accepted although some originators have been required to prepare all the transfers and related schedules as if there were to be a legal transfer. If this information is not listed and kept up to date there could be delays in realising the security. Other originators have argued that bringing the equitable assignment to the verge of a legal assignment would be as costly as a legal assignment. The compromise which is reached in any one case will usually depend on the strength of the originator's covenant and on all the circumstances of the transaction.

Nevertheless, it will not be possible even with an equitable assignment to eliminate all the administrative procedures. Proper records of which mortgages are at any time in the pool are essential and it should be remembered that no disposal of an equitable interest can be effected without writing duly signed by the seller. In other words, computer records will not be sufficient on their own and certain officers of the originator and administrator may find themselves signing even more papers than they had bargained for.

(d) Transfer of assets related to the mortgage pool

The life policies which are taken by the originator as collateral security from the borrower will be assigned to the issuer with the mortgages.

If a life policy was originally only deposited by the borrower with the originator, it is usually a prerequisite of securitisation that the deposit is perfected into a legal assignment of the life policy by the borrower subject to the borrower's right of redemption. The originator usually has power to do this without reference to the borrower by using a power of attorney contained in the mortgage.

Notice of the assignment of the life policy will often be given to the life assurance company. Similarly, all other insurance policies relating to the mortgages (for example, mortgage guarantee indemnity insurance, block building policies, etc) will be assigned to the issuer and notice in writing should be given to the various insurance companies.

(e) Transfer of assets other than mortgages

The nature of credit and charge card receivables, trade receivables and lease and hire purchase receivables when compared to mortgages means that a number of considerations will arise on transfer which are not of concern in the case of mortgage securitisations.

One example is notifying each debtor of the transfer of his debt to the issuer. In the case of trade receivables which represent very short-term debts likely to be discharged in a single payment, it is not practical to give notice within the available time period. Furthermore, the number of trade or credit card receivables constituting a portfolio which is being transferred to a vehicle company may be very large in comparison to a mortgage pool of the same value. The cost associated with giving notices to such large numbers of debtors when combined with the administrative burden may be prohibitive.

The question of set-off (which has been previously mentioned) where the originator remains the lender of record is likely to be a serious concern in the case of credit or charge card receivables. This is because the kind of financial institutions concerned may well have financial liabilities towards borrowers. In the case of trade debts, set-offs might arise as a result of a continuing trading relationship between the originator and the debtor or by virtue of disputes in connection with other contracts between the parties.

2. WARRANTY PROTECTION FOR SPV

(a) Mortgage sale agreement

In the case of a mortgage securitisation the mortgage sale agreement will contain a range of warranties from the originator in favour of the issuer and frequently also in favour of the trustee (or the agent for the syndicate banks in a private passthrough structure) to cover risks in respect of the mortgage pool.

Standard warranty protection will include (at the least) warranties that:

   (i) each mortgage constitutes a valid and binding obligation of the borrower and, subject to completion of any pending registration at HM Land Registry, constitutes a valid and subsisting first legal mortgage over the relevant property;

  (ii) all steps necessary to perfect the originator's title have been duly taken (eg registration at HM Land Registry in the case of registered land);

 (iii) all necessary investigations and searches have been carried out by the originator as would be carried out by a reasonably prudent lender;

 (iv) the mortgage advance is within the appropriate loan to valuation ratio or, if greater, there is in force mortgage indemnity insurance to cover the excess;

  (v) prior to making each advance the originator's lending guidelines were satisfied subject to such waivers as might be within the discretion of a reasonably prudent lender; and

 (vi) each underlying property is adequately insured.

The purpose of such warranties is to ensure that the issuer obtains a mortgage pool which is capable of supporting the issuer's payment obligations to noteholders and which will, itself, constitute adequate security for the issuer's obligations.

Warranties will also be sought in relation to the collateral security being transferred to the issuer with the mortgages. Thus, one would expect to see warranties as to:

   (i) (in the case of endowment mortgages) life policies having been assigned to the originator prior to completion of the sale of the pool, the amount payable on maturity of each policy (without taking account of terminal bonuses) not being less than the original amount of the mortgage and payment of all premiums being up-to-date; and

  (ii) all insurance policies (such as mortgage indemnity policies and further advances policies) which are to be assigned to the issuer being in full force and effect and capable of assignment.

A warranty will also be sought that the originator has complied with the Inland Revenue's published reimbursement and audit requirements in relation to any of the mortgages which is a qualifying loan for MIRAS purposes.

As we have already seen, the trustee will be concerned to ensure that a borrower cannot exercise any right of set-off against amounts owed under the relevant mortgage. Although notice of the transfer will prevent future set-offs arising, it will not affect rights of set-off arising up until the time of notification. Therefore, it will be normal to include a warranty that no right of set-off exists in favour of the borrower which would entitle him to reduce the amount of any payment due under his mortgage.

Obviously, the warranties given by an originator in the mortgage sale agreement will vary from transaction to transaction. The trustee, lead manager (and rating agencies) will generally seek to ensure that every perceived risk is the subject of a warranty. The originator will attempt to argue that certain risks are risks of the mortgage business generally and it should not be obliged to take on such inherent risks. Further, warranties should not be a disguised attempt to make the originator responsible for the creditworthiness of the borrowers in the future. This is particularly important if the desired off-balance sheet treatment is to be achieved.

(b) Repurchase of assets on breach of warranty

In the case of a breach of warranty under a mortgage sale agreement, there will generally be a provision requiring the originator to repurchase the relevant mortgage at its outstanding principal amount (plus accrued interest) at the time of the repurchase. The originator is usually concerned to ensure that this is the only remedy for breach of warranty and it is not exposed to double jeopardy in the form of an action for damages resulting from the breach—such an action could indirectly result in it guaranteeing full and timely payments on the notes which would obviously be commercially disastrous for it.

3. STAMP DUTY

There is an exemption from stamp duty in the case of assignments of mortgages and, subject to certain reservations in respect of equitable assignments, it is generally accepted that the exemption covers the assignments of mortgages which have taken place in mortgage securitisations to date.

This exemption is not available to an assignment of other kinds of receivable. Although there are various stamp duty avoidance techniques which are used in financing structures involving the assignment of receivables, such as executing a written assignment outside the United Kingdom or effecting the assignment by way of a written offer and oral acceptance, these techniques may not prove acceptable in the context of an issue of rated public securities.

On a large portfolio of assets, stamp duty on assignment will be a significant cost in a securitisation and has to date constituted an impediment to the successful securitisation in the United Kingdom of assets other than mortgages.

B. Taking security

Upon the transfer to the issuer of the assets to be securitised the trustee for noteholders (or the agent for syndicate banks in a passthrough transaction) will take security over those assets and the collateral security.

1. NATURE OF THE SECURITY TAKEN

In a mortgage securitisation, the issuer will enter into a deed of sub-charge in favour of the trustee or agent. The issuer will sub-charge the mortgage pool and any related security for the mortgages. It will also charge its right to receive payments from the Revenue under the MIRAS scheme, the authorised investments which are permitted under the transaction documents, its interest in the bank accounts established for the purpose of the transaction and its rights under the transaction documents. It will assign to the trustee or agent its interest under its insurance contracts which relate to the mortgage pool and will also give a floating charge over all its remaining assets and undertakings. The Inland Revenue, the transaction account bank and (usually) the various insurers will be notified of the existence of the relevant charge.

There is some doubt whether MIRAS receivables from the Inland Revenue, which constitute statutory obligations on the part of the Inland Revenue to pay, are capable of being assigned or charged at law. The current practice of the Revenue is to accept and comply with instructions from a party entitled to MIRAS receivables to pay them direct to an account charged to a trustee for the benefit of the chargor's creditors and there has been no indication to date from the Revenue that it proposes to change this practice.

Furthermore, although the charges over the bank accounts established for the purpose of the transaction and the authorised investments will normally be framed as fixed charges, there is some doubt as to whether a court would actually construe charges over transaction accounts and authorised investments as fixed (rather than floating) charges. Floating charges are usually seen as less valuable protection than fixed charges because they can rank behind certain preferential creditors. More importantly, floating charges only 'attach' to the relevant assets when the charge 'crystallises', eg following an event of default. At that time the assets may have been dissipated or be of little value. To protect against this concern, the administration agreement and deed of sub-charge will specify the circumstances in which moneys may be withdrawn from the accounts. It is also worth noting, as a general point, that the trustee's (or agent's) ability to enforce its security over authorised investments and cash will be dependent on its ability to trace the relevant assets.

There may be either a legal or equitable sub-charge of the mortgage pool.

(a) Legal sub-charge

In the case of unregistered land the sub-charge will consist of (i) a covenant by the sub-mortgagor (ie the issuer) to pay the principal sum and interest secured by the sub-mortgage; (ii) a transfer to the sub-mortgagee (ie the trustee) of the mortgage debt together with the benefit of all the powers and provisions contained in or conferred by the mortgage, all securities for the same and generally the whole benefit of the mortgage; and (iii) a proviso for re-assignment to the issuer on payment of the sum secured by the sub-mortgage (ie the principal and interest owing on the notes). Notice of the sub-charge is given to the borrower.

In the case of registered land the same principles apply save that the transfer of the property interest must be completed (if it is to take effect at law) by registration of the trustee (or agent) at HM Land Registry as sub-chargee of the mortgages.

Following a legal transfer of the mortgage pool and legal sub-charge, the trustee (or agent) will be entitled to exercise the rights and powers of the mortgagee in the same manner as the issuer. However, it should be stressed that the remedy of the trustee (or agent) is to sell the mortgage pool in the event of default by the issuer under the sub-charge. Only if the borrower defaults will it have the power of sale of the land.

It should also be borne in mind that, with mortgages of registered land, there will inevitably be a delay between an application to register the transfer to the issuer and the sub-charge, and the completion of registration. Who can exercise such powers during the period between:

(i) the date the transaction is completed and the date HM Land Registry receives the application; and
(ii) the date the application is received and the date registration is actually completed?

The Land Registration Act 1925 deals with certain powers, but what about the ability to make further advances and have them secured under the terms of the charge? This is primarily a question of construction of the mortgage document and, as noted in the context of certain new mortgage products, can be important to resolve. If the mortgage document refers to the originator and its successors in title it will be a question of construction whether the issuer can, at the appropriate time, properly be called a successor in title. Following the legal route, once the mortgage has been assigned to the issuer and then, by way of sub-charge, to the trustee, it is the trustee, and not the originator or issuer, who should be able to make further advances and have them secured under the terms of the charge. This will only be the case for registered land once the trustee has become the successor in title by being registered as the proprietor of the charge under the terms of the sub-charge.

(b) Equitable sub-charge

Equitable sub-charges follow similar rules to those for equitable assignments because the method of creating such sub-charges of property involves assignment subject to an equity of redemption.

Who can exercise the rights and powers of the mortgagee where there is an equitable assignment and equitable sub-charge? The procedures currently adopted, in order to tack discretionary further advances, are to have a temporary release by the trustee of the sub-charge and a reassignment by the issuer to the originator. The documentation may then provide for the mortgage to be put back into the pool once the advance is made. Alternatively, the mortgage may be kept out of the pool and a new one of equal amount substituted. The tacking of mandatory further advances has already been described.

2. REGISTRATION

In the case of a legal transfer of the mortgage pool and a legal sub-charge registration will be required at HM Land Registry.

A Form 395 will also be lodged at the Companies Registry.

Under the Companies Act 1985 the creation of certain types of charge requires registration at the Companies Registry. Those which must be registered include charges 'for the purpose of securing any issue of debentures' (such as the notes) and a floating charge on a company's undertaking or property. If the prescribed particulars of the charge together with the charging document itself are not delivered to the Registrar of Companies within 21 days after the charge's creation, the charge becomes void against the liquidator or administrator and any creditor of the company. This would render completely ineffective the security given to the trustee or agent by the issuer of the notes. As a result, great care is taken to ensure that the relevant details are duly delivered on or as soon as possible after the closing of the issue.

The current English law on charges is not particularly satisfactory and there are often lengthy debates between the lawyers as to the registrability of certain charges and the detail of the particulars which need to be registered. Many of these debates are resolved once the Registrar of Companies issues a certificate registering the charge, which he will do after examining the charging document and the particulars delivered to him. A certificate of registration of any charge is conclusive evidence that the requirements of the Companies Act as to registration have been satisfied. However, registration will not mean that the charge was in fact validly created or that it will have the priority between competing creditors that the trustee would necessarily want to have, namely a first ranking charge. As a result, detailed procedural steps are always taken to ensure that the directors of the issuer have validly exercised their powers in creating the charge and searches are made to ensure that no existing charge has been created by the issuer. This should, of course, not be a problem in practice.

There is an additional requirement of the Companies Act 1985 which is important to bear in mind. A copy of every certificate of registration is required to be endorsed on every note issued by the issuer as the payment of that note is secured by the charge which has been registered. This requirement does not usually cause much of a problem in practice because very few of the securitisations to date have involved the issue of definitive notes. In most cases the global note representing the entire issue has been issued on terms that no exchange is required for definitive notes unless certain events occur such as the closure of the two main Eurobond clearance systems.

The Companies Act 1989 provides for several changes in the current system. While the Act is not intended to reform the substantive law of charges, the changes (which are likely to become effective early in 1991) will have a radical effect on the procedures for and effects of registration. The most significant of these which are relevant to securitisation are (i) the certificate of registration will only be conclusive evidence of the date of submission of the particulars and (ii) if the registered particulars are not complete and accurate at any time, the charge will be void to the extent that any rights are not disclosed by the registered particulars which would be disclosed if they were complete and .accurate. In effect, this will mean that the trustee or the agent will have to exercise extreme care over the details included on the forms submitted to the Registrar of Companies and any changes may need to be disclosed. A further change introduced by the Companies Act 1989 will be the need to deliver details of the date on which the notes are subscribed within 21 days of the closing. It is not yet clear what additional particulars will require to be disclosed but the issuer may have a statutory obligation to disclose the allocation of the notes among the management group. A final, but important, point to note is that, while no fees are currently payable for registration of charges, that will change under the new regime although it is to be hoped that these costs will not be significant.

3. PRIORITIES

Where there is a legal transfer and legal sub-charge of registered land the trustee (or agent) will have the rights of the original mortgagee and will therefore take subject only to overriding interests and interests registered prior to its own.

In the case of an equitable charge over registered land, the trustee (or agent) will take subject to interests registered before it and subject to all interests registered after it but which were registered within the priority period afforded by a search of the Register which did not reveal the trustee's (or agent's) interest. The trustee (or agent) will also take subject to 'equities' created before the borrower is given notice of the assignment such as charges, liens, options and other similar third party rights. Such equities could fall into three categories being those:

(i) created before the trustee's security;

(ii) created before or after the trustee's security but taking priority because of rules governing priority between equitable interests generally or between assignees of choses in action or by statute;

(iii) created after creation of the trustee's security and which are legal interests.

In unregistered land the trustee, if it makes no registration at the Central Land Charges Registry (and it is doubtful whether an equitable sub-charge can be registered as a land charge), will take subject to interests of third parties taking an interest in the property for value without notice of the trustee's interest and will take subject to prior equities as referred to above except that in the case of (iii) the person taking a legal interest would need to be a bona fide purchaser for value without notice of the trustee's equitable interest.

These concerns are usually regarded as being largely theoretical and only passing reference is made to them in the offering circular. They should only arise if there is fraud or mistake on the part of the originator or the issuer and, so far, the balance of convenience has been in favour of equitable assignments and sub-charges rather than the legal (almost) risk-free route.

ADMINISTRATION/SERVICING

It will invariably be the case that the SPV has no employees. While this is obviously easier from a practical point of view, it is also insisted upon by the rating agencies as employees need to be paid and, in an insolvency of the issuer, would rank as preferential creditors. There would also be social security contributions which have to be made for which the Inland Revenue would also rank as a preferential creditor ahead of the trustee and noteholders.

Who better than the originator to act as the administrator of the issuer's assets and of its business? It will act as agent of the issuer and of the trustee to the extent necessary but, while it will have contractual obligations, it will not incur any liability for the debt of the issuer to noteholders and others. The suitability of the originator to play this role will be closely examined by the lead manager (at least on its first encounter) and by the rating agencies. It is common for many of the new mortgage lenders to act as administrator on issues where they have originated the mortgages for securitisation. However, other originators such as banks have found it more cost effective to delegate the administrative function to a highly computerised operation not located in expensive premises on the High Street. The new mortgage lenders have been able to generate useful fee income without any real increase in their own cost base.

The extensive obligations of the administrator are set out in great detail in the administration or servicing agreement. Inevitably these reflect to a large extent the way the administrator's own portfolio is administered. Other chapters describe more fully the need for extensive back office facilities to keep track of the large number of mortgage accounts while keeping costs to a minimum. Certain of the functions of the administrator have already been mentioned—setting the interest rate on the mortgages and handling arrears and enforcement procedures. The contractual powers of the administrator are also expanded by powers of attorney which are given by each of the issuer and the trustee. These are necessary to enable the mortgage to be discharged at HM Land Registry when the borrower redeems in full. It would obviously not be sensible to involve officers of the trustee on a continual basis for this essentially administrative (albeit legally important) function. These powers of attorney also mean that little to no involvement is required by the trustee when substitutions occur or further advances are made.

The way in which the administrator is involved so fundamentally in the transaction could mean that the rating of the notes was dependent upon the rating of the administrator. Typically the new mortgage lenders are not themselves rated. As a result, the insolvency of the administrator could, in the absence of appropriate safeguards, jeopardise the issuer and the rating for the notes. The Bank of England has also imposed a number of wide-ranging restrictions on 'the servicing agent' if it is a bank, in order to ensure that its role is not seen as being more than acting as an agent. If any one of a number of specific conditions is not satisfied the assets administered by the servicing agent will be consolidated with its balance sheet for risk asset ratio purposes. These conditions are set out in Appendix 1 (on page 304). One partial solution is that, on the occurrence of certain events, the administrator's appointment can be terminated and a substitute administrator take over. If no substitute can be found at an acceptable cost or at all, it is usual for an appropriately experienced entity to be 'standing in the wings' ready to act if necessary for an agreed fee as the 'administrator of last resort'.

INSOLVENCY CONSIDERATIONS

It is obviously crucial in a structured financing of this type that the risk of insolvency is kept to a minimum. The issuer's own position must be closely examined to ensure that it can never be called upon to meet liabilities at a time when it has insufficient assets to do so. The position of other parties in the transaction must also be analysed to ascertain whether their insolvency or financial difficulties would have an impact on the issuer. The analysis of these risks is usually undertaken by the lead manager and, in a public transaction, by the rating agencies for the benefit of investors.

ISSUER INSOLVENCY

The issuer is the only person legally obliged to make payments of principal and interest on the notes. In order to meet its liabilities, it has recourse only to its share capital and reserves, the mortgages and collateral security transferred to it and its contractual rights against the other parties, such as the originator and the administrator. The issuer must be protected as far as possible against both asset risk and liquidity risk. These tend to involve mainly commercial rather than legal difficulties. Asset risk will be primarily concerned with the quality of the mortgages and collateral security, the arrangements for deposit and safekeeping of the title deeds, the ease with which the trustee can enforce or realise the security if need be and credit enhancements such as pool insurance or properly constituted subordinated notes. Liquidity risk obviously focuses more on the sufficiency of the issuer's cash flow at any time it is called upon to make payments. These will be payments not only to noteholders but also to third parties such as the trustee, the administrator for servicing the assets, tax liabilities and ongoing auditors' expenses in addition to all of the initial expenses of the issue.

ISSUER'S EXPOSURE TO THIRD PARTY INSOLVENCY

Many of the commercial solutions to asset and liquidity risk depend upon third parties providing to the issuer some form of protection. If the relevant third party becomes insolvent or is experiencing financial difficulties at the moment when the issuer needs it to perform, the issuer's own position will be prejudiced. Typically there will be three or four types of third party to which the issuer will be looking for payment or support at any particular time—insurers (for example, life companies, buildings and mortgage indemnity providers and, in some cases, pool insurers), holders of junior or subordinated notes, bankers and the originator/administrator.

1. INSURERS

The rating agencies will insist either that there is a spreading of risk between a group of insurance companies, eg mortgage indemnity providers, or that there is an appropriate rating for the claims paying ability of the relevant insurer, eg if it is the pool insurance provider. However, whatever the ability of an insurer to pay claims when due, it must not be forgotten that any contract of insurance depends upon the utmost good faith of the insured in disclosing risk to the insurer. The specific terms of the insurance contract must also be closely examined to ensure that claims can indeed be made on the basis and at the times contemplated.

2. HOLDERS OF JUNIOR NOTES

The junior notes will be constituted by the same trust deed and benefit from the same security as the senior notes. However, the rights of holders of junior notes to receive payment and to require the trustee to enforce the security for failure to make payment on time or in full must be properly and effectively subordinated to the rights of the senior noteholders. Subordination techniques in the United Kingdom are becoming increasingly sophisticated to deal with the many difficult problems which can arise in English law but which are beyond the scope of this book. Suffice to say that there can obviously be conflicts between what junior noteholders would like the trustee to do in any default or enforcement and what would be best for the senior noteholders. As junior notes are increasingly sold to third party investors, these conflicts need to be addressed in the offering circular and the trust deed.

3. BANKERS

The issuer will inevitably have at least one bank account into which payments by mortgagors are directed and from which payments to noteholders and third parties are made. The bank at which this account is maintained must not exercise any banker's right of set off in a manner which would prejudice the issuer, eg to claim operating expenses or a refund because a borrower's direct debit had not been met when presented. Other banks may well be involved in the transaction, eg the providers of a liquidity facility to meet shortfalls from temporary failure by borrowers to pay interest on time, or to provide the issuer with funds to pay the initial expenses of the transaction. These banks must either be appropriately rated or have provided all the necessary funds at the outset and their entitlement to receive interest and principal must be effectively subordinated to the rights of noteholders.

4. ORIGINATOR/ADMINISTRATOR

As mentioned earlier, the originator will have sold the mortgages and collateral security to the issuer and will be obliged to repurchase mortgages if these do not conform with warranties given in the mortgage sale agreement. What happens if the originator becomes insolvent soon after the original sale or the repurchase? The administrator will be obliged to ensure proper administration of the mortgage assets but will want to have flexibility in its dealings with borrowers. For example, it may wish to delay an increase in the mortgage rate even though the rate payable by the issuer on the notes has increased. It may wish to substitute new mortgages into the pool or make further advances to borrowers rather than use the redemption proceeds to repay principal on the notes. If the administrator becomes insolvent before or after the interest rate subsidy is paid or the substitution or further advance occurs, what is the position of the issuer vis-à-vis the liquidator or receiver of the administrator? Can the issuer be required to pay back money which it has received but which it needs in order to meet its obligations to noteholders?

These questions have to be satisfactorily resolved if a rating is to be obtained and the transaction to work in all foreseeable circumstances. Their answer depends, in part, on interpreting relatively new and untested provisions of the Insolvency Act 1986. These provide, for example, that the liquidator of a company can disclaim any 'onerous property' such as an unprofitable contract or one giving rise to a liability to pay money or perform any other onerous act. The extensive obligations set out in the administration agreement could well be regarded as an onerous contract. The court can, in certain circumstances, rescind a contract on terms providing for the payment of damages or other amounts as the court thinks just. Other provisions enable the court to make virtually any order it thinks fit if a company has entered into a transaction at an undervalue or given a preference to any person which puts that person into a better position. Various presumptions are made where the persons involved are connected with each other, which is likely to be the case between the originator/administrator and the issuer even if an off-balance sheet structure is employed.

The circumstances of each transaction and party are different and need to be closely examined. However, given the absence of judicial authority on the relevant facts and the requirement to provide legal opinions at the time that the notes are issued in relation to events which have yet to occur, uncertainties are bound to remain.

PROFIT EXTRACTION

It is refreshing to note that, despite the emphasis on insolvency and risk which has dominated the last few pages, these transactions are fairly profitable—and not just for the lawyers. The originator which has securitised its assets clearly wants to be able to retain as much as possible of the profit after payment of noteholders and ongoing expenses. This used to be possible, even in off-balance sheet structures, by the originator receiving dividends on its preference shares or ordinary shares. There are, of course, legal restrictions on what profits are available for distribution by a public company and these occasionally meant that profits which were available in cash terms were not available for accounting or legal purposes until, for example, the initial expenses of the issue had been fully amortised. Nevertheless, the dividend route was a common one and relatively simple to operate. However, even before the Companies Act 1989 came into force, profit extraction methods began to depend almost entirely on contractual mechanisms between the originator/administrator and the SPV. It is in this context that most of the difficult tax issues in securitisations arise. These are addressed more fully in Chapter 3. While each transaction must be considered in detail according to its own facts, it is worth noting here the main methods which have been seen in the markets so far:

(i) the use of an interest rate swap or parallel loans which, in practice, have resulted in the SPV alone making payments to the originator;

(ii) the sale of the mortgages to the SPV at a price above par—this is justified commercially on the basis that the mortgages will generate profit over time and they are therefore worth more than their principal amount at the time of sale;

(iii) the payment of fees such as for providing administration or other services; and

(iv) the payment of interest on the subordinated loan made by the originator to fund the initial expenses or to establish certain reserves.

REGULATORY AND OTHER CONSIDERATIONS

The requirements of the Companies Acts, the Bank of England and the accounting profession for off-balance sheet treatment have already been mentioned, as well as the need for a licence under the Consumer Credit Act and registration under the Data Protection Act. One other statute always needs to be borne in mind in any securitisation, namely the Financial Services Act 1986.

This Act prohibits the unauthorised carrying on of investment business in the United Kingdom. Each aspect of the transaction must be analysed to see whether it involves 'investments', whether the relevant activity constitutes 'investment business' and, therefore, whether authorisation is required under the Act. If authorisation is required but has not been obtained, a criminal offence would be committed and there would be civil sanctions as well. For example, a contract might be unenforceable and any money paid under it might have to be returned. Obtaining authorisation can be a lengthy process and the extensive rules and regulations applicable to an authorised person may make it virtually impossible for the originator/administrator to run its own or the issuer's business. This has been a fear of many new mortgage lenders although the banks and building societies are likely to be authorised anyway because of other aspects of their business.

The basic activity of mortgage lending as well as most of the arrangements made for generating mortgage business have been excluded from the range of investment activities which require authorisation. However, many uncertainties remain—for example, does the transfer by the originator to the issuer of the collateral security for mortgages including endowment life policies (which are investments for the purposes of the Act) mean that there has been a dealing in investments, which is a regulated investment activity? There are various exclusions in the Act which should apply in most circumstances so that authorisation will not be necessary for the mortgage originator or the issuer purely because of the transfer of assets.

What is the position of the issuer when it issues securities in the market? All of the public issues to date have been structured so that the securities are full recourse debt obligations of the issuer with the investor's right to payment being secured on all of the assets of the issuer. This structure was adopted principally for tax reasons but it is also advantageous for the purposes of the

Act. Even though the securities are 'investments', merely issuing them does not of itself require the issuer to be authorised. Although there had been concern that the nature of the security meant that noteholders were participants in a collective investment scheme, the Act was amended at a late stage to try and relieve the difficulties. Collective investment schemes are subject to totally different regulations governing their operation and promotion which could have seriously impeded the development of the market. However, as issuers and their advisers are continually devising new structures, the language of the relevant exemption must be examined to determine whether it applies in the particular transaction.

Section 75(6)(1)(i) provides that there will not be a collective investment scheme if there are 'arrangements under which the rights or interests of the participants are represented by investments falling within paragraph 2 of Schedule 1 to the Act which are issued by a single body corporate which is not an open-ended investment company'. The definition of 'open-ended investment company' is not particularly easy to interpret but it is thought that most issuers should not be caught. However, will the securities which they issue always fall within paragraph 2 of Schedule 1? Again, most of the securities can be regarded as debentures or other instruments creating or acknowledging indebtedness and thus within paragraph 2 but this will not invariably be the case. Further, the exemption does not address the now common situation in most securitisations, namely that a permanent global note is issued and never exchanged for definitive notes. Not only must the terms of the global note be examined to ensure that it itself falls within paragraph 2, but a further (hopefully theoretical) concern must also be addressed. Almost all Eurobond transactions involve global notes and the two main clearance systems, Euroclear and Cedel. Individual investors have contractual arrangements with these clearance systems and do not themselves hold the securities which contain the rights enforceable against the issuer. Is it, therefore, right to say that the rights or interests of the participants are 'represented by investments falling within paragraph 2'?

The Act can give rise to other unpleasant surprises, eg for the administrator. Paragraph 14 of Schedule 1 to the Act describes one type of activity constituting investment business, which could require authorisation, as 'managing, or offering or agreeing to manage, assets, belonging to another person if (a) these assets consist of or include investments; or (b) the arrangements for their management are such that these assets may consist of or include investments at the discretion of the person managing or offering or agreeing to manage them and either they have . . . done so or the arrangements have at any time . . . been held out as arrangements under which they would do so'.

The administrator will, of course, be managing the assets of the issuer in the most economically efficient manner which is consistent with the rating agencies' requirements. This could include, for instance, re-investing monthly payments of interest by borrowers in high yielding but secure investments, such as gilts, prior to the quarterly payment to noteholders. It could also include the administrator deciding to surrender an endowment life policy as part of the enforcement of the security for a mortgage. In either case, is the administrator managing the assets of the issuer such as to require it to be authorised under the Act? The somewhat unhelpful answer is that authorisation could be necessary if certain eminently sensible commercial actions are indeed to be taken by the administrator on behalf of the issuer. It is clearly unsatisfactory that the Act has such a wide application well beyond the contemplation of even the most hard line legislator.

The Act could also require trustees to be authorised. It is a common provision in the trust deed for these transactions as well as for virtually all Euromarket issues that, following an event of default and the receipt by the trustee of insufficient funds to pay at least 10% of the principal amount of the notes, the trustee should have full discretion to invest these funds until such time as it is able to distribute an amount of at least 10% of the notes. Has the trustee thereby agreed to manage assets belonging to the issuer and does it have discretion to invest in 'investments' or have these 'arrangements' been 'held out as arrangements under which they would' consist of or include investments? The answer will probably depend on whether the trustee holds itself out as offering investment management services and there is no guidance in the Act on what this involves. In any one case, the particular facts should be considered (although different lawyers may reach different conclusions) and some trustees have become authorised as a precaution.

LISTING AND SELLING RESTRICTIONS

All the public note issues so far have been listed on either the London Stock Exchange or the Luxembourg Stock Exchange. If the issue is to be listed on the London Stock Exchange, Part IV of the Financial Services Act requires that listing particulars be prepared. The document must comply with The Stock Exchange's own regulations although these are much less extensive than, say, for a domestic share offering. Most issues have, however, been listed on the Luxembourg Stock Exchange because of their generally more relaxed application of the rules and because of a tax advantage (now repealed) for investors which are UK tax resident. Luxembourg listed issues are not subject to Part IV of the Financial Services Act. For the time being, the relevant requirements are set out in Part III of the Companies Act 1985. These relate mainly to the form and content of the prospectus which has to be delivered to the Registrar of Companies. Although there may not in fact be a 'prospectus' for the purposes of the Companies Act, it is usual to proceed as if there is one as the requirements are not particularly onerous. In due course, Part III of the Companies Act will be repealed and replaced by Part V of the Financial Services Act. It is hoped that the generally relaxed approach to securities offered in the Euromarkets to professional and sophisticated investors will be maintained by any new regulations.

If the notes are listed on either the London or Luxembourg Stock Exchange and the appropriate requirements of the Financial Services Act or the Companies Act have been met, the prospectus or other information memorandum relating to the issue can be widely distributed. However, the managers of the issue (who will almost certainly be authorised persons) must still comply with the restrictions in the Financial Services Act (and supporting rules and regulations) on the making of unsolicited calls and the distribution of investment advertisements. In practice, these are unlikely to cause difficulty given the professional nature of the investor market.

RESPONSIBILITY FOR INFORMATION

This has tended to be an area where Euromarket professionals have been much more relaxed than their domestic counterparts. This is changing as investment bankers become more aware of the wide range of criminal and civil sanctions which can apply to them and their clients if the markets are misled or inaccurate or incomplete information is given to investors. The relevant considerations are often no greater in mortgage or other asset securitisations than in normal Euromarket transactions although questions of materiality can be very different when the issuer is a single purpose, thinly capitalised issuer with a limited range of assets rather than IBM or the World Bank.

CONCLUSION

It can be seen that securitisations involve an enormously wide range of legal issues, some of which are common to other Euromarket transactions or structured financings and others which are unique. In such complicated transactions it is inevitable that the documentation is extensive and expensive in terms of management time as well as lawyers' fees. As so many aspects of the transaction link in with each other and the success (and rating) of the deal depends upon their being no unforseen surprises or weaknesses, it is often difficult to divorce the legal from the commercial aspects. The two go hand in hand although a balance must always be maintained between legal theory, commercial convenience and best practice.

Chapter 3

Tax Issues

Ben Staveley
Freshfields

Having regard to the complex and delicately balanced nature of structured financing arrangements of this kind it should come as no surprise that they raise a number of tax issues, some of them rather difficult. In order to understand these issues and their significance it will be helpful to look first at the tax position of the originator before securitisation.

TAX POSITION OF THE ORIGINATOR BEFORE SECURITISATION

Strictly, there is no need for an originator of mortgage loans to be UK tax resident in order to be prescribed by the Treasury as a qualifying lender for MIRAS purposes, though the Treasury will want to see some presence in the United Kingdom to cope with the administration of MIRAS. Building societies automatically achieve qualifying lender status without the need for Treasury prescription. In practice most originators have tended to be UK tax resident, as also have securitisation vehicles.

On that basis it is assumed in this chapter that the originator and any securitisation vehicle will be UK incorporated and resident, as commercially it is normal for the vehicle, like the originator, to be a qualifying lender for MIRAS purposes so that borrowers can continue to receive tax relief on their mortgage interest at source under the MIRAS scheme.

A typical mortgage lending business, involving lending money to individuals secured on property and collateral security, will normally amount to the carrying on of a trade for tax purposes and be accepted by the Inland Revenue as such. The originator will actively seek out and originate new mortgage loans, as well as making further advances in relation to those borrowers and providing remortgage finance.

On this basis, the mortgage loans and related security will generally be treated as held on revenue account for the purposes of the trade, notwithstanding that once the advances have been made they are usually held to redemption or maturity rather than being actively 'turned to account'.

As a trading company the originator will be taxed in a generally favourable manner, as described below.

Interest paid by the originator on its funding, and any other revenue expenditure incurred in originating mortgages and administering its mortgage portfolio, should in the ordinary course of events be allowed to the originator as a deduction for corporation tax purposes against its receipts on the mortgage loans, which it will bring in on an accruals basis. Similarly, bad debts will give rise to allowable deductions for corporation tax purposes. Such deductions will generally also be available on an accruals basis apart from yearly interest paid otherwise than to a United Kingdom bank, when the deduction should strictly be on an interest paid basis.

If the originator makes a loss on its mortgage lending trade then it will on a current year basis be able to relieve that loss against the profits of any other activities which it carries on. It could utilise the loss on the mortgage activities by surrendering it to another member of its group subject to the generally applicable rules on the utilisation of losses and group relief. Finally, if not otherwise utilised, the loss would be available for carry forward and, to a limited extent, carry back against future or past profits of the mortgage trade.

Although, as mentioned above, mortgages are generally held on revenue account for the purposes of the trade, the tax treatment of mortgages tends to differ from the tax treatment of trading stock generally. With trading stock there is a deemed disposal of the stock at the end of each financial year and any diminution in the value of the stock gives rise to an immediate deduction. Sometimes, an increase in value can—at least in the Inland Revenue's view—be immediately taxable as well. By contrast, mortgages are often held on a basis which does not follow that of trading stock to the letter but which has the result that the originator is taxed on any gain or loss only as and when made on their disposal either to a third party or through redemption rather than on the basis of an annual deemed disposal. This 'realisations basis' treatment can make the taxation of the disposal of mortgages appear superficially like the taxation of the disposal of capital assets. However, an important distinction is that there is much greater flexibility available in the use of trading losses within a company and within a group than there is in the case of capital losses. A trading stock or realisations basis treatment is not, however, universal. There are, for example, mortgage lenders who, by agreement with the Inland Revenue, hold their mortgages as capital assets, rather than as trading assets.

As regards value added tax, the supply of mortgage finance to borrowers is an exempt supply. However, mortgage lenders may well be registered for VAT purposes on the basis that they do make some taxable supplies. For example, a mortgage lender might supply mortgage administration services to third parties. The general rule as far as recovery of the originator's input VAT is concerned is that tax will not be recoverable to the extent it relates to the making of exempt supplies. Often, a mortgage lender will have agreed a special method with Customs and Excise which governs the recoverability of input tax and represents a departure from the normal statutory method. Again, the originator may for general group VAT planning reasons be a member of a group for VAT purposes so that any intra group supplies will not be supplies at all for VAT purposes. However, one consequence of a group election is that every member of the group becomes jointly and severally liable for the VAT liability of every other member of the group, which may not, in the rating agencies' view, be acceptable for a securitisation vehicle itself.

If the mortgage lending were not to be treated as a trade, it would fall to be treated as an investment activity. In that event the taxation of the activity and of the company might be markedly different. Deductions would be available for a narrower range of expenses (not, for example, for bad debts). Costs associated with the acquisition of investments will mostly be capital in nature and tax relief would be available only in a computation of chargeable gains. Deductions would be available only as and when paid rather than on an accruals basis, though admittedly receipts would be treated likewise.

The remainder of this chapter looks at the position if a securitisation takes place and complicates the comparatively simple position described above. The analysis can be broken down into the following elements:

(i) taxation effects of the sale of mortgages and collateral security to the vehicle;
(ii) tax treatment of the expenses of establishing the transaction;
(iii) taxation of the vehicle during the life of the transaction;
(iv) tax treatment of the securities issued by the vehicle;
(v) tax implications of returning profit to the originator.

TAXATION EFFECTS OF THE SALE OF MORTGAGES AND COLLATERAL SECURITY TO THE VEHICLE

The mortgages will commonly be sold by the originator to the vehicle for a price equal to the outstanding principal amount of the mortgages. The value of mortgages is generally taken to be their outstanding principal amount plus, perhaps, accrued interest. The entitlement to receive mortgage interest under the mortgages at a rate that is attractive for lenders might suggest a higher value. On the other hand, some indications point the other way. Any borrower could redeem his mortgage tomorrow, thus removing the benefit of the future income stream; the mortgages carry a fairly heavy administrative burden, and there may be a risk of the mortgage rate having to be maintained, for competitive reasons, below the lender's wholesale market cost of funds. The mortgages, however, are generally disposed of at a price which reflects the originator's cost of creating or acquiring the mortgage.

The technical analysis of such a disposal can theoretically be quite complex, depending on a number of variables including the status of the mortgages as capital or revenue assets in the hands of the originator and the vehicle, and whether the vehicle is in the originator's tax group or is otherwise connected with it for tax purposes. However, in principle, the feature that the originator sells the mortgages to the vehicle at cost means that the disposal should be neutral from a corporation tax point of view.

Although it is generally thought that no tax problems arise on a disposal of mortgages at their outstanding principal amount, there are, however, circumstances in which the mortgages might be sold for a price exceeding that amount. The main consequences of this are explained under 'Profit Extraction' below.

Other assets will be disposed of together with the mortgages, such as charges over life policies and interests in insurance policies. As regards the charges over life policies, in which the originator's interest is merely a security interest, these should sensibly be regarded as entirely ancillary to the mortgages and will take their colour as revenue or capital assets from the mortgages themselves. The same will also be true for other insurance policies (such as mortgage indemnity policies), even if the originator owns them beneficially rather than merely owning a security interest in them. It would accordingly not normally be necessary to distinguish them from the mortgages or to try and attribute a separate value to them in determining the tax effects of the transfer to the vehicle.

A. Stamp duty

As with any sale of assets, it is necessary to consider the stamp duty position. As a general proposition stamp duty is chargeable on any instrument in writing which implements the sale of an interest in property, with the duty being charged at the rate of 1% of the value of the property transferred.

If duty were charged on the sale of the mortgage debts to the vehicle, this would be a very severe extra cost to the transaction. However, a transfer of mortgages will not normally be chargeable to stamp duty. This is on the basis that the transfer of mortgages used to fall within a specific head of charge 'Mortgage, Bond, Debenture, Covenant . . .' in Schedule 1 to the Stamp Act 1891. Stamp duty in relation to instruments within this head was abolished by s 64 of the Finance Act 1971. Furthermore, case law and, in this instance, the repealing statute as well indicate that instruments which fall under a specific head which is repealed do not fall back into some more general head of charge. The same exemption should also operate to exempt the assignment of the charges over the life policies or other collateral security from the stamp duty charge. Care is, however, needed to avoid the instruments ranking as the disposal of the equitable interest in the mortgages only, since case law suggests this would not benefit from the exemption.

The position is rather more difficult in the case of an assignment of insurance policies, such as the originator's existing buildings and mortgage indemnity insurance policies to the extent that they relate to the mortgages being sold. It is thought, relying on the case of *Blandy v Herbert* (1829) 9 B & C 396, that an assignment of rights under an insurance policy is not chargeable with ad valorem stamp duty unless a claim has arisen under the insurance policy so that it has some present, rather than merely contingent, value and in many cases such assignments have not been submitted for adjudication. A more cautious view is that such an assignment could be of 'property' the conveyance or transfer on sale of which is chargeable to ad valorem stamp duty even though no claim has arisen.

One stamp duty saving technique that might be considered—if for some reason the above protections were not available—would be for relevant documentation to be executed and retained outside the United Kingdom. This might particularly be considered in a case where the basic subject matter of the securitisation was not an asset of which the assignment was, as in the case of mortgages, specifically exempted from duty and where registration of the document in the United Kingdom was not an important commercial requirement. A good example might be lease receivables which would rank as property for stamp duty purposes but not property which benefited from any particular exemption on assignment. In such a case, duty would arise on the assignment of the subject matter of the securitisation at the rate of 1%, an expense which might significantly reduce the attraction of the proposal. If the relevant assignment documentation were executed and retained outside the United Kingdom, duty would not generally be avoided but merely deferred. However, there would be no need for any of the documentation to be stamped unless and until it needed to be relied on in the United Kingdom, ultimately by bringing it in evidence in court proceedings. Nor would any time limits for penalties and interests begin to run unless and until the documents were brought into the United Kingdom. It would be worth considering dividing the portfolio of assets transferred among several assignments so that the necessity of bringing into the United Kingdom an assignment relating to one asset only did not give rise to duty in respect of the entirety of the portfolio.

B. Other considerations

The disposal of the mortgages and collateral security should not be regarded as a taxable supply for VAT purposes. On this basis, no VAT should be payable by the vehicle on acquiring those assets.

Finally, it should be noted that the so-called 'accrued income scheme' does not apply to the acquisition of mortgages by the vehicle. The accrued income scheme is a body of legislation which, where it applies, operates to treat persons acquiring and disposing of income-bearing securities as entitled, for tax purposes, to the interest arising on those securities as if it arose on a day to day basis during their period of ownership rather than on the actual payment dates. However, because the borrowers under the mortgages will be individuals rather than companies or other bodies, the mortgages themselves will not be securities to which the scheme applies. The effect of this will be that, for mortgages bought by the vehicle part of the way through the (usually monthly) interest period, the whole of the interest payable at the end of the month will be taxable in the hands of the vehicle. The implications of this will need to be borne in mind in considering the vehicle's tax profile, particularly if the vehicle's true 'profit' for that first part month is less than the full interest receipt because it paid the orginator an amount in respect of the interest accrued up to the date of transfer.

TAX TREATMENT OF THE EXPENSES OF ESTABLISHING THE TRANSACTION

The most significant expenses of establishing a transaction can be categorised as follows:

(i) the selling concessions allowed to, and the management and underwriting commissions paid to, the managers of the issue;

(ii) the professional fees of the legal and accounting advisers to the originator, the managers and the trustee;

(iii) the rating fees of the rating agencies;

(iv) the up-front fees payable to any banks providing loan facilities to support the transaction;

(v) the payment of the premium, and the funding of the deductible (or first loss provision), in respect of any pool insurance policy;

(vi) fees of the trustee acting for the bondholders;

(vii) printing and listing fees relating to the issue;

(viii) the fee payable to the administrator of last resort.

The main question is whether these expenses are deductible for corporation tax purposes if borne by the originator or the vehicle. If the answer is that they are deductible by one but not the other, this may indicate the most efficient way of bearing those expenses.

As a general point, quite a number of the expenses will be deductible if they are borne by the originator, provided at least that the originator is itself a trading company (see above). This is on the basis that if the originator agrees with the vehicle to bear the expenses as a term of the agreement to transfer the mortgages, the expenses will represent an incidental cost of effecting a trading disposal and will be allowable on that ground. This may be a satisfactory method of dealing with some of the expenses, but needless to say consideration will need to be given to whether this achieves the desired commercial effect as between the originator and the vehicle, having regard in particular to available methods of extracting profit from the vehicle (see below).

Turning to the position if the expenses are borne by the vehicle, and dealing with the categories of expenses set out above:

(i) the management and underwriting commissions payable to the managers should be deductible as an incidental cost of obtaining loan finance under s 77 of the Taxes Act 1988, whether the vehicle is a trading company or an investment company. If instead a selling concession is allowed to the managers (effectively rewarding the managers by allowing them the right to subscribe the notes at less than par) the concession will not be so allowable (s 77(7)(b)). This strongly points towards rewarding the managers by way of commission rather than concession, particularly given that there should be no difference between the two as far as VAT is concerned—VAT should not be chargeable in either case;

(ii) legal and other professional fees should also constitute an incidental cost of obtaining the loan finance and should be deductible on the basis just outlined. This treatment is available only insofar as the advice relates to the obtaining of finance by the vehicle's issue of the bonds to the market;

(iii) the initial fees of the rating agencies should again be deductible expenses for the vehicle on the same basis, as they relate directly to the raising of finance through the bond issue;

(iv) up-front fees paid to banks providing facilities to the issuer should also be deductible as an incidental cost of obtaining those facilities (and would be so deductible whether or not those facilities were, in the event, drawn down);

(v) the tax treatment of pool policy premiums is less certain. It is perhaps less obvious that the fee is deductible as wholly and exclusively incurred for the obtaining of finance by the vehicle. This is because, arguably, protection of the vehicle's asset portfolio is a step removed from the liability it incurs to finance the acquisition of that portfolio, particularly perhaps if it is seen to be insuring its own assets for its own benefit. As against this, it is certainly arguable that the pool policy premium is in a commercial sense incurred to obtain the finance, since it is a credit enhancement feature which would not have been incurred but for the insistence of the rating agencies. If a claim for a deduction under s 77 is not sustainable, it is possible that a pool policy premium could be deductible as a trading expense if the vehicle was accepted as carrying on a trade, which is itself a difficult question (see below). The deductibility of premiums on this basis might be an easier argument to sustain if the premium was a recurrent payment so as to be more clearly deductible as a revenue expense on a year by year basis. However, such a solution is unlikely to be acceptable to the rating agencies without some means of insuring the annual payments. If the vehicle is regarded as an investment company rather than a trading company, the question will be whether the premium ranks as a management expense. Again, the position is rather doubtful. If a claim for a deduction was made, it would be necessary to argue—contrary to the position to be adopted if a claim for relief under s 77 was being maintained—that the premium related to the preservation of the company's investment asset rather than to the raising of the finance (*Hoechst Finance v Gumbrell* (1983) 56 TC 594).

In addition to the payment of a premium, it is usual for a pool insurance policy to contain a first loss or excess provision whereby the first, say, £1 million of claims are met by the insured. The insurer may require that an amount equal to the first loss provision or deductible is deposited with a bank on terms which entitle the insurer to draw on the account to pay claims under the policy as and when they rise until the account is exhausted. The vehicle itself is unlikely to be able to fund the deductible, which will accordingly have to be provided by the originator. Assuming that the funds deposited continue to be beneficially owned by the originator, interest earned on the deposit will be taxable as income of the originator in the ordinary course. However, the question arises whether any loss suffered by the originator as a result of the pool insurer drawing on the account will qualify as a deductible expense for the originator.

Provided the disposal of the mortgages by the originator to the vehicle is a disposal on trading account and the originator has to effect the deductible arrangements in order to make the disposal, it is certainly arguable that such a loss would be deductible to the originator, although in practice the originator may encounter an increasing degree of resistance to a claim for a deduction if a considerable time elapses before the loss arises. If the originator is not adequately compensated for this expense, further complications could also arise;

(vi)–(viii) the trustee's fees, printing and listing fees and the fee payable to the administrator of last resort should all be deductible as incidental costs of obtaining loan finance under s 77. Perhaps the only doubt relates to the fee payable to the administrator of last resort, since arguably that fee is (like the pool policy premium) a fee related to the asset portfolio rather than the raising of finance. However, the amount of such a fee is likely to be comparatively small in any event, and the availability of a deduction not accordingly of critical importance.

A number of the above expenses will bear VAT, which is likely to be irrecoverable by the company bearing them, whether the originator or the vehicle. The following list sets out the basic position:

(i)   management commission: exempt; selling concession: in practice, not a supply for VAT purposes;
(ii) legal and other professional fees: standard-rated;
(iii) rating agency fees: standard-rated;
(iv) banking facility fees: exempt;
(v)   pool policy insurance premium: exempt;
(vi) trustee's fees: standard-rated;
(vii) printing and listing fees: standard-rated;
(viii) administrator of last resort fees: standard-rated.

TAXATION OF THE VEHICLE DURING THE LIFE OF THE TRANSACTION

To establish the tax treatment of particular items of income or expenditure for the vehicle it is necessary first to consider a more basic question, namely whether the vehicle is a trading company or an investment company. This is broadly determined by its predominant function, although it is certainly possible for the position to be more complicated: a trading company can have an investment activity and an investment company might carry on a trade.

By contrast with the originator, the vehicle will typically be rather passive. It will not carry on any new mortgage lending business or seek out new customers. It will, rather, acquire a single portfolio of mortgages which it will hold to redemption. The only external activities which it is likely to undertake in relation to the portfolio is the acquisition, during a limited period, of further mortgages in substitution for those which have been redeemed and the making of further advances to borrowers on a discretionary basis or, in the case of some new mortgage products, a mandatory basis.

Beyond that, the administration and monitoring activity of the vehicle in relation to the portfolio will generally be comparatively passive, consistent with the role an investment company might undertake in relation to an investment portfolio. Whether a mortgage securitisation vehicle will fall to be treated as a trading company or an investment company is a question of fact to be determined in the light of the facts and circumstances in the particular case. However, because of the importance, in determining the details of the tax treatment of the vehicle, of knowing the answer to the question, a widespread practice has been to invite the Inland Revenue's views in advance. The Inland Revenue have often been helpful enough to give an indication of their likely views. They have been known to accept that a vehicle could be regarded as trading if its activities are effectively limited to acquiring a mortgage portfolio to hold to redemption and even if it does not carry on any very significant extra activity in the way of acquiring further mortgages to replace those which have been redeemed or making further advances. More recently, however, the Inland Revenue have been more inclined to the view that investment company treatment is generally appropriate.

A. Trading company treatment

If the vehicle is regarded as carrying on a trade, as a general matter, its income will be brought into charge to tax, and its expenses allowed, on an accruals basis rather than a cash basis. Its income, which will mainly take the form of interest received on mortgages, will accordingly normally fall to be brought in on an accruals basis. As a trading company, the vehicle will in computing its profit be entitled to deduct expenses in the same way as any normal trading company, subject to the usual statutory conditions and disallowances. For example, the vehicle would have to show that its expenditure had been incurred 'wholly and exclusively' for the purposes of its trade and would not be entitled to a deduction for expenditure which was of a capital nature (s 14 of the Taxes Act 1988). Although fewer expenses would rank as capital than in the case of an investment company, the latter restriction would nonetheless inhibit a deduction for a number of the up-front costs referred to above. However, as described, many of them will rank as incidental costs of obtaining loan finance and thus qualify for a statutory deduction under s 77 of the Taxes Act.

In relation to ongoing expenditure, the position for a vehicle accepted as trading would generally be quite favourable. In relation to expenses other than interest, a trading deduction will generally be available, for example in relation to fees payable to the administrator for administering the mortgage portfolio and other expenses of a revenue nature related to its mortgage trade, such as expenses associated with raising short-term finance of a revenue nature. A deduction is available for bad debts to the extent that a specific, rather than general, provision is made (s 74(j) of the Taxes Act).

As far as interest is concerned, the position is slightly more complicated, though the complications mainly relate to the form in which a deduction is taken rather than to its availability. Short interest (very broadly, where the debt obligation is not expected to be outstanding for as long as a year) will be allowable as a trading deduction on an accruals basis. This will also be the case with yearly interest payable to United Kingdom banks, for example on facilities taken out to enable the vehicle to fund initial expenses or facilities designed to preserve the vehicle's liquidity in the case of mortgage arrears.

Other yearly interest will be allowable not as a trading deduction on an accruals basis but as a charge on income on an 'as and when paid' basis. This includes not only yearly interest paid otherwise than to United Kingdom banks, but also (and more obviously) to interest on the bonds themselves. The bonds will, in a public issue, invariably be listed on the London or Luxembourg Stock Exchange and as such will constitute 'quoted Eurobonds' within the meaning of s 124 of the Taxes Act. The effect of this is that interest can normally be paid without deduction of United Kingdom income tax. In the context of the vehicle's corporation tax position, the significance of this is that a deduction is available for the interest notwithstanding the absence of an income tax withholding, even where the interest is paid to a non-resident (s 338 (4)(b) of the Taxes Act).

A question over deductibility sometimes arises if, as a method of enhancing the creditworthiness of the main issue of 'senior' bonds by the vehicle, a secondary issue of subordinated or 'B' bonds is made simultaneously. Typically, the 'B' bonds will be subordinated as to payment of both interest and capital to the senior bonds. If there is a deficit on any date when interest or capital falls to be paid on the bonds, it will be the 'B' bonds which suffer the deficiency first. Any deficiency will not normally be written off at that time but will be rolled forward and paid as and when funds become available. However, if there is an ultimate deficiency as far as the 'B' bonds are concerned, amounts carried forward as payable but unpaid may be written off at this stage. The question that is sometimes raised is whether amounts payable in respect of those 'B' bonds could somehow be regarded as 'dependent on the results of the vehicle's business'. This could make the interest return susceptible to being characterised as a 'distribution', at least in the case of payments to recipients who are not United Kingdom corporation taxpayers, by virtue of s 209(2)(e)(iii) of the Taxes Act. In that event, the vehicle would have to account to the Inland Revenue for advance corporation tax (currently at the rate of 25/75ths) on the distribution and it would not be entitled to a deduction for the 'interest' paid by it. A further worry is that the vehicle could be 'degrouped' from its parent company, if any, under Schedule 18 to the Taxes Act 1988. However, the generally accepted view is that this treatment is unlikely to be accorded in practice.

In the case of mortgage-backed Euro-commercial paper the position is somewhat different. As with commercial paper generally it is issued at a discount rather than being interest-bearing. As far as the vehicle is concerned, the discount will usually be deductible as a trading expense if the vehicle is itself a trading company, given the short term nature of the paper. Alternatively, even if the discount is not allowable as a trading expense it should be allowable on the statutory basis applicable to 'deep discount securities' in Schedule 4 to the Taxes Act. No withholding tax attaches to the discount.

B. Investment company treatment

If the vehicle falls to be regarded as an investment company, the tax computations must be prepared on rather a different basis. First, all income will be brought in and expenses allowed on a cash basis rather than an accruals basis. Secondly, the categories of expenditure for which the vehicle will be able to claim a deduction are narrower. Apart from charges on income (see below), investment companies are restricted to a deduction for 'management expenses', a term that is not statutorily defined but which case law authority indicates is comparatively circumscribed. In fact, given the vehicle's relatively modest range of expenditure, the treatment may not be too disadvantageous. A deduction should certainly be available for the ongoing costs paid to the mortgage administrator and auditors. Furthermore, a number of items may rank as incidental costs of obtaining loan finance and thus be deductible under s 77 of the Taxes Act as described above. No deduction will, however, be available for the costs associated with acquiring the mortgage portfolio. Although these may count in establishing a higher base cost for the purposes of corporation tax on chargeable gains, it is unlikely to be of much use. If the vehicle suffers a capital loss on redemption of the mortgages at par, it may have no capital gains available to absorb the loss, the use of which may also be subject to statutory restrictions. Moreover, no deduction will be available in respect of bad debts, except perhaps again to establish a similarly unusable capital loss.

The vehicle will normally be able to deduct its interest costs on broadly the same basis as discussed above in relation to a trading company. However, interest relief will always be on a paid basis rather than an accruing basis. Further, investment companies are not strictly able to deduct short interest at all unless it is paid on an advance from a bank recognised as such by the Inland Revenue or certain other categories of financial institutions, whereas (as noted above) a trading company should be able to obtain a deduction for short interest as a trading expense.

C. Tax and accounting mis-matches

As the mortgage rate charged to borrowers will normally exceed the rate of interest paid by the vehicle on its borrowings from the market, the vehicle will tend to make a net profit in commercial terms. This will also represent a profit in tax terms, unless the method by which profit is extracted from the vehicle is by way of a tax deductible fee (see below).

Although the expectation will thus be that the vehicle will normally make a taxable profit, it is nevertheless possible that in some accounting periods amounts deductible for corporation tax purposes might exceed the taxable income available to absorb them, by reason of borrowers' defaults. The flexibility for utilising any such surplus deductions will again depend on the status of the vehicle—trading company or investment company—and the relationship between the vehicle and the originator. If the vehicle is a subsidiary of the originator such that they form part of a group for group relief purposes, it will be possible for the vehicle to surrender the surplus amount to the originator or another group company for relief against its own taxable profits. A tax free payment could perhaps be made by the originator in return if this was desirable to fund the vehicle. If, on the other hand, the necessary group relationship does not exist, the vehicle can only utilise those losses by carrying them forwards (or, in the case of a trading company, backwards to a limited extent) against profits arising in other years. Any such utilisation would be subject to the normal corporation tax rules and restrictions governing the use of losses and other deductible amounts.

The fact that the issuer could have a corporation tax liability of a greater or lesser amount, and the need to ensure that it provides for that liability, is a matter which will need to be taken into account in planning the transaction at its inception. It is particularly useful to identify in advance what will be the accounting periods of the vehicle for tax purposes. These will normally, but not always, match the Companies Acts accounting reference periods. The mis-match of monthly receipts on the mortgages against (say) three-monthly interest expenses on the bonds could give rise to a tax mis-match, and thus an expense, particularly in the first period. A timing problem could also arise if—as will be the case with a vehicle which is a trading company—its interest receipts fall to be brought in on an accruals basis but its bond interest is relieved only on an 'interest paid' basis as a charge on income.

VAT

The VAT position of the vehicle is not very favourable. Usually, the vehicle will itself make no taxable supplies and accordingly will not be, and indeed will not be entitled to be, registered for VAT purposes. It will, however, have standard rated supplies made to it at the outset, eg by the trustee (see above). Ongoing fees may also be standard rated. In particular, the administration fee may be regarded as standard rated. It is possible, however, that it might be regarded as exempt, particularly if supplied by the originator itself (see 'Profit Extraction' below). However, assuming the fee is standard rated and that group treatment is not possible, the administration fee will certainly represent the largest standard rated supply suffered by the vehicle. Fees for administration services could well be charged at up to (say) 0.25% of the outstanding principal amount of the mortgage portfolio being administered from time to time. Thus, on a £200 million portfolio the administration fee might be £500,000 per annum, with VAT of £75,000 at a 15% standard rate. Where the originator is itself the administrator, the rating agencies may require the originator to charge administration fees to the vehicle on an inclusive of VAT basis. This is designed to insulate the vehicle from possibly severe increases in its burden of irrecoverable VAT as a result of changes in the applicable rate of VAT. This obviously represents a cost to the originator, although if the originator is entitled to receive the transaction profit arising in the vehicle by one profit extraction method or another, the cost will to some extent be a timing cost rather than an absolute cost. It represents a cost at the point of supply (because the originator has to account to HM Customs and Excise for part of the fee received) but the effect is that over time the vehicle will make more profit which will in due course be returned in one form or another to the originator.

In those circumstances consideration might be given to mitigating the cash flow cost by reducing the level of the administration fee. However, depending on the relationship between the originator and the vehicle, HM Customs and Excise might be able to charge VAT by reference to an arm's length level of fees if that was different from the amount actually charged.

In any case where the vehicle suffers irrecoverable VAT, it will be of some consolation that the irrecoverable VAT should prove deductible in calculating the vehicle's profits for corporation tax purposes.

TAX TREATMENT OF THE SECURITIES ISSUED BY THE VEHICLE

The securities issued by the vehicle to the market will generally be Eurobonds with a comparatively standard taxation treatment. It will be necessary to describe this treatment in the document offering the securities to the market, though the description generally makes clear that it does not purport to deal with bondholders in a special tax position, eg who are dealers. The major features of the treatment may be summarised as follows.

The bonds will be 'quoted Eurobonds' within the meaning of s 124 of the Taxes Act 1988, being interest bearing securities quoted on a recognised stock exchange. In consequence, as mentioned above, interest will normally be payable to the holder of the bond without deduction on account of UK income tax by the vehicle or any paying agent. The only circumstance in which interest will fall to be deducted is if the bondholder not only fails to confirm to the paying agent either that he or it is non-UK resident or that the bond is held in a recognised clearing system (currently the Euroclear, CEDEL and First Chicago clearing systems), but also presents the bond for payment to a paying agent in the United Kingdom.

Standard Eurobond terms contain a provision requiring the issuer, in certain circumstances, to gross up a payment of interest if a withholding tax is imposed (although an issuer will normally bargain for (and obtain) exceptions which mean that there is no obligation to gross up unless the law changes unfavourably). In the case of securitisation issues, it is common for no such grossing up obligation to be included. This is because normally the vehicle will not have sufficient funds available to meet the potentially significant additional expense of a grossing up obligation. Its source of income is generally restricted to the mortgage portfolio, the interest on which would not be sufficient to support a burden of interest payments on the bonds at, effectively, a grossed up rate. Accordingly, securitisation issues have generally seen the risk of withholding tax accepted by the market rather than by the vehicle. Under current law, however, it is open to bondholders to avoid any UK withholding tax by presenting the bonds to an overseas paying agent or by making an appropriate declaration of non-UK residence or by retaining the bonds in a recognised clearing system.

In the offering circular, it is normal to mention the application of Extra Statutory Concession B13 which, subject to appropriate exceptions, means that the Inland Revenue will not pursue a non-UK resident recipient of gross interest for any residual income tax liability. Furthermore, investors are normally warned about the potential application of the collecting agent provisions contained in s 123 of the Taxes Act 1988.

The bonds will normally have the status of 'qualifying corporate bonds'. Accordingly, disposals will not give rise to chargeable gains or allowable losses for UK tax purposes. The bonds will also normally be securities to which the 'accrued income scheme' provided for in s 710 et seq, Taxes Act 1988 applies, and it is customary to include a brief description of some of the possible effects of that legislation in the offering circular.

Finally, the offering circular normally also deals with the stamp duty and stamp duty reserve tax position in relation to the bonds—there is normally no UK stamp duty or stamp duty reserve tax cost in relation to the issue of the securities or their transfer by delivery. Sometimes, in addition, a description of the inheritance tax position is included although this is not of relevance to most investors as they will be corporate entities. However, even where bonds are owned by individuals, provided the bonds are physically held outside the UK, they may fall outside the inheritance tax net on a disposal by a non-UK domiciled owner.

A typical example of the tax section from an offering circular is given at the end of this chapter.

TAX IMPLICATIONS OF RETURNING PROFIT TO THE ORIGINATOR

As briefly mentioned above, the vehicle will normally generate profits, largely by reason of the differential between the mortgage rate which determines the level of its income and its funding rate on the bonds that it issues. The originator will want to channel those profits back to itself by one method or another. The extraction of profit is an area where tax difficulties have to be carefully watched.

There are two main considerations in relation to profit extraction. The first is that the profits must be taxable once only—and not both within the vehicle and in the hands of the originator when extracted. This points towards two possible methods of extracting the profit: either (i) making a payment to the originator which, whilst taxed in its hands, is deductible for the vehicle or (ii) making a payment which is not tax deductible for the vehicle but is not taxable in the hands of the originator. The problem which must be avoided is the vehicle making a payment which is not tax deductible for it but the receipt of which is taxable in the hands of the originator and against which it cannot set off losses or other reliefs. Unsurprisingly, nobody has yet devised a method of achieving the fourth possibility—a tax deductible payment for the vehicle which is not taxable in the hands of the originator.

The second main consideration is that VAT costs should be kept to a minimum since they are likely to be wholly irrecoverable for the vehicle.

The main methods of extraction which have so far been employed in practice are discussed below.

A. Dividends

The most obvious method of extraction is to take profits out by way of dividend. This is almost certainly the simplest and safest method and has been adopted in a number of cases.

Under this method the profit is taxed in the hands of the vehicle. Provided, as this chapter assumes, both the originator and the vehicle are UK resident, the dividend which extracts the profit will not be taxable income of the originator and therefore any double taxation risk should be avoided.

Generally, the vehicle will have to account for advance corporation tax (ACT) when paying a dividend. This will, however, amount only to a timing problem if the vehicle expects to pay mainstream tax. An obligation to account for ACT can be avoided altogether if the vehicle is a 51% subsidiary of the originator for corporation tax purposes, a test determined by ownership of ordinary share capital. The vehicle must also be, broadly, more than 50% economically owned by the originator. A group income election can then be made between them enabling ACT to be avoided.

Potentially of greater value than the group *income* group is a group *relief* group, enabling losses to be surrendered between the originator and the vehicle. In the absence of a group relief group there is an obvious situation where profit extraction by way of dividend is inefficient from a tax viewpoint. If the originator has current losses or other surplus deductions which could be set against income received from the vehicle in *taxable* form, the 'profit' would not fall into charge to tax at all. However, if the income is received as a non-taxable dividend a tax charge on the profit can be expected to arise within the vehicle. That tax could be avoided if the vehicle were a member of the originator's group relief group, because the excess current losses of the originator could then be surrendered down to the vehicle. In the absence of the group relief group tax will be paid which might be regarded as unnecessary.

For a group relief group to exist the originator must hold 75% or more of the ordinary share capital of the vehicle—and it must again satisfy additional tests which, broadly, have the effect that the originator must own 75% or more of the issuer economically otherwise than on a temporary basis.

Unfortunately, as explained in Chapter 2, with the changes introduced by the Companies Act 1989 and the Bank of England's February 1989 paper, it may not be possible for the originator to own shares in the vehicle and the dividend method of extracting profits may not therefore be feasible. A second possible constraint arises if it is important to start extracting profit early on. It may be that, during the initial period of the transaction, there will be profits in cash terms but insufficient profits available for distribution within the issuer for company law purposes for the required dividends to be paid out. This may be the case, for example, if high initial expenses have to be written off during the expected life of the bonds and this is likely to be very short.

B. Interest

A method of extraction similar to the payment of dividends is for the originator to lend money to the issuer and extract profit by way of interest. While the originator may be unable to hold shares in the vehicle, it may nevertheless be able to lend to the vehicle—and could perhaps do so on terms which give the loan many characteristics of a shareholding. The loan could, for example, be a long-term subordinated loan and could perhaps carry interest which is variable according to the profits of the vehicle.

Extraction by way of interest will be efficient if either the interest paid is deductible for the vehicle and represents taxable income of the originator or (subject to the points concerning dividends discussed above) the interest paid is non-deductible for the vehicle but is not taxable in the originator's hands. There are also some group relief and withholding tax considerations to bear in mind. The basic rules are as follows.

First, given the assumption that the originator and the vehicle are both UK resident, interest should in principle be deductible for the vehicle—and will be taxable income of the originator—even if it varies with the vehicle's profits, so long as the interest rate does not exceed a reasonable commercial return for the use of the borrowed moneys. An important point here, however, is that short interest will not be tax deductible for the vehicle unless, as mentioned above, the vehicle can substantiate a claim to deduct the payment as a trading expense or it is on an advance from a bank recognised as such by the Inland Revenue (or certain other limited classes of financial institutions).

Secondly, to the extent the interest does exceed a reasonable commercial return it will be non-deductible but should be treated as a Schedule F distribution (ie effectively as a dividend) for tax purposes and therefore will not be taxable income of the originator. However, this is subject to a caveat: there is an argument that if interest is excessive it cannot be regarded as consideration given for the use of the borrowed moneys. If this argument is correct, any such 'interest' which is so excessive will not technically even be a Schedule F distribution. As a result, the payment would still be non-deductible for the vehicle but would also be taxable income of the originator. On this basis, double taxation could arise.

Thirdly, interest paid on, say, a long-term subordinated loan which does not exceed a reasonable commercial return will almost certainly be payable under deduction of basic rate tax, unless a group income group exists between the issuer and the originator. To the extent the interest exceeds a reasonable commercial return and is treated as a Schedule F distribution the issuer will have to pay ACT in respect of it (even if there is a group income group in place).

Fourthly, if the vehicle needs to be a member of a group relief group with a person *other* than the originator, the payment of profit-related interest to the originator may easily degroup the issuer from the intended group.

Obviously the scope for interest extraction will be limited by the scope for the originator to lend into the vehicle and it is likely to be of little use if interest is not to exceed a reasonable commercial return.

C. Administration fees

The next main area to consider is administration fees. The issuer, being a special purpose vehicle, will almost certainly have to appoint a third person to administer its business and, in particular, its mortgage portfolio. It is likely to have to pay a substantial fee for that person's administrative services.

The question that arises in relation to profit extraction is whether, if the originator carries out the administration, the fee can vary with the profits and be such that it provides a method for extracting substantially all of what would otherwise be the vehicle's profits. The answer is probably a qualified 'yes', there being two main qualifications.

First, it is of course vital for the fee to be a deductible expense of the vehicle if effective double taxation of the 'profit' is to be avoided. If the fee simply strips out all of the profit but an independent third person could have undertaken the administration for a smaller fee, a risk exists that it will be non-deductible or, a least, will not be wholly deductible. The fee could, in an extreme case, be seen as a *division* of profit rather than an *expense* of earning profit. It is clearly advisable for some profit to be left within the vehicle after payment of the fee and perhaps the vehicle's opportunity to buy the mortgages should be conditional on its accepting the administration fee arrangements.

The second qualification relates to VAT. The practice adopted by HM Customs and Excise does not appear to be entirely consistent or indeed fully formulated at present, although some more or less formal statement of their views is expected to be forthcoming shortly. The difficulty is that, as a technical matter, a fee for administration of the issuer's business or of its loan portfolio might attract VAT and the issuer would be unable to recover any VAT charged to it. Accordingly, if the administration fee was increased in order to be used as a profit extraction method, the irrecoverable VAT might also be increased.

The main question is whether the fees are standard rated or exempt. It is arguable that exempt treatment is appropriate to the extent that the services relate to the 'management of credit' that was first granted by the originator. If this basis is accepted, it becomes relevant to consider whether the position is compromised by the existence of other supplies which are also performed by the originator alongside the mortgage administration. An example might be work done by the originator in dealing with the vehicle's general corporate administration (eg filing annual returns at Companies House) and dealing with matters arising in relation to the bonds which the vehicle has issued (eg arranging for notices to be given to bondholders). These supplies, on their own, might fall to be standard rated. The approach of the authorities where the services combine standard rated and exempt elements would normally be to determine the question of liability on the whole supply by reference to which elements predominate. On this basis, it is at least possible that a VAT problem could be avoided entirely if the mortgage administration element is predominant. Given the element of uncertainty involved, it is often the case that the views of HM Customs and Excise are sought in advance as to their likely attitude towards the question of liability on particular supplies.

VAT could, of course, be avoided if the issuer is in the same VAT group as the originator. This will, however, only be possible if they are holding company and subsidiary for company law purposes. Even if this was commercially possible, it might be simpler to use a different method of profit extraction such as dividends.

D. Broking fees

Broking fees can be used for profit extraction in the same way as administration fees and they give rise to similar tax deductibility considerations.

The particular advantage of broking fees is that, since they should represent fees for *arranging* mortgage lending (rather than for administration of existing loans or other business) they would more clearly be exempt supplies for VAT purposes and therefore should not involve the risk of irrecoverable VAT costs which may attach to the use of administration fees.

Broking fees may, therefore, be a useful method of profit extraction but will be of assistance in limited circumstances only, particularly if the structure of the securitisation is a conventional one. This is because the 'originator' can only really act as an arranger if the originator is not selling its own mortgages to the vehicle, but some other structure is adopted. For example, the originator might not actually lend on its own behalf and then sell to the vehicle but instead act on an agency basis, the actual originator of the mortgage being the vehicle itself. This would give increased scope for mortgage broking fees as a method of extraction.

E. Interest swaps

An interest swap is a possible extraction method which is frequently discussed. In principle it is very attractive but unfortunately both law and practice are somewhat uncertain.

The essential idea behind a swap based method is that the vehicle agrees to pay the originator periodic amounts based on the mortgage rate and the originator agrees in return to pay the issuer periodic amounts based on the Eurobond rate. The main commercial justification for the issuer is probably that, assuming a discretionary mortgage rate, it should be assured through the swap mechanism that it is entitled to an income sufficient to meet its obligations on the bonds. In other words, the swap is one mechanism by which the issuer can be assured of its income even if the mortgage rate falls below an adequate 'threshold' rate.

Although this basic commercial justification for a swap may exist, the swap is far removed from a conventional interest swap. Traditionally, a fixed interest rate is swapped for a floating rate and, if no premium is paid for the swap, the transaction should be equally attractive to both parties. Here, a floating rate is swapped for, effectively, a floating rate. While basis rate swaps have become common in the swaps market, the two rates are usually independently set, eg US Treasuries and prime lending rates. In this case, the originator, if it is administrator, may well have control of the mortgage rate and can therefore procure that it is a net beneficiary under the swap. The swap is anyway expected generally to impose net payment obligations on the issuer (since the securitisation is expected to produce a profitable spread between the mortgage rate and the bond interest rate) and therefore seems, without more, to be a transaction loaded against the vehicle. Furthermore, the vehicle's gross payment obligations under the swap would preferably take specific account of the vehicle's administration expenses as well as the bond interest rate, a rather unusual feature.

The tax treatment of interest swaps is based largely on Inland Revenue practice. The practice is to *treat* swap payments by taxpayers other than banks and swap traders as 'annual payments' for tax purposes. Annual payments generally have to be paid under deduction of tax. But the Inland Revenue practice is not designed to impose a withholding tax obligation. Rather, it is designed to give taxpayers that cannot seek deductions for swap payments as trading expenses (as most cannot, except for banks and swap traders) deductions for the payments as 'charges on income'.

Because of the general uncertainty surrounding the practice, it has generally been felt difficult to predict the treatment applicable to a securitisation swap given that the swap is likely to be so different from the traditional form of swap on which Revenue practice is based. For example, it may be regarded as inappropriate to treat payments by the vehicle as deductible annual payments if they are seen as divisions of profit rather than true expenses of interest rate risk management. Even if they are regarded as annual payments—and so prima facie deductible for the vehicle—a deduction will be denied if they are not incurred for 'a valuable and sufficient consideration', a test which is difficult to satisfy if in commercial reality net payment obligations are expected from the outset to rest only on the vehicle. As in other cases, it has been customary to seek to obtain from the Inland Revenue in advance a degree of comfort on the treatment that will be afforded if swaps are to be used.

Further, as noted above, if the swap payments are treated as annual payments, they will without more fall to be paid under deduction of tax—unless the originator is a bank or a swap trader. Revenue practice is not to treat payments to banks or swap traders acting as principals as attracting an obligation to deduct tax. If deduction of tax has to be avoided, back to back swaps through a bank or an offshore intermediary may have to be attempted—and these will only add to the complexity (and cost) of the transaction.

Finally, the current uncertainty about the use of swaps has, if anything, increased in the light of the Inland Revenue consultative document relating to interest rate swaps which was published in March 1989. That document embodied a welcome attempt by the Inland Revenue to seek views on a possible codification of their current practice. However, the document indicates that the Inland Revenue are alive, and not particularly well-disposed, to the possibility of swaps at inherently uncommercial rates being used as a method of manipulating where profits arise for tax purposes. It must accordingly be rather doubtful, in the absence perhaps of some specific Inland Revenue confirmations, that the use of swaps will continue to be an attractive profit extraction method in a securitisation.

F. Sale for a price exceeding par

Another method of extraction that has been used in practice, despite technical difficulties, is for the originator to sell the mortgages to the vehicle for a price exceeding their par value, the excess being left outstanding and paid over time out of the vehicle's interest rate spread. The commercial justification for this route is that, since the mortgage rate is expected to exceed the note rate and the notes can be issued at par, the mortgages may arguably be worth more than par. There are various difficult tax analyses of this structure depending on the precise status for tax purposes of the vehicle's and the originator's holdings of the mortgage portfolio and their degree of connection for tax purposes. Two possible analyses are explained below to demonstrate the difficulties involved.

First, let us assume that the originator is a trading company whose mortgages are held on revenue account for the purposes of the trade. The tax treatment of sales of mortgages at par has been discussed earlier in this chapter. In summary, sale of the mortgages at par will not normally cause any profit to arise for tax purposes. However, sale for a price in excess of par will give rise to a trading profit for the originator. Furthermore, that profit, at least if it is sufficiently ascertainable, may at least in the Inland Revenue's eyes have to be brought into account as having been earned on the sale to the vehicle immediately, even though payment is only subsequently funded out of the spread. For the vehicle, on the other hand, it is much more likely that the mortgages will be acquired as *capital* assets (as investments of an investment company). If that is the case, the payment of the excess over par will, as described above, be a capital payment only which is not deductible against income profits. It *may* form a part of the issuer's CGT base cost in the mortgages which will ultimately be reflected in capital losses on redemption of the mortgages at par, but these losses are unlikely to be of use. The result is effectively double taxation of the spread out of which the excess over par is paid.

The second possibility is that the vehicle does establish that it carries on a trade and acquires the mortgages as revenue assets for the purposes of the trade. This route is also likely to be inefficient since no profit or loss on such a transaction should be recognised for tax purposes until final realisation— probably on redemption of the mortgages. The originator will bring in income profits when payments of the excess are made (if not earlier) and the vehicle will not obtain corresponding deductions until final redemption.

The technical analysis is different again if the mortgages represent trading stock of the originator and/or the issuer. The best position is where the mortgages are trading stock of both originator and issuer but, without going into detail, problems may still be expected to exist.

Despite these technical difficulties the Inland Revenue have, in one or two cases, taken a fairly sympathetic approach to mortgages sold in excess of par, at least where the vehicle has established a trade and the accounting treatment of the originator's profit on sale and the vehicle's payments of the excess have been favourable. This approach may not be so likely in the future, given that the Inland Revenue seem now to be more inclined to regard the vehicle as an investment company rather than a trader (see above).

G. Other methods

On the basis of the profit extraction methods described above, if the originator sells mortgages into a vehicle, is no longer to administer them and cannot invest in the vehicle so as to extract profit by way of dividends or interest, only interest swaps or sales in excess of par seem to be available. However, both these routes are technically unsatisfactory and it is therefore difficult to recommend them without some specific comfort from the Inland Revenue.

The remaining question is whether there are any other possibilities. In theory there are, but the scope for using them does seem to be limited:

(i) some possibilities are based on avoiding having to extract at all—in other words keeping income out of the issuer altogether. One example is where the originator has become entitled to continuing insurance commissions such as commissions for the placing of renewable buildings insurances in respect of mortgaged properties. There may be no need to transfer the right to these commissions to the vehicle, given that once the income is put into the vehicle it will only have to be taken out again. One might expect it to be possible, if this can be achieved under property law, for the originator to assign only a part of the mortgages, reserving for itself the beneficial entitlement to so much of the income stream as represents what would otherwise be the vehicle's profit. Alternatively, the originator could assign the mortgages outright subject to some form of trust back. Unfortunately, in this case MIRAS is a problem. The mortgage loans will generally have fallen within MIRAS and the Inland Revenue have said that if beneficial ownership of mortgage interest is to be split between two persons, MIRAS can no longer properly be administered;

(ii) one way of avoiding UK problems relating to taxation of the spread might be thought to be to set up the vehicle issuer in an offshore jurisdiction. Here again there is an immediate MIRAS problem. The vehicle will need to be prescribed as a qualifying lender and, as mentioned above, the Inland Revenue will not prescribe a non-resident which is not acting through a UK branch;

(iii) if the profits cannot be extracted fully during the life of the transaction it may be that they have to be accumulated and taxed within the vehicle. If the originator could take a call option over the shares in the vehicle, it might perhaps ultimately be able to buy the shares (perhaps for original cost) and then strip the profits out by way of dividend, having brought the vehicle into its group and made the necessary group income election. Such an arrangement may, however, nullify the off-balance sheet accounting and regulatory treatment which is often critical to the commercial attractiveness of the securitisation.

CONCLUSION

It can be seen that the tax issues in securitisation are often complex and the likely tax treatment can contradict what would otherwise appear to be sensible commercial solutions. The Inland Revenue's approach has, in the past, not been unhelpful even where the technical analysis has left many open questions. Whether this will continue to be the case remains to be seen but it is to be hoped that greater certainty will enable these transactions to flourish and the market to develop as commercial needs dictate.

APPENDIX

TYPICAL TAX DESCRIPTION FROM AN OFFERING DOCUMENT

United Kingdom Taxation

1. TAXATION OF INTEREST PAID

Under current Inland Revenue practice the Notes will be regarded as bearer securities for the purposes of s 124 of the Income and Corporation Taxes Act 1988 notwithstanding that they are represented by the Global Note and accordingly interest payments will be treated as interest paid on a 'quoted Eurobond' within the meaning of s 124. Therefore, so long as the notes are represented by the Global Note and continue to be quoted on a recognised stock exchange within the meaning of s 841 of the Income and Corporation Taxes Act 1988 (the Luxembourg Stock Exchange is currently a recognised stock exchange) and held within a recognised clearing system within the meaning of s 124 (Euroclear and CEDEL have each been designated as a recognised clearing system for this purpose) payments of interest on the Notes by any Paying Agent may, under current law and practice, be made without withholding or deduction for or on account of United Kingdom income tax. This paragraph will not apply if the Notes cease to be represented by the Global Note.

If the Notes cease to be represented by the Global Note and definitive Notes are issued, the definitive Notes will constitute 'quoted Eurobonds' within the meaning of s 124 of the Income and Corporation Taxes Act 1988, provided that they continue to be quoted on a recognised stock exchange. Accordingly, under current law and practice, payments of interest may in such circumstances be made by any Paying Agent without withholding or deduction for or on account of United Kingdom income tax where:

(i) the person by or through whom the payment is made is not in the United Kingdom; or

(ii) the payment is made by or through a person who is in the United Kingdom and:

(a) it is proved, on a claim in that behalf made in advance to the

Commissioners of Inland Revenue, that the person who is the beneficial owner of the Note and entitled to the interest is not resident in the United Kingdom or, where the interest is by virtue of any provision of United Kingdom legislation deemed to be income of a person other than the person who is the beneficial owner of the Note, on a claim in that behalf made in advance to the Commissioners of Inland Revenue by the other person that such other person is not resident in the United Kingdom. Under current Inland Revenue practice an appropriate form of declaration of non-residence provided to the Paying Agent is sufficient proof; or

(b) the Note and Coupon are held by one and the same person in a recognised clearing system (as to which see above).

In all other cases, interest will be paid under deduction of United Kingdom income tax subject to any direction to the contrary by the Inland Revenue pursuant to the provisions of any appropriate double taxation treaty. If interest is paid under deduction of United Kingdom income tax, the Issuer is not obliged to pay any additional amount in respect of the Notes.

Where:

(i) a bank or other person in the United Kingdom obtains payment of any interest (or any warrant for or cheque purporting to be drawn or made in payment of such interest) on behalf of a holder of a Note or Coupon

(a) in circumstances such that payment has not been made by or entrusted to any person in the United Kingdom; or

(b) if the Note in respect of which such payment is made is held in a recognised clearing system (as to which see above); or

(ii) a bank in the United Kingdom sells or otherwise realises any interest (or warrant for or cheque purporting to be drawn or made in payment of such interest) and pays over the proceeds to any person or carries them to his account,

that bank or other person may be required to withhold or deduct for or on account of, or otherwise be assessable in respect of, United Kingdom income tax unless it has been proved, on a claim in that behalf made in advance to the Commissioners of Inland Revenue, that the person owning the Note and entitled to the interest (or, where the Note is held under a trust of which a person is the sole beneficiary in possession or the interest is deemed for United Kingdom tax purposes to be the income of some other person, that person) is not resident in the United Kingdom.

The interest payable on the Notes has a United Kingdom source and as such, whether or not paid gross, will be chargeable to United Kingdom tax. However, under Inland Revenue Extra-Statutory Concession B13 (the application of which to interest on quoted Eurobonds has been confirmed by

Inland Revenue Statement of Practice SP8/84 and which, like all Extra-Statutory Concessions, operates subject to the existence of special circumstances and to its not being used for tax avoidance), no action will be taken to pursue any liability to such United Kingdom tax in respect of persons who are not, for the whole of the relevant year of assessment, resident in the United Kingdom except where such persons:

(i) are chargeable under s 78 of the Taxes Management Act 1970 in the name of a trustee or other person mentioned in s 72 of the Taxes Management Act 1970 or an agent or branch having the management or control of the interest: or

(ii) seek to claim relief in respect of taxed income from United Kingdom sources (insofar as the tax on the interest can be recovered by a set-off against the claim); or

(iii) are chargeable to corporation tax on the interest as income of a United Kingdom branch or agency of a non-resident company or to income tax on the interest as profits of a trade carried on in the United Kingdom.

2. CAPITAL GAINS; ACCRUED INCOME

The Notes will be qualifying corporate bonds for the purposes of United Kingdom capital gains tax and accordingly no chargeable gain (or allowable loss) will arise for these purposes on a disposal of the Notes by a Noteholder.

A Noteholder who is resident or ordinarily resident in the United Kingdom or carrying on a trade in the United Kingdom through a branch or agency with which the ownership of the Note is connected may be chargeable to United Kingdom tax on income on an amount treated (by rules known as the accrued income scheme contained in Chapter II of Part XVII of the Income and Corporation Taxes Act 1988) as representing interest accrued on the Note at the time of disposal (calculated by reference to a formula in the legislation or on a just and reasonable basis). If for any reason any interest due on an Interest Payment Date is not paid and a Note is subsequently disposed of with the right to receive accrued interest, special rules may apply for the purposes of the accrued income scheme.

3. INHERITANCE TAX

United Kingdom inheritance tax may be chargeable on the death of, or on a gift of Notes by, a Noteholder who is domiciled or deemed to be domiciled in the United Kingdom.

The liability to inheritance tax of a Noteholder who is not domiciled or deemed to be domiciled in the United Kingdom will depend on where the Noteholder's interest in the Global Note is treated as situated for United Kingdom tax purposes. The situs of such an interest for tax purposes is not entirely clear and may depend on the nature of the arrangements made by a Noteholder with Euroclear or CEDEL for holding his interest in the Global Note. Such persons are therefore advised to consult their professional advisers.

No charge will arise in respect of absolute gifts of Notes made more than seven years before the death of the donor.

4. STAMP DUTY

No United Kingdom stamp duty or stamp duty reserve tax is payable on the issue of the Global Note or on the issue or transfer of a Note in definitive form. Whether the transfer of Notes while they are represented by the Global Note will fall within the exemptions from United Kingdom stamp duty may depend on the nature of the arrangements made by a Noteholder with Euroclear or CEDEL. In the absence of an exemption, there may be circumstances in which a liability to such duty would arise although a transfer of Notes in such form should not give rise to a liability to stamp duty reserve tax.

The above is not a complete summary of the United Kingdom tax law and practice currently applicable and some aspects do not apply to certain classes of taxpayer (such as dealers). Prospective Noteholders who are in any doubt as to their tax position should consult their professional advisers.

Chapter 4

Profile of a Specialist Mortgage Lender

Robert Weir
Household Mortgage Corporation plc

INTRODUCTION

Household Mortgage Corporation is a privately-owned company established in March 1986. Our shareholders are major financial institutions, divided fairly evenly between domestic and international investors. In the autumn of the same year, the company opened for business and in its first two-and-a-half years of operation has written nearly £1½ billion of residential mortgage business.

HMC was formed to take advantage of the structural changes in the UK mortgage market which were then becoming apparent. The shareholders, and the new management, had a clear vision of objectives which have remained unchanged since formation. Securitisation of the company's assets was seen as an essential tool to help achieve some of those objectives.

Like any new company, the perceived requirement was to build a sustainable competitive advantage in each business activity undertaken. Therefore, we established key objectives amongst which were:

(i) to achieve a satisfactory minimum level of return on gearable capital (*not* return on assets, which is seen as secondary) consistent with a venture capital investment;

(ii) to build customer franchise through quality of service, the product range available, and a knowledge of their needs and preferences;

(iii) to establish a cost base sufficiently low to withstand any future market down turns or industry shake outs;

(iv) to achieve continuity of adequate funding at competitive prices;

(v) to avoid excessive financial risk such as that inherent in funding long-term mortgage assets with short-term banking lines.

At the time of establishment, the ability to securitise mortgage assets was seen as essential to help attain the last three objectives. To that extent, setting up HMC was a shot in the dark, since the ability to securitise UK mortgage assets was unproven. It had, of course, happened in the United States which no doubt was some small comfort to our investors but, at the same time, the impetus for the creation of that market was different and the investor base was well established while it was non-existent in Europe.

Our plans for new business origination were ambitious, and funding available through the interbank markets was seen as inadequate for a number of reasons. First, our appetite for new funding was unlikely to be satisfied since repeated recourse to the banking market for medium/long-term funds would quickly bump up against banks' prudential sector and company limits. Secondly, the majority of committed bank lines would be too short to fund mortgages with a nominal maturity of 25 years. Much is made, quite rightly, of the fact that the average life of mortgages (and hence mortgage-backed bonds) is much shorter than the stated nominal maturity. However, early repayment of a mortgage is at the borrower's option, but not the lender's. Some mortgages (albeit a very few) do last for 25 years and hence bank funding, all of which is repayable, typically, within five to ten years, is inadequate. This may not be a concern for those institutions, such as UK banks, who enjoy the protection of a central bank acting as lender of last resort. However, for a company such as HMC, funding to the nominal maturity of the asset base is an essential insolvency protection. Finally, the company was unlikely to achieve its desired gearing levels through reliance on bank funding and hence we would fail to meet our return on capital targets.

To meet these concerns it was essential for the company to be able to access the long-term securities markets through being able to deliver high credit quality paper which was attractive to a broad spectrum of potential investors, both domestic and international. Hence we made an immediate decision to design computer systems and to underwrite assets with the specific intention of securitising the mortgage business written.

Now that the company has securitised about £1 billion of assets, both through public and private markets, we can look at the results. These show that the shortcomings inherent in the banking markets have been addressed. Quantity and continuity of funding supply is much better through access to securities markets where potential investors can be numbered in thousands rather than hundreds. Bond investors are prepared to look at instruments with a long maturity so long as a reasonably liquid secondary market is assured. Finally, given efficient bond structuring, the gearing capabilities available through the bond markets are infinitely more attractive than through normal corporate debt.

The remainder of this chapter discusses how we organise, structure and administer our bond issues, both for standard UK mortgages and for new products.

ORGANISATION OF AN ISSUE

A. Selection of professional advisors

1. LEAD MANAGER

The most important decision facing a potential issuer is the selection of the lead manager for the issue. The lead manager of a mortgage-backed issue will perform each of the following tasks:

 (i) structuring the issue;
 (ii) negotiating with the rating agencies;
(iii) pricing the issue;
(iv) assembling an underwriting group;
 (v) distributing bonds;
(vi) secondary market making.

The input of the lead manager in each of the above areas will depend on the individual requirements of each issuer. A debut issuer, for example, will require a greater degree of assistance with the structuring of the transaction than an established issuer. In this context, structuring encompasses far more than just determining the terms and conditions of the bonds themselves and will require the lead manager to assist in the development of the issuer's computer systems to produce both initial pool data and continuing surveillance and monitoring of the issue. The latter task should not be underestimated; the market is full of horror stories of lenders who have discovered during this process that the information on their database bears little more than a passing resemblance to detail held on hard copy in their files.

At HMC, we have reached the stage where we have developed a number of tried and tested structures which both work for us and ultimately produce bonds which will be well received by the market. We do not therefore lean very heavily on our lead managers for structuring support, but we are always receptive to new ideas. We take the approach that a bank which provides us with an idea which adds significant value to an issue will be awarded the mandate for the transaction. Here I would also add a word of caution. We frequently receive suggestions for innovative structures which appear superficially attractive but in such instances we ask ourselves two questions: will the market buy the resulting bonds at a price which makes sense and will the cost savings to HMC as issuer of the underlying funding be swamped by ancillary costs such as legal fees? The most cost effective development has often proved to be evolutionary, rather than revolutionary.

One area where we expect our lead manager to provide significant value is in discussions with the rating agencies. This is described in greater detail below, but we find that having, as it were, an independent intermediary discussing rating issues not only saves our management time but also adds a degree of weight to our arguments, since the agency realises that we have done the groundwork by convincing the lead manager of the particular point at issue.

Many issuers would regard the pricing of the issue as being the most important function of the lead manager and some issuers will choose their lead manager on the basis of price competitiveness alone. This is not necessarily a wise strategy in an emerging market like the UK mortgage-backed securities market.

There are two basic methods of determining the pricing of an issue. First, the issuer can invite a group of banks to bid for the bonds. Alternatively, pricing may be negotiated between issuer and lead manager. The latter is the route usually taken with a lead manager appointed well in advance of the issue and who has performed a significant amount of corporate finance work for the issuer.

The problem with running a bidding group on an issue is how to choose the winning bid. It is not simply a question of hitting the lowest bid because other factors come into play. In spite of the recent volume of issuance, the market is still young and the danger for an issuer of choosing a very aggressive bid leading to a poorly received issue is that future access to the market will become more difficult. HMC has had bidding groups on issues, but it has done so with a clear idea of the price at which it wished to see its paper put into the market. Consequently, the bank chosen to underwrite and distribute the paper was that whose pricing most closely coincided with our view of what the correct pricing for the particular issue should have been. This is not a strategy of universal application. We are able to adopt this course because we maintain our own fairly extensive secondary market operation in mortgage-backed floating rate notes. This gives us an accurate feel for the tone of the market at any particular time and consequently for what might be achieved with a new issue. This approach is only realistic when the new issue closely resembles, in structuring terms, a previous transaction preferably by the same issuer.

The alternative to this approach is to reach a negotiated price for the issue with the lead manager. The starting point in these discussions is for the lead manager to give a very firm indication of the level at which it expects to be able to place its underwriting commitment. The difference between that price and the price at which it buys the bonds from the issuer will therefore represent the lead manager's remuneration, both for any corporate finance work that it has provided and also for assuming the underwriting risk on the issue. Each issuer will have its own views on the level of such remuneration, but just as it may be counterproductive to hit the lowest bid in a competitive auction, the issuer should bear in mind that banks need to be incentivised for them to continue to devote resources to this market. Which route is better? A new issuer really has only one choice and that is to follow the negotiated route. Experienced issuers may wish to experiment with bidding groups but a firm appreciation of market conditions is necessary in order to run a tender properly.

Having priced the issue the lead manager's next job is to assemble an underwriting group. In the early days of the market the fashion was to assemble a large underwriting group comprising banks who had aspirations to become market makers in mortgage-backed securities and banks which, at the time, were friends of (or were owed a favour by) the issuer. Appearances in the latter category turned out to be something of a mixed blessing, since just about every issue until January 1988 proved very difficult to place. The trend now is towards smaller underwriting groups. HMC's approach is to leave the final decision entirely to the lead manager. However if our opinion is sought (which is usually the case) we only express a preference for those banks prepared to commit market making capital (and hence aid liquidity) to the market.

Currently we would regard banks such as Barings, Credit Suisse First Boston, J. P. Morgan, Salomon Brothers, Union Bank of Switzerland and S. G. Warburg as active market makers in most issues. We believe our approach is in the best long-term interests of the market as it ensures a good primary supply of bonds to the houses which will provide secondary market liquidity in an issue. We see little point in including banks who have no capability in this particular market and will therefore either hold the bonds to maturity or sell them back to the lead manager via brokers.

As can be seen, while we place a considerable degree of emphasis on the secondary market making capability of our management group, the underlying structure of the bond is also important. In this respect the structural innovation in our first FRN issue (which has now become a market standard) of passing back mortgage redemptions to bond holders via a purchase fund route has proved outstandingly successful. We outline the reasons for this later in this chapter.

The choice of lead manager will depend on the degree of importance that each issuer places on the factors outlined above and the ability of each bank to meet the issuer's needs. Before embarking upon this decision it is essential that the issuer has a clear idea of the factors which are of particular importance to him and to assess the aspirants in the light of those factors alone.

2. LAWYERS

The issuer should be able to influence (but not necessarily determine) the choice of, perhaps, three firms of solicitors involved with the transaction; those representing the issuer, the managers and the trustee. The last two roles may be combined within the same firm although different partners should normally be involved in case conflict occurs. The first general principle guiding the choice of legal advisers is to look for firms who are familiar with what is involved in a mortgage-backed transaction. The second general principle is to ensure that the documentation used on an issue is as nearly as possible re-useable. Both of these are tremendously important in containing costs. For example, the Mortgage Securitisation and Management Deed on a typical HMC issue will run to over 200 pages and the Trust Deed and Deed of Charge will be of similar length. These are obviously very expensive documents, both to draft and to have reviewed, and therefore a degree of consistency in the documentation itself and in the firms who are preparing and reviewing it is highly desirable. These concerns are greater than for a normal corporate debt offering in the bond markets in view of the inevitable legal complexity generated by a structured financing.

HMC has been fortunate in that our general corporate legal advisors, Slaughter & May, have been at the forefront of UK residential mortgage securitisation. They have acted for us in each of our ten issues and have worked with HMC and the other parties to these transactions in preparing relatively standard HMC documentation. We have always requested our lead managers to instruct firms who are familiar with this documentation and they have always been receptive to this request. Not only does this save fees, since the basis for the documentation for a particular issue can be a mark-up of the documentation from a previous issue with which the parties are familiar, but equally importantly it saves a considerable amount of time both in the preparation and in the review of the documentation. This can be particularly important if the issue has been launched opportunistically with a very tight deadline between launch and closing. Structured financings will always involve more legal work than the typical corporate debt issue. However, once satisfactory standard documentation is in place, the temptation to meddle should be resisted since the minor improvements achieved are nearly always outweighed by the costs involved. However, convincing lawyers of the validity of this argument often tests the managerial skills of issuers and lead managers alike!

3. TRUSTEE

The trustee on a mortgage-backed issue will be expected to play a much more active role than the trustee functions normally associated with a conventional eurobond issue. As with the lawyers, the general principle is to aim for continuity and the Law Debenture Trust Corporation has acted as trustee on all of HMC's bond issues.

The nature of the trustee's duties are discussed extensively in Chapter 10 and again I would strongly advise engaging an organisation already familiar with these obligations.

4. PAYING AGENT

The comments in the previous two sections are equally relevant here. The points to watch with a paying agent are the mechanism for passing principal payments back to bond holders and, if a senior/subordinated structure is employed, the mechanics for paying interest on the subordinated notes. The difficulty with this is that, technically, the situation could arise where there is insufficient cash in the issuing vehicle to meet the full interest payment expected to be made on the subordinated tranche. The paying agent may not know until just before the interest payment date whether the subordinated bond holders will be paid in full and, if not, the extent of any shortfall. The timing of payments to junior bond holders can therefore be quite tricky. Obviously it is best to wait until the last possible moment so that the maximum possible cash flow from the underlying mortgage pool can be generated in order to make interest payments. The paying agent on the other hand values certainty and will wish to ensure that he is fully covered for any cash which is disbursed to the subordinated note holders. The lesson is, once again, that there is no substitute for experience.

B. Structuring

1. CREDIT ENHANCEMENT

Credit enhancement is added to the structure of a mortgage-backed securities issue in order to address two principal risks: the risk of a credit loss arising upon realisation of a mortgage in the portfolio; and the risk of the issuing vehicle running short of liquidity, caused by borrowers being in arrears with their mortgage interest payments.

Two basic structures have been developed to address these risks. The most straightforward means of reducing the credit risk on mortgages in a portfolio is to purchase mortgage pool insurance. The insurer, in return for a premium, will agree to cover any realised losses on mortgages within a specific portfolio up to a maximum limit. The insured is generally required to bear the first losses on the portfolio up to an amount typically equal to $\frac{1}{2}\%$ of the portfolio insured. This is normally done by the insured collateralising the first loss provision by placing cash in an escrow account. An interim claims procedure is usually available under the policy, so that claims can be paid before any losses are finally realised. Such policies address the credit risk on the portfolio, but a separate form of enhancement is necessary to address the liquidity risk.

Liquidity risk is often covered by a bank agreeing to make available to the issuer a committed credit facility available for drawing to finance arrears of interest arising on the portfolio. Cash can usually be drawn under the liquidity facility so long as cover remains available under the pool policy in an amount at least equal to the drawings under the liquidity facility.

The main advantage of enhancing an issue by insurance is its simplicity. Like the mortgage-backed market itself, this area of insurance is still young but it shows signs of developing and becoming more competitive. Established issuers can have cover arranged at short notice and although the field of lead underwriters is still small, the reinsurance risk is now taken by a wider spectrum of insurers than was the case in the market's infancy. However, new issuers will probably still experience considerable lead times before the final underwriting commitment is in place.

HMC prefers to provide both liquidity and credit enhancement to its issues by means of a senior/subordinated structure. Liquidity support is provided by the deferral of interest on the subordinated tranche, in the event that insufficient cash has been earned by the issuing vehicle to meet quarterly bond interest. Credit support is provided by the deferral or, potentially, the writing-off of principal payments due to the subordinated bond holders. Obviously these subordinated bonds carry a higher credit risk and interest margin. To date we have not had any problems in finding banks willing to underwrite these bonds, which usually amount to approximately 6% of total issue size. We prefer the senior/subordinated route because we evaluate our mortgage-backed securities in terms of return on capital by constructing a cash flow model based on our standard arrears, default, repayment and further advances assumptions. The fact that a senior/subordinated issue uses very little capital (and here capital is defined in the broadest sense to include all cash outflows for fees and expenses in addition to the capitalisation of the issuing vehicle) means that the returns available from this route are extremely attractive. A second benefit of the senior/subordinated structure is that it serves as a hedge against redemption rates on the portfolio. A pool insurance premium is paid on the closing of the issue and is not rebated if the issue redeems faster than expected. In contrast, the incremental cost of a senior/subordinated issue is the additional coupon on the subordinated bonds. Since the subordinated bonds redeem during the life of the issue, such incremental cost is only borne in proportion to the size of the issue outstanding from time to time.

To date HMC has not had to call upon pool insurers to cover any credit losses on its insured issues, nor has it had to defer any interest, or write off any principal, on subordinated notes in its senior/subordinated issues.

2. SUBSTITUTION AND FURTHER ADVANCES

The initial costs of a mortgage-backed securities issue can be substantial and various techniques have been developed in order to prolong the average life of the issue to achieve the maximum possible period of time to recover such initial expenses.

The most obvious means of extending the average life is to substitute new loans into a securitised portfolio to replace any loans which have redeemed. This was a technique pioneered by HMC in our first mortgage-backed issue, but in that issue substitution was limited by reference to a maximum principal amount of loans that could be added to the pool. Market practice now is not to place any limit on the principal amount of loans being added to a mortgage pool, but rather to place a time limit on the substitution period. A three year substitution period is typical on FRN issues but, as will be seen below, longer substitution periods can be achieved on fixed rate issues.

An issuer can also prolong the average life of a transaction through the treatment of further advances; the market has seen three main methods used.

First, some issuers make further advances on mortgages in the securitised portfolio by way of a second charge. In other words, the original loan stays within the issuing vehicle, but the further advance is retained on the books of the mortgage originator. This tends to be an administratively cumbersome method of making and monitoring further advances. The second method is to treat a loan on which a further advance is made as a redemption and take that loan out of the pool. This is obviously a very expensive process for the issuer, since the redemption rate on the pool as a whole is influenced not only by the underlying redemption rate of loans but also the rate of incidence of further advances. The most efficient method of dealing with further advances is to securitise the further advance along with the original mortgage. The effect on average lives of adding, in effect, a small new loan to the portfolio is minimal, but the real value lies in retaining the full principal amount of the original loan within the issue.

3. REDEMPTION MECHANISMS

Mortgage-backed securities issues have seen two basic means of passing mortgage redemption proceeds back to bond holders. Some issues pay out each bond holder proportionately on a pro rata basis, so that a holder of a £10,000 bond might find that after six months, the principal amount of the investment has reduced to, say, £9,300. This method is said to have the advantage of fairness in that it treats each bond holder equally and assures a bond holder that the average life of his investment will correspond with the average life of mortgages within the pool. In practice, however, the partial redemption of bonds means that a match-funded investor in mortgage-backed securities has continually to monitor his portfolio and ensure that the funding exactly matches the amortisation of the underlying investment.

HMC has pioneered a different method of effecting redemptions. On our issues redemptions are passed back to bond holders by one of two means; either bonds are drawn by lot to be redeemed in full, so a bond holder knows that the full principal amount of each bond needs to be financed on each roll over, or the issuer purchases bonds in the open market using redemption moneys and cancels those bonds. The advantage to the issuer of this route is that it is possible to purchase bonds in the open market at a discount and consequently the issuer may be able to make a small profit by purchasing at, say, 99.90 and cancelling the bond at par. The advantage to the investor is that this mechanism introduces liquidity into the market. An investor wishing to liquidate a position knows that the issuer will always stand ready with a firm bid. This means that investors with short-term maturity horizons can purchase mortgage-backed securities knowing with a reasonable degree of certainty that they will be able to move in and out of the bonds with very limited capital risk. This route provides a better solution for both issuers and investors and it is hardly surprising to note that many new issuers since HMC have adopted this mechanism.

C. Markets

1. PUBLIC ISSUES AND PRIVATE PLACEMENTS

HMC has been a frequent user of both the public bond markets and also the private placement markets. Traditionally, given our concerns about return on capital, we have been prepared to go into the private placement market where margins are a little higher than the rated public bond markets in return for delivering securities with less credit enhancement and/or capital than would be seen in a typical AAA rated public issue. Through time, however, we have been able to refine and reduce the capital element of our public bond issues and, against the background of a very receptive public bond market, we now look unlikely to return to the private placement market simply for reasons of gearing. We see the main advantage of the private placement market as being the flexibility it offers. This is seen not only in the terms and conditions of the bonds—we have arranged private placements, for example, with much longer substitution periods than have been seen in the public bond markets—but also in the underlying mortgages used to collateralise the issue. The private placement markets are much more receptive to non-standard mortgage product, prime examples being pension and Scottish mortgages, where the different legal system in Scotland presents certain difficulties in obtaining a public debt rating for an issue which includes Scottish loans. The trend of our business is towards an ever increasing array of mortgage products. While the first port of call for financing these mortgages will continue to be the public markets, it may be that the private placement market will have a significant role to play in the refinancing of such loans, especially in the early days of the product's life.

2. FLOATING RATE NOTES

The sterling FRN market has, of course, been the market into which the vast bulk of UK mortgage-backed securities have been issued. After a slow start, the market has proved surprisingly resilient both in terms of volume and price. For HMC, as well as many other issuers, this market will remain the core market for issuance.

The FRN market offers issuers two major benefits. First, the market can accommodate very large issues. We have seen individual issues ranging up to an amount of £500 million. Large issue sizes obviously help to recover the very substantial fixed costs associated with a structured public bond issue. The other main benefit of this market is the degree of certainty of funding that it offers to issuers. HMC has been keen to develop alternative markets for issuance in case the sterling FRN market were ever to be closed. However, we are considerably more comfortable with the availability of this market than we were in early 1988 and it seems to us that the sterling mortgage-backed FRN market is now here to stay.

3. FIXED RATE ISSUES

HMC is to date the only institution to issue fixed rate UK mortgage-backed securities collateralised by variable rate mortgages. We had two principal objectives in mind when we launched our first issue, HMC 101. First, we were looking to attract a new class of investor into mortgage-backed securities by offering traditional sterling fixed rate investors a bond which was in all material respects identical to other fixed rate securities in which they already invested. Secondly, we were obviously looking to improve on the returns available to an issuer and in this respect the issue was extremely successful.

The approach that we took to the issue was to produce a conventional AAA rated FRN which could then be swapped to provide the cash flow on the ultimate fixed rate bond. Two problems arise from this approach. First, a traditional mortgage-backed FRN will amortise during the life of the bond. This produces a floating rate cash flow on a declining principal balance, which would mean that the fixed rate issuing company would have to enter into a callable interest rate swap exactly matching the amortisation of the FRN. This would be an expensive transaction if indeed it were possible. The solution to this problem was to make the substitution period on the FRN equal to the life of the fixed rate issue. In the case of HMC 101 this was five years. In order to cover the position where sufficient new mortgages could not be found to keep constant the principal amount outstanding of the FRN, the fixed rate issuer entered into a Guaranteed Investment Contract (GIC). Under the terms of the GIC any redemption proceeds from the FRN could be placed on deposit at a rate equal to the FRN rate. This would then preserve the integrity of the floating rate cash flow, enabling a conventional (in commercial terms) interest rate swap to be written converting the floating rate interest stream from the FRN and GIC into a fixed cash flow to match the coupon on the fixed rate bond.

The second problem to be addressed was how to ensure that fixed rate investors received the full redemption proceeds of the fixed rate bond on its maturity date. This was solved by the fixed rate issuer entering into a takeout agreement under which the fixed rate issuer had the right to sell the FRN to the takeout provider at par on the maturity date of the fixed issue. These sale proceeds would then be passed back to the fixed rate investors on the due date, producing a bullet maturity issue.

The structure can be reproduced in diagrammatic form (page 82).

For an investor, the HMC 101 issue is indistinguishable from any other fixed rate euro-sterling issue with a bullet maturity. Given the AAA rating on the 101's we expected them to trade at narrower margins over the equivalent gilt than building society issues of a similar maturity, none of which carries a rating as high as AAA. The superior credit quality of the 101's has been demonstrated in the fact that they consistently trade ten to fifteen basis points better than comparable AA rated building society issues. This is in contrast to the FRN market where AAA rated mortgage-backed FRNs generally trade at greater

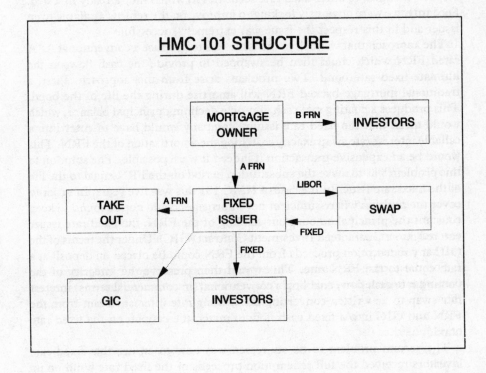

HMC 101 STRUCTURE

```
┌─────────────┐    B FRN    ┌─────────────┐
│  MORTGAGE   │ ──────────→ │  INVESTORS  │
│   OWNER     │             │             │
└─────────────┘             └─────────────┘
        │
      A FRN
        │
        ↓
┌──────────┐   A FRN   ┌──────────┐   LIBOR   ┌──────────┐
│  TAKE    │ ←──────── │  FIXED   │ ────────→ │   SWAP   │
│  OUT     │           │  ISSUER  │           │          │
└──────────┘           └──────────┘ ←──────── └──────────┘
                             │         FIXED
                           FIXED
                             │
                             ↓
┌──────────┐           ┌─────────────┐
│   GIC    │           │  INVESTORS  │
└──────────┘           └─────────────┘
```

discounted margins than building society paper, in spite of the better credit quality of the mortgage-backed securities issues. The difference in pricing in the FRN market is attributable to the uncertain amortisation pattern of the mortgage-backed securities issues. This factor is obviously not present in the fixed rate markets and the market trading levels give a true reflection of the market view of the relative quality of the two types of bond.

D. Timing

In the early history of the UK mortgage-backed market (up to the end of 1987), the question of timing was of crucial importance. Pricing was an allied but secondary problem. Each issue simply offered investors an additional five basis points or so more than the previous issue. In spite of this, the newness of the market and the general lack of awareness amongst the investor community meant that each new mortgage-backed issue was difficult to place and generally left an overhang of paper in the market. Bringing two issues close together simply exacerbated this problem. In the middle of 1988, the situation completely reversed itself. Now, the problem with timing is of getting an issue into the market quickly enough to satisfy investor demand. This situation seems likely to continue for quite some time. Consequently, the comments in this section are directed principally towards timing as it affects the management of an issue, as opposed to the market reception.

For these purposes issues can be segregated into one of two categories, corporate finance driven or opportunistic. Corporate finance driven issues are those where the transaction represents either the first issue from a particular organisation or where an established issuer attempts to introduce a new development in the structuring of an issue. The starting point for a debut issuer is to produce, in conjunction with the lead manager, a detailed timetable. Usually this is done by working backwards from an intended launch date. The timetable will cover not only drafting items such as the prospectus and documentation, but more importantly should identify the system implications of selecting a mortgage pool and managing a portfolio. The lead manager will be able to give fairly detailed assistance and comments on the former, but is unlikely to have a sufficient understanding of a particular issuer's administrative procedures to be able to make a significant impact on the latter. The lead manager should, however, be able to define in great detail the pool information required, both initially and during the life of the issue, and this will form the starting point for any systems development that needs to be undertaken by the issuer.

The invariable experience of the UK mortgage-backed securities market is that this process throws up more problems than had originally been anticipated. First time issuers generally discover two things. First, information held on their database does not coincide with the hard copy information held in mortgage files and consequently many apparently clean mortgage loans will not meet the rigorous warranties required of mortgages used to collateralise issues. Secondly, systems which are perfectly adequate to administer a mortgage portfolio on a commercial basis may need extensive re-programming to provide information required by rating agencies or in the management of a mortgage-backed issue. For example, the typical arrears warranty demanded by Standard & Poor's Corporation is that each mortgage loan has not been more than one month overdue in the previous twelve months. This is not the kind of information which would be readily accessible out of a typical mortgage administration system. HMC was fortunate in that the company was set up with a view to securitising its loans. Our systems were therefore designed with a view to flexibility and to retain evey possible scrap of information concerning each mortgage account.

If the issue involves new structural developments two areas need to be covered before launch. First, it is essential to explain any changes to a previous issue to the rating agencies well in advance of the intended launch date. This may involve the re-working of cash flows and we find that producing new cash flows helps to crystallise abstract concepts. Secondly, the legal implications of any change in structure need to be worked through quite carefully. The problem with the volume of documentation associated with a mortgage-backed issue is that one relatively innocuous looking change can have a knock on effect throughout the documentation of the issue. We like to try to cover this area by producing a mark up of a previous prospectus showing the changes that will be made in the underlying documentation. This can then be sent to the rating agency to help in its credit analysis. This can also be sent to a potential lead manager to clear the market impact of the points.

Experience shows that most people underestimate the time required to sort out the problems thrown up by the processes described above. If an issuer has a particular requirement to put a corporate finance driven bond into the market by a certain date, then the timetabling process described above must allow for a reasonable degree of slippage along the critical path. Our dependence on the mortgage-backed securities market for our funding means we are always interested in improving the efficiency of our bonds and consequently are always looking to introduce refinements into our bond structures. Because of the uncertainty in the timing of this process, we have one or two 'boiler plate' structures which can be used on an opportunistic basis either to meet a funding requirement at short notice or to take advantage of a brief window in the bond market.

There are four basic requirements before considering an opportunistic bond issue. The issuer needs to have confidence in:

(i) its systems both to select a clean pool and also to administer the issue;
(ii) the structure of the issue;
(iii) the certainty of receiving a rating of the desired level; and

(iv) the availability of mortgage assets, either at the launch of the issue or by closing.

In fact this last point is considerably less important now that the market has become more mature. We see, for example, issuers launching transactions without having first selected a mortgage pool or, in the case of some issuers, without having the mortgages on the books at the time at which the transaction is launched. In such cases, the bonds are sold on the basis of the rating and this element assumes a correspondingly greater importance in the new issue process.

HMC has undertaken two opportunistic issues, one in the fixed rate markets and one FRN. In both cases the documentation for the issue was an almost exact replica of a previous transaction. Given the time pressures of a fixed rate issue, the lawyers were instructed to limit their input simply to correcting any errors in the previous transaction, rather than trying to improve on drafting which had previously been regarded as satisfactory. We now adopt the general strategy of retaining a pool of assets within our warehousing company sufficient to collateralise an issue launched at short notice. This enables us to tap pockets of investor demand and is also essential for dealing with the timing uncertainties of the fixed rate markets.

The fixed rate market gives rise to its own particular timing problems. First, the market is considerably more fickle than the FRN market and can be closed for weeks at a time. It is not therefore possible to run a funding strategy on the basis of launching a fixed rate issue at a particular time. It is not simply a question of price. Unlike the FRN market, the fixed rate markets may not be available at any sensible price. Secondly, even if the fixed rate markets are open at an acceptable price, there is the problem of finding a swap in suitable size and with a sufficiently rated counterparty. The uncertainties inherent in the fixed rate markets mean that HMC relies on the FRN markets for its core mortgage backed issuance, but the competitive pricing available in the fixed rate markets lead us to have available both documentation and assets in case a new issuance opportunity should appear.

E. Rating agencies

The contribution made by Standard & Poor's Corporation to the development of the UK mortgage-backed securities market is often overlooked. Mortgage-backed securities are a complicated instrument the credit quality of which most investors would find difficult or impossible to evaluate. By taking the initiative and devoting substantial resources to this market to determine rating criteria, Standard & Poor's have reduced the burden on investors of credit assessment on mortgage-backed securities. Without the initiative of a widely respected rating agency the market's development would have been severely hampered. HMC has to date invited only

Standard & Poor's to rate its issues and consequently the comments in the remainder of this section apply only to the criteria, procedures and policies adopted by that agency.

The starting point for an issuer is to read and understand the agency's published criteria for rating UK mortgage-backed securities. Standard & Poor's publishes a detailed guide to their approach and this can be helpful in assessing the optimum pool selection for rated issues. For example, Standard & Poor's penalise, in terms of credit enhancement, pension mortgages in relation to endowment based mortgages. Although conventional wisdom is that a pension loan portfolio is generally of higher credit quality than its endowment loan counterpart. Given the credit penalty in a rated issue, we prefer to refinance the bulk of our pension loans through mortgage-backed securities placed privately with investors whose credit analysis in this respect more closely coincides with our own.

We are now sufficiently familiar with the way in which Standard & Poor's applies its quantitative analysis to a particular UK mortgage pool that we can run this analysis ourselves in order to calculate the foreclosure frequency and loss severity of a given portfolio. This enables us to calculate the required credit enhancement for a desired level of rating for a pool. We can then accurately estimate the credit enhancement costs associated with an issue before it is in the market. This enables us to evaluate competing issue structures and alternative mortgage pool selections much more precisely than the approach adopted by some issuers of putting a bond into the market and then asking Standard & Poor's to size the credit enhancement associated with it.

This gives HMC a considerable degree of comfort that the statement made on the launch of the bond, that the bond is expected to be awarded an AAA rating, will prove to be accurate. The degree of certainty arising out of the quantitative approach taken by Standard & Poor's to evaluating a mortgage pool is of very considerable benefit to an issuer.

Whenever we attempt to introduce a new structural development into one of our issues, we always discuss this with the rating agency first. An issuer will never receive an absolute confirmation of the rating agency's approach, since their statements have to be qualified by reference to the final agreed documentation between the parties. Perhaps the best way for an issuer to resolve the conflict between broad concepts and detailed documentation is for the issuer to furnish the rating agency with a copy of the draft prospectus for the issue at as early a stage as possible. The prospectus should, after all, be no more than a summary of the underlying documentation and should form the starting point for an analysis of the transaction as a whole.

We have found Standard & Poor's to be very receptive to this approach and offer constructive comments on rating concerns at an early stage of the new issue process. This has proved especially invaluable when we came to launch our fixed rate issue in the autumn of 1988. Popular mythology would lead one to believe that rating agencies seek to place an impenetrable barrier before every structured issue. Our experience indicates that this is a misconception.

ADMINISTRATION OF LIVE ISSUES

Administration of a live issue does not commence on the day a deal is closed. Whilst closing will provide the first accounting transactions, a significant amount of preparatory work must be undertaken prior to that date. Critical tasks include:

 (i) registration of the new company with MIRAS Central Unit as a live entity—this must be done at least a month prior to closing;
 (ii) opening of bank accounts to receive the interest from the newly securitised mortgages and the proceeds of the issue;
(iii) making the necessary adjustments to the computer system to ensure it recognises the existence of a new company;
(iv) in HMC's case, where direct debits are used as a method of interest collection, advising Bankers Automated Clearing Services (BACS) of the intended use of the new bank account.

Having established the administrative framework within which the new company operates, closing requires identification of each individual loan to be transferred to the refinancing company (together with accrued interest at that date), and the change of branch number on the system identifying to which corporate entity that loan belongs. Each corporate branch number has its own unique bank account number held within the system to ensure that interest is collected in the correct account, an important point as the bank accounts of the securitised company are charged to the trustee as protection for the bondholders.

Apart from the normal requirements of maintaining the books of account of any corporate entity, a securitised company requires additional care and maintenance. If the terms of the deal permit substitution of new qualifying loans to cover redemptions and part repayments of existing loans, the computer software must recognise all cases where the capital values of the existing mortgage pool assets are reduced. The report identifying such reductions must be reconciled to cash receipts as a matter of routine. In order to ensure that the average quality of the mortgage pool is maintained at a level close to the characteristics described in the prospectus, the computer software identifies loans available for securitisation within the originator which closely match the characteristics of those redeemed. The list of 'available' loans is reviewed and the branch numbers of those selected are changed to that of the securitised company. A report is thereby generated from the system identifying the value of those loans substituted and the necessary cash transfer made to effect the purchase by the securitised company. An overall comparison must be kept with the maximum value of substitutions permitted and the date after which no further substitutions are allowed must be monitored.

Similar constraints may also apply to the making of further advances. Assuming they are permitted to a specified financial limit, formal procedures must be followed to comply with the legal framework. In HMC's case the transfer of the mortgage from Household Mortgage Corporation to a refinancing company is effected by equitable transfer. As legal registration of the charge remains with HMC, any further advance must also be made by HMC. Accordingly, those loans on which further advances are requested are transferred by the securitised company to the originator, again by changing the branch number. The advance is then made by the originator and the loan, supplemented by the further advance, is sold back to the securitised company for cash. The increased loan must satisfy all the necessary warranties such as income multiples and loan to value. All cash transfers between the companies comprise the loan value and accrued interest to date. Those loans which fail the warranty tests must be reviewed to establish reasons for failure and amendments made to the database where necessary. Any loans which continue to fail will be left in the originator and a new loan substituted.

Regular compliance tests are necessary to ensure both that the tangible capital of the vehicle is at least at the level prescribed in the prospectus and that there is sufficient cash within the vehicle to meet the next coupon payment on the notes. The latter test, called the Threshold Interest Margin test by HMC (and similar phraseology is used by others), is carried out at each coupon fixing on the notes or on a change in the mortgage rate. A comparison is carried out of the resultant new gross margin with the minimum margin permitted. If the test shows a prospective margin less than the minimum, a cash forecast is prepared to the next coupon date of the notes to identify whether the bondholders can be paid. If the test indicates a shortfall in the cash available to satisfy the bondholders the originator must either provide an advance to cover such a shortfall or increase the mortgage rate. Repayment of any advance under this test only occurs when it can be demonstrated that sufficient funds will be generated to pay the next coupon.

LEGAL CONSIDERATIONS

Legal constraints on an issue are contained in various statutes, mainly the Consumer Credit Act, the Data Protection Act, the Financial Services Act and of course the Law of Property Act.

Throughout the life of an issue it is important to ensure that both the originator and the issuing company remain properly authorised under the relevant statutes. If direct financial services are offered, the originator must seek and maintain Financial Services Act registration.

HMC introduced equitable transfers of mortgages, as opposed to a full legal transfer, in its first bond issue. This method avoids the laborious and expensive procedures necessary to record full legal transfer from originator to refinancing company and has since become established as a market standard. By adopting the equitable transfer route the originator remains the legal (but not equitable) owner of the mortgages and therefore retains the ability to deal with the assets in the pool. This is important, so that cumbersome formalities are avoided in the event, for instance, of a further advance or a redemption. The refinancing company's interest, although not perfected by way of full legal transfer, is nevertheless protected by the provisions contained in the management deed entered into between the originator and the refinancing company.

On redemption, if the equitable route is followed, sealing discharges is not a problem as the originator retains legal ownership of the charge and seals the discharge acting as agent for the refinancing company and the trustee. However, if a legal transfer has been made, sealing will usually be effected by the originator company acting under a power of attorney from the trustee and the issuer. This means that either the power of attorney needs to be registered at the Land Registry (and an appropriate facility letter produced) or, for unregistered land, the power of attorney is produced each time a discharge is sealed.

Where mortgages are transferred by equitable assignment the legal title to the mortgage remains unaltered and the borrower still has only one company to deal with.

Requirements of the rating agencies for deeds storage may cause an issuer to change its conventional procedures. The rating agencies may require third party or dual key storage arrangements which can cause problems to originators and issuers. Ability to have access to the deeds of the properties within that issue is often restricted either by time and/or by the percentage levels of removals allowed to ensure that the trustee's security is not jeopardised.

Where substitutions and further advances are made it is important that each loan being transferred meets all the necessary preconditions and that the transfers are effected properly within the provisions of the management deed which embodies the requirements of the Law of Property Act. At the time of each transfer each loan must be capable of matching all the warranties given on the original mortgage pool.

The trustee requires the issuer to notify it of specified events during the life of the issue. These notification events must be observed and the correct notification procedure adopted.

SUMMARY

Specialist mortgage lenders such as HMC will need to capitalise on their strengths to sustain and improve the substantial position they have already created for themselves. These strengths are:

  (i) a low expense base;
 (ii) an ability to make greater returns on capital than is normal in the industry out of smaller margins through efficient bond structuring;
(iii) a more diversified product base through the requirement to deliver into

the hands of brokers and life companies products which address the needs
of customers in different (and sometimes adverse) market conditions;
(iv) highly efficient servicing;
(v) financial protection through the ability to fund to maturity.

We believe that companies structured as centralised lenders able to issue
efficiently structured securities will take an increasing share of the mortgage
market, they will offer a more diversified product range and make better
returns for shareholders.

Chapter 5

What Securitisation can mean for a Commercial Bank

Bruce Gaitskell
CIBC Mortgages plc

COMMERCIAL BANKS AND SECURITISATION

A. Mortgage activities of banks

Until the late 1970s banks showed little interest in the UK mortgage market. Building societies enjoyed relatively cheap retail funds and the mortgage rate was consistently below LIBOR.

As the decade progressed clearing banks began to see the virtue of providing a more complete range of services to retail customers and they began to compete with the societies. Mortgages were a safe asset for banks to hold at a time when lending to corporates was becoming less rewarding and early signs of the third world debt crisis were emerging.

In addition, three overseas banks entered the UK mortgage market; Chemical Bank (1980), Bank of America (1974) and Citibank (1974). The last of these, in particular, had aspirations to provide a complete range of banking services to retail customers. Interestingly the first two subsequently sold their mortgage operations to BNP (1988) and Bank of Ireland (1986) respectively. These three banks were later followed by Canadian Imperial Bank of Commerce (CIBC) and Salomon Brothers (through its subsidiary, The Mortgage Corporation (TMC)). These later two were attracted by the positive spread that emerged during the mid 1980s between inter-bank rate (LIBOR) and UK mortgage rates. This same structural change in the mortgage market (which resulted from increased competition between building societies and National Savings for retail funds) led to the formation of the 'new lenders' (eg National Home Loans Corporation, Household Mortgage Corporation, Mortgage Funding Corporation and First Mortgage Securities).

The entry of banks into the UK mortgage market and their current position is charted in Table 1 on page 92.

Since 1985 major building societies have become increasingly reliant on wholesale funding to supplement retail deposits suggesting that mortgage rates

Table 1.

BANKS AND THE UK MORTGAGE MARKET

UK Clearing Banks

BANK	ENTERED MORTGAGE MARKET	MORTGAGE ASSETS UNDER MANAGEMENT (MAY 1989)
Barclays	December 1980	£8.0 BN
Lloyds	February 1979	£6.1 BN
Midland	June 1979	£4.3 BN
Bank of Scotland	June 1989	£2.1 BN
TSB	July 1979	
Yorkshire Bank	August 1986	£0.2 BN

---

are over a period likely to remain above LIBOR in the future. The average spread of mortgage rates over LIBOR for the period 1985–88 was slightly in excess of 100 bp (1%) (see Table 2 on page 93). Together with the beneficial effects of compounding (collecting interest monthly against paying out interest on funding quarterly) and judicious treasury management, lenders were able to achieve margins of 1.25–1.5% during this period. Since August 1988 three factors have changed this situation. First, societies enjoyed a considerable boost to their retail funding following the stock market crash in October 1987, further boosted by the lack of competition from National Savings. Secondly, banks began to anticipate the half-weighting for mortgage assets adopted by the Bank of England following the Basle Agreement. Thirdly, rising interest rates depressed mortgage demand and allowed societies to fund predominantly through retail sources allowing them to keep mortgage rates close to or below LIBOR. These two factors resulted in the spread falling to an average of only 6 bp for the period September 1988–January 1989 (see Table 3 on page 94) although over a longer period it might be expected to average LIBOR + 60–75 bp.

Whilst the first factor might be expected to be temporary the second is likely to have a long lasting effect, especially as the same half-weighting applies to building societies.

Taking the average 103 bp spread that subsisted between December 1984–December 1988 and assuming a typical overhead cost for running mortgage assets of 30 bp, it suggests that banks can make the same return on capital under the new capital requirements at a spread of 67 bp.

The situation is less happy for the new lenders whose capital requirement is dictated not by the Bank of England but by their lending banks. Whilst a number have permitted gearing ratios of 20 : 1 few have achieved in excess of 10 : 1. Banks on the other hand can effectively achieve 25 : 1 based on the 50% reduction in capital requirement for mortgage assets. Typically new lenders

Table 2.

THE DIFFERENCE BETWWEEN 3 MONTH LIBOR
AND THE MORTGAGE RATE

Maximum Difference +2.91 %

Average

1.03 %

Minimum Difference - 2.04 %

Mortgage Rate Surplus (%)

DEC 84	JUNE 85	DEC 85	JUNE 86	DEC 86	JUNE 87	DEC 87	JUNE 88	DEC 88

4.0   3.0   2.0   1.0   0.0   -1.0   -2.0   -3.0

JP Morgan - Asset-backed Securities

Table 3.

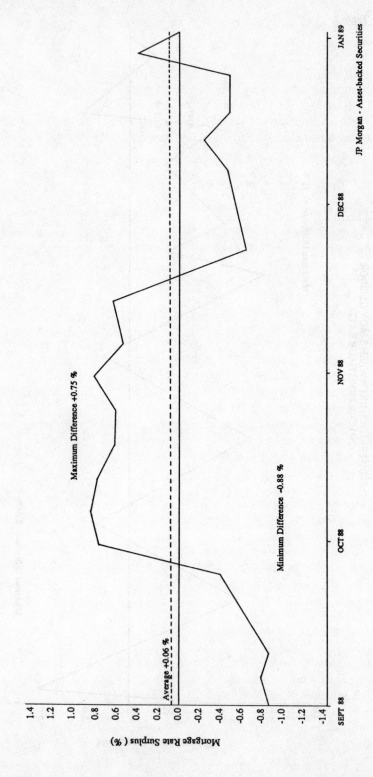

THE DIFFERENCE BETWEEN 3 MONTH LIBOR
AND THE MORTGAGE RATE

Maximum Difference +0.75 %

Minimum Difference -0.88 %

Average +0.06 %

Mortgage Rate Surplus (%)

1.4
1.2
1.0
0.8
0.6
0.4
0.2
0.0
-0.2
-0.4
-0.6
-0.8
-1.0
-1.2
-1.4

SEPT 88   OCT 88   NOV 88   DEC 88   JAN 89

JP Morgan - Asset-backed Securities

borrow committed funds at around LIBOR + 37 bp and have administrative overheads of 30 bp or more; it is difficult to see how average spreads will exceed the total (67 bp) over the next few years.

Over and above the new capital requirements the banks have a number of continuing advantages over the new lenders. Typically they fund at or near LIBOR and are diversified organisations which can survive periods when mortgage spreads are negative. When they come to securitise they have the added advantages of being quality servicers, often having a credit rating.

B. Funding the mortgage book

The major source of funding is provided by the London inter-bank market. Taking a mix of one, two and three month deposits gives a typical average maturity of six weeks. The majority of lenders have the option to change the mortgage rate each month and, on average, are two weeks away from the next re-pricing decision, giving an average interest rate exposure on the asset of six weeks.

It is therefore possible to achieve reasonable match funding of the asset with the liability. Banks are still able to take a view on future movements in the mortgage rate and general interest rates and reposition the funding short or long according to that view. In addition overnight and seven day funds may be cheap relative to longer funding for technical reasons and banks may take these funds and sell forward futures or options to maintain the average maturity they desire on the funding book.

New lenders and, to a lesser extent, building societies are less able to match fund or vary the maturity of their funding book. Typically a new lender's principal funding is provided by committed banking lines with quarterly interest rate setting.

The inter-bank market is substantial but finite and those banks with very large portfolios require some proportion of their funding to be by way of committed facilities. Typically these will cost up to 20 bp more than uncommitted funds taken from the inter-bank market. They also lack the maturity flexibility obtainable in that market.

A number of the banks active in the mortgage market have on-balance sheet Euro-commercial paper programmes which are used, in part, to fund mortgage assets. The all-in cost of these programmes is broadly similar to inter-bank funding.

Unlike UK clearing banks and building societies the overseas banks cannot raise large volumes of retail deposits efficiently. Even when retail rates are substantially below LIBOR the costs of acquisition and administration add a prohibitive additional cost to this type of funding. This inability to raise retail funds presented no problem to the overseas banks until late 1988 or early 1989.

A number of medium sized building societies have limited access to the Euromarkets. The costs of access for them are prohibitive compared to larger societies. In addition they do not need the additional funding at a time when retail deposits are high. They are however at a competitive disadvantage to the larger socieities if wholesale rates once again become cheaper than retail rates. CIBC has been able to address in part its deficiency of retail priced funding by entering into a retail-wholesale swap with a UK building society. By entering into the swap with CIBC the society is able to create a synthetic wholesale borrowing without incurring the issuing expenses associated with a capital-markets bond issue. In the same way the swap gives CIBC a synthetic retail borrowing. Unlike conventional swaps there is no necessity for an intermediary as the credit quality of the counter-parties is generally perceived to be around the AA level. The swap is only attractive where one party is a bank in order that the netted interest payment can be made without deduction of withholding tax.

A small private market has developed during 1989 for these swaps. Typically a bank will pay the society an average building society mortgage rate and receive three-month LIBOR plus a margin. The margin on these swaps moves in line with expected changes in mortgage rate-LIBOR spread and has ranged between 90 bp and 60 bp for a three year maturity.

C. The incentive to securitise mortgage assets

Twenty average mortgages total in excess of £1m and many of the mortgage-lending banks create in excess of 100 mortgages each working day. The funding of such a volume of new assets together with the re-financing of existing deposits presents a formidable challenge to a treasurer.

A number of non-bank mortgage lenders have sought to diversify their funding away from bank investors or lenders by issuing Euro-commercial paper (ECP). Unrated on-balance sheet programmes have generally failed to achieve the desired diversification since banks are the main buyers of such unrated paper.

CIBC's securitisation programme through the A1-P1 rated MAES ECP programme has been successful in attracting a diverse group of investors in Japan, Europe and off-shore US investors around the world. Hence in part it can be said that many banks (in particular those which are not UK clearers) needed to securitise some of their mortgage assets if they were to continue to grow assets of typically £0.5-£1.5 billion each year. However, even without the potential limitation of funding ever increasing levels of mortgage assets, on-balance sheet securitisation would still be attractive to banks.

The most compelling argument for securitisation is the increasing gearing and hence return on capital which is available. In theory it is possible to obtain infinite gearing by borrowing all the capital necessary to securitise a mortgage portfolio although in practice it is more desirable to optimise gearing.

Under the Cooke Committee proposal banks will be limited to gearing of 12.5:1 (although in practice this equates to 25:1 for mortgage portfolios because of the 50% weighting under the BIS proposals). This compares with

30–35 : 1 for building societies and typically 20 : 1 for new lenders (the latter being imposed by covenants under lending agreements). A well structured securitisation gives gearing of around 70 : 1, a three-fold increase over on-balance sheet assets. To increase leverage significantly beyond 70 : 1 risks increasing the marginal cost to the note-issuing company ('issuer') where, in the current low mortgage-spread environment, there is a risk of negative returns.

Table 4 below shows that a structure which is fully leveraged has running costs including administration fees of approximately 75 bp—a figure in excess of where spreads have been over the past 12 months. However, by capitalising the vehicle at 1.35% (as in the example shown in Table 4) the financing and administrative overheads are 47 bp allowing an adequate return of capital even in a low-margin environment.

Table 4.

OPTIMISING LEVERAGE

Up-Front Costs	(%)	(Per Annum)
Insurance		
Deductible	0.50	
Premium	0.30	
Legal	0.20	
Other	0.10	
Managers' fees	0.25	
	1.35	or 0.28%
Per-Annum Costs		
Coupon:	0.20	
Liquidity:	0.01	
Administration:	0.01	
		0.22%
Servicing Fees:		0.25%
Total Running Costs		0.75%

It should be said that there are disincentives to securitise. The process of securitisation involves the transfer of a customer's mortgage from the bank to an unfamiliar funding vehicle not owned by the bank. This disincentive has been softened by the majority of lenders observing the code of practice which was published following the considerations of the 'Working Party on the Secondary Mortgage Market' in 1986 and 1987 and, perhaps more importantly, a bank's ability to maintain the same mortgage rate for securitised borrowers as it offers to the customers it retains. This aspect of potential customer disquiet has probably inhibited clearing banks who are concerned that their multi-financial product approach to customers may be damaged by a mortgage transfer.

A stronger disincentive is the cost of securitisation, both in financial and manpower terms. A first issue takes many months to prepare, involves systems and procedural changes within the organisation and incurs legal costs substantially in excess of the original estimate! For a regular issuer of mortgage-backed securities this high first issue cost is averaged-down by the subsequent use of similar structures. This is not the case for the 'once a year issuer'. Technology in this new market changes rapidly and a structure used 12 months ago is likely to need significant modification.

A solution for the occasional issuer is to access the knowledge of experienced issuers. In the case of an FRN this would take the form of an 'Issuer Consultancy' whilst for ECP the experienced issuer would arrange and manage the programme. This allows the occasional issuer access not only to the structural technology of securitisation but also the more mundane but every bit as important area of pool selection, administrative procedures and systems modifications. It also avoids the need to recruit a securitisation specialist. CIBC has undertaken several such consultancies during 1989. It is also probable they will produce a duplicate of their mortgage-backed ECP structure to allow a number of smaller would-be securitisers access to this market.

D. The choice of markets

A potential issuer has a choice of a number of markets including sterling FRNs, US dollar Euro-commercial paper, sterling fixed-rate bonds or US domestic bond or paper markets. The choice will not only be influenced by price but also market capacity, the possible desire to target non-bank investors (especially for new lenders) and the future intentions of the securitising institution.

Examining each of these markets in turn;

1. STERLING MORTGAGE-BACKED FRNS

In the period from January 1987 to December 1988 issues of mortgage-backed securities totalled some £4.2 billion representing over 50% of the £7.7 billion FRNs issued during this period. Were it not for the relative slowdown in the rate of new asset growth of banks and new lenders during 1989 (due to the depressed mortgage market and the recovery of market share by the building societies) issues of mortgage-backed securities might have been expected to reach £6 or £7 billion in that year alone. Clearly the FRN market has limitations when viewed both against this figure and also the fact that total mortgage debt outstanding at the end of 1988 was some £184 billion.

A further limitation of the sterling FRN market is the fact that the majority of investors in this market are banks and this market therefore offers mortgage lenders limited scope to diversify their funding base. This is particularly acute for the new lenders who are substantial users of the bank syndicated loan market. Typically they borrow from this market at an average cost of LIBOR + 25–30 bp (plus reserve asset costs). The fact that banks advance to new lenders at this level is the probable reason for the relatively high coupon that they demand for highly rated mortgage-backed securities—an AA rated building society issuing an FRN pays some 10–15 bp less than the issuer of an off-balance sheet AAA rated mortage-backed security.

Issues became progressively more expensive in the first 12 months following the first rated mortgage-backed issue from National Home Loans in March 1987 although this trend was subsequently reversed as the market became more familiar with the structure of these issues and the high quality of the assets and associated credit enhancements. This is illustrated in Table 5 on page 100.

It was this high level of FRN pricing which caused CIBC to be the first lender to issue mortgage-backed ECP.

2. MORTGAGE-BACKED ECP

Mortgage-backed ECP offers a number of advantages to issuers. In particular it gives access to the US dollar market which is substantially larger than the sterling market. It also brings investor advantages, most notably the absence of maturity risk that exists with 27–30 year FRNs.

Mortgage-backed ECP securitisations are, however, more complex and expensive to structure. In order to gain the desired credit rating and to guarantee liquidity for holders of paper it is necessary to put it in place a five year sterling backstop for the full amount of the programme.

The combined cost of undrawn committed backstop, the coupon on the ECP (technically the ECP is issued at a discount) and the cost of the dollar-sterling swaps total approximately LIBOR + 15–20 bp. This compared favourably with FRNs which, during 1988, were issued at coupons between LIBOR + 27 bp and LIBOR + 42½ bp.

A further advantage is that paper can be issued continuously during a period for maturities of typically one, two or three months avoiding the event risk which is present with an FRN which only resets four times each year. The maturity and tenure of mortgage-backed ECP can be managed to mirror that of the bank's on-balance sheet mortgage funding. Additionally, the ECP programme can be stepped up over time (subject to provision of additional sterling backstop) without incurring additional structuring or issuing costs.

3. STERLING FIXED INTEREST BONDS

An interesting development occurred in mid 1988 when JP Morgan Securities

Table 5.

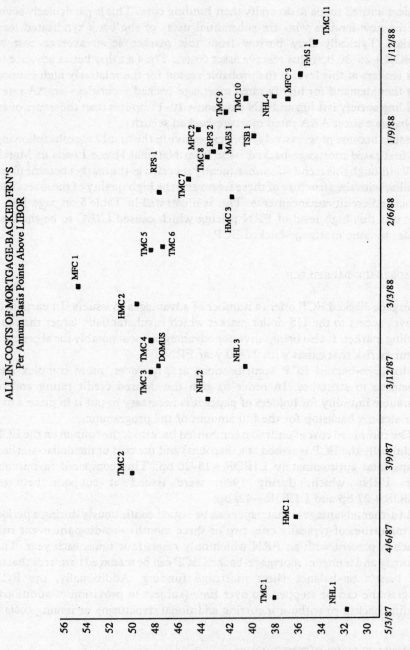

ALL-IN-COSTS OF MORTGAGE-BACKED FRN'S
Per Annum Basis Points Above LIBOR

All-in-costs (per annum basis points above LIBOR)

JP Morgan - Asset-backed Securities

structured a bullet-maturity five year straight sterling issue for Household Mortgage Corporation. A listed 30 year FRN was issued by a special purpose company (SPC) and sold in its entirety to a second SPC. The SPC purchased a five year put on the FRN from American Insurance Group (AIG) and then issued a sterling five year bond. The underlying FRN had five year substitution of mortgages so as to maintain full outstandings for five years.

Although well received the bond issue had two limitations. First, the issue was for only £100 million reflecting the smaller demand for sterling straights and secondly, whilst the funding cost was cheaper than a conventional mortgage-backed FRN, the infrequency with which there is a coincidence of investor demand at the right price, an attractive swap and 'put' availability makes this structure one which cannot be relied on for regular funding needs.

On the positive side the bond achieved a wider non-bank distribution than conventional FRNs and allowed five year substitution compared with the typical three year period seen on recent mortgage-backed FRNs. HMC repeated the issue in early 1989 with another £100 million transaction, AIG again providing the put.

Looking to the future this structure could become more popular, particularly if UK insurers or corporate investors show interest in writing puts on the underlying FRNs and thereby provide a more competitive market for put options. Issue size could also be expected to increase as this new market matures.

4. US DOLLAR DOMESTIC CP

Late 1988 saw MFC and HMC access the US domestic CP market using a AAA rated guarantor. The US domestic market has more depth and liquidity than the ECP market and it seems inevitable that other issuers will tap this market.

The main disadvantages at present are the complexities of meeting SEC regulations and the tendency of the US market to prefer guaranteed deals rather than structured issues. The latter means that a regular issuer will not benefit from the lower pricing that stems from name recognition as investors are focused on the credit quality of the guarantor. This also means that guarantors effectively control the price of access to the US domestic market in much the way that AIG dominated access to the UK straight market.

5. FUTURE DEVELOPMENTS

SG Warburg have pioneered the Sterling Variable-Rate Note (VRN) market in the UK having led on-balance sheet issues for both the Halifax and Abbey National Building Societies. It can only be a matter of time before this structure is used for an off-balance sheet securitisation. The structure has many of the characteristics of ECP; investors bid for the three month coupon on the notes. The unusual feature is that instead of liquidity provided by a back-stop facility investors provide the liquidity by, in an illiquid market, being left with their notes at a coupon of, say, LIBOR + 75 bp. This 'back-stop cost' is presently too high for mortgage issuers at a time when mortgage margins are below 75 bp. The structure would become attractive to issuers if investors were willing to accept a back-stop cost of 50 bp, no doubt in return for a higher coupon in the first three month period.

A further problem with this structure is that the issuer's costs of funding may fluctuate dramatically over the life of the transaction depending on investor demand, whereas an FRN provides a guaranteed cost of funds throughout the life of the issue. While the risk of changing funding costs also exists with mortgage-backed ECP, the market is altogether larger and more liquid and issuers have greater certainty of competitive funding.

E. Structural options

Having selected the market in which one desires to issue mortgage-backed securities there are a number of structural options to consider. Perhaps the three most important are the use of pool insurance or subordinated debt, part repayment upon amortisation or the operation of a purchase fund and whether to issue definitive notes or operate a book entry system.

POOL INSURANCE OR SUBORDINATED DEBT?

The most frequently used type of credit enhancement supporting a rated mortgage-backed security is pool insurance (a fuller description of which will be found in Chapter 9). This is usually purchased to cover the first losses totalling up to 10% (although occasionally it is written for 100%) of the total issue size and is generally subject to a 0.5% deductible put up as a deposit by the originator. As pool insurance only covers losses and not payment delays (ie mortgage arrears) it is also necesary for the issuer to arrange a liquidity facility.

Typically this will be for a sum equating to 2.5–3% of the issue size for a AAA rated transaction.

An alternative to these two separate enhancements is to issue un-rated subordinated debt. This alternative has been successfully employed by both National Home Loans (NHL) and Household Mortgage Corporation (HMC).

In the first case (and until the June 1989 issue by Collateralised Mortgage Securities (No 1) PLC) the subordinated debt was bought and held by NHL thereby providing 'self-insurance' at a considerable cost saving. It is reasonable to suppose that a lender knows the likely performance and credit quality of the mortgage pool better than a provider of pool insurance or an investor in subordinated debt and therefore does not require such a high coupon to reward him for the risk. However, looking forward it is increasingly difficult to see accountants allowing such a transaction to be regarded as off-balance sheet where the originator continues to be exposed to the performance of the portfolio both in terms of losses and note interest delays due to mortgage arrears. The Bank of England guidelines indicate that a regulated institution holding its own (or a connected party's) subordinated debt will not achieve off-balance sheet treatment (for capital adequacy purposes) for the assets sold.

There may be instances in the future where a new lender may find that an on-balance sheet mortgage-backed security incorporating subordinated debt held by itself is a cheaper funding alternative than borrowing in the syndicated loans market. Over and above price considerations such a structure has the advantage of funding to maturity, although in practice most mortgage-backed securities will be called on or prior to the step-up in coupon, typically present in such issues ten years after closing.

By contrast, the second issuer, HMC, sells the subordinated debt in its issues to third party investors who receive a significantly higher coupon than senior noteholders. The advantage to HMC is that the cost of credit enhancement is spread over the life of the issue rather than being an up-front cost as in the case of pool insurance (thereby reducing the capital cost of a securitisation since no pool insurance deductible is required to be financed by the originator). Table 6 on page 104 illustrates the varying returns on capital using the alternative structures.

F. Developments during 1989

1989 started very quietly for mortgage-backed securities reflecting the difficult origination conditions experienced at that time by new lenders and overseas banks. There were, however, a number of issues from July through to September totalling just less than £2 billion.

The first issue was by MAES Funding No 2 plc, a £300 million FRN issue utilising assets from CIBC Mortgages. The issue was significant in a number of respects; with a coupon of 15 bp and fees of 15 bp it was the cheapest mortgage backed FRN to date and, at £300 million, the largest. In addition it features a £200 million tap exercisable in full or in part on any of the first four interest payment dates. The issue did not incorporate substitution reflecting CIBC's view that over the new few years coupons would further reduce. The absence of substitution gave the bond an average life of less than two years and this, together with the liquidity promised by the size of the issue, lead to significantly different investor groups purchasing the paper, notably UK corporates and bank money-market desks.

This issue was closely followed by offerings from Barclays Bank and the National Home Loans Corporation. The Barclays issue ('Gracechurch') was the first seen from the big four clearers and was a conventional issue featuring three year substitution. The coupon of 20 bp and fees of $12\frac{1}{2}$ bp made it marginally more expensive than the MAES issue reflecting the fact that this

Table 6.

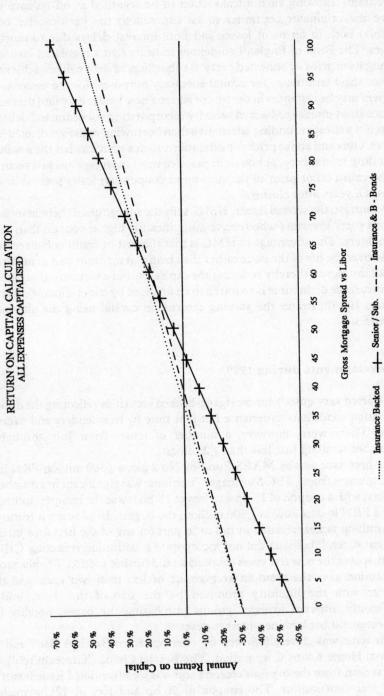

RETURN ON CAPITAL CALCULATION
ALL EXPENSES CAPITALISED

Annual Return on Capital

Gross Mortgage Spread vs Libor

—|— Insurance Backed　　—— Senior / Sub.　　······· Insurance & B - Bonds

JP Morgan - Asset-backed Securities

was a first issue for Barclays and that the smaller size of the issue might lead to less liquidity.

National Home Loans issued through Collateralised Mortgage Securities (No 1) plc a CMO (Collateralised Mortgage Obligation) type of structure commonly seen in the United States. The issue, totalling £225 million, was divided into four tranches; 'fast-pay', 'medium-pay' and 'slow-pay' senior notes and a subordinated tranche. Whilst each senior tranche is pari passu in respect of interest, principal is repaid only to fast-pay notes until the tranche is fully redeemed, then to medium-pay and so on, giving an average life on the fast-pay notes of less than one year (with average lives in excess of five years for the other two tranches). One object of the transaction was to produce, in the fast-pay notes, an instrument attractive to UK corporates thereby giving NHL originated issues a diversification away from bank investors. In this respect the issue was only partially successful since the fast-pay notes appealed to bank money market desks as well as the corporates. Whilst the fast-pay notes had the lowest coupon yet seen in the MBS market the weighted cost of all three senior tranches was higher than MAES 2.

Around the same time The Mortgage Corporation announced the PIMBS programme: an FRN issuance programme of up to £3 billion over a number of years through a series of PIMBS special purpose companies, the first of which, PIMBS No 1 plc issued £250 million in the summer of 1989. The object of the programme is to reduce legal costs associated with note issuance by having a master set of documents covering the majority of the terms of each issue. It was perhaps surprising that a programme of this size and duration restricted itself to both sterling and FRNs but it did have the advantage of embracing a multitude of different mortgage types.

The late summer saw further issues from CMS (No 2) plc, First Mortgage Securities (MS No 2 plc), Household Mortgage Corporation and PIMBS No 2 plc. The common feature of the last three issues was that in each case investors regarded the pricing as rather tight and indicated that it might be some time before the pricing of MAES 2 might be equalled or bettered in the MBS market.

BANK OF ENGLAND NOTICE ON LOAN TRANSFERS AND SECURITISATION

With the increase in loan transfers between banks during the 1980s and the advent of mortgage-backed securities in March 1987 the Bank of England recognised the need to formalise their approach as to when a transferred loan or securitised group of assets could be regarded, for capital adequacy purposes, as being sold without significant retained risk. The preferred approach was for the participants of the BIS—Basle Agreement to extend their work to cover loan transfers and securitisation but there was neither time nor sufficient interest for this to happen. The United States Federal Authorities already had a policy, developed on an ad hoc basis over the previous decade, whilst other participating countries had yet to see securitisation become a feature of their individual markets. It was therefore necessary for the Bank of England to 'go it alone'.

The eventual notice (BSD/1989/1—Loan Transfers and Securitisation) appeared in February 1989, two full years after consultation with interested parties commenced and 15 months after the publication, in December 1987, of a consultative paper.

The policy is broad in its approach, seeking to cover all types of potential securitisation and the transfer of any type of banking loan or commitment.

The notice makes a simple distinction between the transfer of a single loan and the transfer of a group or 'package' of loans, the latter being described as securitisation.

Much interest at the time of the notice's publication centred on the impact it would have on the securitisation of mortgage assets. Interestingly mortgages are not once mentioned in the notice. It is thought that the advent of mortgage securitisation had not caused undue concern at the Bank—the assets were relatively low risk and the presence of credit ratings suggested the transactions were well structured. Nevertheless it has been practitioners in the mortgage securitisation area that have been predominantly, but not exclusively, concerned with the practical effect of the Bank's notice.

The Bank's policy is not to operate a graduated scale where a sold asset with some limited recourse is regarded, for example, as 90% sold with 10% risk retention, but rather an absolute decision—sold or not sold. The paper effectively sets out a list of requirements and exclusions each of which has to be fully met if the asset is to be disregarded for capital adequacy purposes.

The Bank does acknowledge that certain risks exist even when all the rules have been met. The principal retained risks are moral and operational/ administrative. In the first case the Bank needs to make a subjective judgement about how likely it is for a vendor bank to rescue a securitisation vehicle rather than risk, in some way, its own reputation or relationship with its former customers. It might be felt that a UK clearing bank with its substantial retail customer base would be more inclined to rescue a failing securitisation company which it had sponsored compared with, by way of example, a US bank which had effectively withdrawn from UK retail and mortgage banking. In the second case it has to be acknowledged that administrators/servicers of securitised assets have strict obligations with regard to standards of adminis- tration and these are generally supported by indemnities against loss through administrative error. In both of these cases the Bank does not lay down a formal methodology for such calculated risks but prefers to build such considerations into the broad and subjective decision which needs to be taken on a bank by bank basis; that is, by how much should a bank be required to exceed the minimum capital requirements set out in the BIS/Basle paper.

Much has been said, sometimes critically, about the Bank's regulatory approach to securitisation. It should be said, however, that the requirements are not impossible to meet and that securitisation has continued to take place involving regulated banks since the publication of the notice. In the long run practitioners of securitisation all gain by maintaining high standards of transaction integrity. The rating process helps to ensure the achievement of such standards and this is reinforced by the Bank of England's policy statement.

Chapter 6

Securitisation and Building Societies—a Threat or Benefit?

Robert Neill
Leamington Spa Building Society

Securitisation has had a significant impact on building societies, not directly but through the activities of the new lenders. The additional capacity it has afforded these new organisations has enabled them to capture an important share of the mortgage business. Borrowers have undoubtedly benefited from the more intense competition generated by the new entrants to the market. There has been greater product innovation and interest rates are lower than would otherwise have been the case. It has resulted, however, in an over-capacity of mortgage funds, especially since August 1988, which has inevitably led to a squeeze on margins. This trend is not helpful to any lender and positively dangerous to the weaker players.

These events have naturally influenced the views of building societies on securitisation which are as varied as their views on estate agency, the Financial Services Act and conversion to public company status to name but a few topical issues. Even casual observers, who used to regard the industry as one amorphous mass differentiated only by size, now acknowledge the variety of strategies and styles unimaginable in the days of the cartel. Many of the recent activities have only been possible since the Building Societies Act 1986. Why in all this mêlée of activities have societies so far shown very little interest in securitisation? Is it pre-occupation with mergers, conversion, independent or tied status, defence against hostile predators or are there more fundamental economic reasons?

Building societies are portfolio lenders with the majority of their income generated by the margin between the cost of funds and the mortgage rate. Until the early 1980s, as there was excess mortgage demand, the two main restraints on asset growth were capital and the ability to attract retail funds at an acceptable cost. This would seem an ideal environment for securitisation since this would have allowed the excess mortgage demand to be satisfied without asset growth and without additional retail funds. Apart from the legal problem that it was not within the permitted range of powers under the Building Societies Act 1962 the technology for securitisation did not exist in the UK at that time. Societies were not, however, campaigning for any change in legislation on this point or showing any interest in the subject whatsoever. The real problem was that the necessary pre-requisite for mortgage securitisation, a mortgage rate at a relatively consistent premium over money market rates, did not exist. In 1974 and again in 1980, the mortgage rate was more than 2% below money market rates for some months making securitisation non-viable.

From 1983 until 1988, however, the interest rate environment has been favourable for securitisation with the mortgage rate premium over LIBOR averaging more than 100 basis points. This gives rise to two questions; why did this development occur and, even more important for the future of securitisation, will it continue? To answer these questions, an understanding is required of the relationship between three rates, the mortgage rate, the cost of retail funds and the cost of wholesale funds.

In the early 1980s, the clearing banks re-discovered the retail customer and started to compete with societies for both mortgages and retail investors. Even if the clearing banks' objectives were to capture customers rather than retail funds, interest rates similar to building societies' rates had to be offered to attract the customers in the first place. Since both groups could raise funds in either the retail or wholesale market, although societies operated within restricted wholesale limits, the effect was to bring the cost of the two sources of funds much closer together than had been the case previously. The net result of this was that the mortgage rate became more closely tied to the wholesale money rate providing an environment for the birth of the new lenders. This situation continued until early 1987 when the stock market boom left societies short of retail funds. Competition for these funds drove the price up above the cost of wholesale funds as shown very clearly in the graph of LIBOR against the cost of retail funds (page 110). This was a very favourable development for wholesale funded lenders and resulted in building societies' share of the mortgage market dropping below 50%.

The flood of retail funds back into societies since the stock market crash has reversed the situation with the cost of wholesale funds significantly above retail funds which is also illustrated by the graph. Societies have approximately similar levels of funds invested in and borrowed from the money markets and, therefore, the cost of wholesale funds is not in itself critical in determining the mortgage rate. Societies will, therefore, do everything within their power to ensure that the cost advantage of retail funds existing in 1989 lasts as long as possible, enabling them to regain mortgage market share. The margin between the general mortgage rate and LIBOR will, probably, therefore, be well below 100 basis points as long as there is an over-supply of mortgage funds. While this persists, the new lenders accept either squeezed margins or uncompetitive mortgage rates, and it is obviously not a good environment for securitisation.

Building societies cannot, however, expect this cost advantage to last forever because at some point there will again be fierce competition for retail funds. With both banks and building societies able to move to some extent between retail and wholesale funding, the cost of retail funds (plus collection costs) must

Table 1.

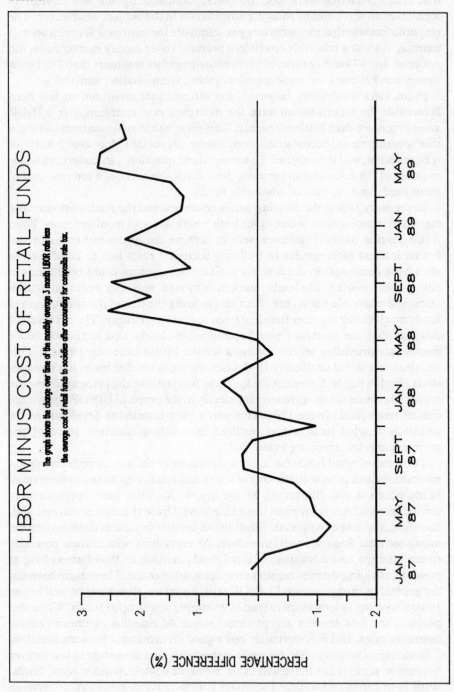

LIBOR MINUS COST OF RETAIL FUNDS

The graph shows the change over time of the monthly average 3 month LIBOR rate less
the average cost of retail funds to societies after accounting for composite rate tax.

on average be comparable with money market rates. The future for securitisation, therefore, looks promising but there may be considerable periods when lenders are left with insignificant margins on their securitised assets.

To return to the original question, if societies did not securitise when there was excess mortgage demand because of legal restraints and the margin over LIBOR made it impractical, why have societies generally not shown more interest recently? The basic reason is that the cost of funds is less than the yield on mortgage-backed securities and, therefore, it is more profitable to hold mortgages on-balance sheet, if there is sufficient capacity, than to securitise. The mortgage market has been so competitive in recent years that not only have mortgage queues disappeared but societies have not been able to generate profitably more mortgage business than could be accommodated on their balance sheets. There has, therefore, been no economic case for securitisation for societies to date.

The only societies that have made public moves in this direction have been outside the largest 12 because their smaller capital base gives rise to the possibility of origination of mortgages exceeding balance sheet capacity. Securitisation is not the only solution to this business opportunity. Several societies have chosen the agency lending route and arranged to originate loans directly onto the balance sheet of foreign banks. This has several major advantages to societies over securitisation. Only two parties are involved in each arrangement and systems and procedures are far less complex than those necessary for securitisation. Birmingham Midshires has made an arrangement with Banque Parabas, the Skipton with Société Générale, the Scarborough with Algemene Bank Nederland, Sussex County with the Danish bank Privatbanken and the Mornington with various organisations. The societies generally originate and administer the mortgage for either a fee or a share of the profits generated. Some societies, including the Skipton, have set up subsidiaries to specialise in mortgage administration with other parties providing the funds and the mortgage business. This has the advantage of earning fee income without asset growth.

One disadvantage of agency lending, however, is that the society does not have complete control over decisions that can vitally affect marketing, and this has certainly been a problem in one arrangement. Another disadvantage is that once the original foreign bank has sufficient mortgage assets, another bank has to be found to continue the programme and they cannot be expected to be committed long-term to the UK mortgage market in the same manner as are building societies. Agency lending also does not provide experience in mortgage securitisation which the Leamington Spa wished to develop to assist in managing the asset side of the balance sheet. It was for these reasons that the Leamington Spa chose to pursue the more difficult route of setting up United Mortgage Corporation (UMC), an off-balance sheet vehicle especially designed for securitisation.

For over 20 years the Leamington Spa had operated in a niche market by offering more flexible lending terms at greater multiples of income than generally available. The margin above the industry average interest rates charged for accepting the greater risk involved with this policy generated significant additional revenue. This additional revenue not only exceeded the mortgage losses incurred, but funded higher investment account interest rates. These in turn attracted a good flow of retail funds to ensure a consistent high growth rate.

This strategy was extremely successful and the society always obtained sufficient mortgage business at these higher interest rates to achieve the maximum growth rate capital would allow. Therefore, standard mortgage business could not be accepted on the balance sheet since this would reduce profitability. Securitisation, a word unfamiliar to the society only two years earlier, offered the possibility of marketing a standard mortgage product to complement its existing niche products and this was the main objective behind the establishment of UMC.

Discussions started with several parties in 1987 with the purpose of jointly setting up an off-balance sheet company owned by a charitable trust. Chemical Bank became the chosen partner largely because it had already been involved in one securitisation issue and it was hoped to launch the company in February 1989, when the mortgage market was still very buoyant. By that time, however, Chemical Bank had decided for strategic reasons to withdraw from the UK mortgage market and so after a short delay the project was continued with Baring Brothers. For similar reasons of return on capital as the society, Baring Brothers did not wish to hold mortgage assets on-balance sheet, but were interested in the securitisation process.

UMC was innovative in many respects but especially for its structured financing designed to give assurance to banks providing funds to a company with only nominal capital. The mortgage portfolio was primarily funded through the issue of mortgage-backed US Dollar-denominated Eurocommercial Paper simultaneously swapped into sterling. For liquidity purposes should ECP not be available, and in order to achieve the desired A-1 rating by Standard and Poor's Corporation and P-1 by Moody's Investors Service, a £180 million five year revolving extendable Note Issuance Facility was established. In addition, a £20 million committed bridging facility was necessary in order to fund an initial pool of mortgages prior to the issue of ECP. When the mortgage portfolio had grown to a sufficient size, the intention was to separate an individual pool and fund this to maturity through mortgage-backed securities.

Although Leamington Spa produced the mortgage offers, it was decided to appoint Chemical Bank Home Loans (later acquired by Banque Nationale de Paris) as administrator because of their experience of securitisation. The society's systems were not designed to produce the detailed analysis or implement the more rigorous controls necessary for securitisation, nor to account for separate pools of mortgages. Building societies' flexible approach to mortgage arrears was also less appropriate for securitised mortgages. In addition, it was felt that the Building Societies' Commission would be less concerned over potential contingent liabilities if the administration was conducted at arm's length from the society.

The plan was to market UMC mortgages through intermediaries and over the branch counter in the same manner as the society's traditional mortgage products. Since wholesale funds were cheaper than retail funds during this time, it was anticipated that the product could be priced under the normal building society rate. All marketing literature and mortgage documents had to be branded UMC in order to make it clear to mortgage applicants they would not receive a normal building society mortgage with membership rights and that the mortgage could be securitised. Although this distinction was readily understood by most intermediaries and in practice was of little concern to borrowers, the different branding and application forms caused considerable confusion.

The project took over 12 months of negotiations with all of the parties involved including Sun Alliance as pool policy providers, the charitable trustees, security trustees, mortgage administrator, rating agencies, legal advisors, accountants, regulators and a multitude of banks. Valuable experience in many areas new to the society was gained during this period which has since been of benefit. The schematic on page 114 outlines the structure of the company which was eventually launched in August 1988 just as the mortgage boom ended.

Regulatory aspects were critical to the design of UMC and are obviously important to the future of securitisation for building societies. The main point of securitisation is lost unless the society achieves a nil or very low partial weight for capital adequacy purposes. UMC was designed to ensure that the society was absolved from any credit risk and not compelled to support the company if difficulties arose, that mortgages never passed through the society's balance sheet and that mortgage administration was performed by a third party. The fact that the society did not have the power to contribute capital to UMC complicated its structure and increased the cost of funding.

The Building Societies' Commission issued a consultative paper in October 1987 on capital adequacy requirements for off-balance sheet lending by societies and, after discussions, this resulted in Prudential Note 1988/2 published in May of that year. It defined the characteristics of various schemes that would be eligible for a nil weighting including agency lending and service contracts. The first two paragraphs stated 'In order to satisfy the Commission that no capital need be held for a particular group of loans, a society needs to demonstrate that for all practical purposes it is absolved from any continuing credit or interest rate risk, and that it will not, in practice, feel compelled to support the off-balance sheet arrangement if difficulties arise: for example, it might feel obliged to do so in the case of a special purpose mortgage finance vehicle set up by the society and publicly identified with it.'

'The Commission will accept schemes as not requiring capital backing which are agreed with:

Table 2.

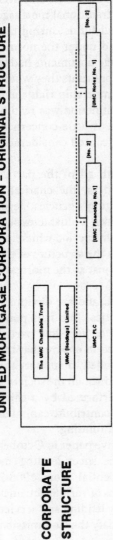
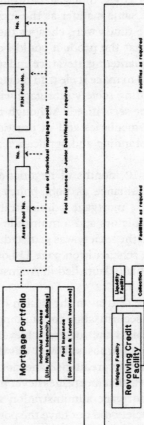

UNITED MORTGAGE CORPORATION – ORIGINAL STRUCTURE

CORPORATE STRUCTURE

- The UMC Charitable Trust
- UMC (Holdings) Limited
- UMC PLC
- [UMC Financing No.1]
- [No. 2]
- [UMC Notes No. 1]
- [No. 2]

ASSET STRUCTURE

- Mortgage Portfolio
  - Individual Insurances (Life, Mtge Indemnity, Buildings)
  - Pool Insurance (Sun Alliance & London Insurance)
- Asset Pool No. 1
- No. 2
- FRN Pool No. 1
- No. 2

Pool Insurance or Junior Debt/Notes as required

sale of individual mortgage pools

FUNDING STRUCTURE

- Bridging Facility
- Revolving Credit Facility
- ECP
- F/X
- Liquidity Facility
- Collection Account
- Expenses Facility

ECP Investors

Purchasers — Facilities as required

FRN Investors — Facilities as required

Marketer, Broker & Processor:	Leamington Spa Building Society
Administrator:	BNP Mortgage Administration Services Limited
Security Trustee:	The Law Debenture Trust Corporation p.l.c.
Charitable Trustee:	Eagle Star Trust Company Limited

either

(a) a regulated institution of good standing (eg, bank, building society or insurance company) which is able to carry the credit and other risks involved without recourse to the society arranging or servicing the loan;

or

(b) a mortgage finance vehicle, providing that it has the characteristics set out in the Annex, so that it is fully distanced from the society and also carries the credit and other risks involved without recourse to the society.'

Since UMC was a mortgage finance vehicle, amongst other conditions, it had to comply with those listed in the Annex as detailed below:

   (i) the vehicle is registered in the United Kingdom;

  (ii) the society's name is not reflected in the name of the vehicle;

 (iii) the society should have no proprietary interest (either directly or through a nominee) in the vehicle, or any company associated with the vehicle;

 (iv) either there is no representation of the society on the board of the vehicle, or only one officer from the society is a director. If more than one society is transacting business with the vehicle, there should be no more than one from each such society and officers of societies who are directors of the vehicle should be in a minority. No officers of the society can act as trustees of a trust with a proprietary interest in the vehicle;

  (v) the vehicle is financed independently from the society and the society does not offer any guarantees to the vehicle;

 (vi) the offer particulars of notes issued by the vehicle make it clear that noteholders have recourse only to the security offered by the pool of mortgages, and not to the society even if it is the originator;

 (vii) it is made clear to other providers of funds to the vehicle that the institutions which are transferring assets to the vehicle bear no legal obligations—beyond their stated legal obligations—to make good losses arising in the vehicle;

(viii) the finance vehicle bears all its expenses. For example, the vehicle rather than the society pays any relevant insurance premiums etc (eg, pool indemnity policies);

 (ix) the society's auditors confirm that they are satisfied that it does not have to record on the face of its published accounts any liabilities (contingent or not) in relation to its interest in the finance vehicle.

The most positive development for building society interest in securitisation is the new power available from 1 July 1989 to own, invest in and support a new type of subsidiary known as an 'appropriate mortgage company' (AMC). From that date societies can establish an AMC which will allow them to:

  (i) acquire mortgage debts;

(ii) make advances secured on mortgages which were designed for subsequent securitisation;
(iii) make further advances to existing borrowers from the associated body;
(iv) count mortgage loans transferred to, or made by, such an associated body with its class 1 or class 2 assets, subject to the loans meeting certain criteria and to an upper limit on the amount which may be counted with class 1.

Appropriate mortgage companies, however, are not able to avail themselves of the exemptions from the regulated secured lending provisions of the Consumer Credit Act 1974 available to building societies. They are also not prescribed as qualifying lenders for the purposes of the mortgage interest relief at source (MIRAS) arrangements unless and until they have been included in an order made by the Treasury by statutory instrument under s 376(5) of the Income and Corporation Taxes Act 1988.

Prior to the advent of AMC powers, a society could only take over an existing mortgage book from another society, using full or partial transfer of engagements, but not from any other type of body. Prospects for securitisation also improved with Building Societies Order, SI 1988 No 1141 which included a provision enabling a society to take back the rump of a package of loans originated by it and subsequently securitised. After 1 July 1989 loans will be able to be transferred in many directions but society membership rights can still prove a hurdle if the loans are ever included on the society's balance sheet. If the loans are destined for securitisation, however, they could be originated directly onto the AMC balance sheet avoiding the membership problem.

Although the UMC type of structure may be repeated for other organisations, societies are likely to take the AMC route since it is more straightforward, and the accumulation of a mortgage pool in preparation for a securitisation issue can be funded from normal society sources. The capital backing required for mortgage assets held by an AMC is similar to that required for comparable loans on the society's main balance sheet. In order to preserve the nature of societies as mutual institutions where the majority of borrowers are members, the amount of loans held by the AMC which could be aggregated with the society's class 1 assets will be limited to not more than 15% of the total commercial assets of the society. Any balance of loans eligible for aggregation with class 1 over this limit would be aggregated with class 3 assets. These aggregation rules are still under discussion and the final version is yet to be published but the effect is to limit the size of the mortgage book held by the AMC. For societies with total assets over £1 billion, this restriction should still allow a sufficiently large pool of mortgages to be accumulated to make securitisation viable.

The liabilities of the AMC would simply be aggregated with those of the society and, therefore, the current wholesale funding limit would still apply. If the AMC raised money on the wholesale market in its own name, rather than borrowing from the parent society, that would count against the limits for the society.

The Statement of Practice on Transfers of Mortgages below dealing with the information to be given to borrowers when seeking general or specific consent to the transfer of mortgages has been accepted by societies. There is an additional code of practice that is applicable only to societies because of their special nature and compliance with this code is also expected.

DRAFT CODE OF PRACTICE ON CERTAIN ASPECTS OF THE TRANSFER OF MORTGAGES BY BUILDING SOCIETIES OR THEIR ASSOCIATED BODIES

1. A building society will not rely solely on any written consent to the transfer of a mortgage unless it is made clear to the borrower before the mortgage is completed:

 (i) that it may subsequently transfer the mortgage to another body which may not necessarily be a building society or an associated body of a building society; and
 (ii) the implications of a transfer for the borrower's membership of the society.

A society can, however, ask for the borrower's consent to the transfer of his mortgage at any time after the completion of the mortgage, making clear points (i) and (ii) above.

2. The implications of a transfer for the borrower's membership of the society should also be made clear at the time of any transfer (even if the transfer is only to an associated body of the society). Where the transfer is to an associated body of the society, the associated body's status as a separate legal entity from the society should be made clear at that time.

3. Where an associated body of a society makes mortgage advances which are capable of transfer to another body it should be made clear to the borrower, before the mortgage is completed, that:

 (i) it may subsequently transfer the mortgage to another body which may not necessarily be a building society or an associated body of a building society;
 (ii) it is a separate legal entity from the parent society; and
 (iii) the borrower will have no membership rights in the parent society.

4. Where an associated body of a society acquires mortgage debts originated by other lenders it should be made clear to the borrower, before the transfer is completed, that:

 (i) the associated body is a separate legal entity from the parent society; and
 (ii) the borrower will have no membership rights in the parent society.

5. It should be made clear to the borrower, at the time of any transfer, who will be administering the loan after transfer.

6. At the time of any transfer the borrower should be reminded that the transferee body may subsequently transfer the mortgage again. Where the transfer is to an associated body of a society, the borrower should also be reminded that any subsequent transfer may be to a body which is not necessarily a building society or an associated body of a building society.

7. A society or an associated body of a society should pass on to the borrower, at the time of any transfer, any information it may have received from the transferee, in response to a request, concerning the transferee's policies which may affect the terms of the loan after transfer (including policies on interest rates, the administration of arrears and the availability of further advances), and state whether such policies are different to those of the society or associated body. If no information is received about the transferee's policies, the society or associated body should tell the borrower that this is the case and that, accordingly, the transferee's policies might be different to those of the society or associated body.

Societies planning public issues of mortgage-backed securities have to address many problems relating to systems and administrative procedures of a far more detailed and precise nature than is their normal custom. The requirements of the rating agencies and auditors for securitisation issues produce a very different environment for mortgage processing departments, but one to which societies can easily adapt once they have a thorough understanding of what is involved.

Our experience with UMC is that customers do not seem too concerned on whose balance sheet the mortgage resides or whether it is securitised or not. The public may become aware of the possible windfall that could accrue if they had membership rights should a society decide to convert to a public company but it is unlikely that such issues occupy an applicant's mind when seeking a mortgage.

The volumes of mortgages anticipated for UMC during the negotiations in the early part of 1988 have not in fact materialised, mainly due to the reasons detailed below. The complexity of the structure and the change of partners prolonged the negotiations delaying the launch until August 1988 when the mortgage market went into decline with the change in MIRAS regulations. Secondly, the lending criteria necessary to achieve the top ratings at an acceptable cost for the ECP were even stricter than those normally required for securitisation and this made the mortgage product difficult to market in the new environment. To resolve this problem, during September 1989, UMC was acquired by Leamington Spa Building Society converting it into the first AMC. Since it is now funded from the society's resources, the lending policy can be made more flexible although mortgages must still be of securitisable quality.

The regulatory environment is becoming favourable for societies to take a greater interest in securitisation. Although societies generally have sufficient capital for their current activities, it could be useful to those concentrating on mortgage lending, especially if the current situation leads to a shake out amongst lenders. If a sustained period of cheap wholesale funds occurs again, it could be a very profitable facility to have in place.

Chapter 7

A Merchant Banker views the Market

Paul Orchart
S. G. Warburg & Co Ltd

The purpose of this chapter is to analyse the role that a merchant bank fulfils
with issuers and that which it fulfils with investors, and then to look at new
products and innovations that are currently being developed in the UK market
in particular.

By way of introduction it is perhaps worth remembering the basics of
securitisation:

(i) the process represents a re-packaging of financial assets;
(ii) a re-packaging which is into a readily tradeable form;
(iii) it represents publicly traded, open market debt;
(iv) which can be underwritten by securities firms.

The fundamental importance is to aim for simplicity by ideally eliminating
or at least reducing both intricate credit and structures. Developments will take
place, and greater value will be extracted, by separating the funding and the
underlying technology. The importance of simplifying structures as much as
possible cannot be underestimated in order to overcome significant legal,
accounting and regulatory obstacles to successful securitisation.

Benefits which are brought to the issuer can be highlighted as follows:

(i) the removal of assets from the balance sheet;
(ii) the reduction of interest mis-match and maturity risks;
(iii) the 'risk free' income from administering the assets;
(iv) the potential cost savings to volume issuers; and
(v) a new funding source representing diversification; this is particularly
important for new mortgage lenders as a move away from dependence on
bank and quasi-bank funding markets.

The growth of the market has been underpinned by the following factors:

(i) pressures upon banks to improve capital ratios;

(ii) securitisation technology becoming more widely understood;

(iii) investors' demand for liquid, high quality financial assets with predictable and high yielding cash flows. The importance of cash flow manipulation should be emphasised in the context of the European markets. Perhaps trends here will be similar to US arrangements where, for instance, there has been a collapse of all principal repayments following an interest only period into a single five year bullet repayment in a credit card receivables financing. In other words, the cash flows that the investor receives can be markedly different from those of the collateral; and

(iv) vogue.

The areas which securitisation can cover, inter alia, in the UK are as follows:

(i) residential mortgages where the UK market is in excess of £190 billion of which over £6 billion has been securitised;

(ii) commercial mortgages—much has been done in the private or public syndicated banking market. Since the early 1970s the sector has had a good credit record and this is a sector where enhancement structures are available;

(iii) computer, auto and healthcare leases;

(iv) auto loan instalment credits where the UK market size is approximately £3.5 billion;

(v) credit card receivables where the UK market size is approximately £11 billion;

(vi) consumer loans; and

(vii) others.

At this stage it is probably appropriate to examine briefly the role of the merchant bank in the securitisation process. The role may be viewed as one which is both adviser and arranger to the issue. The following are the major areas of consideration in which a merchant bank can be of service:

(i) to analyse the commercial advantages for both originators and investors to enter into securitisation;

(ii) to assess the various impacts that regulatory constraints may have on the securitisation process; these include accounting considerations, Bank of England rules, and tax and legal issues;

(iii) to review with lawyers various legal aspects of securitisation including the sale of the mortgage portfolio, the security interest created by the issuing company over its assets, the Administration Agreement, MIRAS, and the provisions of the Consumer Credit Act 1974; and

(iv) to review pricing and structuring in the context of the degree of receptivity amongst investors for mortgage-backed securities; features such as nature of mortgage product, yield to average life, substitution policy, and provision of certain support facilities to the issuing company have to be analysed.

I shall now focus on a number of funding markets which are available, actually or potentially, to support asset-backed financings. This focus will tend to be on areas of development and innovation rather than on the more mature funding markets such as the mortgage-backed floating rate note sector.

There have been two fixed rate mortgage-backed issues to date, HMC 101 and HMC 102, both by Household Mortgage Corporation and both of five year maturity. The first issue, HMC 101, in October 1988, was originally placed at a spread of 82 basis points per annum over five year gilts and subsequently traded to as low as 50 basis points per annum. The second issue, HMC 102, launched in February 1989, was priced more aggressively at 72 basis points per annum over gilts.

The structure which has been used on these issues is that the special purpose company which issues the fixed rate bonds purchases an entire issue of mortgage-backed Floating Rate Notes (FRNs). The FRNs collateralise the fixed rate bonds. The FRNs are AAA rated by virtue of subordinated debt. The fixed rate bonds achieve their AAA rating by virtue of the AAA FRN collateral and a AAA rated guaranteed investment contract (GIC), a AAA swap and a AAA put as explained below. The floating rate receipts on the FRNs are exchanged via a AAA swap for fixed rate receipts equal to the payments on the fixed rate bonds. Full substitution of mortgages in the portfolio which pre-pay is envisaged, to allow the value of the mortgage portfolio, and hence the FRNs, to remain unchanged until the maturity of the fixed rate bonds. In the event that substitution is not possible, FRNs will be redeemed and the proceeds placed in the AAA GIC which guarantees a rate of return equal to that on the FRNs. At maturity of the fixed rate bonds, the issuer is able to put the FRNs to a AAA rated third party at par, the proceeds being used to repay principal on the fixed rate bonds.

A weakness or complication with the HMC structure is the need for each of its elements (FRN/Swap/GIC/Put) to be AAA rated, which restricts the number of counterparties available to provide them and can therefore result in disadvantageous pricing. For example, AAA rated swap counterparties may not provide the most attractive swap rates at the time of launch. An alternative approach would be for a third party to guarantee the fixed rate bonds, eliminating the need for the FRNs and enabling an issuer to approach a range of swap providers other than those rated AAA to achieve more competitive pricing.

In favourable market conditions, it is felt a well timed issue should achieve a swapped cost for the fixed rate bonds of between LIBOR and LIBOR less five basis points per annum. The cost of the put and certain other expenses could generate an all-in cost of financing of LIBOR plus 10 to 15 basis points per annum. As the cost of such issues is critically dependent on a conjunction of suitable issuing conditions in the fixed rate market and attractive swap spreads, it is recommended that an issuer develop an appropriate structure in advance which can then be used on an opportunistic basis.

In recent market conditions, the most attractive opportunities for Euro-sterling issuance have existed in longer maturities (25 to 30 years) for two reasons. First, the government's policy of not issuing new gilt-edged stock and of repurchasing outstanding issues has created a shortage of supply of long-dated gilts, which is the traditional home for institutional liquidity. Consequently demand is strong for long-dated high quality corporate bonds. Secondly, the government's recent tightening of monetary policy through driving up short-term interest rates has caused the gap to widen between the cost of short-term and long-term funds to approximately 1.25% per annum.

As a result, substantial demand could exist for an appropriately structured, long-dated mortgage-backed bond issue. To achieve the finest pricing, the issue would have to be either a bullet maturity or have a scheduled repayment of principal. In the same way as for a standard FRN, the mortgage portfolio would need to contain appropriate income multiples, loan to value ratios and a good geographical spread to insulate it from long-term exposure to the property market. Assuming the prepayment problem can be solved, in normal market conditions we believe an AAA mortgage-backed long-dated issue could be launched at a spread above the benchmark Treasury 9% 2008 which would be attractive to institutional investors. It is felt that a yield would have to be offered which is comparable to the current yield on first mortgage debentures.

It should be emphasised at this point that a large private market exists for, say, heterogenous mortgage portfolios or mortgage types with particular characteristics—100% loan to value mortgage products or long-tail, low-start mortgages and where there are technical and legal complexities to securitisation.

Of course, private placements can range in form from a domestic banking structure through to more esoteric structures employing, say, the Japanese leasing company market and on both subordinated and senior bases.

As far as other assets are concerned there have been many years of non-recourse bank syndicated financing employed to finance, for instance, consumer receivables portfolios. Since August 1985, the Bank of England has been supportive of the acceptance market resulting in effective sub-LIBOR funding.

Over the past three years in particular a lengthening list of international banks have become involved in the residential mortgage market in the UK. During this period an increasing variety of funding techniques has been employed including pass-throughs, sub-participations, mortgage sales and syndicated loan financings. Each technique has involved somewhat differing legal considerations and ramifications but each has sought to deal where necessary with the major risks associated with mortgage funding—namely, credit, basis, liquidity and refinancing.

At the present time, and in the nearer term, there is a dearth of quality mortgage business which is being presented to the banking community in the public financing markets. At the same time, there are two significant regulatory influences which are having, and will continue to have, an impact on bank pricing in the mortgage funding sector. The first is a general hardening in the returns required by the banks as a result of the minimum capital ratio guidelines to be met by 1992. The second is a 50% capital weighting which attaches to mortgage-backed financing conducted in such a fashion as to meet certain central bank criteria. A number of major central banks have yet to clarify their position in this respect, but it is to be hoped that their criteria will be broadly similar to those laid down by the US Federal Reserve Bank and the Bank of England.

The judgement at the moment is that the overall impact of all the factors mentioned above is a beneficial one for a mortgage originator as far as pricing is concerned with regard to bank-related funding. Over the past 18 months we have seen a variety of structures with varying pricing according to the structure used.

Mortgage sales and sub-participations have been concluded in the main to yield LIBOR plus 50 basis points per annum up to LIBOR plus 90 basis points per annum to the purchaser and depositor respectively depending upon level and cost of pool insurance, the characteristics of the mortgage portfolio and the manner of dealing with the administration expenses. There remains scope to introduce a competitive element to this source of funding by organising an informal 'tender panel' of selected banks to bid for the purchase of a portfolio via the mortgage sale route, or to make available matching deposits via the sub-participation route. Both techniques take care of the refinancing aspect.

The 'pass-through' technique has been employed successfully over the past two years at margin pricing of between 37.5 and 50.0 basis points per annum. The potential for expansion of this market may remain somewhat limited given the size of the bank population which is prepared to participate in a financing structure with, perhaps, only a partial assured take-out or put option.

The syndicated loan market has been extremely active over the past two years in, essentially, providing flexible warehousing finance for a variety of the newer mortgage originators. Margin pricing has varied from 35.0 to 50.0 basis points per annum depending upon structure, maturity, mortgage product and timing of transaction. Because of a dearth of new financings over the recent past, a stage of maturity reached in the warehouse financing of the centralised mortgage companies and the 50% capital weighting attaching to appropriately structured transactions, opinion is that there will be a downward pressure on pricing in the near term. A number of mortgage companies may take this opportunity to refinance/restructure their medium-term debt book.

We now turn our attention to the relative attractions of employing the commercial paper markets to finance asset portfolios. The growth of the Commercial Paper (CP) market occured during the 1970s in the USA. Current US CP outstandings are well in excess of US $400 billion. Current Euro-CP outstandings are in excess of US $75 billion, a market which has doubled in the last two years. Current sterling CP outstandings are in excess of £3 billion.

What are the characteristics of the various CP markets?

The depth, size and liquidity of these markets mean they can take, and need, large-scale issuers and on a regular basis; one cannot underestimate the importance of keeping paper in front of investors.

The CP markets are quality-conscious, with the real depth of the markets tapped when dual ratings are present.

CP can provide extremely cost competitive short-term funding: US domestic A-1 + /P1 rated paper can be placed regularly at levels below the Fed Composite (say, at around LIBOR—20 basis points); Euro-CP rated A-1/P1 or A-1 + /P1 can be issued on occasion at below LIBID; and rated sterling CP can be placed sub-LIMEAN.

However, one has to note the additional and, at the outset of a dollar paper programme, unquantifiable foreign exchange costs of swapping the net dollar proceeds into sterling.

There can be pricing flexibility achieved by issuing into investor demand.

There can be a spreading of interest rate resetting risk; various maturity dates can be managed in a rolling programme rather than having regular reset dates for the entire financing as in the case of an FRN issue.

There is a reduction of reinvestment risk.

Finally, the CP markets can represent funding diversification for, say, those mortgage originators who are already using other markets heavily.

Various structures have been employed in order to tap the CP markets:

(i) a banking group designed both to guarantee the issuer and to provide standby liquidity as in the case of the US Domestic Commercial Paper programme for Household Mortgage Corporation;

(ii) mortgage-backed transactions, such as for United Mortgage Corporation (UMC) and for Mortgage Asset-Backed Eurosecurities (MAES), where banks are purely providing standby liquidity to highly structured financing vehicles; and

(iii) mortgage-backed private placements, involving non-bank enhancers such as Financial Security Assurance and Columbus Capital, and where banks are purely providing standby liquidity to entities with corporate substance.

A consistent requirement which is present in all of the above financings is the need for quality, committed enhancement and/or liquidity supplied by banking groups. The level of running costs associated with this banking involvement is obviously key to the cost-effectiveness of a financing scheme employing commercial paper. Perhaps some important areas for consideration should be highlighted.

The overall trend in the banking markets is for there to be a move towards higher returns. It must, of course, be remembered that capital ratio requirements have come into increasingly starker relief over the past two years.

Many international banks in London remain unclear as to the capital weightings which will attach to various commitments which they enter into because their central banks have yet to clarify the position in this area. Minimum returns on regulatory capital are, therefore, difficult to gauge at the moment. The picture is further clouded by the move to assign a 50% capital weighting to activity in the mortgage sector should that activity fall within certain criteria laid down by the Bank of England. Certain questions then arise: should guarantees provided by banks in support of mortgage-backed transactions receive a 50% rather than a 100% weighting, should standby lines of liquidity receive a 25% rather than a 50% weighting and should a fronting bank (receiving the benefits of several counter-indemnities from various guaranteeing banks) look to a 10% rather than a 20% weighting?

There may be considerable merit in looking at a structure which involves a fronting bank providing the guarantee on the issuance of CP supported by the counter-indemnification of a variety of banks who, in turn, take the credit risk of the mortgage portfolio or issuing vehicle. This structure is in preference to several guarantees from a number of banks. This thinking is based on the following considerations:

(i) the universe of rated institutions is considerably smaller than that of both rated and unrated institutions; and

(ii) with one fronting bank the structure of the credit to be presented to CP investors is simpler, and should result in better prices being obtained in that market.

The vast majority of funding structures employing the commercial paper markets have tended to elevate the enhancers rather than the mortgage originators with a consequent dilution of the latters' names as far as investors are concerned. Front end and recurring costs have been heavy in the cases of mortgage-backed and private placement transactions respectively. We feel this is likely to continue in view of both the complexity of the structures and the minimum returns on regulatory capital required by certain enhancers. The liberalisation of the sterling capital markets will mean there is an additional market to tap.

The quality, capacity and availability of the take-out market remains an underdeveloped area, particularly in the area of mortgage-backed commercial paper financing. The alternative route, which has been used as a commercial option to a formal refinancing, is to decelerate the outstandings under the programme ahead of a known reduction of the support funding provided by the banks. The put or maturity guarantee market has tended to have been dominated by Japanese institutions to date.

However, the importance of non-bank enhancers in the future (particularly where the rating agencies have not established standards which can be readily applied to a transaction) cannot be underestimated. This results from the desire to achieve simplicity, integrity and durability: but at what cost is this to be achieved?

Recently a new structure, which is a variant on a medium-term note, has been introduced to the market called the variable rate note (VRNs). This structure permits the issuance of notes with five year maturities that will pay interest quarterly in advance at a variable margin at, above or below LIBOR which is determined quarterly by note holders and other investors bidding under an auction procedure. There is no auction clearing rate, the successful investor attains the coupon for which he has submitted a bid, with a hold order given preference over a non-noteholding investor. Each issue has a maximum holding rate and a minimum holding rate. Bids are to be tendered within this range and, if an investor is unable to sell his notes at the auction, a penalty coupon of the maximum holding rate will apply to that noteholder's paper for the next interest period to compensate him for the illiquidity factor. The Halifax Building Society has issued a £100 million, five year facility and the National Provincial a £150 million, 10 year facility.

There is a continuing belief that good demand would exist for mortgage-backed VRNs. The VRN auction process is relatively complex and it has undoubtedly taken some time for investors to become acquainted with it. With better understanding the market has become increasingly popular and participation in the auctions is broadening. The average margin over LIBOR at auction on these issues has been declining steadily. It is expected that the success of recent auctions will encourage further VRN issuance during 1990, both in sterling and other currencies, particularly if FRN spreads widen.

There are two scenarios we can envisage where the maximum holding rate may be reached. The first is when, for whatever reason, the VRN market or the auction process breaks down, in which case the issuer would or could itself be able to bid at the next auction and retire the issue. The second scenario occurs when a deterioration in either the issuer's credit standing or the UK housing market causes the margin to be bid up to the maximum holding level. That capped rate could, in these circumstances, represent cheaper funding than alternatives available at the time.

In concluding this section, interesting developments are emerging from the recent liberalisation by the Bank of England of the sterling markets. We are seeing the use of sequential pay tranche financing to produce potentially a lower blended cost of funding in the mortgage-backed market. The shorter-pay tranches are of interest to money market investors while longer-term investors are attracted to medium- or slow-pay tranches.

In addition, the sterling markets are open for CP issues up to five years.

In looking at the opportunities to securitise or finance assets other than mortgages, one has to analyse the historic position in the UK.

There is a tendency for there to be a concentration of business in the UK within a small number of high quality and rated, well-capitalised entities without portfolio concentration concerns.

This situation poses real questions as to the scope for development:

(i) why should those entities access capital markets at the all-in cost of AAA or AA collateralised deals?;

(ii) capital considerations are of decreased relevance;

(iii) there is no or little problem in match-funding many of the classes of consumer finance business; and

(iv) there is no obvious pressure to diversify funding.

Therefore, there may be a concentration on markets which are more fragmented, which are good quality, and where there are reasonable levels of credit history and statistics: namely auto loans, lease receivables and trade receivables. In any event, such assets are likely either to represent short-term indebtedness repayable in whole with the precise timing of the repayment being somewhat uncertain in practice (as in the case of trade debt receivables) or they represent medium-term indebtedness carrying regular scheduled repayment obligations (as with lease receivables and auto loans). Both kinds of receivables are suitable to be financed in particular through an asset-backed CP programme because the structure of such a programme is not particularly sensitive to the maturity profile of the underlying assets.

Varying structural considerations would have to be dealt with depending upon the class of assets to be securitised.

In the case of trade debt they clearly will not attract interest during the credit period. The net result would be over-collateralisation and the debts discounted and factored to the securitisation vehicle on a non-recourse basis.

In the case of lease receivables, considerations such as the problems of residual values, frequency of early terminations, and legal complications caused by retention of title by the originator would have to be handled.

In addition, there are many other structural considerations relating to, inter alia, tax, legal, accounting and regulatory issues which are either common or specific to both mortgage-backed and non-mortgage-backed financings.

With regard to tax matters there is, for example, 1% stamp duty on an assignment of receivables. There are ways around this by going offshore or by way of a sub-participation of receivables. However, by employing these measures there is a knock-on effect as to structuring.

Additionally, one has to consider the present asymmetric tax treatment on foreign exchange gains and losses resulting from swapping net dollar proceeds of CP issuance back into sterling. Is there tax liberalisation in the wings for companies with investment status? It would be much welcomed.

As regards legal matters, should the form of assignment be legal or equitable? What about any existing rights of set-off? What about the burden of giving notice to clients? What about the Consumer Credit Act 1974 with regard to the conduct of regulated credit business?

In concluding, it is probably appropriate to highlight the major consider-ations associated with the securitisation of various classes of assets in order, at least, to emphasise the need for both simplicity and for a level playing field to exist for all types of issuers. The complexity of all the interacting influences and considerations below demonstrates the continuing requirement for there to be a greater standardisation of approach to achieve a wider understanding of the benefits of securitisation. Essentially, these considerations are made up of the following:

(i) the securitisation process mitigates risk: bad debt risk is handled by insurance and/or subordinated debt, late payments by a liquidity facility, reinvestment risk by a guaranteed investment contract, if needs be, administration risk by a third-party administrator, basis risk by the fact that the mortgage originator retains the ability to set the mortgage rate, and the refinancing risk by the fact that funding is to maturity;

(ii) credit enhancement has been achieved via the employment of a number of techniques: pool insurance, unrated B-Bonds, and rated B-Bonds. Various additional enhancement elements have included liquidity support and start-up loans; a number of considerations are present when analysing the relative attractions of either using insurance or subordinated bonds: cost of capital, leverage, ease of implementation, capacity, and any possible moral obligation which might be felt to attach to the issuer with regard to the performance of subordinated bonds;

(iii) various mortgage products have been securitised which, to date, include endowment mortgages, pension mortages, non-status mortgages, and low-start mortgages; one needs to take care in terms of assessing the relative composition of a pool of mortgages to securitise, and the impact that the various characteristics of the mortgage products will have on the securitisation structure;

(iv) a detailed review has to be undertaken as to the legal, accounting and regulatory framework which is in existence in order to achieve an appropriate funding strategy, and account has to be taken of provisions contained in the following:

   (a) the secondary mortgage market working group's statement of practice on the transfer of mortgages (initially April 1986);
   (b) Exposure Draft 42 (Accounting for Special Purpose Transactions (March 1988));
   (c) the Companies Act 1989 and the amendments contained therein to the Companies Act 1985; and
   (d) the Bank of England Notice regarding Loan Transfers and Securitisation (February 1989);

(v) the rating agency considerations which, inter alia, include:

   (a) operating systems audit to cover financial performance, historical information, origination process, servicing arrangements, mortgage documentation, computer systems, and insurance;
   (b) information requirements which include loan to value ratios, income multiples, geographical concentration, seasoning, and an analysis of insurance policy providers; and

(c) structuring considerations to include credit enhancement (pool insurance/B-Bonds), liquidity support, cash flow models and a review of legal documentation.

The area of asset-backed financing continues to be one where constant development and innovation are taking place with new challenges facing banks, issuers and investors alike. In order for those processes to move along in a logical manner, it would seem appropriate for there to be trends towards increasing simplicity and decreasing fragmentation to take place. At the present time, for instance, it would be of considerable value to all parties concerned for there to be an elimination of the atmosphere of uncertainty which remains concerning certain aspects of securitisation in the UK including, inter alia, accounting and regulatory concerns.

Chapter 8

How Rating Agencies view Asset-backed Debt

Lionel J. Marsland-Shaw Standard & Poor's Corporation
Donald E. Selzer Moody's Investor's Service Inc

STANDARD & POOR'S CORPORATION'S PHILOSOPHY

The aim of this part of the chapter is to provide an insight into the fundamental concepts on which Standard & Poor's Corporation (S&P) bases its views of the risks inherent in structuring asset-backed issues, and to expand on those ideas by reference to selected topics. It is not the intention within the confines of this brief chapter to detail all the areas which come under scrutiny when undertaking a rating analysis, but to highlight specific points. It should also be remembered that this exposé is, of course, written with an emphasis on the UK market, particularly on mortgage-backed securities. The principles behind the criteria, however, will apply to a variety of countries and assets. Although criteria will not necessarily be identical, they will be comparable, since the underlying consideration behind their inclusion will be that of consistency. As far as criteria generally are concerned, no one item is immutable—all are subject to change if the evidence warrants it.

Rating topics relevant to asset-backed securities can be segregated by type: asset quality or liquidity for example. In this chapter, however, S&P has focused on those topics unique to credit analysis of the issues which have been identified as having aroused particular interest. These topics range from the nature of issuing vehicles, with the protection they require, and S&P's approach to testing asset quality, to certain structural points which flow as a consequence of creating an asset-backed security.

The 'weak link' theory and ratings' consistency are two principal tenets of S&P's rating philosophy. The first of these two principles implies that the chain, or structure, of a transaction is as strong as its weakest link—this has important implications when considering not only the overall integrity of a structure but also the parties involved and the functions and responsibilities they undertake. It is for this reason that the potential insolvency of the special purpose vehicle, which is created solely for the purpose of an issue, is of such importance and that so much attention is paid to the ability of that vehicle to be as far removed as possible from becoming insolvent (see below—'Special Purpose Criteria').

The concept of weak links is relevant because S&P may not rate all parties to a transaction. Consequently, S&P must assume that the unrated entities become insolvent, but rated bonds are expected to perform regardless of the insolvency of any unrated party to the transaction (see below—'Supporting Ratings').

The second principle of consistency is necessary in order to enable investors to compare ratings on a worldwide basis. An investor in a AAA English mortgage-backed security should have the same degree of confidence as investors in AAA rated securities in the USA, in France, or anywhere else in the world where S&P rates bonds.

A. S&P ratings

A credit rating assesses the ability of an issue to pay principal and interest on the debt instrument in full and on time, in accordance with the terms of the issue. It is not a recommendation to buy or sell a security and gives no indication of the aptness of a given security for any investor's portfolio. S&P uses letter symbols to rank debt from the highest surety of repayment (designated by the letter rating AAA) to the lowest (designated by the letter rating D) for bonds in default.

The range of rating symbols, distinguishing between investment grade and speculative grade, as well as between long-term and short-term securities are shown in the table opposite. Ratings above BB + are considered investment grade ratings, while those at BB + and below are considered speculative grade. The table also shows the correlation between short-term and long-term ratings.

The definitions applicable to each of the rating categories are as follows:

1. LONG-TERM DEBT RATING DEFINITIONS

A Standard & Poor's corporate or municipal debt rating is a current assessment of the creditworthiness of an obligor with respect to a specific obligation. This assessment may take into consideration obligors such as guarantors, insurers, or lessees.

The debt rating is not a recommendation to purchase, sell, or hold a security, inasmuch as it does not comment as to market price or suitability for a particular investor.

The ratings are based on current information furnished by the issuer or obtained by S&P from other sources it considers reliable. S&P does not perform an audit in connection with any rating and may, on occasion, rely on unaudited financial information. The ratings may be changed, suspended, or

STANDARD & POOR'S RATING SYMBOLS

LONG-TERM RATINGS	SHORT-TERM RATINGS
(maturity > 1 year)	(maturity < 1 year)

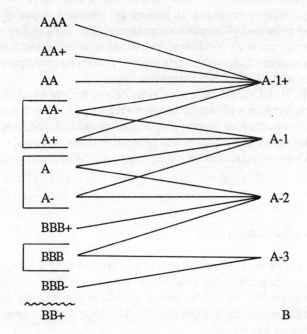

withdrawn as a result of changes in, or unavailability of, such information, or for other circumstances.

The ratings are based, in varying degrees, on the following considerations:

(i) likelihood of default—capacity and willingness of the obligor as to the timely payment of interest and repayment of principal in accordance with the terms of the obligation;

(ii) nature of and provisions of the obligation;

(iii) protection afforded by, and relative position of, the obligation in the event of bankruptcy, reorganisation, or other arrangement under the laws of bankruptcy and other laws affecting creditors' rights.

AAA Debt rated AAA has the highest rating assigned by Standard & Poor's. Capacity to pay interest and repay principal is extremely strong.

AA Debt rated AA has a very strong capacity to pay interest and repay principal and differs from the highest rated issues only in small degree.

A Debt rated A has a strong capacity to pay interest and repay principal although it is somewhat more susceptible to the adverse effects of changes in circumstances and economic conditions than debt in higher rated categories.

BBB Debt rated BBB is regarded as having an adequate capacity to pay interest and repay principal. Whereas it normally exhibits adequate protection parameters, adverse economic conditions, or changing circumstances are more likely to lead to a weakened capacity to pay interest and repay principal for debt in this category than in higher rate categories.

Debt rated BB, B, CCC, CC and C is regarded as having predominantly speculative characteristics with respect to capacity to pay interest and repay principal. BB indicates the least degree of speculation and C the highest. While such debt will likely have some quality and protective characteristics, these are outweighed by large uncertainties or major exposures to adverse conditions.

2. SHORT-TERM RATING DEFINITIONS

A commercial paper rating is an assessment of the likelihood of timely payment of short-term debt obligations. Short-term obligations are those which have a maturity of less than 365 days. The rating measures the issuer's ability to provide funds to repay outstanding principal and interest at maturity and is not a recommendation to buy or sell.

Although the analysis involved emphasises short-term factors, there is usually a strong correlation between Standard & Poor's long- and short-term ratings.

S&P's short-term ratings are defined as follows:

A Issues assigned this highest rating are regarded as having the greatest capacity for timely repayment. Issues in this category are delineated with the numbers 1, 2 and 3 to indicate the relative degree of safety.

A-1 This designation indicates that the degree of safety regarding timely payment is either overwhelming or very strong. Those issues determined to possess overwhelming safety characteristics will be denoted with a plus (+) sign designation.

A-2 Capacity for timely payment on issues with this designation is strong. However, the relative degree of safety is not as high as for issues designated A-1.

A-3 Issues carrying this designation have a satisfactory capacity for timely payment. They are, however, somewhat more vulnerable to the adverse effects of changes in circumstances than obligations carrying higher designations.

B Issues rated B are regarded as having only an adequate capacity for timely payment. However, such capacity may be damaged by changing conditions or short-term adversities.

C This rating is assigned to short-term debt obligations with a doubtful capacity for payment.

D This rating indicates that the issue is either in default or expected to be in default upon maturity.

B. The overall approach

Issues which depend on collateral to repay investors are analysed in a different manner from unsecured debt. An unsecured rating takes into account, among other things, the financial strength and flexibility of an issuer to adapt to changing economic and financial circumstances.

A collateralised vehicle has no such flexibility, and therefore needs to have protection in place at the outset in order to be able to adapt to changing conditions. A secured transaction, by altering the degree of the protections put in place at the start, can target a desired rating for the issue. To do the same for an unsecured issue would entail long-term financial planning in order to adjust strategies and financial ratios, something which may sometimes run counter to shareholders' interests. For this reason, it is important to recognise that in an asset-backed transaction S&P *rates the issues* and *not* the issuers. An AAA rating on one collateralised bond issue does not mean that other transactions by the same issuer would necessarily be rated at the same level, nor does it say anything about the issuer's unsecured creditworthiness.

On any occasion that S&P looks at a transaction backed by a pool of assets, it seeks to be satisfied with three primary aspects of the transaction:

(i) the quality and sufficiency of the collateral;
(ii) the mechanisms that ensure that the cashflow from the collateral gets to the investors; and
(iii) the legal structure of the transaction which ensures that the investor is paid, regardless of the insolvency of any party to the issue.

One concern in assessing the quality and sufficiency of collateral is the actual asset used. Here, the ability of the security to pay the bondholders is the fulcrum of the issue. It is important to understand the potential credit risks inherent in that asset and how the asset can be used to assure value to the investors. S&P uses a variety of overcollateralisation scenarios depending on the assets and whether they are marked-to-market or cash flow based.

To date, all of the UK transactions have been cash flow based, but this does not rule out the possibility of a market value transaction if parties can be found to make a price in the relevant assets. Regardless of the technique used, if the collateral in itself is insufficient to cover the requirements of the transaction, there must be some means of covering any shortfall.

It is vital to understand how the security is to be structured to ensure that the investor receives interest and principal in full, under all conditions. It is also important to consider the funds flow and where there might be a liquidity shortfall. Liquidity needs can occur due to a number of events. For instance, liquidity shortfalls may arise due to a timing mismatch of payments on the collateral relative to payments on the notes, resulting from a mismatch in the interest rate on the funding versus the interest rate on the notes. Similar shortfalls may also occur as a result of market related risks, such as an inability to re-market short-term debt, or to reinvest cash from the assets at the rate required to pay the investors.

The legal jurisdiction of both the issuer and the assets should be addressed in all cases at an early stage. S&P expects structured issues to be unaffected by the insolvency of any party to the transaction, as discussed later in 'Special Purpose Criteria'.

Once the credit evaluation is completed, attention can then be focused on the documentation. S&P will examine all draft documents relevant to the rating of the transaction and comment on aspects which affect the full and timely payment of the issue under all foreseeable circumstances. While final documentation is unavailable until signing, it is wise to have the tacit approval of the documents from S&P prior to launch, and, at a minimum, on all aspects which could be considered material in an offering circular. Should the documents be subject to substantive revisions at any stage, S&P would expect to see the revised drafts prior to submission of final documentation. Drafts of all necessary legal opinions should also be submitted to S&P and its legal advisers and approved prior to signing of the documents.

A public rating from S&P is subject to surveillance for the life of the issue. The issuer, the administrator of an issue or the trustee is expected to provide regular reports on the issue as itemised in the documentation. The rating may be subject to change if the performance of the assets varies from expectations, if any party to the transaction fails to perform as expected, or if rating changes occur on supporting issues (see below—'Supporting Ratings'). S&P will also, from time to time, revisit the administrator of the collateral to ensure that its ability to service any rated issues remains unimpaired.

A thorough understanding of S&P methodology helps to streamline the rating procedure at all stages. The process is iterative and interactive, but it must be remembered that each additional iteration can add to the passage of time between the inception of a deal and its completion. However, once the hurdles have been cleared for the first new transaction of any type, subsequent transactions based on the same scheme become a much more straightforward process for all parties concerned.

C. Selected features of a rating analysis

The following topics are those on which issuers and investors have expressed most interest. They are intended to highlight some of the key aspects of secured issues upon which S&P focus.

1. SPECIAL PURPOSE CRITERIA

Most originators of mortgages, who have tapped the UK mortgage-backed market, have created individual or special purpose companies (SPC) to act as issuers. These issuers do not generally carry an S&P rating and, therefore, from a rating perspective, risk becoming insolvent.

The need for such Special Purpose Criteria depends on the insolvency laws of the issuer's legal jurisdiction. In the United States and the United Kingdom the constraints imposed by legislation such as the US Bankruptcy Code and the Insolvency Act 1986 make such structures key rating considerations. Clearly, however, these insolvency concerns may vary from country to country, given that different national laws may allow creditors and debtors greater or less freedom of action, depending on the legislators' approach.

Consequently, in order to protect investors, and to avoid as far as possible the likelihood of an SPC's assets being attached by any creditors, thus interrupting cash flow and timely payment, the SPC must be made as 'bullet proof' as possible. This assurance can be provided by the issuer demonstrating to S&P that it is insulated as far as possible from becoming insolvent. The SPC must also be able to demonstrate that in the event it does become insolvent the pool of collateral supporting the issue would not be available to creditors of the issuer other than the holders of the rated bonds, and that the debt, which has been sold on the strength of those assets, would not become involved in any such insolvency proceedings.

In order to achieve this situation certain criteria need to be met, usually referred to as insolvency-remote or special purpose criteria. The following are the principal criteria, but the list is not exhaustive and certain other items are also often incorporated in the documents, such as a restriction on the SPC having any subsidiaries. These criteria are of equal importance and are not ranked in any particular sequence:

(i) the issuer's business must be restricted to the purchase of the receivables and the issue of the rated debt;

(ii) the issuer may not incur any additional debt other than debt that:

    (a) is rated the same as the rated debt; or

    (b) (i) is fully subordinated to the rated debt; and

        (ii) is non-recourse other than with respect to proceeds in excess of the proceeds necessary to pay the rated debt; and

        (iii) does not constitute a claim against the issuer to the extent that the excess proceeds are insufficient to pay such debt; or

(c) will not result in a reduction of the existing rating.

(iii) the issuer may not sell or assign the receivables arising from the assets to any entity, unless such entity meets S&P's special purpose, insolvency-remote criteria, and such sale or assignment is subject to the security interests of the debt holders.

2. STRESS TESTING

Having established a vehicle that is an SPC, consideration must be given to the ability of the assets to withstand any deterioration or dilution in quality, as well as any changes in interest rate or pre-payment environments.

Having ensured that there are no obvious legal flaws in the transaction which could cause the structure to stop payment to the investors, S&P will look to ensure that the assets will continue to pay the bonds under the worst foreseeable circumstances. This is because the vehicle has no ability or capacity to adapt to changing financial and economic conditions, such as interest rate changes or increased default rates. S&P will test structures under a series of situations called 'stress tests' or 'worst case scenarios', designed to ensure that the assets will perform to a level of stress dictated by the rating to be applied. The higher the rating required, the greater the severity of the test. It is very important to remember that this is an assessment of risk and *not* an attempt to simulate reality—it is not practical within the confines of a rating assessment to factor into any analysis all the possible permutations and probabilities that may occur.

Clearly, however, some assets proposed for inclusion may be of a new type or of a nature not used before in asset-backed transactions. In these instances, S&P will find whatever data is available on the performance of those assets within the relevant jurisdiction and utilise its worldwide experience to draw as close a parallel as is reasonable to existing and comparative assets to form a basis on which to begin its review of the criteria and stresses applicable (see also below—'Non-mortgage assets'). While a stress test may be different and particular criteria items may vary slightly from country to country, the purpose behind the latter's inclusion in the tests will be the same.

In the United Kingdom for example, the asset that the market has become most accustomed to seeing securitised has been residential mortgages. Behind each rating assessment and calculation for these issues is a three year stress test period. S&P, for its rating purposes, assumes that its 'worst case depression scenario' will last for three years, but that those three years could occur at any time in the life of, say, a 27 year bond. It follows, therefore, that the transaction must be able to sustain the losses envisaged for the whole of its existence because nobody can predict when the possible 'depression' will occur or, indeed, if it will occur at all.

Debt obligations for short-term transactions, such as commercial paper, mature within a year, although the programme is ongoing. In such a case it would be too pessimistic to impose a three year stress on a pool of assets that may only have to support an issue for one year. Consequently, the stress test is modified to the extent that, while based on the concept of a three year depression, the end assumption is reduced in order to reflect the shorter term nature of the issue. This adjusted stress cover must be in place for every year of the programme.

A further distinction is also drawn between stress tests for issues using pool insurance cover and those with a senior/junior note structure. In the former, the tests will calculate the amount of insurance cover and liquidity support required for the transaction, using current criteria and a variety of factors weighted according to the composition of the pool of assets.

In the case of a senior/junior structure, the issuer produces a series of cash flow simulations which reflect the income and payment streams dictated by the transaction documentation, and which will need to incorporate assumptions supplied by S&P. These assumptions will include an expected level and frequency of defaults, variations in LIBOR, reinvestment rates and the value of asset recoveries, as well as the intervals at which such factors are expected to impact cash flow. The purpose of the simulations is to assess the levels of over-collateralisation and credit enhancement necessary to support the issue since the extra collateral being incorporated into the structure is not liquid.

3. REINVESTMENT RISK

The cash flow stream of any asset-backed transaction is always subject to four distinct areas of risk: reinvestment risk, maturity, interest rate and prepayment risk. The last of these four describes the potential repayment of a loan prior to its expected maturity but is an unquantifiable risk since the inflow of prepayments cannot be accurately forecast. Reinvestment risk is one result of prepayment risk and arises from S&P's assumption that cash in hand is likely to earn less than the interest rate return on the underlying collateral in the transaction. Based on the jurisdiction, the rate setting mechanism in the structure and the savings conventions in the country of issue, S&P will make assumptions about the lowest likely reinvestment rate available to an issuer. Before looking at how to quantify and handle such a risk in an issue, a review of the underlying causes and effects is necessary. In the UK, for floating rate assets, S&P presumes that cash can only be invested at 500 basis points less than LIBOR, due to the interest rate reset mechanism which subjects the structure to spikes and troughs in LIBOR, which historically have occurred over relatively short timespans.

Most loans made against assets, or indeed loans generally, give the borrower an option to repay the loan before its specified maturity date, albeit that such early settlement or pre-payment might incur some form of financial penalty to compensate the lender for receiving repayment of its funds earlier than originally anticipated.

This gives rise to a twofold problem in a secured transaction—the first is whether or not the servicer knows in advance that funds are being repaid and the second is how to handle any adjustment to the mortgage interest rate arising because of the pre-payments.

Since each borrower has the ability to pre-pay, it is conceivable that the pre-payment would be made one day after an interest payment date on the issue. If many borrowers settle early at the same time, the issuer may not have enough money to meet the next interest payment. S&P assumes that a great many borrowers will pre-pay simultaneously at the least convenient moment for the issuer. The consequence is that an issuer is then holding cash which has to generate income to the same extent that the collateral was expected to do. Clearly, for the issue to receive its rating in the first place, S&P needs to be certain that there are ways and means to satisfy this potential shortfall from the outset, so that S&P can be sure that the investors will be paid.

One way of achieving this position is to structure the assets, and the issue, so that even where borrowers exercise their rights to early settlement, the issuer has a notice period before this occurs. Thus, while an early settlement 'penalty' or 'premium' can still be required, the issuer will know the extent of the forthcoming income reduction and will also be in a position to know whether it has to make any adjustment to its interest charging rate on the underlying collateral to compensate.

This assessment is made in the threshold interest rate formula, incorporated in most structures, which calculates the rate required, and therefore the adjustment necessary to existing charging rates, in order to maintain income in the next interest period. Alternatively, a guaranteed investment contract can be used (see below—'Supporting Ratings').

However, two things in particular should be noted in this situation as far as a rating is concerned. First, any adjustment mechanism in the transaction structure which is designed to take account of such shortfalls must be included in the documentation at the outset, and the mechanism itself should incorporate S&P's current worst case reinvestment rate criterion. Second, even where pre-payments can be estimated, by virtue of the borrower giving notice, it is still conceivable, from a rating perspective, that the early settlement problem will recur in the last quarter of the life of the bond.

This last quarter problem might occur, for example, because all outstanding debts, or a very large proportion of them, pre-pay at a point, say, one month into the last interest period of a quarterly pay transaction, leaving a period of two months during which income has to be earned to pay the investors. However, there may be either no, or few, remaining assets to bear the burden of a rate increase and thereby make up the income deficiency.

As a consequence, S&P will make certain assumptions as to the amount of collateral debts outstanding, combined with its reinvestment risk assumptions, and provide the issuer with a specific figure which S&P deems to be adequate to offset a worst case shortfall. This amount then has to be included in the structure from the outset, to act as a cushion in case this event occurs, and be in a form which can be drawn upon quickly, such as a cash reserve fund, committed facility or insurance cover.

4. SUPPORTING RATINGS

The inability of an institution to fulfil its role in a rated asset-backed transaction could cause the payment chain to collapse. S&P evaluates the likelihood of a failure in the payment chain by looking at the 'supporting ratings' to a transaction. The term 'supporting rating' refers to entities which play a monetary role and which carry an S&P rating. The requisite level of supporting rating will be dictated by the rating sought for the transaction and the nature of the function, that is short- or long-term, which that party fulfills.

Here again, insolvency law is important, since S&P will not necessarily rate all the parties to an issue and, from the rating perspective, unrated parties cannot be relied upon to perform their functions. Therefore, knowing the strength of the supporting entity, by virtue of the rating already applied, helps in assessing the various aspects of the structure where that party is involved. From S&P's standpoint, were this not the case, and an unrated entity were an essential link in the chain of the structure, its ability to perform its responsibilities to the requisite level of stress would be unknown.

However, that does not preclude an entity with a lower rating, or even without a rating at all, taking a monetary role in the issue; what it does mean is that such parties may need to have a form of credit support available to reassure S&P that the overall strength of the structure is not impaired.

One of the most common functions performed by a supporting rating is that of being a provider of a liquidity or a revolving credit facility. This position is usually taken by a bank where it sustains the availability of funds for the issue for items such as short-term arrears. Similarly, a Guaranteed Investment Contract (GIC) provider is a supporting rating—the purpose of a GIC is to assure the issuer of a guaranteed rate of income on excess cash, thereby boosting income levels sufficiently to match the rate necessitated by the level of the coupon on the issued securities. The third use is for bond issues with a maturity shorter than that of the assets. There must be a provision that an entity rated as well as the banks will buy out remaining assets before the bond issue matures.

5. ENDOWMENT POLICY PROVIDERS

One other aspect of secured issues which is frequently discussed is the assurance companies which provide the collateral life policies for many of the securitised mortgages.

Due to the majority of UK mortgages being backed by 'endowment' policies it became necessary, when S&P first developed its UK benchmark underwriting criteria, to take account of the ability of the assurance companies providing those policies to provide payment of the sums due, when called upon. This situation was complicated by two factors. First, few of the life funds which support the policies had S&P ratings and could not therefore be accepted as supporting ratings in a structure. Secondly, since many mortgage lenders had not previously been concerned with the solvency of the policy providers, some had significant proportions of their mortgage portfolios backed by policies from unrated assurers.

This guideline in no way implies an inability on the part of unrated companies to meet their commitments. However, since S&P has not been requested to provide a rating it feels that it is unable, based solely on publicly available information, to make the necessary judgement required in assessing an assurance company's ability to perform to the level needed in a rated issue. Once again this criterion does not preclude the participation of an unrated assurance company in a structured issue, but the transaction must be constructed so as to provide the necessary credit support in one form or another in order to achieve the desired rating.

The perceived risk may be considered by some to be remote since what is implied is the failure of a company at a point when a borrower needs the funds to repay his debt. However, from the rating perspective this is a risk that needs to be handled by the structure as the policy is the third line of defence after the borrower and the property. S&P believes that the more assets in a pool that are supported by one unrated assurance company the greater that risk. At present, the maximum level of concentration that can be provided by one unrated assurance company, without additional cost of credit enhancement, is 25% of the value of the pool. Minor variations above that level may be tolerable, but significant deviations from that figure are not possible without credit support for the whole of that unrated assurer's proportion.

Additionally, current criteria require that bonds mature, at a minimum, two years after maturity of the last mortgage. This is because maturity of many endowment policies is often later than the related mortgage as a consequence of delays in completing policies relative to property completions and the beginning of the loan. The two year period ensures not only that all policy proceeds are available, but also that, if they are not available, the lender will have sufficient time to take enforcement action before bonds mature.

As the depth of the UK mortgage-backed securities market increases and as greater performance experience is acquired this element of the criteria may evolve to become a less stringent requirement but this is a process of development and not an overnight occurrence.

A further distinction needs to be drawn between policies backed by an assurance company's usual investment funds, as opposed to those policies which are 'unit linked'. The argument in favour of making this distinction is that the isolation of the managed funds, which support the unit linked policies, segregates them from normal investment moneys and, therefore, diminishes the possibility of the unit linked funds being attached by creditors who would otherwise be able to seek payment from a company's general investment funds.

D. Variety in structures and asset types

The foregoing review has been concerned with various aspects of transactions seen to date. Financial markets are continually evolving and it is evident that this evolution will affect securitisation, taking it into structures and using assets not seen before. The following is a guide to presenting new structures and assets to S&P.

1. STRUCTURES

A summary of the proposed structure from the potential issuer or its investment banker is frequently received early in the proceedings and this is often the forum in which new and untried structures are developed.

This can be a useful method of discussing potential problems. A client would want to know the feasibility of a transaction before it gets to the stage of spending expensive management time and resources in investigating a particular financing method which may, ultimately, have legal or technical difficulties that S&P believes cannot be satisfactorily accommodated in the structure. If, however, it is possible to resolve any such problems, the cost of so doing may then make the economics of the transaction unattractive to the issuer.

By way of background to the sort of structural difficulties that can be encountered, examples can be found from among existing UK mortgage-backed deals. The majority of transactions to date have been floating rate note issues, but there have also been two commercial paper transactions. These two commercial paper issues gave rise to different concerns because of their short-term nature and the fundamental mis-match between the term of the funding and that of the underlying asset.

Such an apparent basic incompatibility that arises in commercial paper issues, between the term of the funding and that of the asset, has to be accommodated within the transaction structure. An important area of consideration is how to assure investors of payment, in the event of an issuer's failure to issue new paper to pay off maturing paper. At the time of writing, the only satisfactory way of coping with this takeout requirement for UK mortgage assets, as far as an S&P rating is concerned, is to use a standby or backstop facility to provide full cover to take out the issue should this be necessary. Some form of backstop to meet maturing rated debt will always be required when such a mis-match exists.

Structural concerns have also arisen where an issuer has not used harmonious rates. This means that the interest rate being charged on the underlying collateral is not of the same tenor as that being paid on the securities. Thus, to use floating rate assets to support a fixed rate bond requires the use of some form of interest rate swap to assimilate floating rate income to the fixed rate liability and vice versa. Some transactions already rated have employed methods to 'convert' fixed to floating or vice versa, so that the two rates are synthetically aligned to ensure a consistent income flow to support the issue. In addition to the need for a form of swap, these types of issues will also require a suitably rated swap counterparty since the latter is a supporting rating for the issue.

Given its wide and diverse experience S&P believes it is in a position to evaluate the consequences of a variety of structured transactions and will attempt to respond in a timely fashion whenever new ideas are proposed.

2. NON-MORTGAGE ASSETS

The use of new or different types of assets in a secured issue will necessitate reviewing representative data for such assets. The intent of this method is to obtain a view that is sufficiently broad to enable S&P to establish a generic performance record for the particular asset and to make a statistical analysis from which criteria can be derived; this view would hold true for any non-mortgage asset.

It is important to note that the need for adequate supporting information from the local market of the potential structure is essential. S&P would not impose criteria on one market based on conclusions drawn from similar assets in another country because domestic practice in each market will determine the nature and performance of those assets, which are almost certain to vary from country to country.

The nature of the asset may conceivably make it more difficult either to collate the necessary data or to establish its performance record, but that difficulty does not in itself prevent that asset from being eligible for securitisation. However, inadequate data will always be compensated by more severe worst case assumptions.

E. Conclusion

Consistency and comparability of criteria are essential in rating assessments, but there is also a need to recognise that separate jurisdictions and local markets and practices may require a different or modified approach from that previously adopted elsewhere. Without that consistency a rating could not be seen to imply the same qualitative judgement wherever it was applied.

This consistency is essential to the utility of credit ratings. Different concerns are going to arise when dealing with different countries and S&P will always research the local market and national laws before drawing its conclusions in order to be certain that all necessary conditions have been anticipated. S&P is always willing to review structural proposals in the light of changing market conditions and the advent of innovative financing instruments. Similarly, while maintaining consistency, rating criteria may need to be modified to reflect the inclusion of new or unusual assets.

MOODY'S INVESTORS SERVICE INC'S APPROACH

A. Overview

Over the past several years, the securitisation of assets has become much more frequent, presenting significant investment opportunities for investors. These instruments are often quite complex. Rarely does the investor have the time or the expertise to analyse the associated credit risks. Moody's credit analysis, summarised in the form of a rating, is a useful tool to be used for the investor's own risk/return evaluation, thus decreasing the investor's cost of investment and enhancing market efficiency.

The process for rating a structured transaction—whether it be a mortgage-backed floating rate note or a Eurocommercial paper note programme backed by automobile loan receivables—and rating a corporation's debt issue is very different. In the analysis of a corporation seeking a rating, Moody's analysts study and review the financial condition and performance of the company, assess management's input on this performance as well as their prospects for the future and then arrive at a rating conclusion. In the short run, there is virtually nothing the management of a company can do to the company's financing structure to change a rating conclusion.

In a structured transaction, the process typically starts with the rating desired; in other words, the issuer or merchant banker may believe that to market an issue successfully an AAA or AA rating is needed. The question then becomes what legal, structural and credit supports are necessary to achieve that rating. In these transactions, Moody's has a more active role representing the interests of investors. In short, Moody's goal is to ensure that the structure, the legal risks and the credit risks result in a composite risk level to the investor that is consistent with the rating requested. Of course, when the risk to investors is greater than that represented by the desired rating, Moody's expresses its opinion whenever possible. In that process Moody's is an advocate for the investor.

B. The rating process

In general, one or more analysts are assigned to each transaction. The analyst is responsible for the review and analysis of all documents and legal opinions and of any relevant financial data. At the time of the pricing or offering of the security, a 'prospective' rating may be issued as an indication of the final rating that is expected to be assigned to the transaction upon completion of Moody's review. When the draft documents are in final form, the analyst presents the transaction to the rating committee. Each rating assignment and the development of rating standards are made by consensus of the rating committee after a review and consideration of the transaction.

There are three basic types of securitised transactions in the market today. First, there is the pay-through or cash flow structure, in which the cash flow from the securitised assets will be used to pay all principal and interest to the investors. The security is created when the originator sells the assets to a thinly capitalised, special purpose vehicle company or trust that is 'bankruptcy remote', which, in turn, issues securities collateralised by the assets. This structure has been used for long-term debt programmes, intermediate-term note programmes and, in a few cases, commercial paper programmes, issued by special purpose companies or trusts.

The second type of structure is known as an asset-backed bond or market value transaction. In this type of structure, the liquidation value of the assets ensures the ultimate payment of the bond. The originator sells the assets to the 'bankruptcy remote' issuer, which must maintain the liquidation value of the receivables at a certain level. These receivables are then sold in the event of a default. In these programmes, cash flow from the collateral is typically used to purchase new receivables to maintain the liquidation value. This structure has been used for intermediate-term mortgage-backed bonds issued by (predominantly) US savings and loan associations, commercial paper programmes of special purpose companies and issues of preferred stock by investment companies.

The third type of structure is the fully supported structure, where the investors rely on a letter of credit, a guarantee or insurance policy for repayment of principal and interest. This structure has been used for both commercial paper programmes and intermediate-term note programmes. The issuers of these types of transactions may be of all types.

In making rating decisions, Moody's reviews all potential weak points of the structured transaction and analyses each in terms of the probability of its occurrence, the amount of loss that might be incurred if the event actually takes place and the amount of certainty regarding the evaluation of the probability and the amount of the loss. This is what we call the 'composite risk approach'.

The three general areas of risk to which this approach is applied in the review of a structured transaction are the following:

   (i) collateral—the risk of loss on any assets, the cash flows of which are relied on to provide interest and principal payments to investors;

  (ii) legal—structural weaknesses resulting from legal considerations, primarily insolvency issues relating to third parties;

 (iii) cash flow—structural weaknesses resulting from mis-matches in the timing and amounts of cash inflows and outflows of the issuer, especially in stressful economic environments.

As residential mortgage loans have been the primary asset securitised for sale in the United Kingdom, the discussion will focus, in general, on these transactions. However, many other types of assets will be securitised so, to the extent possible, our rating analysis of them will be described as well. The issues and techniques of rating analysis outlined in the following paragraphs are applicable in many respects to the securitisation of almost any other asset.

C. Collateral analysis

The fundamental issue that must first be addressed regarding the transaction is whether the cash flows to the investor are dependent on the cash flows from the collateral. In a fully supported transaction, an insurance company, bank or other party absorbs the risk of the collateral and makes payment to the investor if the issuer does not. It is essentially a guarantee of the investment and the only relevant collateral issue is whether the rating of the guarantor is sufficient to support the rating on the structured security.

Much of the analysis in this kind of structure centres on whether there are any exceptions to the guarantee, whether the guarantee is enforceable and whether the guarantee will pay within the necessary time frame.

If principal and interest payments to investors *will* be dependent on the timing and amounts of cash flowing from the collateral, the analysis is much more complex. In addition to the analysis of the guarantee, letter of credit or insurance policy providing credit enhancement, we must assess the predictability and variability of the cash flow generated by the assets and thereby assess the adequacy of the credit enhancement level. To qualify for Moody's highest ratings, the credit quality of the assets that collateralise the issuer's obligations and the amount and quality of any credit enhancement protection against arrears and losses on such collateral must be sufficient to withstand an extremely harsh economic environment.

The first step of this process is to examine the track record of the originator and the administrator by looking at their history of arrears, defaults and recoveries. If the structure is a pay-through obligation, Moody's also considers the credit quality of the administrator of the loans to determine whether it is capable of fulfilling its obligations at all points during the potential life of the transaction.

The second step is to determine whether the track records provided are a reliable indicator of future performance. The predictive value of the historical data is directly related to the consistency of the originator/administrator's underwriting standards and collection procedures and to the economic environment during which the portfolio performance was measured.

The final step in the process is to apply a stress test to the receivables in question, with the severity of the test depending on the rating level. In those cases where the receivables are generated in conjunction with the manufacture of a product—and assuming the rating of that manufacturer is less than the rating requested for the transaction—we must consider the impact on the quality of the receivables pool in the event the manufacturer becomes insolvent.

The distinguishing features that differentiate the risk profile of United Kingdom assets from other markets include the economy, the regulatory environment and the assets to be securitised. Therefore, Moody's approach to the analysis of United Kingdom-sourced collateral incorporates these distinguishing features.

1. PRIOR PERFORMANCE AND ADMINISTRATOR CREDIT QUALITY

The issuer of an asset-backed or pay-through security relies on the originator to originate the assets it purchases and generally has neither the employees nor the facilities to administer the asset pool and to collect arrears. A designated party, often the originator that sold the assets to the issuer, is responsible for the ongoing administration of the portfolio. The responsibilities of the administrator may go beyond normal duties, such as setting interest rates, operating the direct debiting scheme and managing collections. Such additional responsibilities may include advancing funds to the issuer to provide liquidity to it if borrowers are in arrears, obtaining all necessary insurance policies, remitting cash flows to the trustee and the issuer, reinvesting temporarily idle cash in short-term investments and administering the day-to-day affairs of the issuer.

In rating such a transaction, the originator's quality is important in determining how the securitised pool of assets will perform during adverse economic conditions. The administrator's quality is relevant from two perspectives: first, the administrator's operational quality; that is, how well equipped is the administrator to carry out its day-to-day responsibilities; and, secondly, the administrator's credit quality, that is, its capability to fulfil the financial responsibilities it takes on as administrator.

The prior performance of the originator and the administrator, as demonstrated by arrears and losses on their portfolios of similar assets, are used in part as a proxy for their quality. To understand the statistics provided in such a review, Moody's studies their policies on underwriting and the administration of their assets.

The most accurate way to analyse a receivables portfolio is by using a 'static pool' approach. A static pool analysis uses data either from a pool of receivables previously sold or historical repossession and loss severity data, which is then modelled to simulate a pool of sold receivables. The idea is to capture the actual losses that would occur in a pool of receivables once they have been securitised. This provides an initial approximation for expected loss if the portfolio has the same characteristics as the receivables to be securitised and is a much more accurate indicator than the losses-to-liquidations or losses-to-portfolio out-standing ratios often used, both of which can be heavily influenced by how fast the portfolio is growing.

To assess the operational quality of the administrator, Moody's often visits the offices of the administrator to review its procedures and the experience and professionalism of its staff. We look at the degree to which the process is automated, the capacity constraints that exist and their audit and review systems. A critical factor is the administrator's collection methods. If the administrator has efficient and effective collection procedures, both the frequency of defaults on the collateral and the severity of resultant losses will be favourably influenced.

If the administrator's financial strength is not adequate (in view of the rating to be assigned to the security) to ensure its continued financial viability for the life of the transaction, contingency arrangements should be made for a back-up administrator and for its financial obligations to be supported and taken on by other parties as required.

The minimum credit quality of the administrator that we would look for depends on several factors:

(i) the maximum maturity of the deal. Clearly, the shorter the maturity, the greater the differential can be between the rating of the administrator and the rating of the transaction;

(ii) the capability of the substitute administrator to take on the operational responsibilities of the contract. An important aspect is the availability to the substitute administrator of relevant data required to assume its duties in a timely manner. Another aspect is the financial strength of the substitute administrator; that is, will the substitute be available if needed and will it be able to comply with the financial obligations it will be required to carry?

(iii) the strength of the legal structure. In other words, how likely is it that principal or interest due to the investor would be delayed as a result of actions of a third party in the event of the administrator's insolvency? Additionally, what is the likelihood that a liquidator or administrator of the insolvent administrator could use provisions available under the Insolvency Act to require the issuer to return to it sums previously paid by the administrator to the issuer (eg, interest rate subsidies)?

(iv) the availability of regulatory protections. How will the regulator treat executory contracts such as the administration agreement? In certain markets, regulators have indicated to us that it is likely such a contract *would* be honoured after the institution came under the control of the liquidator or administrator (or their equivalent). In other countries, including the United Kingdom, this is less certain.

If the administrator is not of sufficient credit quality, we determine the maximum amount of cash flow that could be adversely affected by its insolvency. For AA or AAA transactions, we insist that the loss exposure be adequately covered either by cash reserves, through a letter of credit or by a third party guarantee from an appropriately rated institution.

When the asset administrator's sole line of business is the origination and administration of assets similar to those being securitised, Moody's recognises the potential link between a high level of arrears and losses on the asset pool and the insolvency of the administrator. A poorly performing pool increases the cost of administration and therefore decreases the likelihood that a replacement willing to bear this expense can be found. Unless a third party is obliged to be administrator of last resort, no one may be willing to act in this capacity upon insolvency of the original administrator. Even when the asset administrator's financial strength is not solely dependent on the origination and administration of the assets securitised, an administrator of last resort may be needed if the original administrator is rated at a level that does not support the rating on the security.

2. VALIDITY OF PAST PERFORMANCE AS PREDICTOR

The financial services sector has witnessed many changes in the past few years. Increased competition among lenders has caused an extensive change in the environment in which mortgages and other consumer receivables are originated. In response, many lenders have modified their origination practices to make them more attractive to consumers by accelerating the lending process and decreasing the amount of information requested so that they may maintain market share and attract new borrowers.

These modifications may result in dramatic changes in the risk profile of the loans they originate. Thus, such changes must be reviewed carefully and the predictive value of the historical performance of the originator's portfolio reviewed accordingly.

The state of the economic environment during which the data was collected is also relevant. For instance, much of England has experienced dramatic increases in housing prices in the post war period, with housing occupancy rates also increasing. With such significant increases, a mortgage lender's underwriting mistakes may be hidden, because borrowers could sell their homes as necessary and, if the lender did take possession, the property could be sold at a profit. The factors underlying this growth, however, appear to be changing and the growth has not been sustainable. Therefore, a lender that would have had significant arrears and losses if it were not for such growth may no longer have house price increases to obscure its risky underwriting practices. Increased competition and stabilising house prices may both contribute to the invalidating of historic results as a predictor of the future.

3. STRESS TESTS

If the debt secured by a securitised asset pool is to be rated in one of Moody's highest rating categories, the pool not only must have sufficient credit enhancement to cover expected arrears and losses in the current economic environment but also must have enough to protect the investor in extreme economic environments. The maximum arrears and losses expected in both a hyperinflationary environment and in a severe recession or depression must be covered by the credit enhancement. Different types of assets have different stress tests, which may vary significantly depending on the average life of the assets, their specific characteristics and the rating category.

If the collateral must be sold to allow the issuer or the trustee to make payments to investors (eg, in a market value structure), the market liquidity and interest rate sensitivity of the collateral is reviewed. The minimum resale value of each collateral type is determined by an analysis of the historic trading pattern of the asset in question and the effect of market interest rate changes on its pricing. In such an analysis, the volatility of the trading prices are quantified. We also examine relevant market conditions that might affect trading prices in severe economic environments and try to determine whether the market will be broad enough to absorb the collateral without prices being driven down. We use such information to quantify the amount of resale value the structure can rely upon to pay investors all principal and interest as required by the terms of the issue. The amount of collateral required for a given issue is often called the over-collateralisation level.

Not all types of collateral can be used in a market value structure. If investment grade, publicly placed corporate bonds are securitised, the secondary market for such debt is often very broad and very liquid, even if the bonds must be sold quickly. Therefore, we usually can rely on the ability to sell the bonds to repay all or part of the obligation to investors and a market value structure is possible. If, on the other hand, the collateral is residential mortgage loans that were not underwritten using standard underwriting practices, a secondary market may not even exist. In such a case, Moody's would assume little or no value upon the sale of the collateral and a market value structure is not viable.

It should be noted that the structure may have a significant impact on the way in which the collateral is assessed and on the amount and type of credit enhancement that will be needed to qualify the transaction for Moody's highest ratings. Some structures need less credit enhancement because interest received on the underlying collateral is disproportionately greater than interest due on the security. These margins are sometimes available to offset cash shortfalls of the issuer. Other structures build up cash reserves, which decrease the size of the credit enhancement needed to fund losses or arrears on the assets, or require additional payments of principal to investors if certain events occur (see the discussion of payout events in 'Credit Card Receivables' below).

4. MORTGAGES

Moody's developed its credit support guidelines for mortgage loans based on its research, which indicates that several primary factors contribute to arrears and defaults, including (1) negative equity, which occurs when housing prices fall below the total amount of the borrower's mortgage plus selling costs, and (2) borrower's financial difficulty, usually due to loss of job, change in his or her domestic situation or excessive use of credit.

These factors interact with each other in differing ways to affect arrears and losses depending on the characteristics of individual loans and on the properties securing them. The characteristics of mortgage loans and their security which Moody's considers to be significant include the following:

   (i) loan-to-value ratios;
  (ii) quality and amount of mortgage indemnity insurance;
 (iii) high values of the properties securing the loans in relation to their market areas;
 (iv) loan seasoning;
  (v) type of properties securing the mortgages;
 (vi) use of mortgage proceeds (purchase of home, compared with remortgage of home for additional liquidity);
 (vii) method of setting mortgage interest rates;
(viii) type of mortgage, that is, whether the loan is, for example, a pension-linked or endowment-linked mortgage and, if the latter, the type of endowment insurance and quality of its providers.

In addition, certain factors that affect arrears and losses on the pool are susceptible to change and thus must be considered in evaluating the riskiness of the mortgage pool, including the following:

  (i) further modifications of the Mortgage Interest Relief At Source (MIRAS) benefit;
 (ii) a decrease in the availability of unemployment benefits from the Department of Social Security or otherwise;
(iii) increases in possession and sale costs, most likely resulting from lengthier possession and sale proceedings.

Certain features of the transaction may also increase or mitigate the risk of arrears and losses that the credit enhancement must bear, including the following:

  (i) geographic concentrations of properties securing the mortgages;
 (ii) ability of the issuer to make further advances and/or substitutions out of the funds generated by redeeming loans;

(iii) ability of borrowers to convert to a repayment or index-linked mortgage without the loan being repurchased by the administrator or issuer;

(iv) likelihood that rates on the mortgage loans may need to exceed market rates to cover the expenses of the issuer;

(v) amount of excess margins available to offset arrears and losses;

(vi) allocation of all borrowers' redemptions to the senior tranche of a senior/junior structure first, thus reducing the expected average life of the senior tranche.

Moody's has developed credit enhancement guidelines for each 5% loan-to-value (LTV) range of a benchmark pool and compares all rated pools against these guidelines. The benchmark pool is comprised of 300 non-amortising, variable-rate mortgage loans, underwritten in accordance with standard origination and underwriting practices. The loans are used to purchase, and are secured by, first mortgages on one- to four-family detached or semi-detached properties spread throughout England and Wales. The loans carry mortgage indemnity insurance if LTVs are in excess of 80%, down to 75% LTV. The provider of mortgage indemnity insurance is rated at least as high as the structured transaction. All the mortgage loans are assumed to finance homes that have values that are less than Moody's standard for the region in which the homes are located. None is assumed to be secured by endowment policies. All the properties are owner-occupied.

Moody's has developed adjustments to the benchmark guidelines to allow an assessment of each pool's unique characteristics that mitigate or increase the credit risk of the pool. The most common adjustments relate to the following:

(i) quality and type of endowment insurance policies;

(ii) amount and type of low-start mortgage loans;

(iii) quality and coverage of mortgage indemnity providers;

(iv) property values that exceed the standards for the region in which they are located;

(v) geographic concentrations in higher-risk regions or within postal code areas;

(vi) different property types;

(vii) purpose of loan;

(viii) number of index-linked or capital repayment mortgages.

Deviations from the above characteristics, and their associated impact on credit risk, are considered on a case-by-case basis if they have not previously been assessed.

Mortgage loans are often securitised in cash flow transactions, so liquidation value is frequently irrelevant. In some markets they are used in market value transactions, but we believe their liquidation value is very uncertain in the United Kingdom, where there is no established secondary market for residential mortgage loans.

5. AUTO LOANS

Credit enhancement in an auto receivables backed structured programme is usually provided by a guarantee or repurchase commitment of a highly-rated entity. The agreement commits the guarantor to repurchase defaulted receivable contracts at a price equal to their remaining principal balances (inclusive of interest), up to a specified maximum amount. The maximum amount of the commitment will be a major determinant of the rating assigned to the certificates.

The research conducted on the historical performance of auto loan receivables in severe economic environments is very similar to that previously described for residential mortgages. We reviewed the performance of the portfolios of different lenders, using the static pool method, and a model was built to allow analysts to compare pools submitted for review with the historical interaction of different loan characteristics in a severe economic environment. Again, the differences between the auto loans in the pool to be rated and the auto loans on which the research was conducted are noted and the credit risks associated with those differences quantified.

In examining the adequacy of the proposed credit loss coverage, Moody's focuses on the following key statistics:

(i) the frequency with which contracts may be expected to go into default in the future;

(ii) the loss that will be realised, net of all collection costs, on the repossession and sale of the automobile;

(iii) the likelihood of any significant recovery of such losses following legal action against the borrower;

(iv) the potential size of any other claims against the credit loss policy, such as required advances for arrears.

Typically, default frequency of auto loans is greatest in the first 18 months of a contract. Although we do not expect that pattern to vary dramatically from one lender to another, lenders with different underwriting standards will have significantly different expected default frequencies.

Our analysis of the frequency of default for each transaction focuses on the stability of the underwriting standards and on the originator's and administrator's arrears and default records during periods of up to five years. We adjust these numbers based on a review of the loans supporting the notes. In particular, we evaluate the seasoning of the pool, the expected effect on any change in underwriting standards, the types of automobiles in the pool (new or used), the sensitivity of the pool to changes in the economic climate and the policies of the administrator limiting modifications of contracts. Geographic concentrations are very important in assessing the frequency of default, as are the original maturities of the loans.

In analysing the expected loss from a defaulted receivable, we examine additional information. The actual loss rate is a function of several factors, including the speed and cost of repossession, the quality of the administrator's sale procedures for repossessed cars and the market for used cars of the type in the portfolio. Furthermore, some receivable contracts provide for recourse to the auto dealer if the underlying borrower defaults. When it is relevant, we will examine the financial strength of the dealer network in general and raise or lower the expected loss rate accordingly.

6. CREDIT CARD RECEIVABLES

Frequently, a securitised pool of credit card receivables is composed of a discrete set of cardholder accounts. Except under limited circumstances, no additions will be made to the initial set of accounts, an important factor when evaluating a pool's potential performance because the underwriting and payment history of the accounts is known at the outset.

The securitised credit card receivables include those receivables initially existing under the cardholder accounts as well as any receivables arising under the accounts thereafter. Receivables will consist of principal balances and finance charge balances; the latter may include such items as interest charges, annual fees and service fees.

Some transactions allow the addition of new accounts to the securitised pool. The assessment of the adequacy of credit enhancement for these pools must recognise the potential increase in risk that may be associated with this feature.

We believe that unsecured credit card receivables carry a greater loss risk than auto receivables or mortgage loans. In addition, industry losses are growing and vary widely by originator. Furthermore, historical loss performance may understate future loss potential, depending on a number of factors. Therefore, it is important to understand fully the key characteristics that are predictive of future losses on credit card portfolios.

The following list identifies key predictive variables, as well as some specific questions and concerns Moody's might have when assessing a particular portfolio:

(i) *type of credit card.* Is the card a retailer's card, a travel and entertainment card or a bank card? Since losses may vary significantly, depending on both the relationship between the cardholder and originator and on the type of credit card, we categorise and analyse each separately;

(ii) *cardholder concentrations.* What cardholder concentrations exist by region? Moody's recognises that some regions are more economically stable than others. Are there, for example, affinity groups (endorsements by fraternal, professional or business organisations) or marketing programmes in the portfolio that produce portfolio concentrations in certain cardholder characteristics, such as occupation or level of income? Demographic concentrations may also increase credit risk;

(iii) *historical loss performance*. Loss performance of the accounts in the portfolio may be an excellent indicator of credit quality, particularly for the more seasoned accounts;

(iv) *portfolio underwriting*. Moody's determines when and how the current portfolio was underwritten. For example, some typical questions may be whether the portfolio contains pre-approved accounts and, if so, when and how they were originated and what percentage of the portfolio they represent. Pre-approved accounts are generated from issuer mass mailings and are inexpensive ways to build volume. However, except for an initial screening to determine the mailing list, these accounts are not underwritten. Although such a marketing approach may be valid for business reasons, it generally increases credit risk and Moody's will assess each mailing separately.

Other questions might be: what percentage of the portfolio is composed of solicited or 'take-one' accounts? We will be concerned about how 'take-one' accounts were underwritten. Is there, for instance, a credit scoring model in place? If so, what is its predictive validity and reliability? How does the verification process work? Does it include credit referencing agency checks, income confirmation and employment verification?

Finally, what underwriting changes have been implemented by management during the portfolio's history? Significant changes in underwriting tend to invalidate previous loss history;

(v) *servicing/collection quality*. The ability of the administrator to 'work' the portfolio effectively is critical in minimising credit losses. We focus on the credit strength of the administrator and on the quality of the administrator's collection system.

Once we complete our analysis of the key predictive variables, we evaluate the credit enhancement features that protect investors from credit losses on the portfolio.

The approach for evaluating credit enhancement features is prospective in nature and is a function of Moody's view on how the particular portfolio would perform under a variety of stressful economic conditions. Based on our analysis of the underwriting process, seasoning and the loss history associated with each segmented category, initial estimates of future portfolio performance are developed in a stressed economic environment, with the degree of stress varied by rating category.

The estimates of portfolio performance assume a highly diversified portfolio. Geographic and demographic concentrations are reviewed for deviations from this assumption and any concentrations are assessed as to their potential impact on future portfolio losses. If portfolios are geographically or demographically concentrated, they need greater credit enhancement for a given rating category.

Finally, we conclude our assessment of the credit quality of the pool based on an evaluation of the administrator and on the relationship between the originator and the cardholder. Moody's determines the likelihood of an administrator default and the resulting impact on losses.

Credit card portfolios have very dynamic performance characteristics. Portfolio growth, yield and payment rates can change significantly. To provide additional protection against these changes, the structures used to securitise these assets often include amortisation events or payout events, that, when triggered, necessitate an amortisation of the principal to investors before the scheduled amortisation date. Payout events have included the following:

(i) losses on the pool rising above a certain level for a specified period of time;
(ii) yield on the pool falling below a certain level for a specified period of time;
(iii) originator insolvency;
(iv) administrator default;
(v) credit enhancement to cover losses on the pool falling below a certain percentage of the total outstanding pool.

Payout events are, in essence, credit enhancement features, protecting investors from the continuing effects of portfolio deterioration and from other potentially adverse events. By preventing the continuation of the non-amortisation period that credit card transactions usually incorporate, payout events can act to reduce investor exposure to an adversely performing pool. The pool loss potential is essentially capped because additional losses are limited to those occurring during the amortisation period. Instead of needing protection for any level of losses during the entire non-amortisation period, a payout event can limit loss exposure and, if losses increase above such a limit, amortisation begins. As credit enhancement features, these events reduce the amount of credit protection necessary for a given rating category.

7. COMMERCIAL REAL ESTATE

The evaluation of the sufficiency of credit enhancement levels for commercial mortgage-backed securities varies considerably depending on the number of properties contained in the securitised pool. The process Moody's uses to evaluate one property securing a debt issue revolves around the analysis of cash flows from the leases of that building. The analysis of a large pool of properties, although less intensive than for a single property, is conducted on a loan-by-loan basis with the degree of analysis for each loan depending on loan concentrations.

In general the analysis consists of three parts, beginning with an assessment of the stability of the local commercial real estate markets. In the second phase, the project and lease risk analysis, if the securitisation consists of a single or a small number of mortgage loans we meet with building owners and management, visit the site(s) and review valuations, engineering reports, lists of tenants, and other documents to assess risks associated with the project(s) and their lease structure. Simultaneously, Moody's assesses market conditions to determine the discount rates to be applied to cash flow in estimating market values. In the third phase, we use a computer based sensitivity model to analyse cash flow and market value projections, which provide the basis for calculating the amount of credit enhancement needed, if any.

The assessment of the stability of the local commercial real estate markets involves an intensive and ongoing analysis of demand-side and supply-side risk and results in classification of each market on a scale of five categories ranging from very weak to very strong. The objective of our demand-side analysis is to evaluate the potential risk of a significant decrease in demand for the given property type over the bond term, which is accomplished through an examination of vulnerabilities within the local economic base. Specifically, the economic base is judged in terms of (1) historical growth performance, (2) volatility characteristics and (3) diversification of industries. These attributes are then compared with those of other cities and serve as the basis for classifying these cities in one of the five risk categories.

The objective of our supply-side analysis is to determine the degree to which a local market is prone to over-building. That analysis, as with the demand side, is designed to identify the specific vulnerability of each real estate market to depressed conditions in the future. Based on the historical development pattern, current market conditions and the potential for over-expansion in the future, Moody's again has classified major cities into five risk groups. These supply-side classifications are then considered in developing the assumptions used to project cash flow.

The objective of the second phase of the analysis—evaluating project and lease risk—is to gauge the competitive advantage or disadvantage of the buildings under rating review with comparable buildings in the same market (project risk) and to highlight potential shortfalls in debt service coverage resulting from the variation of terms of existing lease contracts (lease risk). Market data supports the premise that, under adverse economic conditions, a building that possesses superior attributes should maintain a higher level of occupancy and effective rental rates than competing buildings. Therefore, such a building will be subject to less severe assumptions in forecasting cash flows.

The project risk analysis includes a review of location, engineering and other reports, construction quality, presence of toxic materials, functional layout, amenities, ownership, building management and other factors. The lease risk analysis entails applying the assumptions formulated as a result of the review of the project and comparing projected cash flow under the various leases (including renewals or relets) to debt service. Where shortfalls exist in any year, Moody's looks for credit enhancement to cover the shortfall.

Taking into account all of the commercial real estate analysis, the third phase involves the use of a sensitivity model to calculate the amount of credit enhancement, if any, needed to ensure full and timely payment of principal and interest on the bonds. The sensitivity model involves a two-step approach, with the first step a cash flow analysis. The second focuses on the relationship of the building's market value to the amount of outstanding debt. Moody's sensitivity model essentially gauges the capacity of a building to withstand extremely soft market conditions and a simultaneous increase in interest rates while continuing to meet the contractual obligation under the bonds held by investors.

Commercial real estate portfolios lend themselves fairly well to cash flow securitisation structures. If a market value structure is used, commercial real estate may be difficult to liquidate in a short time period in most markets; thus, adequate protection must be available for any potential delay.

8. LEVERAGED BUY OUT DEBT AND CORPORATE BONDS

A review of the collateral risk for pools of investment grade corporate debt, junk bonds or leveraged buy out (LBO) debt relies in part on a study by Moody's of defaults and losses on rated securities. The study reviews historical defaults and losses, over various time periods, on debt initially rated in each of Moody's rating categories.

The pool of assets to be rated are compared with the results of the study. The amount of credit enhancement (or overcollateralisation) needed for the transaction depends on the distribution of the pool among the various rating categories and on the probability of default for each category, with the adjustments as discussed below. The number of firms are very important to the analysis, as are the number of industries to which these firms belong. Anything that would cause defaults to be correlated, such as common customers, industries whose well being is tied to one supplier or even similar vulnerability to escalating interest rates or energy prices, can substantially increase the likelihood of multiple defaults in the collateral pool and are therefore considered by Moody's.

It should be noted that bond portfolios must be actively managed, especially those that contain bonds or debt at the lower end of the rating scale. Therefore, the expertise of the manager and the rules that govern the manager's options can affect risk and must be factored into the analysis.

Corporate debt, whether highly rated bonds or unrated LBO bank financings, can be securitised using either the cash flow or market value structures. However, the liquidity of markets for each may differ significantly among the different types of debt in a market value transaction.

D. Legal analysis

A number of legal concerns must be considered in rating a receivables-backed transaction. Normally, these are insolvency and conveyancing issues that are applicable to any type of structure. They are:

(i) the impact of the insolvency of the originator, the administrator or other third party on the ability of the issuer to meet its obligations to investors;

(ii) the impact of an insolvency of the issuer on investors;

(iii) the potential impact of various forms of assignment of the assets from the originator to the issuer (and trustee) on payments by the issuer to investors;

(iv) the consumer protection laws under which the assets were originated, which might cause the assets to be unenforceable in accordance with their terms;

(v) the impact of regulators and their rules for off-balance sheet financing on the credit quality of the issuer. We also look at the corporation tax implications for the issuer.

1. INSOLVENCY OF THIRD PARTIES

The insolvency of third parties may have a significant impact on the ability of the issuer to meet its obligations to investors for many reasons, in addition to those discussed above. The insolvency of the originator of the assets might result in the liquidator or administrator for the insolvent entity being able to reclaim certain assets sold, or moneys paid by the insolvent party, to the issuer. The insolvency of the administrator of the loans might result in the delay or loss of funds passing through the accounts of the administrator. In a few cases, the insolvency of the administrator may result in the acceleration of the debt obligation of the issuer.

Our analysis is based in part on the various powers available to:

(i) the court on the application of a liquidator or administrator of an insolvent third party to set aside transactions with the issuer:
  (a) it determines to be at an undervalue; or
  (b) to be an extortionate credit transaction; or
  (c) where it determines the issuer (as a creditor of the third party) has been preferred over another creditor; and

(ii) a liquidator to disclaim unprofitable contracts with the issuer (or other onerous property);

and the validity of floating charges and the unenforceability of security interests in certain circumstances.

If any of these remedies will potentially be available to the liquidator or administrator for an insolvent third party, the amount of potential loss must be very small or the risk must be substantially mitigated. Transactions at an undervalue may arise as a result of the administrator subsidising the rates charged by the issuer on the collateral so that the issuer is not required to raise its rates above the current market rate.[1] As these subsidies often do not have any limitation on their size, in certain circumstances the risk can be substantial.

In the circumstances where the transaction is structured to offer both senior and subordinated debt (senior/subordinated transactions are discussed below) and the originator or related third party purchases the subordinated debt from the issuer, Moody's examines the impact of the purchase on the issuer. In particular, we determine whether the sale of the assets coupled with the purchase of the subordinated notes could amount to a transaction at an undervalue giving the court, on the application of the liquidator or administrator, the power to set aside the whole transaction.

2. IMPACT OF THE ISSUER'S INSOLVENCY

In a market value transaction, the credit risk associated with an issuer's insolvency is that the collateral cannot be liquidated at a price sufficient to cover the issuer's obligations to investors in the time period required. Our analysis of such risk has been discussed previously.

In a cash flow transaction, the credit risk associated with an issuer's insolvency is much more complex; therefore, the analysis of the collateral and the cash flows are very important. Insolvency may result under two circumstances: (1) cash flows into the issuer from the collateral or any other sources are not sufficient to meet the obligations of the issuer; or (2) the liabilities of the issuer (including contingent and prospective liabilities) exceed its assets. The first is addressed in our analysis of collateral and cash flow. The second, however, may result from the way in which the accountants and lawyers for the issue structure the various liquidity and funding facilities of the issuer. If loan facilities are worded improperly, or are paid down at speeds that do not match the amortisation of the capitalised initial expenses, the issuer may become insolvent because its liabilities exceed its assets, even though it has enough cash flow to meet debt service. The loan facilities must not create a liability of the issuer that is not perfectly matched by an offsetting asset.

Moody's has been advised that for the issuer not to include its obligation to repay these loans (generally loans used to fund start-up costs and expenses) in its calculation of assets and liabilities for funding purposes, the obligation of the issuer to repay the loan must be subordinated and be enforceable only to the extent funds are available. These loans are generally only repayable after all the senior debt has been retired.

---

[1] Subsidies may occur when the administrator (which is also the originator of the mortgage loans) wishes to keep the mortgage interest rates charged by the issuer at the same level as all other mortgage loans originated by it and originated by other mortgage lenders, in order to remain competitive. The special purpose issuers of securitised debt are often required to charge an interest rate to borrowers sufficient to cover all of their funding costs and expenses unless certain third parties contribute cash to them to cover part of these costs.

3. IMPACT OF VARIOUS FORMS OF ASSIGNMENT

The analysis of the impact of various forms of assignment varies considerably, depending on the type of collateral securitised. With each type of asset, Moody's analyses the extent to which the borrower and others retain rights with respect to the originator. These rights, if significant, may seriously impede the ability of the issuer or the trustee in a securitised transaction to enforce the obligation of the borrower and the cash flows between the borrower and the investor.

Typically, each of the mortgages in a mortgage pool contains three constituent parts, namely, the mortgage debt, the legal mortgage of the property and the charge over the endowment policy. Each of the three may be transferred from an originator to an issuer by way of either legal or equitable assignment. Equitable assignments, although less costly, and operationally easier as between originator and issuer, can add significantly higher levels of risks to noteholders than legal assignments. These risks, which broadly centre on whether borrowers are aware of the transfer of their mortgage, as well as on fraud or mistake on the part of the originator, include the following:

(i) *notice*. Legal assignments of the relevant rights will, usually, require that notice is given to the necessary parties of the issuer's and then the trustee's interest in the securitised loans. Notice is given to the relevant borrowers and insurance companies and, in the case of registered land, the transfer is recorded on the register of title at HM Land Registry. No such notices are typically given in connection with equitable assignments. Consequently, third parties, including the borrowers, not realising that some or all of the originator's mortgage assets have been assigned to an issuer may attempt to attach (or exercise some right of set-off in respect of) the mortgage collateral in satisfaction of the originator's outstanding debts. That would increase the likelihood of delays in the receipt of scheduled payments under the rated notes as the matter is debated through the courts. Furthermore, the originator may, either by mistake or by fraud, purport to assign collateral that has already been assigned in equity without the purported assignee being aware of the prior assignment. In the case of registered land, such third party assignees will search against the property at HM Land Registry and, if the issuer's interest in the underlying mortgage collateral is not recorded there, the third party would not thereby discover the prior assignment and could take free of it.

(ii) *priority of rights*. If the equitably assigned mortgage collateral is capable of being transferred to another third party, whether by mistake or by fraud, the third party's claim to the underlying mortgages could take precedence over the issuer's claim if the mortgages were assigned to the third party by a legal assignment;

(iii) *borrower's right of set off*. A borrower may have the right to reduce payments to the issuer to the extent that the originator owes a borrower money if the borrower has not been given notice of the transfer of the mortgage.

Providing that borrowers are made aware of the transfer of their mortgage or that borrowers waive all rights of set off, this risk can be eliminated. Neither of these practices, however, has been actively used in sterling mortgage-backed securities incorporating equitable assignments of the securitised mortgage collateral;

(iv) *direction of mortgage payments.* In the absence of notification to a borrower, the borrower may legally pay the originator instead of the issuer without the issuer having any legal recourse to block such payments. Should the originator become insolvent or fail to remit these moneys to the issuer, noteholders would be likely to suffer delays or losses under the notes because the borrower would have no further obligation to the issuer for the sums paid to the originator.

Moody's considers each of the risks associated with equitable assignments in light of the credit quality of the party granting the equitable assignment. In certain circumstances, the issuer may procure insurance that provides protection against delay and loss resulting from the equitable assignment or may use some other means to achieve that result. Moody's will consider each support mechanism in its analysis of the risks.

4. IMPACT OF CONSUMER PROTECTION LAWS

Consumer protection laws may have a significant impact on the ability of the issuer and the trustee to enforce an obligation against the borrower. If a consumer protection law is systematically violated, even inadvertantly, the entire collateral pool may be rendered unenforceable against the borrowers.

If loans are less than £15,001, they may fall within the Consumer Credit Act 1974 which, among other things, provides for licensing and other control of traders concerned with the provision of credit or the supply of goods on hire or hire purchase. If the licensing requirement has not been met, the debt may be unenforceable. Many mortgage-backed transactions avoid this Act by excluding mortgages of this amount from the securitised pool, which may not be an option for many other types of collateral.

Other consumer protection risks that must be considered include the ability of the borrower to cancel the loan agreement if it is less than one month old and the ability of a consumer to terminate his or her contract and return the asset it was used to purchase after a certain amount has been paid under the contract. These are only a few of the risks that must be reviewed when evaluating the impact of these laws on a securitised transaction.

5. IMPACT OF REGULATORS AND THE INLAND REVENUE

The Bank of England and the Building Societies Commission have both actively formulated rules regarding what constitutes an 'off-balance sheet' financing for institutions regulated by them. These types of rules often stimulate changes in the structures of proposed transactions that may create additional credit risks unless adequate protections are in place.

The way in which the issuer is taxed must also be considered. Stamp duties or higher tax rates may cause liquidity problems. Withholding or interest deductions rules may result in difficulties in meeting cash payments. The administration of MIRAS payments may create cash flow delays. Many other aspects of the regulatory environment in which the issuer exists must be considered as well. These tax considerations have already been explored more fully in Chapter 3.

E. Cash flow analysis

For certain types of collateral, the third phase of our analysis is modelling the structured transaction. A flexible computer model is built that allows one to run many different stress tests using varying assumptions. Because structures are often complex, the ramifications of various environments and nuances in the legal documentation may not be readily evident, unless this modelling is undertaken.

There is no one 'worst case' environment, because what is stressful to one structure may be a strength in another. Therefore, the interactions of many different variables need to be reviewed at all points in the potential life of the transaction.

Moody's uses its own models to evaluate structures, in addition to models developed by issuers and intermediaries. The accuracy of the latter computer models is assessed through interviews with program designers, an examination of the program code, a partial re-creation of relevant cash flows and/or a letter from an accounting firm stating the model's accuracy. Once satisfied that the model reflects the structure outlined in the legal agreements, various loss, arrears, redemption and interest rate scenarios are used to stress for liquidity shortfalls and interest accruals on shortfalls. Structures permitting a reduction of credit enhancement before full redemption of the rated securities are stressed during periods when enhancement is low.

The securitisation of certain other assets are modelled on a case-by-case basis, depending on the type of the structure and the coverage of the credit enhancement. In each transaction, however, the question is the same—will mis-matches in the timing or amounts of cash flow between the collateral and the investor result in a delay or default in payment to the investor?

Shortfalls resulting from structural defects or weaknesses could occur under many different circumstances. One of the more substantive risks for mortgage-backed securities occurs because the notes pay interest on a quarterly basis while the underlying assets pay interest on a monthly basis. As borrowers can pre-pay their loan at any time, the amount of interest earned on receivables during any quarter may be less than the amount of interest payable on the notes.

Some structures are more susceptible to risk of credit losses on the asset pool than others. For instance, mortgage-backed securities that are solely reliant on mortgage interest rates to cover noteholder payments, as well as the issuer's expenses, are more susceptible to mortgage default losses than those which rely on third parties to cover expenses. This is because the financially more able borrowers are likely to pre-pay their existing mortgage loan in favour of another lender having lower interest rates when costs of the issuer are high in relation to the pool of mortgage loans outstanding. Moody's will review that incremental risk and its mitigating factors in assessing the support level needed. That risk is not as great in programmes that provide for some form of shortfall contingency fund, because the reserve gives the administrator latitude to set market related mortgage interest rates.

SENIOR/SUBORDINATED STRUCTURES

Senior/subordinated structures (also known as A/B or senior/junior structures) use certain cash flows and principal distributions, otherwise due to holders of an obligation of the issuer which is subordinated to the rated security, to provide credit enhancement for the collateral backing the securities. This type of structure is adaptable to the securitisation of residential and commercial mortgage loans, credit cards, automobile receivables and other assets. However, they are complex and require sophisticated computer models to evaluate fully the credit protection available for the benefit of investors.

Currently, three variations of the senior/subordinated structure are being used in the various securitisation markets: one employs an initial deposit and reserve fund for liquidity and maintenance of credit support, another maintains credit support by shifting interests in the collateral pool between the junior and the senior note holders as redemptions and losses occur and the third (most commonly used in the United Kingdom) maintains credit support by using all interest and principal cash flows from the collateral to pay the interest and principal due on the senior obligations before paying interest on the junior.

Some senior/junior structures do not place any restrictions on the amount of credit losses the subordinated security will bear, while others limit the credit enhancement to the original principal balance of the subordinated security—a significant distinction that must be recognised when modelling the structure. The structure that does not place any restriction on the credit enhancement available from the subordinated tranche has all cash flows that would otherwise be paid to the junior security available for this coverage. In a transaction where the mortgages pay 13% interest, and no credit losses occur, this cash flow would be as large as 425% of the par amount of the junior security. The structure that does restrict the credit enhancement would only have 100% of the par amount of the junior security available for credit protection.

The timing of arrears and losses, and whether they occur within a short time period or over the entire 25 years of the transaction, will have a significant impact on the difference between the two structures. For instance, if principal losses on the pool of assets in an amount equal to the par amount of the subordinated security occur very soon after completion of the transfer of the assets to the issuer, very little interest will be due to the subordinated security and available to cover interest arrears that are subsequently deemed losses before the subordinated security is reduced to nil.

Moody's has also rated the A and B securities of related structures that are known as A/B/C structures, where A is the senior obligation of the issuer (rated Aaa or Aa2), B is a rated junior obligation providing part of the credit enhancement (often rated Baa1 or Baa2), and C is an unrated obligation, junior to both A and B, that provides the initial level of credit enhancement. We understand that these structures, to date issued only in the United States, offer significant benefits to issuers seeking a way to reduce the costs of securitisation.

F. Conclusion

Moody's is always willing to review new structures or different types of collateral. The extent to which new structures and collateral can qualify for our highest ratings depends on their ability to withstand the type of analysis described above. These new ideas can often be implemented if the credit risks to investors are adequately addressed and the investor is willing to buy the investments they create.

Many different structures have been rated by Moody's. Adjustable rate securities have been backed by fixed rate collateral. Assets with uncertain redemption speeds have been used to back investments with fixed redemption dates. Interest and principal paid by the securitised assets have been used to create two separate bonds, one repaid only out of interest on the collateral, the other only via principal redemptions.

In each circumstance, to qualify for Moody's highest ratings, the investor must be assured of receipt of principal and interest in the amount and on the due dates promised. All structures rated at the AA and AAA level must meet this standard.

Chapter 9

Opportunities and Risks—an Insurance Company Perspective

Stephen Haines
Commercial Union

Securitisation offers a plethora of opportunities for insurance companies. However, it is unlikely that any particular insurance company will be in a position, or even be willing, to avail itself of the whole range of products on offer. Insurance companies are by their very nature conservative entities and will play to their strengths. This means that some products will not easily fit their strategic thrust whilst others may offer a logical enhancement to current product thinking.

The most obvious new business opportunities range from providing pool insurance on a pool of mortgages to be securitised to help enable the issuer to effect a satisfactory rating from Standard & Poor's or Moody's to writing contingency policies, standard bricks and mortar policies, endowment policies and the much quoted mortgage indemnity policies which bring the loan to value ratio down to a satisfactory level for risk/rating purposes. Obviously any insurance company that surrounds a pool of securitised mortgages with the level of comfort required by the rating agencies will itself need to have a claims payment rating at least commensurate with that of the required level of the issue itself. If the insurance company rating is below that level, the ratings of the reinsurers will need to be of sufficient quality so as not to affect adversely the overall rating of the pool. Originally there was a problem with a non-rated insurance company providing more than 25% of the endowment policies on any rated pool of mortgages. However, this problem is less likely to occur in the future as the rating agencies are becoming more comfortable with UK mortgage exposure and the real level of risks the investor is exposed to. Further, the rating agencies recognise that if the average life of an issue is five to seven years, an endowment policy will not have attained sufficient value by that time to offer the investor any additional comfort if the mortgage is being enforced so early during its term.

Before considering further whether the new business opportunities are attractive to insurance companies, it is important to remember that some originate their own mortgages. An understanding of why an insurance company wants to originate mortgages and what the company's relationship or involvement is with current mortgage providers enables one to see more clearly the nature and attractions of the actual insurance products provided.

MORTGAGE ORIGINATION

One of the main concerns an insurance company will have if it originates mortgages is to control the origination of mortgages in a formal and structured environment thereby ensuring that a life policy is tied around every mortgage originated through the efforts of either the company or its tied intermediaries. The structured environment may entail the establishment of mortgage specialist desks within life branches where mortgage desk staff are comprehensively trained to understand all the various products on offer from the mortgage funders, namely those specialist lenders, banks and building societies with whom the insurance company has a special relationship. The funders will be called the insurance company panel or in the case of building societies the tied relationship. The mortgage desk sales staff are trained to analyse the applications for mortgages from the tied intermediaries who channel their applications either through the life inspectors to the mortgage desks or approach the mortgage desks directly. A direct sales force will, of course, have personal contact with the clients whereas the life inspector has to act in an intermediary role between the tied intermediary and the mortgage desk. The mortgage desk staff will pre-package the mortgage requests by obtaining credit checks, and proof of income where appropriate, take up references and arrange for a valuation. These pre-packaged mortgages are then carefully fed into the panel member whose criteria are best suited for a particular application. Where a direct sales force is concerned, there may be only one or two centralised mortgage desks where complete advice is given on how to obtain and fill in any required information on the forms provided to the direct sales force. These applications are submitted to the mortgage desk for checking and final submission to the funding panel members.

In times of high levels of liquidity in the market any originator of mortgages who is not competing in the funding of mortgages is much in demand from both panel members and the tied building societies clamouring for their quota of mortgages to fund. In times of high mortgage demand but limited funding availability due (inter alia) to balance sheet constraints, securitisation offers continued funds availability for panel members and societies who might otherwise have temporarily to turn off the tap on the originator insurance company, a disastrous scenario for the flow of life business. Obviously in the case of the new special purpose mortgage lenders or funders who are members of an insurance company panel, securitisation is already the established funding route thereby ensuring the flow of mortgage funds as long as the investor base continues to purchase these issues.

RELATIONSHIP WITH FUNDS PROVIDERS

The relationships that exist between the insurance companies as mortgage originators and the panel members or tied societies as providers of funds cover a broad spectrum. They include building societies where a local branch relationship is strong or a tied national relationship exists where the society receives commissions from the insurance company in excess of 100% of the LAUTRO commissions. The insurance company promises to fill a quota of mortgage origination applications and submit these to the society and in return the society recommends only the insurance company's products. In essence, this gives the society an added benefit of only having to understand and sell one brand of products rather than a whole range of products that an independent society would have to sell. Together the society and the insurance company may develop bespoke products to cover niche markets or even develop products for securitisation which will retain a separate identity from the society's brand name mortgage products so as not to confuse the market. This would be for the sole purpose of achieving off-balance sheet funding thereby enabling the society to fund these products without making demands on the society's current funding sources.

Although a few insurance companies do fund some mortgages on their own books it is unlikely to be a major development which would compete with other funders such as the societies because the main *raison d'etre* for any insurance company is clearly insurance products. Mortgages are a vehicle to the insurance business.

Other relationships include the panel members where there may not necessarily be a formalised tie but rather a relationship where the insurance company is one of a number of insurance companies originating mortgages for a particular lender who may also be on the panel of another insurance company. In the case of some of these panel members funding is in part facilitated through securitisation. Depending on the volumes of mortgages introduced by an insurance company to the mortgage lender or panel member, the lender will dedicate staff to look after the insurance company, train the insurance company's mortgage staff and liaise with members of the insurance company's marketing and training staff to develop new products such as low start mortgages, 100% mortgages or even currency mortgages if they fit the demand and distribution network of the insurance company. Panel members could include the specialist mortgage lenders who were the first to reap the benefits of securitisation or banks who, in addition to acting as panel members, may participate in agency agreement lending. In such cases the insurance company originates the mortgages which a third party processor promises to service and the bank, either foreign or UK, offers funding. A foreign bank may want sterling asset exposure; a UK bank may have the eventual structuring of off-balance sheet funding in mind. The processing service is already offered by some special purpose lenders and independent processors; however, it is unlikely that insurance companies, even with their large back office administration systems for the collection of endowment and general insurance policy premiums through the direct debit system, will wish to compete in this by-product of securitisation.

Finally, there is the involvement of a particular insurance company, Commercial Union, with The Chase Manhattan Bank, NA in a joint venture where an important avenue for securitisation has been further developed and refined. This is particularly helpful in approaching both tied and non-tied societies with ideas that may enable a society to achieve off-balance sheet funding in a favourable interest rate environment as well as enabling the insurance company to lock into a source of mortgage funding and to develop niche and specialised products that promote the life business.

The relationship of insurance companies with the funds providers (the building societies, the special purpose lenders and the banks) all depends upon the enormous distribution network insurance companies have at their command. Building societies may have over 7,000 branches, and banks over 13,000. Insurance companies, however, can tap into an estimated 14,000 broker firms, many of which are already tied, thousands of sales persons who are commission driven and tens of thousands of solicitors and accountants who can have substantial influence over what mortgage a client eventually takes. Life companies, through their salesforce, their tied intermediaries and through independent brokers, are constantly talking to clients about their financial needs, including mortgages. The potential distribution system is enormous.

INSURANCE PRODUCT OPPORTUNITIES

The second main area of new business opportunities for insurance companies in securitisation is in the realm of insurance products that help to enhance the credit of a pool of mortgages about to be securitised. These products include the mortgage indemnity guarantees, contingency insurance and pool insurance. Following on from the credit enhancing products are the general products which increased funding/origination through securitisation helps to foster. There are the products distributed to the mortgagor, such as endowment policies, building insurance, house contents and redundancy cover, and those products distributed to the lender, such as block cover for buildings insurance.

Not all insurance companies will take the same view that mortgage indemnity guarantees (MIGs) are good business. Some companies may have written large amounts of these policies previously to help them to enter the mortgage origination market through a type of block policy; however, as the market and hence the risk exposure has grown exponentially in the past few years, the insurers are scrutinising these policies much more closely and some have increased their prices. In essence, these policies reduce the exposure of the lender to an acceptable level of the outstanding loan to property valuation. This may be in the region of anything from up to 100% down to 75% depending on the rating requirements for a particular pool of mortgages. The premium, of course, varies dramatically if the risk is 100% and falls off sharply from 95% down to the acceptable level of, for example, 75%. The premium is paid by the mortgagor and is a one-off payment. In the event of a mortgagor's default and a claim by the lender, the portion of the loan covered by the insurer is paid out to the lender thus mitigating the lender's liability on the insured portion. Where the insurance company is not rated and the mortgages covered by the MIGs are to be securitised, the MIGs will need upgrading through a rated insurance company, which may well be through the rated provider of the pool policy.

Contingency insurance comes in a number of forms. Basically, contingency policies are taken out to protect against certain remote physical, legal and commercial risks involved in residential mortgage lending activities in England and Wales. These risks may include potential fraud by professionals involved in the house purchase. Contingency insurance is also effected to cover losses arising in circumstances where a mortgage does not conform to the warranties given by the lender on the sale of the mortgage to the special purpose vehicle for securitisation. If the rating for a pool of mortgages is to be AA or AAA, the rating agency or agencies may insist on a commensurately rated insurance company providing the contingency policy.

POOL INSURANCE

The other area of credit enhancement is, of course, the pool policy. This is certainly an area which may fit the product thinking of some insurance companies but not others. If the rating of the pool provider is not commensurate with the issue rating, there must be further enhancement by appropriately rated reinsurers. The rating agencies will set the level of cover required having exhausted their worst case scenario tests to see what cover is needed to enable the note holders to emerge whole out of a catastrophe. The cover may typically range from 6 to 8 or 9% cover for losses sustained within the pool. However, at a certain level, once the risk element has been covered, it is relatively inexpensive to insure the whole pool for 100%.

In assessing the risk in writing pool insurance the insurance underwriters will need to take a number of factors into their calculations. These include:

  (i) the economic conditions in the territory, particularly those that affect the domestic housing market and the specific history of house price fluctuation;
 (ii) the lending policy of the mortgage funder including status enquiries, the borrowers' credit history, ratio of income to debt service, other debt and a breakdown of eligible property categories;
(iii) the lender's policy for dealing with arrears;
 (iv) the profile of the pool of mortgages which will include LTV information, the geographical spread, the number and size banding of the mortgages,

the percentage element, if any, of unconventional mortgages (low start etc) and leasehold/freehold proportions;

(v) the 'cut in' point for specific underlying mortgage indemnity guarantees;
(vi) the maturity analysis of the pool and the proposed policy on substitution and further advances;
(vii) the lender's past experience;
(viii) the existing arrears and default position;
(ix) the results of the rating agencies' review of the pool.

If the underwriters are comfortable with the risks assessment, the insurers of the pool policy will calculate the premium required properly to reflect the risk undertaken by the insurance company. This involves the application of the historic arrears/repossession data which will be adapted for any changes in economic conditions and adjusted for any positive or negative features of specific pool characteristics. The calculations will show a 'maximum loss within reasonable profitability'. This figure will be grossed up for acquisition and handling costs and a profit margin. To this figure the insurer will add a risk factor for losses between the maximum probable and the indemnity limit representing the catastrophe element.

When the very first securitised issues were launched over two years ago there was some talk in the insurance market of capacity problems. As the market has grown and more reinsurers have entered the market through the efforts of insurance brokers, this capacity has also grown to the point where there would appear to be no immediate problems for new issues using insurance cover. As these securitised issues have an average life of five to seven years, and as the issues pre-pay at an average of perhaps 15% per year, tied insurance capacity will be released for new policies thus freeing up some of the market. In addition, with an improvement in the loan to value ratio of well seasoned mortgages some three or four years into the life of a pool, insurers may be more comfortable with a higher risk exposure to the market. Certainly some insurance companies not currently in the market are examining their appetite for such business which will, perhaps, further extend insurance capacity.

POOL INSURANCE VERSUS SENIOR/SUBORDINATED STRUCTURES

The current debate in the market for asset-backed structures is whether the issuer is best served by using 'wrap around' pool insurance or by using senior/subordinated structures where the unrated junior portion of debt takes the first loss on any defaults. Obviously there is no clear cut 'best advice' as to which route to follow. One may well expect an insurance company to advocate the former at all costs. That should not be the case as there are good reasons for using both routes.

The senior/junior route which involves the junior notes providing insurance for the senior notes by absorbing any mortgage defaults and liquidity shortfalls is especially applicable to those issuers where the opportunity cost of capital is of prime concern. If the issuer is concerned to achieve the highest possible return on capital, the senior/junior route is very attractive. There are no upfront insurance premiums to pay and the return on capital can be up to 30% higher than using a conventionally structured security backed by pool insurance. The cost of credit enhancement in such a transaction is paid over the life of the issue in the form of a higher coupon on the subordinated bonds thus appealing to issuers with limited capital available. The cost differential between the senior/junior route and pool insurance including (respectively) the incremental cost of the subordinated tranche, the cash cushion in the form of a deductible or capital fund held in escrow and the pool insurance premium is somewhere in the region of 0.15% per annum for senior/subordinated debt versus 0.17% per annum for an insured structure. This assumes pricing (including commissions) of LIBOR + 0.25% per annum for the AAA rated FRN with a seven year life and LIBOR + 1.09% per annum for the subordinated tranche (equal in size to 10% of the AAA rated FRN issue) with an average life of ten years.

While the cost differences are not large on a per annum basis, the real advantage in using the subordinated structure as opposed to the insurance route is where any initial outlay of capital represents not just a capital cost but an opportunity cost to the issuer. If the amount either in the form of a deductible or capital fund or the amount of the pool insurance premium could be used as capital to support the debt that continues to finance the mortgage loans made by the issuer, the opportunity costs will equal the lender's capital costs. This in essence means capital will be tied up and not be available to fund mortgages. If, however, the issuer has a high degree of liquidity, the opportunity cost becomes less important. Subordinated tranches are not always easy to sell in the market, although this is improving, and pool insurance can be more accommodating for an issuer where there is a steep increase in the amount of loss cover required by a rating agency. The amount of the subordinated tranche may have to grow to cover the increase in direct proportion to the increase whereas insurance cover may be proportionally less expensive and more accommodating as the insurer may take a view both on the risk and the relationship with the issuer. If the investors in the junior notes ever suffer a delay in receiving interest or receive only part of their interest on the due date, even though they are aware they assume any first losses, this could make such issues uneconomic and much harder to sell. The question also arises as to whether, in such a case, the issuer feels morally obliged to support the issue even though this is certainly not legally required. Such a question does not arise in an insured issue.

The return on capital requirement, the availability of capital, the average life including further advances and substitution, the relationship with an insurer, the make-up of the mortgage products to be securitised and, perhaps, the concern of the issuer having a moral commitment may all determine the issuer's choice of credit enhancement. The important consideration for the issuer as a whole is that there is an alternative to pool insurance which will not only contribute to competitive pricing for credit enhancement but will also free up insurance capacity in the market.

CONCLUSION

In conclusion one needs to ask whether insurance companies would be likely themselves to undertake the issue of mortgage-backed obligations, a natural progression from originating mortgages, whether they would invest in these securities and what capital adequacy requirements, if any, there would be.

There is certainly no reason why an insurance company should not issue such obligations. Some are already deeply committed to doing so through a third party funder or funds arranger, such as the Mortgage Funding Corporation with its in-house Treasury operation, both using its own mortgages or on a shared basis with another originator as we have seen in one of the recent HMC issues. This can cause problems with panel members or tied societies if the insurance company has such relationships and uses its own brand name mortgages, especially in a flat market with suppressed demand. However, what is unlikely is that an insurance company will wish to use its own balance sheet to finance its mortgage business and, if it does, certainly for no great length of time. Until very recently the market had not seen an issue directly by the XYZ insurance company—instead we have seen issues of XYZ insurance company mortgages issued by a special purpose vehicle such as Mortgage Funding Corporation No 1 plc which is managed and administered by MFC. This issue is clearly at arm's length from the insurance company whose mortgages comprise the pool of mortgages within the issue. There is, of course, no reason why an insurance company could not set up its own finance vehicle for the sole purpose of issuing mortgage-backed obligations either under another name or its own name, although there could be balance sheet accounting implications in using the insurance company name. However, in December 1989 Legal & General securitised some of its mortgage portfolio through a £175 million issue by Temple Court Mortgages (No 1) plc, an off-balance sheet vehicle. Whether more insurance companies will follow suit and issue securities through a third party or through their own finance vehicle is difficult to say. It really depends on the sensitivities with existing tied relationships.

Presently relatively few life and general funds invest in mortgage-backed obligations and for each issue in the market there are only three or four insurance companies who may take up to 5% of the issue into one of their funds. Insurance companies are not governed by the same rules and regulations as set out by the Bank of England for banks investing in mortgage-backed instruments. However, they are required to maintain certain minimum solvency requirements calculated in terms of net assets as a percentage of new life premium income. In calculating what the net assets are the insurance company applies accounting rules as set out by the Department of Trade and Industry. Any intended investments above a certain size are deemed inadmissible for solvency margin purposes. The minimum solvency margin under EEC requirements for non-life business is approximately 16%. The admissibility rules are the same for the life business but the solvency requirements are calculated differently. In essence, insurance companies have to bear in mind the effect any investment would have as to whether the investment would or would not be deemed inadmissible. Certainly as the securitisation market continues to grow and deepen and as the gilts market contracts it seems probable that the managers of the life funds will seriously consider investing in such securities once the accounting requirements have been clearly defined within the company. This would also possibly apply to any general funds once the liquidity of the secondary market is fully developed. The stability of the housing market, the credit enhancements due to the strict stress tests applied by the rating agencies and the historically low default rates offer a solid investment opportunity. One can only assume as the market continues to mature that these facts will be appreciated by more and more investors including insurance companies.

Chapter 10

The Role of the Trustee in Issues of UK Mortgage-backed Securities

Anthony G. Buckland and Julie Craik
Bankers Trustee Company Limited

INTRODUCTION: THE CONCEPT OF CORPORATE TRUSTEES

A. The fundamentals of trusteeship: duties, principles and discretion

It was Albert Camus who said,

'Integrity has no need of rules.'

Obviously the drafters of the Financial Services Act thought integrity needed a little help. Professional integrity, the kind you pay for, now has many rules. Their enforcement is the responsibility of many agencies from the Bank of England to the self-regulating organisations such as The Securities Association or IMRO.

In fact, one financial 'guard of honour' has been around for centuries. For trustees, rules are nothing new; nor are financial markets and services which have long been a major employer of their services.

It is particularly interesting that the trust has once again come into its own as a central part of the MBS structure and therefore part of a structure based on the ownership of real property. In this sense it is returning to its English roots. By the thirteenth century, the trust concept was certainly known and may have originated in Roman law. However, early records show that the 'use', as it had been known since the ninth century, was, in the thirteenth century, a method whereby land was conveyed to boroughs for the use of Franciscan friars, who could not otherwise own property. Obviously, the holding of assets off-balance sheet is no new idea.

The hallmarks of the involvement of a trustee in bond issues and other financing structures are often stated to be flexibility and protection, primarily for the lenders but, by virtue of their joint representation by a single entity, also for the borrowers. Trustees are widely recognised to be an enhancement to a variety of financing structures and they are considered a necessity for asset-backed finance such as mortgage securitisation.

Several fundamental principles govern the activities of trustees and enable the corporate trustee to provide a unique business service. Developed over centuries, these principles are now more relevant than ever with the pressures on the contemporary banking and finance systems to be highly progressive and at the same time cope with increasing government regulation.

For their part, trustees, being endowed with wide discretion, can make a major contribution in facilitating the progressive approach. At the same time they assist in responding to the demands of the regulators because trustees must observe legal and equitable duties and principles in the exercise of their discretion. Conversely, this does not produce a rigid system. The constant inter-action between duty and discretion means that the actions of the trustee are not necessarily determined but may instead be guided by such principles. In essence they must give careful and impartial consideration to the exercise of both discretion and duty in the knowledge that, at any time, they may be called on to justify their decisions.

A paid trustee is expected to exercise a higher standard of care than an unpaid trustee, particularly where the service offered is that of a professional trustee, which is the subject of our discussion here. As such, he is expected to deal with a trust in the same way that any prudent person in business would deal with his own affairs, and to do so with 'honesty, integrity and fairness'. Phillip Wood states:

'the fiduciary must act with due diligence, in the best interests of the beneficiaries, in good faith and must not allow his interest to conflict with his duty.'

As an exercise of their discretion, trustees are given power to agree to modifications of documents and to waive breaches of their terms. The guiding rule here is that neither must be deemed to be materially prejudicial to the interests of the noteholders. In practice the trustee will consult with a lawyer and seek an opinion to this effect as part of the process of exercising this discretion. The trustee may also require expert advice in other areas, particularly in relation to financial alterations.

PRIVATE PLACEMENTS

It is worth mentioning at this point that trustees are not appointed to act solely for public Eurobond issues but also for private placements. This is where the issue is never publicly launched but is created as an investment vehicle for an individual bondholder or small group of holders. A number of privately placed, mortgage-backed issues have subsequently been publicised such as Blue Chip Mortgage Pass-through Securities and MFC Finance No 1 plc.

The role of the trustee is unlikely to differ from that for a public issue, the major difference being that, in general, where an issue is a private placement, the trustee cannot disclose the fact of its appointment for the issue.

B. Trustees and issuer default

It is interesting that much of the comment on the role of the trustee naturally emphasises their protection of the noteholders or lenders, particularly in the event of default by the issuer.

Why would a borrower see this as a good reason to be the party which should appoint a trustee and, more importantly, pay for the privilege?

Defaults leading to enforcement against the borrower are certainly not everyday events but one case provides a dramatic example.

1. FIRST CASE STUDY

In 1987, a much troubled Canadian oil company, Dome Petroleum, found itself in default on loans amounting to C$6.3 billion. It was attempting (and reported to be succeeding in) worldwide negotiations with bondholders and bank lenders for interim payment waivers in order to gain time to restructure its debt. The negotiated agreement was conditional on there being no enforcement action by any bondholder. Despite having reached agreement with 53 out of 54 banks and a clear majority of the public noteholders, Dome found itself being sued by the Swiss holder of a SFr 50,000 Note in a Zurich commercial court. There was no trustee on the issue; instead, there was a fiscal agent, an agent of the borrower.

Dome had already had to contend with threatened action by a West German bank lender owed $4.8 million and Swiss holders of C$240,000 of unsecured issues. At a meeting of Swiss lenders, a majority voted to permit the waiver sought by Dome. Non-voters, however, remained free to act.

Dome argued that, given time, the re-financing and re-structuring of its debts would enable a greater amount to be paid than would be the case if the company were liquidated at that stage. The majority of lenders was prepared to agree. The action which ensued jeopardised not only the agreements in relation to the Swiss debt but all the agreements.

Leaving aside, at this stage, jurisdictional problems in relation to trusts, what the borrower and most of the lenders had witnessed was the impact of the fundamental difference between a fiscal agent and a trustee.

As we have said, a fiscal agent is the agent of the issuer and, in reality, a paying agent. He does not represent the bondholders. Fiscal agency agreements are, consequently, more restricted in their scope. The Swiss issue documents did not provide for bondholder meetings nor impose any restriction on the activities of an individual holder nor render a decision of the majority binding on non-voting or dissenting bondholders. What is even more startling is that, even in the absence of a major default, a simple, technical default could open the way to litigation against an issuer by any single bondholder, the consequences of which could be disastrous for the issuer. It is obvious that the interests of noteholders must be paramount for a trustee but when we come to discuss this in more detail, we will see the techniques and methods by which, had there been a trustee in the right place at the right time, the vast majority of lenders and Dome itself might not have found themselves subject to the wishes of a solitary noteholder.

Of course, these events were happening to a company in a notoriously volatile industry against a background of heavily falling oil prices. Surely, asset-backed securities ought to be more soundly based.

2. SECOND CASE STUDY

A recent American case may serve as a warning that all participants in this market should be vigilant to the risks.

The case involves the California Student Loan Finance Corporation whose loans are guaranteed, within certain terms and conditions, by the United States Federal government. According to the reports, when the servicer converted from one computer system to another, there was a massive loss of data and, as a result, failure to service the loans within those terms. In particular, delinquent loans were not pursued. In this case, the Federal government may not be liable under its guarantee and there is, therefore, some doubt as to whether banks which provided CSLFC with letters of credit will be repaid. Losses may run as high as US$400 million.

The trustee has since replaced the servicer. The case also illustrates one reason why trustees, perhaps seen by some as a procedural rather than substantive requirement, truly earn their living. That they are not in a comfortably immune position is shown by the action which is being taken against the trustee itself, partly, it is said, in an effort to increase pressure on the trustee to reach agreement with the US Department of Education over the guarantee. It should be made clear that no conclusions have yet been reached as to the liability, if any, of the trustee or where liability should properly fall.

The fact is that trustees have one of the best reasons in the world to perform their function to the necessary standard; in doing so on behalf of beneficiaries of that trust, trustees also protect their own interests and in the event of litigation (which is a risk for any business) receive vindication.

C. Trustee perspective on the securitisation market

Bankers Trustee Company Limited is a trust company which was established in England over 50 years ago. The name reflects the fact that the company is a subsidiary of an American bank within which it is part of the Corporate Trust and Agency Group which operates from New York, Luxembourg, London and the Far East.

The company acts as trustee for many types of complex financing structures including mortgage-backed securities based on both domestic and foreign mortgages.

High on the list of priorities for trustees of mortgage-backed securities is contact with the market. It is essential to stay in touch with developments both in the retail mortgage market and in securitisation. If the retail market is slow, securitisation may decrease until business picks up again.

From a client service point of view, the fact that a securitised issue is made, for example, by an insurance company as opposed to a building society is unlikely to determine in principle the trustee's approach to dealing with that issue. In the event of a trustee acting for any of these entities it is essential and, hopefully, reassuring to be aware of the regulatory systems and rules which they must observe.

From a marketing point of view, regulatory systems governing each group are just one factor which enable us to understand changes in their participation in the market and in meeting their funding needs and consequently provide opportunities for trustee services.

Mortgage funders and providers fall into four main categories which are, of course, building societies, banks, insurance companies and specialist mortgage companies. As far as securitisation is concerned there are still relatively few active participants. All the public mortgage-backed securities and various private placements have, in the main, been lead managed by a small group of investment banks. Most public issues have been the product of specialist mortgage companies established over the last few years.

TRUSTEES AND TRUST COMPANIES

A. English corporate trustees

In many ways the advent of securitisation has prompted new focus on the identity of the trustee and the quality of service it will bring to the role. To many involved with securitisation, what was previously just a name on the prospectus has emerged as a real company or independent group within a major bank or insurance company. Over the centuries of evolution of the trust, where the emphasis was on those for private, family or charitable purposes, trustees themselves were, of course, individuals and frequently professional advisers.

In the United States there are in excess of 3,000 trust companies. In the United Kingdom, there are 120 members of the professional body, the Association of Corporate Trustees or TACT for short. Apart from unit trusts and pension funds, relatively few of these provide corporate trust services at any level, and fewer still offer this as a specialised and independent business in relation to domestic loan stock and Eurobonds, let alone structured and secured finance. Those that do are staffed by full time trust officers and administrators who have specialist knowledge of the capital markets.

In the United Kingdom trustee companies are regulated mainly by the Public Trustee Act 1906, the Trustee Act 1925 and the Trustee Investments Act 1961.

Since 1988 trustees have been subject to the new system of regulation under the Financial Services Act and most have sought membership of IMRO, one of the self-regulating organisations. The main thrust of the regulation of trustees now seems to be aimed at controlling any investment activities. This is likely to be rare for bond trustees but the impact of the FSA on trustees in this respect has been discussed further in Chapter 2.

B. Comparison between US and English trustees

The philosophy of trustees in the United States and the regulation of US trustees has developed in a noticeably different direction to that in the United Kingdom.

Looking specifically at US corporate trustees, their role was increased in order to provide greater protection for bondholders in the face of increasing corporate defaults on their debt. Following the 1929 financial crash, there was a complete review of all markets and the result was the Trust Indenture Act of 1939, known to all in the business as the TIA.

Fundamentally, as long as a bond issue progresses in the normal way with all payments made as they fall due, the discretionary authority of US trustees may be much more precisely defined than for English trustees. After a default, however, it appears to be the case that discretion may be more broadly construed in the trustee's favour.

Pre-default, trustees apparently have to adopt a 'text-book' approach in their dealings with respect to any trust. For example, US trustees have always been very much more circumspect about powers of investment and will expect to be provided with highly specific instructions, usually within the Trust Indenture. Trustees have been more directly regulated and face reasonably heavy reporting obligations in respect of the trusts for which they are responsible and they may also face greater liabilities for any failure to adhere to the strict conditions of the Trust Indenture.

In the United Kingdom the courts have tended to examine the approach of the trustee in dealing with a particular problem and then decided whether the trustee could be seen to have acted prudently and properly in the circumstances and in good faith.

Under the TIA, the 'prudent man' standard must be included in Trust Indentures specifically in relation to the trustee's actions on default by the issuer. Robert Landau comments as follows:

'It is axiomatic that imposition of responsibility should be accompanied by the grant of sufficient power and authority to discharge it properly. Yet what occurred was the establishment of a new standard of conduct for indenture trustees without any change in its limited authority. The prudent man in managing his own affairs can take any action that seems to be indicated by the circumstances. The same is generally true with reference to the classes of fiduciaries to which the rule has been applied heretofore. As applied to indenture trustees, it will be noted that the trustee is limited to the exercise of the rights and powers vested in it by the indenture.'

US trustees, in taking what may be considered as appropriate action in default circumstances, may, therefore, find that they are having to do so on the basis of power that is implied to their position rather than expressed within the Indenture and, in this way, putting themselves beyond its protection. They are thus facing two levels of uncertainty: first, the existence of their authority to take particular action and, secondly, that of the standard to which they must act and the principles they may follow in exercising such authority or discretion.

This is a complex area to which we have only provided an introduction here but this serves to highlight one of the key aspects of the role of trustees, the nature of their discretion.

THE STRUCTURE OF MORTGAGE-BACKED SECURITIES

Each of the two possible trustee appointments can be seen in the diagram opposite. The structure of certain issues has resulted in the shares in the vehicle company being held by one trustee (the trustee shareholders) with a different trustee acting as the issue trustee.

In the lower half of the diagram is the traditional Eurobond role of the trustee. A professional corporate trustee or trust corporation is appointed by the issuer to represent the bondholders. Their initial investment provides funding for the issuer for the purchase of the mortgages. The issuer also appoints, as *its* agent, a principal paying agent. The trustee ensures that the principal paying agent pays both interest and principal to the bondholders and that the issuer observes the terms and conditions of the notes issued. For the trustee, the key documents are:

  (i) the prospectus or offering circular including the terms and conditions of the notes;
 (ii) the Trust Deed;
(iii) the Paying Agency Agreement;
(iv) the Agent Bank Agreement.

However, in a securitisation, the trustee has an equally important role. It holds the security for the issue which is designed to ensure that the noteholders are paid in full and on time. This security consists of all the assets of the issuer including the pool of mortgages and the rights it has against various parties such as the mortgage servicer who administers the mortgages and collects

STRUCTURE OF BOND ISSUE
MORTGAGE - BACKED SECURITIES

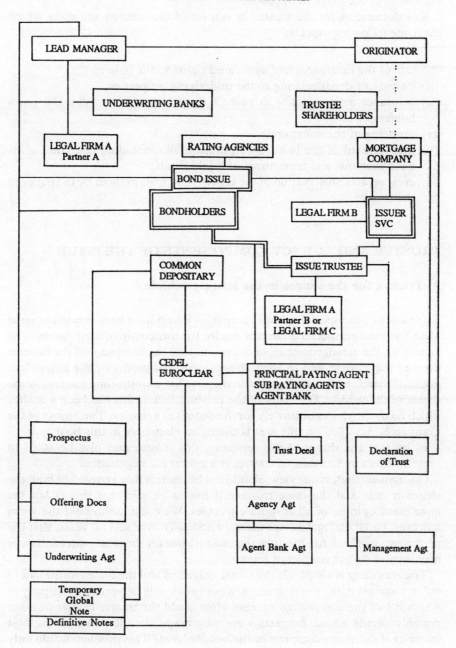

interest, principal and other payments on behalf of the issuer. This is illustrated in the diagram opposite.

Key documents for the trustee in respect of the security are those which cover the following aspects:

  (i) sale of the mortgages and associated rights to the issuer;
 (ii) custody of deeds relating to the underlying properties;
(iii) insurance arrangements to protect the issuer (and thereby the note-holders);
 (iv) servicing of the mortgages;
  (v) management of the issuer's corporate affairs including operation of its bank accounts and investment of liquid funds;
 (vi) creation and preservation of the security interests granted by the issuer to the trustee.

TRUSTEE AND AGENCY COMPONENTS OF THE ISSUE

A. Trustee for the shares in the issuing vehicle

The nature of the special vehicle companies which have been created to issue MBS has entailed special arrangements for the ownership of their shares. The motive for the arrangement is, of course, to take the company off the balance sheet of the 'parent' and to allow the extraction of profits by the latter. It is essential therefore that an independent entity has a controlling interest in the shares of the vehicle. On many of the existing issues, this has been a trustee which holds the shares ultimately for the benefit of a charity. The impact of the Companies Act 1989 on this area is discussed elsewhere in this book.

In holding the shares of the company, this trustee may also be asked to provide directors but this, of course, is a matter for negotiation.

One request that, in our view, should not be made is that a trustee be both the shares trustee and the issue trustee. It has to be said that this is not the unanimous opinion of all corporate trustees. We continue to hold the view, however, based on legal advice taken periodically over several years, that the performance of both functions by the same trustee for the same issuer and issue may involve a clear conflict of interest.

The reasoning is simple. If the issuer defaulted and the issue trustee had to enforce against it, the ensuing action would obviously be against a company in which it had the controlling interest. How could the trustee in that position possibly decide whose interests were paramount, let alone act in the best interests of either the company or the bondholders? This problem would only be intensified if the trustee had also provided the directors of the issuer as, in that case, the trustee group would effectively be suing employees of the same organisation.

STRUCTURE OF SECURITY
MORTGAGE - BACKED SECURITIES

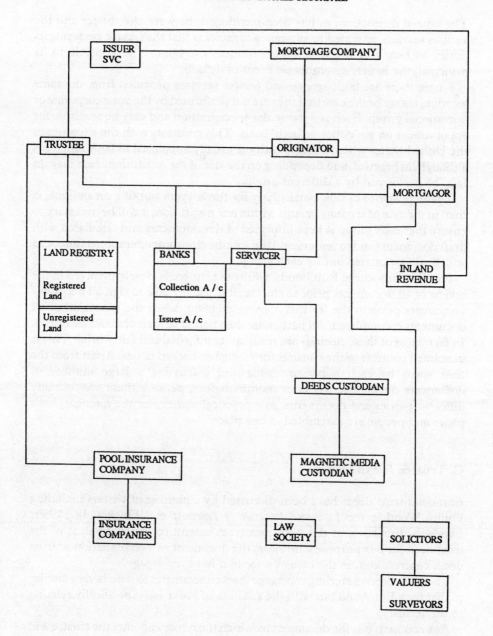

B. Agency services

The crucial distinction, as has been mentioned, between the trustee and the various services provided in an agency capacity is that the trustee performs its duties on behalf of the noteholders whereas the agent is responsible to its principal, the issuer, assuming no event of default.

Where there are both agency and trustee services provided from the same location, it may be the case that they are not performed by the same corporate or operational group. Each is a particular specialisation and may be available for appointment on an 'either or both' basis. This contrasts with the situation in the United States where a single entity is usually appointed to both functions although, in practice, and depending on the size of the institution, each may, in fact, be performed by a different group.

The importance of this, particularly for the lawyers working on an issue, is that, in the case of separate groups within one institution, it will be necessary to ensure that each group is kept informed of developments and circulated with draft documents and to understand the specific closing or operational functions which will be carried out by each group.

For most unsecured Eurobonds, whilst the trustee is closely involved in the review of all documents prior to closing, it is usually able to sign all necessary documents prior to the 'formal' closing meeting, when the execution of all documents is completed. All parties are then bound to their contractual duties. In fact, most of these closings are really quite informal and fairly brief. This is in marked contrast to the closings for mortgage-backed issues. Apart from the time spent by each party reviewing and discussing a large number of documents during the weeks or months before, because there are so many different parties and documents, as a practical matter, for the moment, both paper and people are assembled in one place.

C. Trustee for the issue

Eurobond trust deeds have been discussed by a number of writers including Phillip Wood in the *Law and Practice of International Finance*. In Robert Landau's discussion of the American trust indenture, the equivalent of the trust deed for our purposes, he views the document as a combination of trust deed, contract and, in the case of a secured issue, mortgage.

The trust deed in sterling mortgage-backed securities to date is very similar to that for a Eurobond but with the addition of provisions specifically relating to the security.

As a contract, it is the document by which the issuer appoints the trustee and details their respective rights and duties. As a trust deed, it incorporates the terms and conditions of the issue as direct obligations between the issuer and the trustee and is, therefore, enforceable by the trustee. The trustee's security interests are constituted by the deed of charge.

On the trust aspects, the corporate trustee is distinguished from the personal trustee in a number of important respects:

(i) the corporate trustee may not take possession and deal with any security until after an event of default;
(ii) it cannot exercise the same control over the issuer as that by a personal trustee over its trust property and is not, theoretically, under the same duty of care;
(iii) a personal trustee deals directly with his beneficiaries. The bond trustee may never see his beneficiaries. Most contact is with the issuer.

A number of the terms and conditions of the notes themselves draw the attention of the noteholder to the more detailed provisions contained in the trust deed. A standard format is as follows:

(i) general summary of the issue;
(ii) form (almost always bearer only), denominations of individual notes and title to the notes;
(iii) the secured status of the notes;
(iv) summary of the nature and creation of the security interests in respect of the notes;
(v) negative pledge covenant, whereby the issuer undertakes not to permit charges to be created on any of its assets and not to incur any indebtedness other than relating to the notes;
(vi) covenants not to engage in any other business or have subsidiaries;
(vii) interest payments, fixing and publication of interest rates;
(viii) final redemption, optional and mandatory redemption;
(ix) form and method of payment to noteholders;
(x) prescription (limitation) periods for payments on the notes;
(xi) payment of withholding tax and no grossing up obligation;
(xii) events of default and methods of enforcement of notes by the trustee;
(xiii) provision for noteholders meetings and, in respect of the trustee, power to agree to modification of terms and substitution of principal debtor and to waive breaches of terms of all connected documents;
(xiv) indemnification of the trustee including for the trustee's fees, costs and expenses;
(xv) replacement of damaged notes and coupons;
(xvi) provision for giving notice to noteholders;
(xvii) governing law.

Certain terms are provided in greater detail in the trust deed including the following:

(i) limitation on the principal amount of the notes, details of the form of the notes and the mechanics of their issue;

(ii) covenant by the issuer to pay principal and interest and provision for this to be effected through the paying agents;

(iii) covenant by the issuer to observe the terms of the issue and the provisions of the trust deed;

(iv) covenants by the issuer in favour of the trustee such as those:

    (a) to maintain paying agents in appropriate locations;

    (b) to keep proper accounts;

    (c) to give notice of any event of default;

    (d) to supply certificates signed by directors of the issuer confirming that there have been no events of default and that the issuer has observed all the terms of the issue;

    (e) to supply accounts and other information as requested;

    (f) to ensure that the principal paying agent notifies the trustee in the event of any failure duly to receive funds from the issuer;

(v) provisions supplemental to the Trustee Act 1925 in favour of the trustee including the right to obtain and rely on professional or expert advice and details of the exoneration of the trustee from liability except in the case of its own negligence or default;

(vi) exoneration of the trustee from liability for obligations or warranties in respect of the security interests and the trustee's entitlement to assume due performance of obligations by the servicer and others in the absence of actual knowledge of any default;

(vii) provisions for the appointment, removal and retirement of the trustee.

The above summaries are intentionally brief but some issues to which they give rise are discussed further below.

TRUSTEE RELATIONSHIPS: THE ISSUE

A. The noteholders

Of all the people affected by a bond issue, the group which the trustee may be least likely to see is the noteholders. Trustees may occasionally see bondholders when they personally present coupons to the principal paying agent if they are both at the same office location. In addition, bondholders may be able to inspect copies of issue documents at the offices of the trustee.

The nature of the relationship of trustees to the noteholder beneficiaries in respect of a bond issue is essentially a formal one. Obviously this contrasts with the position for personal trustees where the relationship is much more likely to be just that. The trustees will try to gain an understanding of the specific and individual needs of their beneficiaries.

As a Eurobond is usually a bearer instrument, there can be no definitive conclusion on any factor as to the identity of their holders or investors including financial strength and sophistication or nationality. Sterling mortgage-backed securities are held by banks and large institutional and corporate investors in the UK and abroad but they may also be held by the 'Belgian dentist'.

BONDHOLDER MEETINGS

The most important possibility of contact is the bondholders' meeting. There may come a time during the life of any issue when the trustee cannot find justification within the limits of its discretion to agree to certain proposed amendments or to waive certain breaches of the terms of the issue. The trustee may, nevertheless, feel that it would not be right to reject the proposals without ascertaining the views of the bondholders.

Typically there will be provisions in Eurobond trust deeds for the calling of meetings by the issuer, the trustee and a specified number of noteholders. There will be a separate schedule detailing the methods of holding meetings, giving notice to bondholders and voting by proxy or in person. In addition there will be provisions detailing special matters which require both a high quorum and high majority vote in favour.

The latter may include any proposals to alter the form or dates of payments, alterations to the security for the bonds or alterations to the meetings provisions themselves.

Issuers may obviously prefer it if a decision is such that the trustee can agree without recourse to the bondholders but the presence of the meetings and majority voting provisions in the Trust Deed is designed to protect both investors and issuers.

For issuers such provisions can be seen as a 'limitation of liability' as opposed to the unlimited liability which might result from their absence in that any bondholder could take action against the issuer, even for relatively trivial reasons.

For investors, as we have seen in the Dome case, if a majority decision is legally able to bind all the bondholders, this should prevent a minority taking or succeeding in an action to the detriment of the majority, if not everyone.

B. Lead managers and issuers

Our introduction to an issue commences when we are contacted by the lead manager or directly by the issuer (in practice, those creating the issuer). Trustees prefer to be involved earlier rather than later even if a project is at a tentative stage and does not ultimately lead to the planned issue actually launching. Trustees, by the nature of their business, maintain the confidentiality of such information because it is on this basis that they are able to keep their place in the market.

Even if the issue does not proceed, the exchange of information at this point can prove valuable and informative for future projects. The trustee keeps in touch with the market and the lead manager or issuer gains a better understanding of the functions a trustee can perform. Trustees are also in a position to provide useful guidance on the appropriate strategy to avoid practical problems which could delay completion or arise from the proposed structure. They are likely to have been involved in many complex deals and so bring a different perspective to any discussion.

It is particularly the case with MBS that potential trustees should be carefully interviewed prior to the final appointment decision being made, although this does not always appear to happen. It is obviously essential to establish that the relationship will 'work' between the personalities involved and that the trustee has the necessary technical expertise, administrative systems, resources and sheer commitment to do the job.

C. Rating agencies

On rated issues, the importance of the trustee's position has led, for the first time in the United Kingdom, to the trustee itself coming into contact with the rating agencies. They do not maintain or provide official ratings of trustees as such, but, as can be seen from their published issue rating procedures, Standard and Poor's and Moody's appear to put a high priority on their analysis of each participant in an issue. For trustees, their ratings or assessment of key parties such as the pool insurer and the servicer and of the structure of the issue are important and instructive factors.

For issuers and lead managers, the rating agencies' knowledge of a trustee should also be an important determinant in the selection process.

Trustees and rating agencies have been able to derive benefits from establishing what could be termed a 'dialogue' although, clearly, there is never a question of either breaching their duty of confidentiality.

As closings draw near, particular problems crystallise and require resolution. In many ways, the rating agencies and the trustee share mutual concerns. Where the issues impact on these areas, direct discussions between the two can produce swift, practical and satisfactory solutions.

D. Lawyers

The choice of lawyers is a vital consideration because their role is fundamental in bringing an issue to its conclusion. Certainly, the lead manager and the issuer must be advised by different firms. In theory, trustees should use a third firm and do so in a number of cases. This may be particularly appropriate where a particular firm advises the trustee on multiple issues by the same issuer (and consequently retains the trustee's standard documents for that issuer on file and is completely familiar with the history) and also where the issuer works with several different lead managers, each using their own, customary legal advisers.

A Eurobond tradition has developed, however, whereby trustees use the same firm as that advising the lead manager (never the issuer), each being advised by different partners. The advantage here is the natural 'short circuiting' which should be possible by virtue of this arrangement.

The trustees and consequently the position of their legal advisers in any negotiations is to ensure that both their own rights and interests and those of future noteholders are protected and enforceable.

The protection by the trustees of their own interests is not a contradiction in terms, although this does, of course, include the simple commercial one of ensuring that they are entitled to payment for the duration of the issue. The protection of their 'rights' is obviously crucial for trustees must be put in a position where they can perform effectively in terms of discretion but (where necessary) agree guidelines for certain procedures to avoid protracted discussions in those areas during the life of the issue. One particularly important right (which also protects noteholders) is that of the trustee to consult lawyers, appoint agents or obtain other professional advice and to be reimbursed all such costs and expenses.

Operational, structural and business aspects of the issue are all proper areas of concern for the trustee to the extent that these have an adverse effect on such rights for technical, legal or practical reasons or represent a risk factor. Trustees are aware that there is a fine line to be drawn between this and the perception by lead managers and issuers, which trustees prefer to avoid, that they are 'interfering' in the deal itself. Where the concerns of the trustee are perfectly legitimate, however, and it is not possible to change the relevant term or terms of the issue, the trustee will wish to ensure that there is either sufficient emphasis on, or warning about, these aspects.

Once an issue has closed, it is down to the issuer and the trustee to establish their working practices. Contact will be much more regular with the issuer of mortgage-backed securities than with the issuer of a straight Eurobond and the trustee may have to continue in contact with his legal adviser as the issue progresses.

TRUSTEE RELATIONSHIPS: THE SECURITY

The trustee will want to know as much as possible about the companies carrying out the various functions which affect the security for the issue and it is advisable to visit them prior to closing if possible. In fact, a formal due diligence check should, in any case, be completed by the lead manager at this stage and the trustee has the further comfort of the initial and subsequent auditing processes. We believe that the trustee should continue to make such visits regularly after an issue has closed. It is through such visits that the trustee will learn about and understand the techniques used by the servicer and the custodian. Such meetings also provide the opportunity to establish a working relationship and discuss possible or actual problems.

A. The servicer

The growth of the mortgage servicing business has largely been due to a combination of increased demand for mortgages and the development and availability of computer systems with sufficient capacity to meet the demand. Trustees are not appointed to undertake systems reviews, as such. Practical demonstrations by the servicing staff, however, are helpful and instructive in gaining an overall appreciation of the servicing operation.

It is useful to start by looking at the key stages in processing mortgages from initial applications through routine collections and arrears procedures. It is when we come to this last aspect that the operation is likely to require a more personal approach and to be carried out by a special group or team.

In particular, prior to closing, it is useful for trustees to make a point of confirming with the issuer and the lead manager that technical staff of the servicer have been fully briefed as to what will be required, particularly in terms of data, both in time for the closing of the issue and subsequently.

Stated very briefly the servicer will carry out those duties detailed in the agreement appointing him including:

(i)   setting the mortgage interest rate;
(ii) the general monitoring of each mortgage and collection of interest payments and other moneys;
(iii) dealing efficiently and in an acceptable way with arrears;
(iv) enforcing the security, if this becomes necessary;
(v)   ensuring the safe custody of documents;
(vi) ensuring that all appropriate insurance policies are maintained;
(vii) managing/operating the investment and flow of funds and certain special funding or insurance arrangements such as those to cover shortfalls in receipts.

POSSIBLE PROBLEMS

An important aspect here is that trustees should ensure they have power to set the mortgage rate, if the servicer fails to set it at a sufficiently high level or if the need arises for any other reason. This can cause servicers some concern at the negotiation stage but the fact is that trustees do not act capriciously and would only expect to have to take such a step in the most extreme circumstances.

In the trustee's interests, there should be reasonably extensive reporting requirements on the servicer including in particular reports on arrears and action taken, periodic minimum lending rate and any estimated shortfall or surplus in receipts against the moneys required for payments on the notes. Bank statements on the collection and issuer's accounts will probably be sent directly by the appropriate banks but it should be for the servicer to ensure that this is done.

In relation to computer data tapes, we find it preferable for an agreed number of 'spare' sets always to be in the hands of a specialist magnetic media storage agent. This agent undertakes that he will never allow the release of tapes so that the remaining number of sets will be reduced below a fixed minimum. By the nature of the article, they must be updated regularly, so all the tapes are likely to be out on rotation at some point.

The trustee should also have the power under the servicing agreement to remove the servicer if there is due cause within the terms of the servicer's appoinment, for example, if the servicer:

  (i) fails to make payments when due;
 (ii) fails to carry out its duties or observe its covenants and does not remedy this within a specified time;
(iii) ceases business or is wound up or put into liquidation;
(iv) is incompetent or unable to carry out its duties to a satisfactory level.

Certain terms in the documentation attempt to provide for the aftermath of such a dismissal including the question of access to computer tapes, facilities and information. A trustee should, however, be alert to the possibility of complex problems in this area; particularly, where the compatibility of different computer systems is concerned and any resulting difficulties in accessing data or ensuring that the integrity of data is maintained during the process of transferring it from one system to another.

B. Servicer of last resort

The ultimate step would be for the trustee to assume direct responsibility for the servicing function based either on in-house resources or contingency arrangements made with alternative servicers; this is the so-called servicer of last resort agreement. Whilst agreement with the trustee on this point remains a matter for negotiation with individual issuers, the rating agencies may place increased emphasis on this aspect in future. In the United States, as a practical matter it is 'industry standard' for trustees to offer mortgage servicing and, as a legal matter, if they are not themselves the servicer, they are usually bound to act as servicer of last resort.

C. The deeds custodian

It is preferable for this to be an entity which is completely independent although the servicer will require reasonable access to collect deeds. However, the officers of the deeds store itself should retrieve deeds from their storage site and log them out and vice versa on their return.

The concept of most deeds storage systems is relatively simple. At the simplest level, trustees should make periodic visits to check that a random sample of deeds which are supposed to be present are, indeed, there. Provided there is a logical numbering sequence it should also be possible to check that deeds marked out are not there but, short of going through every deeds packet, not to mention the entire deeds store, such a check can never be perfect. It may be worthwhile to confirm that a sample of deeds packets which are marked out are actually at their intended location, if not in transit.

The custodian should also supply regular deeds location reports.

Like the servicer, the trustee can dismiss the custodian subject to the conditions of the appointment.

FUNDING ARRANGEMENTS

Again, we will look at particular aspects which may concern the trustee depending on the structure of an issue.

A. Insurance

It is essential to obtain a clear picture of the range of insurance cover available to the issue, to understand any special claims provisions or procedures, such as those available for shortfalls in receipts.

Possibly the most important aspect as far as the trustee is concerned is the form and level of pool insurance for an issue. This is generally intended to cover against default by the underlying mortgagors and should make up any shortfalls in principal or interest following the enforcement of the mortgages and the sale of the mortgages involved. The precise terms of pool insurance cover will, of course, vary from one issue to another and levels of cover have included limits ranging from 10% to 100% of the principal amount of the issue.

Above all, the trustee should be satisfied that the insurer is rated at a sufficiently high level. In fact, although this should never be assumed, the latter is more than likely to be the case in view of the requirements of the rating agencies.

Another key issue for negotiation is whether failure by the pool insurer to pay should be an event of default. The outcome will depend on the strength of the parties' negotiating positions although it is usually accepted that exhausting the level of cover under the pool policy will be an event of default.

B. Senior/subordinated structures

One area which does not appear to have received a great deal of public discussion is the position of the trustee in relation to structures which, in effect, self-insure using a subordinated issue of notes of perhaps 10 or 15% of the principal amount of the senior notes. The subordinated notes bear shortfalls or losses on the mortgage portfolio and effectively provide a cushion in respect of such losses to the senior noteholders. As a practical matter the trustee may not have any real problem where the subordinated issue is purchased by a company within a group of which the issuer is a member or which is otherwise connected with the issuer.

The concern to trustees arises where external investors purchase the subordinated notes because, strictly speaking, he is acting as trustee on two secured bonds of the same issuer, albeit senior and subordinated. Despite the nature of both notes being made clear prior to their issue, trustees are alert to the disruption which could be caused if the notes actually failed to pay in full. The trustee could face a conflict of interest in its attempt to represent both groups of noteholders in an action to enforce against the issuer. If the trustee judges that a conflict has indeed arisen, the documentation usually provides that the trustee will have regard only to the interests of the senior noteholders. If it became impossible for the trustee to continue to act in relation to both the senior and subordinated debt, the trustee might have to resign from one appointment in favour of a substitute trustee.

C. Investments and deposits

At the negotiation stage, the trustee should fully understand the nature of any investment or deposit arrangements and the types of entities through whom these will be effected. For example, there may be a set of objective, minimum standards or criteria drafted. It is certainly worthwhile for the trustee to ascertain for itself or ask for information about the availability of institutions meeting the criteria and, in practice, those that are likely to be used. One pitfall can occur where the bonds are to be rated by more than one rating agency but the relevant entity, which may in all other respects be acceptable, has been officially rated by only one agency.

D. Bank accounts

One particular area which trustees see as a weak link in terms of control, because increased vigilance is required by the servicer and by bank staff, is the use, on some issues, of separate collection and issuer accounts.

The collection account is usually for all receipts by the servicer and inevitably means that the issuer's funds are co-mingled with other receipts into that account. Such an account system may then rely on 'manual' transfer across to the issuer's account of its own receipts.

The trustee would obviously prefer it if mortgage payments due to the issuer could be paid directly into the issuer's account as this would avoid the weak link which arises where reliance is placed on human intervention to transfer funds into the issuer's account.

As the vast majority of mortgage payments appear to be on a direct debiting system, it would certainly appear to be possible for receipts against the appropriate portion to be diverted to a specified and approved destination. However, trustees are also realistic enough to understand that what may seem to them to be technically possible, may not be practical.

THE SECURITY INTERESTS OF THE TRUSTEE AND ENFORCEMENT OF THE ISSUE

It is the security side of MBS issues which mean increased responsibility for the trustee and an increase in practical involvement with both the issuer and parties which carry out the various functions mentioned previously. A detailed examination of the various documents is beyond the scope of this chapter. We will confine our review to the areas of particular importance to the trustee.

A. The security interests of the trustee

One of the most fundamental aspects for the trustee is the nature of the security interests which he and the issuer will acquire through the sale and charging of the mortgages and the actual conveyancing mechanics used.

Typically, the originator or owner of the mortgages enters into an agreement for the sale of the mortgages to the issuer and executes transfers to the issuer in respect of all its rights (ie the charges by way of legal mortgage over the borrowers' properties) in both registered and unregistered titles. Trustees should ensure that they are in possession of the documents of title which will enable registration and, consequently, the perfection of the issuer's and the trustee's interests at HM Land Registry. The trustee will also require an irrevocable power of attorney in its favour for this purpose.

The crucial aspects of this process for the trustee in many ways mirror the constitution of the issue itself. The contractual element which establishes the issuer's rights in the mortgages and, therefore, the property in which the trustee will have its security interests pursuant to the issue, is found in the sale agreement to which the trustee may be party.

The trustee looks to the deed of charge for its own security interests vis-à-vis the issuer and the mortgages. It is through this document that the trustee must obtain first, fixed, legal or equitable assignments by way of security of all the issuer's rights in the mortgages.

Assignments in favour of the trustee should also cover the issuer's interests in all forms of investments and deposits, insurance policies, including any pool policy and the issuer's rights in respect of bank accounts (both the servicer's collection account and the issuer's own account), all agreements and documents which form part of the issue and the MIRAS payments due from the Inland Revenue.

LEGAL AND EQUITABLE CHARGES

Specifically, registration is 'enabled' rather than effected if the issue is structured in such a way that both issuer and trustee acquire equitable rather than legal interests. In this case, the issuer under the sale agreement and the trustee under the deed of charge are bound not to file for registration until the occurence of events given rise to the need or right to do so.

It is, however, vital that the trustee ensures it is put in the best possible position to effect registration within the shortest time if it ever came to this. For this purpose it should obtain from the issuer (or in reality the servicer) all the essential components, such as title numbers, which the Land Registry requires to be present on the applications for registration. It is useful if the trustee makes direct contact with the Central Land Registry periodically to check on current waiting periods. If registration had to be effected, the formalities would obviously be carried out by lawyers on the trustee's behalf.

Most issues have gone the equitable route, though not all. Certainly, legal charges are preferable for a number of reasons which are discussed in Chapters 2 and 8. However, they may mean the direct involvement of the trustee in servicing procedures, for example, if the trustee begins to receive a regular weekly, if not daily, flow of correspondence in relation to the mortgages which form part of the pool. These may be letters from solicitors requiring to know balances payable on redemption (ie on the sale by the mortgagor of the underlying property) and require to be followed up with a telephone call to the relevant firm if the case appears to be urgent and subsequent forwarding of the mail to the servicer.

This does represent an increased administrative work load for the trustee but, more importantly, because the trustee is now a link in the servicing chain, it does not want to become a source of delays. It is, therefore, imperative that, from the outset, the trustee works with the servicer to develop a routine way of handling various different items.

B. Enforcement by the trustee

Whilst remedial action by the trustee may be limited to replacement of the servicer, the specific failure by the servicer may also be an event of default under the terms of the issue and, as such, may require more severe action by the trustee.

There should also be an event of default in respect of the issue where:

(i) the issuer fails to pay principal and interest when due;
(ii) the issuer fails to carry out its duties or observe its covenants and does not remedy such failure within a specified period;
(iii) either of the issuer or the pool insurer ceases business, is wound up or put into liquidation.

The trustee may respond to an event of default by declaring the notes immediately due and payable. In all cases except where there is failure to pay principal and interest, the trustee must decide whether or not the event in question is materially prejudicial to the interests of the noteholders. Alternatively, it must also accelerate the issue if requested to do so by a set proportion of the noteholders (for example, 20%) or if directed by an Extraordinary Resolution.

The trustee will want to be able to exercise the right to perfect its security interests in the mortgages. It should also be able to do this where it considers that the charged property is in jeopardy or where it is legally obliged to do so as a result of a court order.

In any of these circumstances, it is likely that the trustee would consult with the lead manager, with lawyers and any other specialist adviser as necessary.

Following the trustee's declaration that the notes are immediately due and payable, it may serve an enforcement notice and, at the request of the noteholders, will have to do so.

The trustee's remedies will include:

(i) the appointment of a receiver;
(ii) an action for the debt, for the sale of the security as a complete package or in part or the enforcement of it; and
(iii) taking possession of the charged property.

The trustee will have a floating charge which will entitle it to appoint an administrative receiver ahead of the appointment of an administrator. Of the above options, the trustee may well select that to appoint a receiver and for this purpose would employ a specialist firm, possibly an accountancy firm.

Trustees might consider it inappropriate to take possession themselves, because they would then become responsible for the property. In any case, trustees would not usually have the systems or administrative infrastructure to deal with the mortgages. They would prefer to be able to find a purchaser for the whole mortgage portfolio but this may not be feasible in the economic environment at the time. If not only the issuer but also the borrowers are in default, the trustee may well have to proceed against several hundred borrowers and try to realise the security as best it could. This is likely to be a cumbersome and time-consuming process. It is possible that the issuer would be in default but the servicer would not, in which case the trustee may not have to involve itself too closely in the day-to-day enforcement procedures against borrowers. However, it is more likely that the servicer will also be in default and instead an alternative servicer would have to be found to take on the task. What steps a trustee will actually have to take in these circumstances can never be known in advance and it is to be hoped that the matter is never put to the test.

Chapter 11

Topical Issues in a Developing Market

Nigel Terrington
National Home Loans Holdings plc

This chapter considers four topical but unrelated issues—market development versus diversification, pre-payments, profit extraction and off-balance sheet considerations. Each illustrates how the market is developing and the participants are becoming more experienced.

MARKET DEVELOPMENT VERSUS DIVERSIFICATION

Issuers of mortgage-backed securities have varying motives in arranging such transactions. At the one extreme is The Mortgage Corporation which generates assets for sale as soon as a reasonable size has been achieved. The original motive was quite clearly a means by which its parent, Salomon Brothers, was able to establish a footing and develop the sterling market enabling it to underwrite and trade in securities. After all Salomon is a securities house not a savings and loans institution. This position was exemplified by the launch of TMC No 11, a £500 million FRN with four separate tranches. At the time of launch many of the mortgages did not exist and were originated subsequently.

Some few months later TMC announced the launch of its PIMBS structure—a £3 billion two year mortgage-backed security programme. A permanent dealer group was established consisting of Salomon, Baring, Warburg, Morgan and CSFB and one of the main aims of this arrangement was to establish a 'commodity' type approach with low issuance costs to the mortgage-backed transactions.

A different approach has been adopted by many of the less regular issuers, including NHLC.

National Home Loans Holdings is a mortgage portfolio lender. With a capital base in excess of £200 million, economic theory suggests that you should securitise only when the capital becomes scarce. However, this is a question of timing. In a rapidly developing and changing market and with a major diversification programme substantially underway the balance sheet capacity could change within a relatively short period. Notwithstanding this we perceive the mortgage-backed securities market as a strategic means to achieve our treasury goals:

(i) diversification;
(ii) reducing costs;
(iii) matching maturities.

NHLC has been criticised as being the champion of innovation at the expense of assisting in the development of the home market.

Sterling as an investment currency has been volatile. The floating rate note market has been affected by this volatility but also by the seeming illiquidity of the mortgage-backed securities, over supply of paper by the building society movement and other external factors.

The early transactions by NHLC, TMC and HMC were launched into a market without an investor base. They were of a relatively small size, illiquid and generally placed in the banking sector because of the lack of a natural investor. It could take weeks for the lead manager to distribute all of the securities, compared to a matter of hours now. Some were sold with puts to a third party at five and seven years essentially converting securities into banking assets.

The participants in the banking community perceived very little difference between a loan to NHLC or HMC and an investment in a rated mortgage-backed security, originated and serviced by the same company. There were two main results:

(i) banks would aggregate investment in these securities with straightforward corporate loans to the originator/servicer, thereby restricting capacity for further on-balance sheet borrowing. One of the fundamental principles of securitisation is to free up bank lines and transactions were therefore falling at this first hurdle;
(ii) the banking community began to dictate that these securities should pay margins in line with those achievable under bank lines. The result was that mortgage-backed pricing moved up. This development coincided with the substantial demand by the new wave of mortgage lenders of loan facilities to finance on-balance sheet mortgage portfolios. The relationship of supply and demand between borrower and lender moved heavily in favour of the latter. Banks were being shown proposals on a seemingly daily basis and were able to dictate pricing.

At about this time one or two issues came to market with prices leap-frogging over each other and the distribution mechanism was highly questionable. The market was looking frail.

Despite originating high volumes of new mortgage business, many of the centralised lenders restrained themselves from issuing into this market. It was also during this period that the investment banks began actively cultivating a new wider non-bank investor base. Interest developed from Japan and the continent (with an element of currency strategy behind certain plans). The UK corporate sector, which was experiencing record levels of liquidity and a retracting gilt market, became active participants. A number of particularly large accounts inspired new life into the demand for these assets. Banks remained a large taker of the assets but the move was more towards the treasury desk rather than the corporate banking department.

During the late summer and autumn of 1988 issuers re-emerged from hibernation. The additional paper fed confidence to the investor community. Several more investment banks appeared on the scene, all claiming to make markets and all claiming to distribute the lion's share of every issue. Yields over LIBOR fell rapidly and deal after deal brought new confidence of market capacity.

During this period we were able to watch a new market being born, coughing, spluttering and stumbling in its formative years but quickly to become one of the brightest, healthiest adolescents around. However, there is still a way to go before the market could be described as having long-term stability and until that time it will remain exposed to internal and external influences. For example, only recently a series of sell orders and, more importantly, unfounded gossip of selling was enough to make prices move quite sharply and one or two investment banks temporarily hid from the market-making scene. Investors must be given confidence that the players will be there through the good and bad times.

It is likely we will see a period of consolidation in the near future with a slower narrowing between the mortgage-backed and building society FRN spreads. The ball, as ever, remains firmly in the investment banker's court. They must widen the investor network and provide it with additional confidence by making firm prices and at narrow spreads.

At the time of the early transactions, NHLC decided to commence a diversification programme. Whilst the mortgage-backed FRN market appears healthy today, one must question whether a series of events could dramatically turn this progress into retreat.

This diversification is both offensive and defensive. Offensively we have gone to the US to establish commercial paper and bond transactions, to the Far East for private placements and regional bank funding and to Europe to develop whole loan portfolio sales. The result has been substantial research and development work and large legal bills. However, we now have half a dozen or so products, which we could safely describe as sitting on the shelf waiting to be pulled down. Our bankers must now compete in pricing terms, not in a local market but globally. We can compare a US commercial paper drawing with a tranche of a private placement in Japan or whole loan sale to a French bank. Transactions are in short supply and consequently diversification has created competition and assisted in the downward pressure on funding margins. The relationship between lender and borrower has changed.

On the defensive side, NHLC does not want to be exposed to one market. The volatility of the FRN market is well documented. If you, as a matter of policy, maintain a prominent position in the market regarding mortgage origination volumes, then somewhere down the line a degree of reliance will be placed on securitisation. If the FRN market were suddenly to become expensive or the availability of new funding was becoming doubtful, we do not want the generation of new assets to be interrupted. Hence, the need to diversify.

This being said, one should not ignore the home market. A substantial level of securitisations will continue to be funded through the FRN market. The maintenance of a regular issuing programme will encourage investors and investment banks on the liquidity of the paper, an area that has been an emotive issue in the past. However, NHLC will also be continuing to explore alternatives.

WHOLE LOAN SALES

Whole loan transactions are essentially the sale of a portfolio of mortgages without the benefit of certain structuring aspects such as credit enhancement and ratings. As such, trades are conducted bi-laterally and generally kept private. There are no available figures for the size of this market but . estimates approaching the size of the sterling mortgage-backed FRN market have been made. The market in the US is well developed. Assisted by homogeneity and high volume levels whole loans are tradeable assets (with markets being made!) rather than their private placement equivalent here in the UK.

There are many reasons why the whole loan sale makes sense:

(i) front-end costs of public securitisations remain high. Simplification of structure while achieving a similar goal reduces this expense;
(ii) a formal structured transaction is clumsy and involves severe inflexibility. Consequently the not so straight forward originator may run up against product or administrative constraints he will find commercially unacceptable;
(iii) the lack of commerciality of a certain party to a typical transaction can be avoided. The stress tests imposed by the rating agencies are unrealistic. They produce protection far in excess of what is required in reality. Consequently additional cost is incurred;
(iv) credit enhancement can be eliminated. The acquirer should be someone who can make value judgements on the UK mortgage market, rather than a rating driven investor. As a result, the acquirer would undoubtedly prefer a higher margin passed through rather than paying for either pool insurance or subordinated notes or indeed any of the other potential nuts and bolts that could be added.

There are several ways of structuring a whole loan sale. They range from an outright sale to a financing arrangement:

(i) *whole loan sale*. The acquirer purchases a portfolio without enhancement and is exposed to all of the risks. He receives all of the income and agrees to pay the originator/servicer a fixed administration fee. This may look like giving away too much but the structure provides substantial benefit to the originator/servicer in times of margin pressure and adds to stability and quality of earnings;

(ii) *guaranteed margin*. As above except the acquirer receives a fixed margin with the originator receiving what is left. Essentially this is a funding route with the basis risk being retained by the originator;

(iii) *profit share*. The portfolio is sold and both the originator and acquirer receive a fixed administration fee and margin respectively. Income over and above this level is shared in accordance with a pre-agreed formula. The relationship on the profit share is dependent on fee/margin structure and whether there are any inducements to keeping the gross LIBOR/mortgage rate spread as wide as possible.

CMO

At the time of the 1989 Budget the Bank of England announced that the rule restricting the issue of capital market instruments with maturities of less than five years was thereafter abolished. The Bank had previously considered that even if the security had a final maturity of 27 years they would consider the expected average life, as marketed by the investment banks and perceived by the market as a whole, as the determinant for qualification within the five year rule.

Mortgage-backed securities launched to date have final maturities of between 27 and 30 years depending on whether substitution is included or not. However, the average life of the mortgage portfolio is in the region of five to seven years.

MAES Funding No 2 plc, a vehicle established by CIBC, was the first to take advantage of the relaxation of the Bank's rules with a £300 million FRN with a call at four years and using a 25% per annum pre-payment assumption to create an average life of two years. The pricing on this transaction was the finest coupon then achieved, LIBOR + 15 basis points per annum.

MAES was able to sell the view that the four year call was likely to be exercised by the inclusion of a substantial hike in the coupon to 50 bp per annum.

Shortly afterwards, National Home Loans (though Collateralised Mortgages Securities (No 1) plc) launched the UK's first CMO, a structure which (whilst not new to the financial markets) had not been used previously to finance UK mortgages, again for the same five year rule reason.

A CMO or collateralised mortgage obligation is a technique invented in the United States in 1986. Since that time a total of US$200 billion has been issued domestically and US$50 billion into the Euromarkets.

In its simplest form the CMO involves the creation of a number of tranches or classes within a transaction and directs the cash flow from redemptions to the various classes in a certain pre-determined order.

In an FRN every £1 of redemption proceeds is used to pre-pay the noteholders, either pro-rata or selected by lot. Consequently, each noteholder experiences the same pre-payment experience. In the CMO that £1 of redemption proceeds may be directed to certain of the noteholders depending on their particular class.

The following diagram explains the most straightforward of the structures:

	A-1	A–2	A–3
Redemptions ———→			

Time

As redemptions occur they are initially applied to tranche A-1 until A-1 noteholders are prepaid in full. When complete paydown of this tranche has taken place, the subsequent proceeds are all directed to tranche A-2 noteholders, again until full paydown. Proceeds are then directed to tranche A-3.

The result is that the investor in tranche A-1 experiences a very fast pay-back period. Assuming tranche A-1 represented 50% of the total pool and pre-payments occurred at the rate of 20% per annum, investors would experience an average life of 18 months and a final maturity of 3.2 years. This is as compared to an investor in a standard FRN who would experience an average life of five to eight years (depending on whether substitution was included or not) and a final maturity of 13–16 years.

Tranche A-2, assuming it constituted 30% of the total portfolio, would experience an average life of five years. The final tranche, A-3, would experience an average life of 9.6 years.

It is immediately clear that by recasting the cash flow into a fast, medium and slow-paying tranche, it is possible to appeal to different types of investors. The fast-paying piece should appeal in particular to the money market investor. The slow-paying piece to the investor who prefers his note maintaining its value, with the option of writing asset swaps to convert the note into a five year gilt/US treasury linked instrument.

It is quite apparent that the CMO structure assists with one of the problems identified by investors with the FRN. Investors now have a substantial degree of certainty with which to establish their credit and return horizon.

A derivative of the CMO has extended this certainty even further. This is by means of the Planned Amortisation Class—or PAC tranche.

Diagrammatically this is presented as follows:

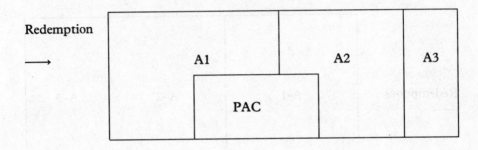

Time

As redemptions occur, in common with the previous example, they pay down tranche A-1. However, in year three (for example) any redemptions that take place are passed through to the PAC tranche up to the (say) £10 million limit for that year. Any pre-payment flow proceeds over and above this amount are passed through to tranche A-1 (until it is paid down in full). The same takes place in years four and five. If there are insufficient funds to pay down the PAC tranche within any particular year then the tranche is effectively carried over to the following period. The shortage of funds does not create an event of default but just defers pre-payment of the notes.

The PAC tranche gives substantial prepayment certainty to investors and it is structured to ensure the annual limit is achievable under most circumstances.

Mortgage-backed securities have to date traded at a premium over building society FRNs, including those of the somewhat smaller societies. The mortgage-backed securities have virtually all been rated AAA compared to the building societies who range from AA, at best, to not rated. One of the principal reasons for the mortgage-backed sector trading outside the builders has been pre-payment uncertainty. With changing and developing structures the spread will have to narrow, if not invert.

PRE-PAYMENTS

The majority of debt issued into the capital markets is structured with a bullet maturity. However, mortgage-backed securities are structured to pay down in line with the underlying mortgage pool.

The final maturity of most mortgages is 25 years. This is, however, seemingly irrelevant as the borrower has the ability to redeem his outstanding mortgage at any time prior to final maturity, in most situations without penalty. This might appear a statement of the obvious; however, in analysing the position further in pure financial terms the lender has sold or given the borrower a 25 year call option, most probably without cost. There is indeed a cost to the issuer because as previously mentioned one of the reasons why mortgage-backed paper trades above the lesser credit rated building societies is the uncertain repayment rate brought about by this borrower call.

Mortgage-backed bonds can pre-pay for a number of reasons related to the borrower's actions:

(i) *moving house.* This is by far the biggest reason for pre-payment. One wonders whether the creation of a portable mortgage, ie the mortgage loan that stays with the borrower irrespective of his house would effectively eliminate pre-payments. Discussions as to what makes a borrower change house and when are obviously beyond the scope of this book;

(ii) *further advances.* Transactions launched to date have included most options relating to the application of further advances. They include:

   (a) a limited level of funds being held available in the original pool to lend on further advances;
   (b) unlimited substitution (new mortgage lending or further advances) during a limited time period—usually the first three years;
   (c) removal from the pool through a repurchase by the originator, so that the originator would lend the whole amount;
   (d) lending of the further advance amount by the originator on a second charge.

   This is generally considered to be a potentially major contribution to pre-payments. Building society statistics of the 1980s indicate that an average of 7.3% of borrowers seek further advances each year. These statistics were borne out by TMC in their early mortgage transactions and resulted in them rewriting certain provisions so that further advances in later transactions did not automatically invoke a pre-payment;

(iii) *other demographic and economic factors*:

   (a) death;
   (b) job relocation;
   (c) a change in the borrower's financial status;

(iv) *refinancing.* The mortgage market is now highly competitive and borrower mobility has never been more active.

One point worth mentioning here is that senior/junior deals will tend to pre-pay faster, everything else being equal. The reason is that pre-payments from the whole mortgage portfolio are applied to pay down the senior notes, ie £107 million is used to pre-pay £100 million of debt. With a pool insured deal the size of the portfolio equals the senior notes, ie £100 million pays down £100 million.

ACTUAL PRE-PAYMENT EXPERIENCE

The CMO has certainly focused attention on the speed with which the securities have, and are likely to, pay down. Until recently investors had not regarded the issue as important, although issuers certainly did. Extending the average life from, say, five to eight years has helped the issuer amortise his fixed front-end costs over a longer period. Many of the transactions that have included three years of substitution have been executed at seemingly little or no extra cost. The issuers have effectively had a costless option.

Despite this, market analysis of the pre-payment experience remains limited. In part it is not as critical, as compared to the US, where through fixed rate mortgages and securities, a changing interest rate scenario can dramatically affect the pre-payment speed and ultimately the yield on the notes and cost to the issuer.

If we look first at the mortgage/housing market, it is apparent that data published for the benefit of investors to date is based on building societies research which suggests an average mortgage life of approximately 6.6 years. This research is from a Building Societies Association Survey in 1986 and covered 1,102 people.

This is a very small sample when compared to the total population which now includes in excess of seven million borrowers. The actual results of the survey are set out, for background purposes, in Table 1 below.

Table 1.

AVERAGE TIME SPENT BY OWNER OCCUPIERS IN CURRENT PROPERTY

	%
Up to 1 year	10
1 to 2 years	10
2 to 3 years	8
3 to 4 years	8
4 to 5 years	6
5 to 10 years	22
More than 10 years	36
	100

This average life figure is often used as an industry standard and yet, for a number of reasons, it was never representative and is certainly no longer applicable to the mortgage market of today. The experience to date for securitised issues is that pre-payments are much faster than was originally predicted and average lives will be much shorter than 6.6 years.

Since the Building Societies Association research was published, the mortgage market and, particularly, the borrowers' understanding of the market has matured. As a result of increased competition amongst lenders, mortgages are now more portable and borrowers will more frequently re-mortgage to utilise the increased availability of finance to achieve greater flexibility and cost savings.

It is interesting to note what information is currently available and in what context it should be applied.

The Building Societies Association provides gross redemption statistics for the building society movement. These show, during the period from 1970 to 1987, a comparatively narrow range of results (see Table 2 on page 210) with an average of 10.5% per annum. This suggests an average mortgage life of approximately 6.25 years.

It is interesting to note that during the first ten years of that period the rate of redemption was fairly constant and there was no apparent trend. During the latter eight years, however, the rate has gradually increased from 8.1% in 1980 to 14.6% in 1987. The 1987 figure would produce an average life more in line with our market experience to date of approximately 3.86 years. This trend justifies our belief that there is an increasing tendency for borrowers to re-mortgage more frequently.

Experience soon told us that, perhaps because of the changing environment, the speed of redemptions was faster than first thought and an average life of 4.5 to 5 years was more in line with reality.

The mortgage securities market has now begun to use Constant Pre-payment Rates (CPRs), a concept imported from the United States. This is an assumption that the mortgage portfolio will pay down at a certain percentage rate on its declining balance. This has been typically regarded as 15 and 20% CPR.

The graph on page 220 reflects the position of a pool declining at 20% CPR.

An alternative to the CPR is the straight line method, most recently used in MAES Funding No 2. This structure uses equal paydown based on the original principal balance, not the declining balance. MAES 2 assumed an aggressive 25% straight line pre-payment rate, ie

	Closing Outstandings	Pre-payments	% Outstandings
Year 1	£300 m	£75 m	25
Year 2	£225 m	£75 m	33
Year 3	£150 m	£75 m	50
Year 4	£ 75 m	£75 m	100

Table 2.

BUILDING SOCIETY REDEMPTIONS

	Redemptions as Proportion of Gross Redemptions	Redemption as % of Opening Balance
	£ billions	%
1970	0.7	9.1
1971	0.9	10.2
1972	1.1	10.6
1973	1.3	10.3
1974	1.1	7.5
1975	1.8	11.2
1976	2.0	10.6
1977	2.1	9.3
1978	2.7	10.2
1979	2.9	9.1
1980	3.0	8.1
1981	4.4	10.3
1982	5.1	10.4
1983	6.1	10.7
1984	7.4	10.9
1985	9.1	11.0
1986	14.1	14.5
1987	17.1	14.6

However, whether you ascribe to the CPR principle or the straight line, both concepts are purely theoretical and do not actually exist in the real world.

The graphs on pages 221 to 224 show the pre-payment experience of NHL 1st, 2nd, 3rd and 4th Funding. The annual average of the monthly pre-payments for the period from launch to end-June 1989 together with the projected average lives based on this speed is:

	Pre-payment Rate	Average Life
NHL 1	18.90%	6.198 years
NHL 2	18.74%	6.202 years
NHL 3	16.34%	6.205 years
NHL 4	12.51%	5.937 years

However, this in no way reflects the changes that have occurred over that time.

A trend that is apparent from the diagrams is absent from the theoretical figures the market works from. However, it reflects logic that the pre-payments accelerate in the early years. Assuming that there is no significant seasoning in the pool, it is unlikely that borrowers will choose to move house for at least 12 months or so. Consequently, we should expect a low pre-payment speed, building up over a period of time.

This point can be reflected in another way. NHL 2nd Funding pre-paid quite rapidly in the early part of its life, indeed more quickly than its sister transactions both public and private. The reason, we concluded, was that the average seasoning of the pool at some 14 months was much older than most and consequently borrowers were already thinking about moving. Investors should perhaps consider this statistic in future, if it is provided in the prospectus.

During 1988 we experienced an explosion in the mortgage market. Three factors acted to create our version of the 'triple witching hour':

(i) the 1988 Budget reduced the top rate of tax to 40%;
(ii) the Budget also announced the abolition of joint MIRAS on a single property, but with effect from 1 August 1988;
(iii) the rapid reduction in sterling interest rates.

The result was unprecedented volumes in housing turnover and mortgage demand. House price inflation, already high, accelerated, which encouraged more people to move. The availability of funding was no problem.

It is therefore hardly surprising that 1988 experienced redemptions at such high levels.

Just as quickly as the bubble was blown up in 1988, it burst in the autumn, as the Chancellor (fearing a rekindling of inflation and pressure on the pound through a rapidly deteriorating trade balance) hiked interest rates back to and above the pre-summer levels. During the winter months housing turnover decelerated rapidly and estimates for house price increases fell from the buoyant 20/30% level to single figures or lower. 1989 has continued to experience the depressed turnover levels and price inflation has fallen to zero and, in parts, backtracked.

However, and somewhat surprisingly, the level of redemptions did not collapse, although they did fall. This, we surmise, was due to a number of reasons:

(i) the shock treatment was directed at the south of England. The rest of the country continued to enjoy relatively buoyant conditions;
(ii) borrowers were beginning to hurt (as the Chancellor had intended) and would be prepared to shop around to get a better deal through refinancing. Supply of course was readily available;
(iii) a plethora of new mortgage products hit the market ranging from low start to currency mortgages. Many were designed, such as the low start, to assist the budgeting process by enabling the borrower to pay 3% below the going rate and rolling up the shortfall. This product was ideal for the consumer in the prevailing interest rate environment;
(iv) some of the mortgage-backed securities included clauses requiring a redemption from the pool should a further advance be required. In an

environment of stagnant housing turnover borrowers may have a tendency to remain in the property and redecorate or develop it, eg an extension, which they would fund by borrowing.

What does the future hold? It is obviously difficult to predict whether the economic gyrations experienced to date will continue. However, in a standard environment we would expect low redemptions in the first two years increasing in years three, four and perhaps five and gradually tailing off thereafter. The tendency for a borrower to remain in his home after five years is substantially higher compared to the below five year bracket.

PROFIT EXTRACTION AND OFF-BALANCE SHEET CONSIDERATIONS

Profit extraction has been one of the areas where the greatest attention to detail has been paid by issuers, investment banks, legal and accounting advisers. No one method has emerged as the most efficient primarily because the corporate structuring behind the originators, and regulations affecting them, has been different.

Additionally the rapid development in non-recourse funding techniques in recent years has resulted in regulators increasingly seeking to establish appropriate rules and guidelines. Consequently, the framework has been constantly changing.

During this period we have seen the EEC 7th Directive imposing its will on the UK legislative procedure through the medium of the Companies Act 1989. The aim of certain provisions of the Act is to redefine the meaning of subsidiary to relate essentially to 'control' or 'dominant influence' as a matter of fact rather than just looking at equity participation.

The Bank of England, after a long gestation period, released in February 1989 its guidelines to UK banks on the treatment of Loan Transfers and Securitisation for capital adequacy purposes. The Bank has focused not just on the legal risks involved but also on the moral risks to the originator, ensuring it felt no obligation to rescue a failing special purpose vehicle. Consequently, it has established a series of rules, which have to be adhered to if the sale is, for capital measurement purposes, to be treated as having taken place. These rules range from no equity participation to the divorcing of certain associations between issuer and originator, even down to name.

Both of these areas of regulation point to a certain treatment based on defined positions. They both appear to permit the sale of mortgages but allow the retention of profit arising from those same mortgages.

The accounting profession has moved down a separate track. Through ED42 (which now seems to have been a year in redrafting) they were seeking to establish a principle not previously used before. It was acknowledged that legally a sale of the mortgages had taken place and that the liability for the debt did not rest with the originator. However, the accountants were seeking to reflect the 'economic' reality of the transaction, ie if the originator through one means or another received the benefit of the mortgages in the same manner as if they had remained on the balance sheet, the accounts should reflect this.

Bearing in mind all these complications, and indeed uncertainties, in addition to the 'clarity' of our taxation system, one begins to understand why these transactions take a substantial amount of planning and result in the individuals associated with the deal developing senility before closing.

The taxation aspects cannot be emphasised enough. Many of them are described in Chapter 3. The result of some of the legislative requirements is diametrically opposed to the optimal tax treatment. The point should be made that, in most cases, the intention is not to reduce one's tax liability through the inclusion of bells and whistles but to eliminate double taxation on the same profit stream and the imposition of withholding and to ensure that any tax or VAT leakage is minimised and appropriate advantage can be taken of group relief.

The method of profit extraction used will be dictated by the above points and perhaps by corporate policy. Naturally for bank issuers such as Barclays and TSB the overriding area for concern will be the Bank of England's requirements; likewise for CIBC and Bank of Ireland with their respective central banks. For issuers such as MFC and HMC the situation is not that straightforward and indeed both have adopted a different approach.

NHLC has created two off-balance sheet groups. The first, Finance For Home Loans Holdings, in which it effectively has a 50% stake, involved a mixture of ordinary and preference shares which enables the vehicle companies to fall outside the Companies Act 1985 definition of subsidiary, but within the definition of the NHLC group for tax purposes. The equity stake allows NHLC to be the beneficiary of most of the profit in the vehicle companies. The second structure involves Collateralised Mortgage Securities (Holdings) Limited and is designed to meet the Bank of England's requirements. For National Home Loans the need for off-balance sheet treatment arises for three reasons:

 (i) it is a publicly-quoted company and is part of a group containing an authorised institution regulated by the Bank of England;
(ii) its bank lenders impose gearing constraints restricting the level of debt to equity;
(iii) an inability to leverage outside the balance sheet defeats one of the principal reasons for securitising, namely to free up capital and thereby enhance returns on that same level of capital.

HMC on the other hand has adopted a much simpler approach. The concept of limited liability exists even within a group. Parents are not necessarily liable for debts of subsidiaries and vice-versa. Many corporations raise debt centrally for the group through a captive finance company subsidiary. Commonly it is nominally capitalised and may benefit from a parent company guarantee, but quite often from just a letter of comfort or continuing ownership clause.

Ultimately in the latter situations there is only a moral obligation for the parent and, legally, it could walk away from the debt of its subsidiaries.

HMC Holdings, the parent, owns a number of subsidiaries. One is the mortgage originator and asset holding company. This institution sells its mortgages to a sister subsidiary, which issues the mortgage-backed security. HMC Holdings, through a 100% equity participation in the special purpose vehicle, is able to achieve the best of all worlds:

(i) profit in cash terms is lifted by way of dividend directly to Holdings;
(ii) irrespective of cash distributions a consolidated profit statement would include the earnings contribution from the SPV;
(iii) a group income election for tax purposes is easily achievable which results in an ability to avoid some of the more complicated structures, especially where VAT is concerned (see below).

The NHL and HMC structures both work. For NHL there is a particular desire to remove them from the balance sheet. For HMC the issue is not so important. The major difference between the two is that NHL is publicly quoted whereas HMC is privately owned.

Some people may question both companies' decisions and consider that this emphasis on off-balance sheet treatment is excessive.

Does it matter if the accountants present a set of figures that reflect a consolidated position? Do stock market analysts really focus on the matter? For a manufacturing company, high gearing levels are certainly a negative point but is there a real market benchmark which is considered prudent in terms of leveraging and the effect of investors' exposure to, say, changes in the LIBOR/mortgage spread?

The answer to these questions is yes if it costs money either directly or indirectly. For example:

(i) if a bank securitising a pool of mortgages were to fail to comply with the Bank of England's rules, it would be required to maintain the same level of capital as if the mortages had never been sold. The business would not be able to grow to the same extent and, arguably, the transaction could not be justified in terms of resource, cost and pricing. In this instance, there is a clear cost to not removing the asset effectively from the balance sheet;
(ii) if the stock market down-rated the shares as a result of what is considered an imprudently leveraged balance sheet, there will be an immediate cost in terms of investor relations. Should further equity be required to expand or diversify the business, there could then be a real cost in the relative price of new stock;
(iii) if banks consider that mortgage-backed securities should be included in the mortgage company's calculation of gearing, the benefit of freeing up capital

is lost. Both NHLC and HMC have been successful in convincing bankers that this is not the correct analysis, largely because of the absence of the risk to the originator from the mortgage portfolio.

Any new participants in the mortgage-backed securities market who also raise money from the banking community should do one of two things:

(i) define gearing as borrowings of the company (and subsidiaries), but clearly exclude debt raised by securitisation. Care needs to be taken with the different definition of subsidiary for accounting purposes under the new Companies Act. A banker will have a different perspective on assets and liabilities than accountants;
(ii) establish a structure where the corporate policy is quite clearly marked out and bank lending to the originator is on a stand alone basis. The use of SPVs elsewhere in the group, whether a subsidiary or sister company, produces no moral risk and it must be made clear that assistance will not be provided in the event of a problem.

As mentioned previously, there is no one particular method of profit extraction which has dominated. However, the following briefly summarises the options available.

SERVICING/ADMINISTRATION FEE

The originator of the mortgages is usually the servicer. It needs to charge a fee for this service in any event, even though some may regard it as robbing Peter to pay Paul. The rating agencies would expect a market fee to be payable to the servicer as they consider that if this fee, which is the only certain level of income available to an administrator, is too low, the motivation to manage the pool properly is compromised.

Administration of mortgages to an SPV are considered by Customs and Excise as the supply of a service and subject to VAT at the standard rate of 15%. The nature of both the originator and the new mortgage pool owner is likely to mean that neither can charge VAT on the supplies it makes. As a result no, or insufficient, VAT receipts will be available to offset the payment of VAT on administration fees. Therefore a servicing fee calculated on all of the remaining profits is not an efficient route. A valid group income election for corporation tax purposes does not necessarily mean that a VAT group election is available.

To avoid this VAT leakage it has been suggested that the servicing fee should be minimised, as overall it does not detract from the aggregate level of income available to the originator/servicer. However, Customs and Excise have the ability to impute a value (at market rates) irrespective of the actual charge and then impose 15% VAT on that level.

DIVIDENDS

Regulated banking institutions and institutions seeking to comply with the new Companies Act will not be able to extract profit by way of dividends. In seeking to comply with off-balance sheet treatment for both sets of regulations the originator must have no direct or indirect equity stake, either actual or beneficial.

In any case, the payment of a dividend requires the payer to account to the Inland Revenue for advance corporation tax (ACT). Briefly, this would result in an effective withholding of 25/75ths of the distribution and a consequent timing delay and cash flow cost. However, this cost can be mitigated through:

(i) a group income election, if available;
(ii) the receiver of the dividend also being profitable and within the same quarter paying a dividend (of sufficient size) to its own shareholders, thereby enabling the benefit of the ACT payment made by the issuer to be realised immediately.

Dividends are by far one of the most straightforward methods of profit extraction but in the new regulatory environment their use could become obsolete for many originators.

SUBORDINATED LOAN INTEREST

Subordinated loans can be provided by the originator for the following reasons:

(i) to finance the start-up costs of the special purpose vehicle. These could include the pool insurance premium, underwriters' management/selling commission, legal fees and rating agency fees. Typically they are repaid out of profit over a number of years;
(ii) to finance contingency/shortfall funds, usually in respect of transactions utilising the senior/junior method of credit enhancement.

As these loans are subordinated the interest rate payable is naturally higher than that on the senior notes. The originator is probably the most appropriate person to make these loans as it, above everyone, should be happy with the credit quality of mortgages sold from its balance sheet. As such it provides the originator with an ability to receive an element of the profit achievable in the vehicle. There are, however, one or two points worth mentioning.

If the originator is not carrying on a banking business for tax purposes, the interest payments on any loan in excess of 12 months are subject to withholding at the basic rate by the SPV. However, this problem is eliminated if the originator and the SPV can benefit from a group income election.

If the Inland Revenue considers the rate of interest charged on the loan excessive, the portion in excess of a market rate is treated as a deemed dividend and subject to the same ACT provisions as a dividend payment to a non-group member. Given the rather small level of transactions which have included subordinated loans from third parties it is rather difficult to tell what is excessive.

Under Bank of England rules the originator is permitted to make the subordinated loans and still obtain off-balance sheet treatment. However, there are two adverse affects:

(i) any loan made on a subordinated basis to 'your own' securitisation SPV results in that debt being deducted from capital in the Bank's capital adequacy and ratio calculations. This obviously restricts balance sheet capacity. For example, in meeting the Bank of England's minimum capital measurement of 8%, a bank would be able to gear up to 25 times its capital base on its mortgage assets alone (8% = 12.5 multiplied by 0.5 risk asset weighting = 25 times). Therefore if a £1 million subordinated loan was established in relation to a securitisation of £100 million, the bank in question would be restricted from making a further £25 million of additional mortgage lending (or £12.5 million of straight commercial lending). Consequently, the structure has been relatively inefficient in freeing up capital. As a separate point, should the interest margin on the mortgages be 100 bp, the subordinated loan would need to be priced at 25% above the cost of funds to achieve the same return on capital;

(ii) should a bank make the start up loan, the Bank of England rules do not permit any pre-payment of this loan until the scheme has been unwound completely. This is highly inflexible and creates an accounting problem for the originator. As the provider of that loan, it has to justify to its auditors where the source of repayment will be. Previously, the loan has been repaid from future profit. However, maintaining the loan outstanding until final maturity will result in a loan without any assets being allocated to make repayment. Consequently, UK auditors could require that this loan be written off by the originator and this would apply not over the life of the scheme but possibly on the day the loan is made. This is the position for a UK bank. If the originator is not so regulated, banks lending to that company may not be happy for their funds to be exposed to assets with a lesser credit quality than first mortgages. The result could be reduced gearing or some other formula established to restrict balance sheet capacity. Additionally it could affect the pricing of the bank debt.

MANAGEMENT CHARGES

Similar to administration fees the originator can provide two management functions:

(i) straightforward management fee of the SPV's business in return for a fee—this could be subject to VAT;

(ii) treasury management—if the originator arranges finance for the SPV, this service could be considered not to attract VAT. Nevertheless, it cannot exceed a reasonable level.

SERVICING STRIP

In the US it is common practice for the servicer to take his profit virtually out of the top slice by only passing through an agreed margin (naturally the level passed through has to meet the rating agency tests). Effectively, the servicer retains the right to receive a portion directly from the borrower and the SPV only receives net. The Inland Revenue has objected to this method as it creates administrative complexity under the MIRAS Scheme.

BROKING FEES

Some schemes involve on-going mortgage origination arrangements either directly with the SPV or with its immediate off-balance sheet parent. An originator who undoubtedly maintains a position in the origination side of the mortgage market could act as the issuer's (or parent's) agent in raising new assets. Naturally the originator could expect a fee for such a service.

Complications may arise surrounding the tax treatment of this arrangement and the need to ensure the recipient of the asset is a trading company for tax purposes.

DEFERRED CONSIDERATION

The originator can sell the portfolio to the SPV at a premium, such premium being the product of a calculation based on the actual profit performance of the mortgages sold rather than what was expected on closing.

The charging of an up-front known premium is certainly an option but variable factors in the mortgage interest rate spread, pre-payment speed and certain types of costs make it virtually impossible to determine accurately the present value of the future profit stream from the mortgages.

The deferred consideration route avoids this problem because it is calculated and paid in arrear, after the profit has been achieved.

There are some important tax angles that need close consideration most notably the treatment of the deferred consideration payer being treated as a trading company for tax purposes. It is questionable whether SPVs are trading companies and therefore an intermediate company may be necessary.

The creation of a trading company for tax purposes certainly has some commercial disadvantages. It will need to originate itself a significant portion of the total securitisation pool. This may necessitate, amongst other things, separate funding lines and adapting existing computer and related systems.

INTEREST RATE SWAPS

Under this method the originator and the SPV enter into an interest rate swap whereby the SPV agrees to pay the mortgage rate to the originator and in return receives an amount sufficient to cover the SPV's cost of funds (the note rate) plus other running costs.

The Inland Revenue has questioned the treatment of swaps for some time and at the time of writing a general consultation is in process.

The Bank of England has accepted this method of profit extraction and indeed Barclays Bank has since taken advantage of their treatment, irrespective of the tax uncertainty mentioned above.

The use of a swap is realistically restricted to banks as the payer to a non-bank must withhold tax at the basic rate, unless the parties are in the same tax group. If the two counterparties are not banks, a bank could, at a cost, be found to stand in the middle.

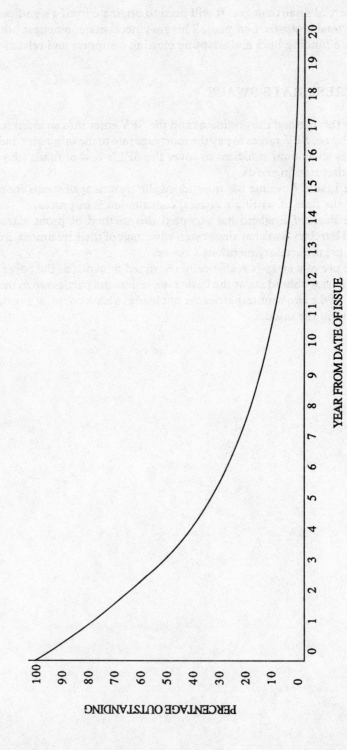

REPAYMENT PROFILE AT CPR 20 %

PERCENTAGE OUTSTANDING

YEAR FROM DATE OF ISSUE

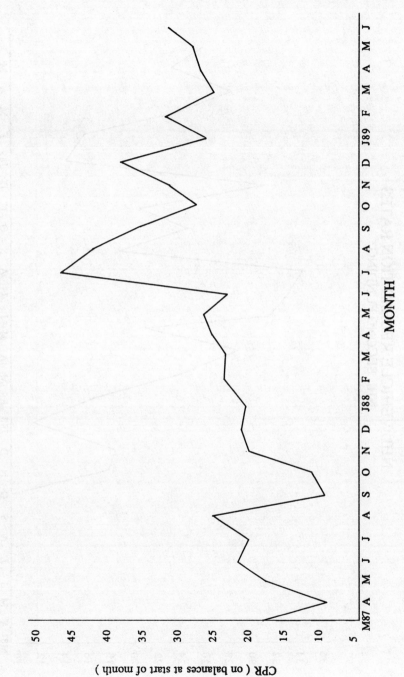

NHL VEHICLE REDEMPTION RATES
NHL FIRST FUNDING

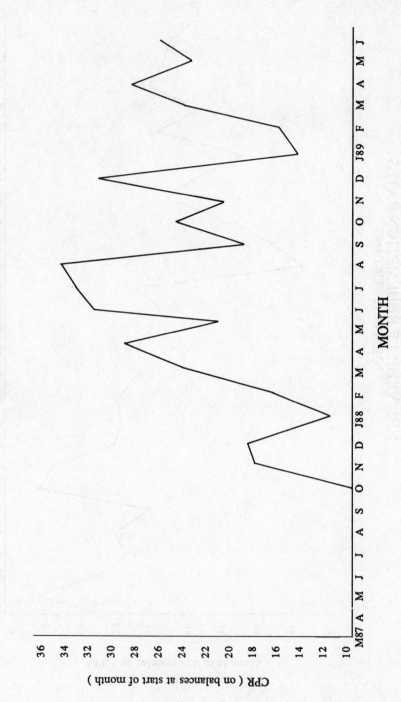

NHL VEHICLE REDEMPTION RATES
NHL SECOND FUNDING

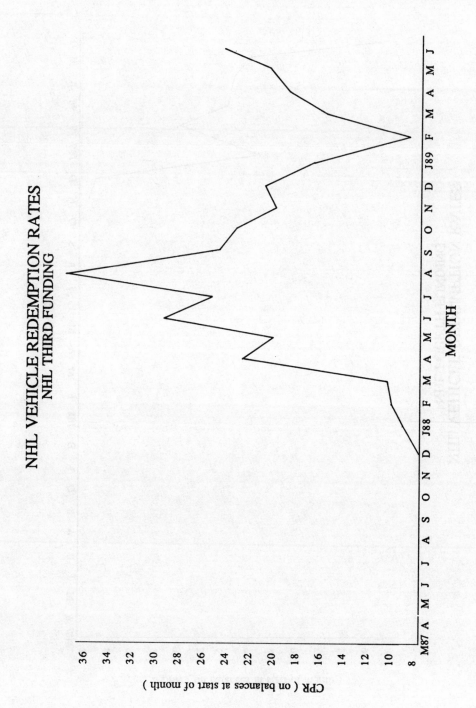

NHL VEHICLE REDEMPTION RATES
NHL THIRD FUNDING

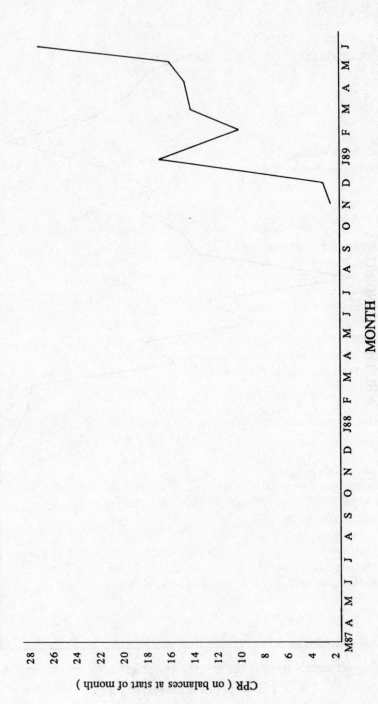

Chapter 12

Accounting Treatment*

Michael Wildig
Arthur Andersen & Co

INTRODUCTION

The development and growth in the number and volume of securitisation transactions has raised important accounting issues for the various parties to the securitisation process. Existing accounting literature in the UK provides little definitive guidance on many of these issues, although the proposed introduction of an accounting standard on off-balance sheet finance (as currently embodied in ED42 'Accounting for special purpose transactions') will have an impact on various aspects of the accounting for securitised products.

Why accounting treatment is important

1. OFF-BALANCE SHEET TREATMENT

In addition to the many finance-related factors that underlie the attractiveness of securitisation, such as improved asset/liability management and access to new funding sources, the increasing focus by bank and other regulators on capital adequacy and risk-based capital guidelines has emphasised the benefits of removing assets from the balance sheet. Similarly, for all entities, securitisation can improve gearing and other ratios provided that the securitised assets are in fact removed from the balance sheet. One of the key questions, therefore, is whether and under what conditions can securitisation be treated as a sale as opposed to a financing arrangement, not only from an accounting standpoint but also from a regulatory point of view.

2. CONSOLIDATION

Many securitisation structures make use of special purpose vehicles (SPVs) which acquire securitised assets and issue the related collateralised debt.

Whether these SPVs need to be included in the consolidated accounts of the originator has in the past depended on the strict legal structure and ownership of the vehicle and it has been a relatively straightforward task to achieve non-consolidation. With the introduction of the Companies Act 1989 which has widened the scope of consolidation, and the likely further reinforcement by the accounting profession of the requirement to consolidate controlled entities, this is changing.

3. PROFIT AND LOSS RECOGNITION

Whether sale or financing treatment is appropriate for the originator, consideration needs to be given to the profit and loss impact, both so far as the original securitisation transaction is concerned and as the securitisation process continues, including such matters as the extent and timing of recognition of income and related expenses.

This chapter will discuss the following accounting considerations:

  (i) an overview of the key accounting issues;
 (ii) current and proposed accounting and banking supervisory rules;
(iii) application to specific transaction structures and arrangements;
 (iv) overview of US generally accepted accounting principles;
  (v) the future.

The chapter will not cover accounting issues faced by buyers or investors in securitised products.

OVERVIEW OF KEY ACCOUNTING ISSUES

The principal accounting issues which arise from securitisation transactions in the UK are:

  (i) *sale* versus *financing* treatment of the segregated pool of assets for the originator, seller or sponsor ('Originator');
 (ii) consolidation of the issuing vehicle (the 'Issuer') by the Originator;
(iii) profit and loss recognition by the Originator and the Issuer.

A. Sales versus financing

Potentially, there are many different types of securitisation transaction. At one extreme there are outright sales of assets or interests in assets. At the other extreme there are borrowings collateralised by assets. In the middle ground there are sales of assets with degrees of recourse to the seller and non-recourse borrowings collateralised by assets. The transactions at each extreme are generally easy to account for because their substance equates with their form. The accounting issues arise primarily because the transactions in the middle have characteristics of both sales and borrowings and raise the question of whether the Originator should continue to include the assets on its balance sheet or record a sale.

It is generally accepted that a *sale* has taken place for accounting purposes *where the risks and rewards of ownership of an asset have been transferred*. In ED42, which when finalised will become the Accounting Standard for off-balance sheet transactions in the UK, it is re-affirmed that a review of the allocation of the inherent risks of an asset between parties to a transaction is often a significant indicator of whether or not the transaction has resulted in the acquisition or disposal of an asset by an enterprise. If an entity transfers legal ownership of an item to another entity but does not significantly alter its position with respect to the specific risk or reward characteristics embodied in the transferred item, the item should not be taken off-balance sheet.

On this basis, therefore, there has to be a significant transfer of both the risks *and* rewards arising from the item in order that the transfer can be treated as a sale. It has been argued that more emphasis should be placed on risks being transferred rather than rewards that are being retained in considering whether a sale has been achieved for accounting purposes, particularly if those risks can be identified and quantified at the outset and suitable provision made including, for example, to cover against bad debts or interest rate exposures.

The Bank of England's attitude as to when a sale has been achieved for capital adequacy purposes is considerably more onerous and, for example, precludes the seller having any residual beneficial interest in the principal amount of loans transferred and does not allow the buyer to have formal recourse to the seller for losses incurred. Further, the Bank has expressed concern with the moral and operational risks where banks originate and/or service loans under these schemes.

B. Consolidation

Because of the use of SPVs and the need to keep a group relationship for tax purposes, a number of complex structures has grown up. The assets that are being securitised can be held by a corporation, trust, partnership or other legal entity. The securities or ownership interests issued can therefore take the form of, for example, debt, common stock, preferred stock or limited partnership interests. The economic substance can be the same irrespective of the legal form, although until now the regulatory, tax and accounting implications have often depended on legal form.

The majority ownership of equity capital is usually indicative of control. However, control can exist without majority ownership and this has led to the redefinition in the Companies Act 1989 of the parent/subsidiary relationship.

The Companies Act 1989 will have quite significant effects on a number of existing securitisation structures because:

(i) it gives greater emphasis than before to voting and other methods of control; and

(ii) it widens the scope of consolidation.

C. Profit and loss recognition

1. BY THE ORIGINATOR

If the securitisation transaction qualifies for sale treatment, the transferred assets are removed from the balance sheet and, in the simplest case, a gain or loss arises and is immediately recognised by the Originator, being the difference between carrying value and sales proceeds.

Adjustments to this gain or loss may be necessary at the outset or subsequently to reflect such matters as:

(i) any liability of the Originator under any recourse provisions;

(ii) any abnormal servicing fees retained by the Originator;

(iii) any interest rate differential on the assets sold maintained by the Originator;

(iv) any surplus moneys within the SPV which are likely to be repayable to the Originator;

(v) the impact of overcollateralisation of assets sold;

(vi) the treatment of issue and other expenses incurred or borne by the Originator;

(vii) the recoverability of any amounts advanced to the Issuer by the Originator.

The accounting implications of these adjustments are discussed further below.

2. BY THE ISSUER

So far as the Issuer is concerned, income from the securitised assets and the related loan finance costs will be recognised on the normal accruals basis within the SPV.

Consideration will need to be given to:

(i) provision for bad debts or non-recoverability of securitised assets at their book amounts net of proceeds from any recourse provisions, insurance or other recoveries;

(ii) amortisation policy for issue and other initial costs incurred by the SPV;

(iii) recognition of any surplus moneys generated by the vehicle that are to be paid away, typically to the Originator of the securitised assets.

CURRENT AND PROPOSED ACCOUNTING AND SUPERVISORY RULES

Now that the key accounting issues have been identified, it is appropriate to see whether, and to what extent, the current and proposed legal, accounting and supervisory rules address these issues as they apply to the securitisation process.

1. COMPANIES ACT 1985

The Companies Act 1985 gives guidance on how to account for assets and liabilities but does not define what constitutes an asset or a liability. Similarly, the Act embodies the overriding requirement that accounts should give a 'true and fair' view, but does not provide detailed guidance on what this means, nor how it should be applied. This falls to the professional judgement of the accountant.

The Act does have greater relevance in determining whether a company should be included in group accounts. The general rule requires inclusion of all subsidiaries where a parent has a majority of the *equity* share capital or otherwise controls the composition of the board. It should be noted that group accounts do not require consolidation of all subsidiaries but can be achieved, for example, by inclusion of separate sets of accounts for each subsidiary.

A number of securitisation structures to date have sought to avoid the Companies Act definition of a subsidiary by the establishment of SPVs, often with different classes of shares, with varying voting rights or profit entitlements and with the majority of equity shares and board members allocated to non-related companies or trusts. The use and perceived abuse of these so-called 'controlled non-subsidiaries' has led to a much wider definition of those entities requiring consolidation as reflected in the Companies Act 1989.

2. COMPANIES ACT 1989

The Companies Bill was issued in late 1988 and was enacted at the end of 1989. It will apply to financial years beginning on or after 23 December 1989. The Act implements the terms of the EEC Seventh Directive dealing with group accounts. The Act redefines the criteria for qualifying as a parent or a subsidiary and also broadens the types of entity which may be regarded as members of a group to include partnerships, but probably not trusts.

Group accounts must now be consolidated accounts and the reliefs from producing group accounts have been tightened.

An entity will be a subsidiary and therefore fall to be included in the consolidated accounts where the parent has:

(i) control of voting rights;
(ii) control of the board of directors;
(iii) control of operating and financial policies of the entity;
(iv) control through dominant influence;
(v) control through common management.

In certain cases the Act requires a shareholding or other participating interest to be present.

There is no intention to require UK partnerships to prepare consolidated accounts and therefore a parent undertaking is only required to prepare consolidated accounts if it is also a UK incorporated company.

The Act does not allow for any grandfathering provisions and accordingly many of the existing securitisation structures and off-balance sheet arrangements which have made use of 'controlled non-subsidiaries' may need to be included in future in the consolidated accounts of the Originator.

3. STATEMENT OF STANDARD ACCOUNTING PRACTICE 14 (SSAP14)— GROUP ACCOUNTS

The rules contained within SSAP14 generally follow those contained in the Companies Act 1985 before its amendement by the Companies Act 1989. It is probable that the revised ED42 will amend the consolidation rules of SSAP14 and amplify the requirements of the 1989 Act.

4. STATEMENT OF STANDARD ACCOUNTING PRACTICE 18 (SSAP18)—ACCOUNTING FOR CONTINGENCIES

Securitisation transactions may include contingent items where the criteria for inclusion in the financial statements will depend on the differing degrees of probability that are required before a loss as opposed to a gain is to be recognised.

In general contingent losses should be included rather than merely disclosed in the financial statements where it is probable that a future event will confirm a loss which can be estimated with reasonable accuracy at the date when the financial statements are approved by the board of directors.

Contingent gains, on the other hand, should not be accrued in financial statements and should only be disclosed if it is probable that the gain will be realised. In those cases where an Originator has a residual interest in any surplus generated by an SPV the question therefore arises as to whether this amount represents a contingent gain such that the recognition must be deferred until the events giving rise to the contingent nature of the amount have been resolved, for example full repayment of all sums owing to investors.

5. ED42—ACCOUNTING FOR SPECIAL PURPOSE TRANSACTIONS

ED42, issued in May 1988, sought to deal with the perceived problems and accounting and disclosure deficiencies arising from off-balance sheet finance transactions, often where these involved controlled non-subsidiaries.

The main provisions of ED42 are that:

(i) accounting for a transaction in accordance with its substance is central to the concept of 'true and fair'. Accounting for substance means that the treatment should fairly reflect its commercial effect;

(ii) no amount of disclosure will remedy a failure to account for the substance of a transaction. However, disclosure may be required in addition to the accounting, for example of the special nature of the asset or liability;

(iii) special purpose transactions package rights and obligations in ways that make it difficult to discern the substance and therefore the appropriate accounting treatment. For example:

   (a) legal title may be separated from the rights to benefits and the associated risks;

   (b) there may be a series of transactions such that the commercial effect is only apparent if all of the transactions are considered together rather than separately;

   (c) the package may include options whose conditions make it probable that they will be exercised;

(iv) a key step in analysing special purpose transactions, in order to determine their substance, is to see what effect they have on the 'assets and liabilities' of the company as defined below and also to consider what is most likely or probable to occur;

(v) an asset is a 'probable future economic benefit controlled by and accruing to a company as a result of past transactions or events';

(vi) a liability is a 'present obligation of a company entailing probable future sacrifices of economic benefits by transferring assets or providing services in the future';

(vii) assets and liabilities, as defined above, should be shown separately and not netted off, even if there is a legal right of set off;

(viii) controlled non-subsidiaries should be included in the group accounts, or, if there are no group accounts, pro forma group accounts, together with a summary of their accounts and an explanation of their treatment in the group accounts. A controlled non-subsidiary is a company, trust or other vehicle which, though not fulfilling the Companies Act 1985 definition of a subsidiary, is directly or indirectly controlled by and a source of benefits or risks for the reporting enterprise or its subsidiaries that are in substance no different from those that would arise were the vehicle a subsidiary.

ED42 includes a section dealing specifically with securitised mortgages and raises, as the key question, whether any benefits and related risks remaining with the Originator are of a kind that is best indicated by retaining the securitised assets on its balance sheet. Five categories of risk associated with securitised mortgages are identified:

(i) bad debts;
(ii) delays in collecting repayments, which the Originator may have to make good;
(iii) basis risk, which represents the difference between the interest rate receivable on the assets and that payable on the debt and where such differences may be borne by the Originator;
(iv) reinvestment risk, which represents the interest rate differential on investing early redemptions;
(v) administration risk, where the Originator continues to administer the mortgages and is exposed to negligence suits and to public or moral pressure to ease repayment obligations in the event that economic or other conditions deteriorate.

If the combined effect of these risks represents a significant risk or benefit to the originator, the ED suggests that the assets should be retained on its balance sheet with a corresponding liability for the amount due.

What is meant by a significant risk or benefit is not defined, nor is there any attempt to distinguish between the retention of risks as opposed to the retention of benefits, whether contingent or otherwise.

6. PROPOSED CHANGES TO ED42 PRIOR TO ITS ADOPTION AS A STANDARD

It was apparent from many of the comments received on ED42 that there was wide support for an accounting standard on off-balance sheet finance. It was also agreed that given the complexity and number of transactions or arrangements, including securitisations, that need to be covered, the standard should be based on a general approach, appealing to concepts rather than prescriptive rules.

It has been argued that securitisation arrangements really do change the underlying subject matter from the point of view of the Originator and that it would be misleading to reflect both the securitised assets and a corresponding liability on the balance sheet of the Originator, particularly where all the risks have been effectively covered by insurance or other arrangements.

It was further suggested that a distinction could be made between monetary and non-monetary assets and sale treatment would be allowed for the former provided the risk element has been removed or otherwise adequately provided for.

Suggestions as to specific disclosures that may be required of assets transferred under securitisation arrangements included:

(i) consolidation of all similar balance sheet vehicles (as a note to the financial statements);

(ii) description of profit extraction;
(iii) income derived by the Originator distinguishing normal servicing fees from residual profit;
(iv) any contingent gains or losses not yet recognised and the circumstances by which they may crystallise.

Certain aspects of ED42 have been largely overtaken by events, in particular the Bank of England's Notice (see below) and the Companies Act 1989. It is probable that a further exposure draft will be issued and it is possible that the definite Standard will not be effective until accounting periods commencing on or after 1 January 1991. The revised exposure draft is likely to differ from the original in a number of ways, including, it is anticipated, the treatment of securitised assets, where specific guidance notes are expected to be given. Until this matter is finally resolved, accountants will continue to look to the underlying substance of ED42, particularly the need to ensure that the accounting reflects the economic substance of transactions and that appropriate disclosure is given to support the accounting treatment.

7. BANK OF ENGLAND'S NOTICE ON LOAN TRANSFERS AND SECURITISATION

An important and attractive reason for entering into securitisation transactions is to achieve off-balance sheet treatment for capital adequacy purposes.

The Bank of England's Notice on Loan Transfers and Securitisation (see Appendix 2 on page 312), issued in February 1989, provides detailed guidance to UK authorised institutions as to the factors the Bank will consider in determining whether or not a sale of an asset or bundle of assets has taken place for capital adequacy purposes.

The Bank identified the following areas to be considered when determining whether or not the risks and rewards of an asset or bundle of assets have been transferred:

(i) method of transfer, ie:

    (a) novation;
    (b) assignment (legal or equitable);
    (c) sub-participation.

The Bank has indicated that all of these methods, if properly contracted and subject to certain conditions, can achieve sale treatment;

(ii) conditions of the sale agreement, including:

    (a) no contravention of terms of original loan agreement;
    (b) residual beneficial interest in principal must have passed;
    (c) no recourse by buyer to seller for losses;
    (d) no obligation by seller to repurchase assets or support losses;
    (e) rescheduling or renegotiation affects buyer, not seller;
    (f) funds do not need to be remitted to buyer until received by the seller.

The Bank also sets out a number of different conditions to be met by a bank acting as servicer or administrator of loan packaging schemes, in order to ensure that its role is not seen as being more than acting as agent:

(i)   the servicer's auditors and legal advisers must confirm that the terms of the scheme protect it from any liability to investors in the scheme;

(ii)   the servicer must be able to demonstrate that it will not feel obliged or impelled to support any losses suffered by the scheme or investors in it;

(iii) the servicer must not own any share capital in the SPV or otherwise control it;

(iv)   the servicer should have no more than one representative on the Board of the SPV which must be independent of the servicer;

(v)   the SPV's name should not include the name of the servicer;

(vi)   the servicer must not bear any of the recurring expenses of the scheme, although it may make a one-off contribution to enhance the creditworthiness of the SPV;

(vii) the servicer should not intentionally bear any losses arising from interest rate movements;

(viii) the servicer should not provide a liquidity facility to the vehicle in order to cope with cash shortfalls caused by arrears other than an initial one-off payment;

(ix)   the servicer may not retain an option to repurchase, or refinance, loans except where the portfolio has fallen to less than 10% of its maximum value and the option only extends to fully-performing loans.

The consequence of not satisfying the Bank on any of the above conditions is not an accounting resolution but rather an impact on the institution's capital requirement or minimum risk asset ratio.

It is therefore possible that the accounting treatment will differ from the somewhat harsher supervisory treatment, for capital adequacy purposes, of securitised asset transactions by banks. However, it is clear that the auditors will need to be satisfied that, from an accounting point of view, the transaction qualifies for sale accounting treatment.

APPLICATION TO SPECIFIC TRANSACTION STRUCTURES AND ARRANGEMENTS

This section deals with a number of the accounting issues that arise from various securitisation structures and arrangements.

A. Adjustment to profit or loss on sale

Assuming that sales accounting treatment is deemed to be appropriate, the Originator may need to record a number of sale adjustments at the date of sale, which may be adjusted during the life of the securitisation issue as circumstances change.

1. RECOURSE ESTIMATES

Recourse obligations may take many forms and their existence, terms and conditions will be a key determining feature as to whether sale treatment is indeed appropriate or not. The revised ED42 may suggest that the total element of receivables covered by recourse provisions should continue to be kept on-balance sheet even though this amount exceeds the anticipated bad debt experience of the Originator.

Some of the various forms of recourse include the following:

(i) the Originator has to reimburse the Issuer in cash for losses caused by bad debts through delinquencies or ineligible receivables. This represents a loss to the Originator and should be initially provided at the time of sale and may need to be adjusted as actual loss experience develops;

(ii) the Originator replaces defaulting receivables with 'good' receivables. Again this will represent a loss to the Originator which should be provided as in (i) above;

(iii) the Originator does not receive the full purchase price for the assets sold but a 'holdback' reserve is established against which defaulting receivables are set. In this case the amount of the reserve that is estimated to be ultimately recoverable would be reflected as a receivable by the Originator and that portion that is needed to cover losses from defaults is provided for at the time of sale;

(iv) senior/junior structures where the junior, subordinated debt is retained by the Originator and bears the defaults and other losses. Provided such junior debt is deemed to be adequate to cover future losses, there is no impact on the sale of receivables supporting the senior debt. There may of course be a need for a provision on the junior debt;

(v) overcollateralisation of the assets sold where assets are sold at an amount greater than the value of the related securities issued. As with (iv) above the surplus assets which are used to meet any defaulting receivables should be provided for and any surplus amount should be treated as a receivable by the Originator;

(vi) a reserve or spread escrow account is established, into which is passed the excess of interest earned on the receivables transferred over the interest passed through to the investors together with a normal servicing fee. This account, which may be established at the outset by the Issuer using the proceeds of an advance from the Originator, is used to meet any default on the receivables. Some or all of the balance on the account may revert to the Originator during the period of the securitisation as the underlying receivables are collected. The recognition of the amounts that will be repaid to the Originator (including any original advance) should be recorded when recoverability is certain.

The fundamental accounting issue is whether the Originator is able to make a reasonable estimate of such recourse obligations or recoveries so that they can be recorded as a liability or asset at the outset. This can normally only be achieved where there is reliable historical experience and often only where there is a large portfolio of relatively small and homogeneous accounts to consider. If this is lacking, sale accounting treatment will be difficult to justify. It is, of course, appropriate that these estimates should be reviewed and adjusted throughout the securitisation issue on the basis of actual experience.

Under US accounting requirements, it should be noted that sale accounting is specifically not allowed unless the collectibility and repossession are subject to reasonable estimation. It is not sufficient to provide the maximum exposure—instead a reasonable estimate of the actual exposure is necessary.

2. ABNORMAL SERVICING FEES RETAINED BY THE ORIGINATOR

If servicing of the transferred receivables is retained by the Originator and if these fees differ from the current, normal rates, the sales price should be adjusted using the estimated present value of the differential. This accrual will be written back over the period of the servicing.

3. INTEREST RATE DIFFERENTIAL RETAINED BY THE ORIGINATOR

If receivables are sold with an interest rate differential retained by the Originator, for example if high yielding credit card receivables are sold to yield a lower rate, the present value of the interest rate differential, based on the estimated life of the underlying receivables, should be recorded as part of the sales proceeds.

The carrying value of the interest differential will be released to income over the life of the receivables and should be reassessed regularly to adjust for actual pre-payment and delinquency experience.

4. ISSUE COSTS

Where these have been incurred by the Originator and sales treatment has been adopted, it is not appropriate to defer these costs but rather they should be taken as an expense and included in the computation of profit or loss on sale.

B. Accounting issues arising from various profit extraction methods

An important factor in considering differing securitisation structures is the effectiveness (primarily from a tax point of view) of extracting any residual profits from the SPV. In most cases the accounting is relatively straightforward and should typically be recognised on an accruals basis by both the Issuer and the Originator.

1. SALE OF ASSETS TO THE SPV AT A PRICE EXCEEDING PAR

This will give rise to a realised profit by the Originator, although the full proceeds of sale will only be received over time assuming that a sufficient spread is generated by the SPV. This gives rise to the accounting issue of whether the recoverability of the receivable is sufficiently certain to be included in the Originator's financial statements.

2. INTEREST SWAPS

In these situations, the SPV agrees to pay the Originator interest based on the rate of interest earned on the securitised assets (for example the mortgage rate) in return for the Originator paying the SPV interest based on the SPV's funding rate (for example the amount paid to the SPV's bond holders).

The SPV and the Originator will accrue interest income and interest expense inclusive of the effects of the swap and establish a liability or asset for amounts payable or receivable from the swap counterparty.

3. PARTIAL SALE OF INTEREST IN SECURITISED ASSETS

Consideration has been given to the transfer of only a partial interest in the securitised assets, such that any residual remaining in the SPV belongs to the Originator. Assuming that this is achievable from a legal and tax standpoint, the accounting will follow the normal accruals and prudence concepts, ie recognition when recoverability is reasonably assured. This may be at the outset or during the life of the securitisation.

4. ADMINISTRATION AND OTHER FEES

These will be accounted for on the accruals basis in the normal way.

OVERVIEW OF SECURITISATION ACCOUNTING UNDER US GAAP

A general US accounting postulate is that accounting follows the economic substance (as opposed to the legal form) of a transaction unless a specific authoritative accounting pronouncement prohibits it. Securitisation, however, is one area where the *form* of a transaction is more important than the economics. Two transactions with similar economics, but different structures, may be accounted for very differently.

The FASB has issued two accounting standards that are specifically relevant but that also provide conflicting guidance: Statement of Financial Accounting Standards No 77, 'Reporting by Transferor for Transfers of Receivables with Recourse' (Statement 77) and FASB Technical Bulletin No 85–2 'Accounting for Collateralised Mortgage Obligations (CMOs)' (Technical Bulletin 85–2). Although Technical Bulletin 85–2 addresses only mortgage transfers, it is generally applied to all other types of receivable.

Securitisations generally fall into two categories: those that purport to be sales or participations and those that are borrowings. The fundamental difference is the legal ownership of the underlying receivables.

Transactions which purport to be sales generally involve a pass-through structure, in which the Issuer sells pass-through or participation certificates that represent a pro rata ownership interest in the underlying receivables.

Transactions structured as borrowings appear as collateralised debt, with the receivables pledged as collateral.

The choice of which accounting policy applies depends on the form of the transaction. If the transaction purports to be a sale, Statement 77 applies; if the transaction purports to be a borrowing, Technical Bulletin 85–2 applies. Either form can receive sales treatment if properly structured, although the economic requirements are very different.

A. Statement 77—sales structures

In practice, sales accounting is not difficult to achieve under Statement 77, particularly for large pools of homogeneous receivables. The necessary conditions are as follows:

(i) the seller surrenders control of the future economic benefits embodied in the receivables; the transferor has no call option to repurchase receivables previously sold except pursuant to the recourse provisions. However, a right of first refusal is permitted;

(ii) the seller's obligation under the recourse provisions can be reasonably estimated. Lack of experience with similar receivables generally precludes sales treatment because of the inability of the transferor to estimate credit losses and the related recovery costs under the recourse provision;

(iii) the buyer cannot require the seller to repurchase the receivables except pursuant to the recourse provisions or a 'clean-up call', which permits the seller to repurchase the outstanding receivables when the amount outstanding is nominal.

If all of these three conditions are satisfied, the transaction is accounted for as a sale. Any retained interest in the assets would be maintained on the balance sheet, net of any recourse provision.

B. Technical Bulletin 85–2—financing structures

Technical Bulletin 85–2 applies to transactions structured as borrowings with the receivables pledged as collateral. The Issuer owns the underlying receivables and the securities created are the debt obligations of the Issuer which are secured and funded by the underlying receivables.

Technical Bulletin 85–2 provides that such transactions should be recorded as financings unless all of the following conditions are met:

  (i) neither the Issuer nor its affiliates have the right or obligation to substitute collateral or to obtain it by calling the obligations;
 (ii) the expected residual interest, if any, in the collateral is nominal;
(iii) the investor can look only to the Issuer's assets or to third party insurers or guarantors for repayment of both principal and interest on the obligation and neither the sponsor nor its affiliates are even secondarily liable;
 (iv) there is no requirement to redeem the obligations before their stated maturity other than through normal pay-through of collections on the mortgage collateral.

If all of these conditions are met the transaction should be accounted for as a sale of the assets.

With regard to condition (ii), the expected residual is defined as the present value of all amounts expected to revert to the issuer or its affiliates (including reinvestment earnings). Excess (above average) servicing fees and any overcollateralisation are considered part of the expected residual interest. In practice, 'nominal' has been interpreted as 1% to 2% of the fair market value of the collateral.

Under Technical Bulletin 85–2, it is reasonably easy to assure financing treatment for the Issuer. However, the transaction can be taken off-balance sheet by the Originator by selling a majority ownership interest in the Issuer to a third party and thereby avoiding consolidation as explained below.

C. US consolidation issues

In the US, Statement of Financial Accounting Standards No 94, *'Consolidation of All Majority-owned Subsidiaries'*, requires consolidation of all majority-owned subsidiaries unless control is expected to be temporary or control does not rest with the majority owner. Technical Bulletin 85–2 concludes that the Issuer is merely a conduit for the Originator and the financial statements of the Issuer should be consolidated.

Off-balance sheet treatment may be achieved in two ways. First, the Issuer can structure and account for the issue of certificates as a sale. In this case, consolidating the Issuer will not cause the assets to come onto the consolidated balance sheet. Secondly, the Originator can sell its residual or equity interest in the Issuer, avoiding consolidation altogether, so long as that sale is substantive.

If the Issuer or special purpose vehicle (SPV) is not owned by its sponsor but by another party (so-called 'orphan subsidiaries'), the existing accounting literature is not clear. The other party might be a 'not-for-profit' entity or an individual. The Securities and Exchange Commission (SEC) has announced that they will publish a staff accounting bulletin which will require consolidation of orphan subsidiaries by their sponsors unless 'the majority owner (or owners) of the SPV is an independent third party who has made a substantive capital investment in the SPV, has control of the SPV, and has substantive risks and rewards of ownership of the assets of the SPV (including residuals)'.

D. The EITF and the FASB financial instruments project

The FASB is in the relatively early stages of a major project dealing with financial instruments and off-balance sheet financing. The project, which some believe is the most complicated project ever undertaken by the FASB, is expected to last about five years. It may create sweeping changes in accounting and the conclusions ultimately reached could have a significant effect on asset securitisation transactions and the enterprises that participate in them. Until the FASB develops guidance, the FASB's Emerging Issues Task Force (EITF) and the SEC will continue to address specific issues as they arise.

THE FUTURE

The securitisation industry in the UK is expanding in size, scope and complexity at a time when the legal and accounting framework is undergoing a number of significant changes which will have a major impact on both existing and proposed securitisation structures.

The new Companies Act and the Standard on Off-Balance Sheet Finance will probably take effect from 23 December 1989 and 1 January 1991 respectively. Whilst there are likely to be transitional provisions in the Standard, the Act does not contain any grandfathering provisions and existing securitisation structures may require different accounting treatments for the future, particularly the inclusion of previously non-consolidated entities in the consolidated accounts. The effect that this will have on gearing ratios and on existing loan covenants has not been addressed, but it is clear that Originators and their advisers will seek alternative structures that achieve the basic objectives of off-balance sheet treatment without foregoing the rewards from the securitised assets.

It is apparent that there will be much debate as to whether sufficient of the risks and rewards have been transferred to justify sales treatment and much of this debate will centre around the continuing influence that the Originator has in such matters as the setting of interest rates, the follow up on delinquent receivables and the right to share in any residual in the SPV. All or some of these elements remaining may suggest that the Originator has not complied with the basic objective of the passing of all risks *and* rewards commensurate with the risks being transferred.

Some of these problems may be overcome by the establishment of joint ventures or consortium companies, perhaps owned individually less than 50% by a number of Originators, servicers and even investment banks, so as to avoid the consolidation rules. These companies will manage and operate the SPVs within prearranged and tightly prescribed rules, covering such matters as:

(i) entitlement of Originators to service, fee and other income generated by the SPVs, including any residual income;
(ii) setting of interest rates charged on securitised assets;
(iii) procedures for following up and collecting delinquent receivables;
(iv) repayment of any surplus moneys to Originators held within spread accounts or as a result of over-collateralisation.

The impact of the proposed changes in the US in this area will also influence the accounting treatment to be adopted, but the UK is still as far away as ever from following the example of the US in having a detailed accounting rulebook, which may bring some certainty but also provides the opportunity for avoiding the rules.

Chapter 13

Asset-backed Securitisation

Joseph D. Smallman and Michael J. P. Selby
The London School of Economics and Political Science

INTRODUCTION

Securitisation offers traditional and non-traditional financial intermediaries a source of low cost funds. By packaging homogeneous receivables for sale to investors via the capital and money markets, this new method of financing has grown exponentially because of the utility (savings and benefits) it offers issuers and investors. Therefore, finance professionals must gain an understanding of this new system in order to stay competitive.

The purpose of this chapter is to give the reader a general overview of non-mortgage securitisation. All non-mortgage securitised debt instruments are referred to as asset-backed securities (ABS). This chapter presents three main sections. The first section presents a general overview of the US ABS market and examines the reasons for its rapid growth, the legal structures of ABSs and credit analysis considerations. The second section examines the pricing and cash flows of ABSs with detailed illustrations of certain issues. Additionally, in this section we compare and contrast the ABS cash flows with mortgage-backed securities. In the concluding section we discuss the potential development of asset-backed securities in Europe.

OVERVIEW OF ASSET-BACKED SECURITIES (ABS)

A. Growth of asset-backed securities

When Mark McCoy, Salomon Brothers' asset-backed specialist, was asked what assets were appropriate for securitisation, he replied, 'If it flows, securitise it!' By this he meant that any receivable that generates a cash flow can be considered for structured financing. At present, the following receivables have been securitised:

credit cards	utility leases
auto loans	computer leases
boat loans	municipal equipment leases
marine loans	trade receivables
furniture loans	health care receivables
home equity loans	Euro trade receivables
non-performing loans	junk bonds
unsecured consumer loans	insurance premiums
manufactured housing loans	recreational vehicle loans
auto leases	political subdivision bonds
truck leases	utility debt and common stock.

Currently, American Telephone & Telegraph Co is considering securitising its customers' bills, whilst investment bankers are considering structured financing as a solution to third world debt. The potential for asset securitisation is only limited by the imagination.

Issues of asset-backed securities are growing at a dynamic rate (see Figure 1 on page 244). Over £17 billion of public and private issues were placed in 1988, a 70% increase over 1987, with the cumulative growth exceeding £36 billion. Standard & Poor's Corporation (S&P) predicts that this trend will continue. S&P is predicting that in 1989 rated issues will surpass £20 billion, with total market growth exceeding £100 billion by 1992.[1]

The forces motivating this rapid growth are twofold: economic and regulatory. The economic and legal environment will continue to help spur the growth of ABS. The freeing of capital and lower intermediation cost are the two primary economic benefits that are fuelling ABS market growth. Ensuing regulatory reform will continue to motivate securitisation in both the US and Europe. These areas are covered in detail in this section.

1. ECONOMIC MOTIVATION

Securitisation offers the following economic benefits:

  (i) low cost source of funds;
 (ii) fee income;
(iii) off-balance sheet financing;
 (iv) lower intermediation costs;
  (v) risk management—interest rate
                       —credit rate.

(a) Low cost source of funds

Securitisation lowers the cost of funds by isolating risk. With asset-backed

---

[1] Standard & Poor's 'Asset-Backed Securitisation Credit Review' 16 March 1987 and 27 March 1989.

Figure 1.

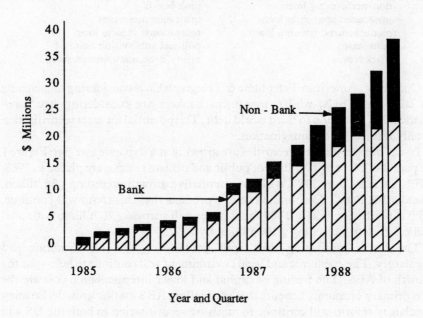

ABS Market Cumulative Issue Volume
Bank vs Non-Bank Assets

securities, investors buy a specific set of receivables with a known amount of risk. This is far safer than investors lending to the company which can then, at its discretion, fund existing assets or purchase riskier ones. This uncertainty leads investors to demand a higher rate of interest for general obligation bonds than for ABS. Additionally, issuing ABS allows companies with low credit ratings to borrow funds at AAA rates.

On the surface, ABS financing appears to be dearer than traditional financing methods. As shown in Table 1 opposite, the ABS cost appears to be 25 basis points (25/100 of 1%) dearer than a comparable traditional corporate issue.

This price differential, currently ranging between 20 and 25 basis points, is based on three factors. The first is that payments are received monthly as opposed to half-yearly. This increases the owner's administrative costs. Secondly, the embedded call option which is inherent in most ABSs adds value. Investors demand to be compensated for the pre-payment uncertainty which exposes them to reinvestment risk. Finally, ABSs are stated in terms of average life which means that the actual maturity could far exceed the stated one.

Table 1.

Security	Average life	Rate %	Spread over Treasury
Treasury	2 years	8.06	–
AAA Corporate	2 years	8.73	67 basis points
AAA ABS	2 years	8.98	92 basis points
Incremental cost of the ABS			25 basis points

Source: P. Zweig, *The Asset Securitisation Handbook*

When considering the cost of capital, it appears that the ABS is dearer, but this analysis fails to consider the aggregate cost of capital. Traditional debt financing must have equity to support it when evaluating credit quality; ABSs are valued on their internal structure, independently from the company's balance sheet. In most cases the cost of structuring ABSs is less than the cost of equity to support the debt issue.

To illustrate, let us re-examine the previous example. Assume that the ABS has a 7% recourse rate. That is to say, in the event of default the originator will repurchase up to a total of 7% of the ABSs principal balance, thus giving the ABS a 14 : 1 debt to equity ratio. Additionally, suppose that the corporation has a 10 : 1 debt to equity ratio and the cost of equity is 25% on a pre-tax basis. As shown by Table 2 (page 246), by identifying the all-in cost of capital, the ABS actually offers a savings of 18 basis points to the issuer.[2]

(b) Fee income

Fee income represents a large portion of the net present value of revenues when evaluating consumer loans. Fee income may include the fixed charges for cash advances on credit cards, annual membership fees and servicing fees. Additionally, revenues are generated through the net positive funding over the life of the asset. By securitising assets, companies are able to earn up-front fees and servicing fees without blowing up their balance sheets. Another benefit to fee income is that it is immune from interest rate risk. Increasing fee income shifts portfolio earnings from interest rate-sensitive spread income to fixed fee income.

(c) Off-balance sheet financing

Securitisation takes assets off the balance sheet, allowing banks with a tight capital structure to free capital. Taking assets off the balance sheet can significantly improve return on equity.

---

[2] This example was adapted from Phillip Zweig in *The Asset Securitization Handbook*, Dow Jones-Irwin, p. 28.

Table 2.

		Rate %	Spread over Treasury
COST OF ADDITIONAL $100 RAISED THROUGH CORPORATE DEBT			
Debt	$100	8.73	67 basis points
Equity	10	25.00	
Total	$110		
Weighted average cost of capital		10.21	215 basis points

		Rate %	Spread over Treasury
COST OF ADDITIONAL $100 RAISED THROUGH ASSET-BACKED SECURITISATION			
Debt	$100	8.98	92 basis points
Equity	7	25.00	
Total	$107		
Weighted average cost of capital		10.03	197 basis points
Savings through ABS			18 basis points

Source: P. Zweig, *The Asset Securitisation Handbook*

(d) Lower intermediation cost

From a macro-economic view, securitisation lowers intermediation costs.[3] Securitisation is simply a type of wholesale financial intermediation (see Figure 2 opposite) which re-bundles existing financial instruments into new securities. This process re-routes disintermediation, represented by the broken line, at the wholesale level. The intermediary's economic function is to reduce transaction and information costs between borrowers and lenders. Intermediaries that provide this service at the lowest cost stay active in the market, while other intermediaries fade away.

Via securitisation intermediaries are able to perform their service without the burden of interest rate risk management. It is, therefore, a form of disintermediation with regard to interest rate risk. By not being burdened with interest rate risk management, intermediaries are exposed to less risk and are able to lower their costs.

(e) Risk management

(i) *interest rate risk.* Companies transfer the interest rate risk to the holder of the ABS. This can be extremely beneficial to finance companies that are highly sensitive to interest rate fluctuations;

(ii) *credit risk.* Risky assets can be transferred off-balance sheet, and this can

---

[3] Hess, A. C. and C. W. Smith, Jr., 'Elements of Mortgage Securitisation', The Journal of Real Estate Finance and Economics, Vol. 1, No 4, December 1988, pp. 331–346.

Figure 2.

Wholesale Financial Intermediation

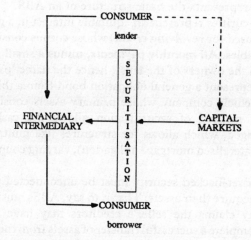

help a company's overall credit standing. For example, Credit Commercial de France used the ABS structure to improve its credit posture by removing $500 million of high risk third world loans from its balance sheet in March 1989.[4]

2. REGULATORY MOTIVATION

US banks share the target date of 1992 with their European cousins in regard to a new wave of regulatory reforms. The new risk based capital rules in the US are scheduled to take full effect in 1992. These capital rules will require US banks to include the total dollar amount of credit cards, automobile loans, boat loans and other consumer loans when calculating capital requirements. These loans require a risk weighting of 100%; mortgage loans, treasury securities and other types of bonds will have a lower risk weighting. The risk based capital rules have caused banks to sell their high risk weighted assets and invest the proceeds in lower weighted ones. As mentioned earlier, even after taking consumer credit off their balance sheets, banks can still earn fee income by servicing the loans.

B. Legal structure

Asset-backed securities share similar legal structures with their mortgage-backed counterpart. Either a AAA or AA rated trust or special purpose

---

[4] American Banker, Asset Sales Report, 20 March 1989, 'French Bank Securitizes Third World Debt Portfolio', p. 3.

corporation is formed to hold the assets. This protects them in the event that the seller becomes bankrupt or is unable to continue to service the receivables. Figure 3 opposite represents the basic structure of an ABS.

Pass-through securities represent an equitable interest in a grantor trust or credit card trust (used for revolving credit) whose corpus consists of a pool of designated receivables. All monthly payments, minus a small service fee, are passed through to the owners of the trust; hence the name 'pass-through'.

Pay-throughs represent a general obligation bond from a thinly capitalised special purpose vehicle company whose primary assets consist of a pool of receivables. This method of securitisation allows the cash flows to be dynamically managed, which allows for structures like multiple class notes (similar to the collateralised mortgage obligation), varying coupon periods and bullet maturities.

Issuers of the asset-backed security must be unconnected with the entity from which they acquire their assets. That is to say, ABSs must be completely immune from any claims the seller's creditors may have in the case of bankruptcy. To complete a successful transfer of assets from the 'Originator' to the 'Issuer' they must establish a 'true sale'. This topic will be further discussed below under 'Legal Issues'.

1. NEW LEGAL DEVELOPMENTS IN THE US

On 19 December 1988 Judge Kevin Duffy overruled Security Pacific Bank in *Security Pacific Bank v Securities Industry Association (SIA)* which put a halt to US banks' underwriting their own assets. Security Pacific had received a letter from the Comptroller of the Currency supporting their underwriting of mortgage-backed securities and confirmed that they were acting within the confines of the Glass-Steagall Act.

The Glass-Steagall Act prohibits banks from actively engaging in the securities underwriting industry. The SIA filed suit against the Comptroller of the Currency in the US District Court for the Southern District of New York in June 1988 and Security Pacific Bank later intervened as co-defendant. Judge Duffy's ruling halted banks from actively underwriting in the asset-backed securities market. However, on 8 September 1989 Judge Duffy's ruling was reversed by the United States Courts of Appeals for the Second Circuit. These legal ambiguities will force United States' law makers to make comprehensive legal reforms.

2. NEW LEGAL DEVELOPMENTS IN THE EUROPEAN COMMUNITY (EC)

One of the major nations in the European Community is starting to clear the way for asset-backed securitisation. The United Kingdom 1989 Budget cleared away one of the major hurdles for asset-backed securities. Prior to this new regulatory approach sterling-denominated debt issues were limited to a five

Figure 3.

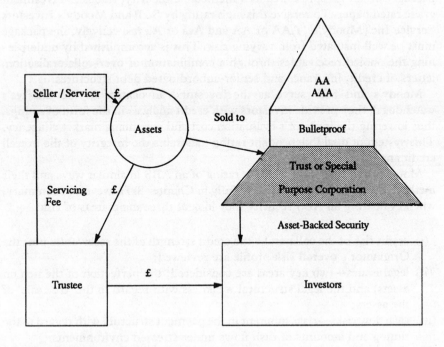

Basic Structure of an ABS

£ = Receivables cash flow

year minimum maturity. This restriction limited securitisation to long-term debt receivables. Mortgages were the only long-term homogeneous debt instrument that had enough depth to permit the securitisation method of intermediation. Now that short and intermediate maturities are allowed, it will be interesting to see how the sterling market reacts given this new freedom.

Another predominant government force in the EC has started supporting and promoting securitisation. French legislators, in December 1988, laid the ground work for *titrisation* (French for securitisation). This new French law will allow underwriters to securitise many types of amortising debt. The two aims of this legislation are: first, to provide additional methods of improving capital ratios for banks; and secondly, to aid free market consumer credit. As the UK and France start developing their markets, other European Community members should follow suit.

C. Rating agencies considerations

Securitisation offers traditional and non-traditional financial intermediaries a source of low cost funds by packaging homogeneous receivables, and then selling the package to investors via the capital and money markets. The package, which is represented as a marketable security, trades as investment grade rated paper. To receive this high rating by S&P and Moody's Investors Service Inc (Moody's), AAA or AA and Aaa or Aa respectively, the package must be well insulated from varying risk. This is accomplished by underpinning the pooled receivables through a combination of over-collateralisation, letters of credit, insurance and senior-subordinated debt structures.

Moody's and S&P serve as the investors' advocates. As the 'market's watchdogs', they provide investors with credit analysis in the form of ratings, thus lowering the investor's evaluation cost and enhancing market efficiency. This system of dual independent rating maintains the integrity of the overall credit analysis.

Moody's and S&P approach the rating of an ABS in similar ways and their methods have been described more fully in Chapter 8. However, in summary, when evaluating an ABS security they look at three main areas of risk:

(i) credit risk of the collateral—the credit strength of the receivables plus the Originator's overall risk profile are reviewed;
(ii) legal issues—two key areas are considered; the perfection of the lien on assets; and the legal structural weakness with regard to the 'true sale' of the assets;
(iii) cash flow risks—risks inherent in the payment structure with regard to the timing and amounts of cash flows under stressed environments.

1. CREDIT RISK

The risk analysis is achieved though the rating process. This starts when the issuer approaches the agencies before it registers the ABS with the Securities and Exchange Commission (regulatory authorities) to discuss the rating parameters. The issuer, or its investment banker, meets each agency to discuss the structure of its transaction and to introduce the agency to the nature of the issuer's business and its operations. Prior to this meeting, the issuer submits a package containing the company's background, strategy, operations, systems and five years of portfolio performance data.

During this preliminary meeting the parties discuss the viability of the issue, the level of rating required and any potential weaknesses of the issue. When the parties agree that the issue is likely to achieve its rating goal, the issuer sends the agency a formal letter requesting a rating. Additionally, they agree to keep the rating agency fully informed of any alterations in the legal documentation or the asset-backed security's structure.

Following the rating request, the issuer forwards all initial drafts of the documentation, including:

(i) the pooling and servicing agreement;

(ii) the prospectus, if it is a public issue;

(iii) a private placement memorandum for a private issue; and

(iv) an indenture when applicable.

After reviewing the documentation, the agency performs an on-site examination. This involves meeting management to review the overall efficiency of the organisation. It is accomplished by interviewing the senior financial management, lending division managers, the underwriting or credit managers, collection managers and the computer systems management. The control functions of accounting, auditing, documentation and management information systems are reviewed. This enables the agency to determine the efficiency of the credit and collection processes.

Furthermore, a delinquent receivable is traced through the system, from the first notification through collection, charge-off and liquidation of the collateral (if applicable). Particular attention is given to the work load of each collector, the duration of the process and involvement of upper management in the more difficult cases. Upon final assessment of the Originator's system, the agency will make recommendations on procedures to segregate the pooled receivables for tracking and reporting purposes.

2. LEGAL ISSUES

When assessing the legal structure of an ABS, it is crucial for the transaction to be 'bulletproof' because the issuer could be exposed to losses if the Originator went bankrupt. Under the US Bankruptcy Code, transfer of assets from the Originator to the Issuer must pass the 'true sale opinion' which is attained from independent legal counsel. When different independent legal counsellors are given identical transactions to consider as a 'true sale', opinions can vary. Therefore, when evaluating the 'true sale' of a structure, S&P considers the following as key considerations:

(i) The transfer is treated as a sale for accounting and tax purposes.

(ii) The level of recourse (direct or indirect) to the Originator is less than a reasonably anticipated default rate based primarily on historical default data. Recourse may take several forms including:
—repurchase of defaulted assets;
—substitution of good assets for defaulted assets;
—reimbursement of third party credit provider;
—retention of subordinated notes.

(iii) The Originator retains none of the benefits of ownership of the transferred assets, ie the Originator is not entitled to any appreciation of the assets and the Originator does not have the right to use the proceeds of the assets.

(iv) The documents are consistent and evidence the parties' intent that the transfer be characterised as a sale.

(v) Neither the assets nor the proceeds of the assets are commingled with property of the Originator.[5]

3. CASH FLOW RISKS

The cash flows of an ABS are predominantly dependent on the cash flows from its underlying receivables. If for some reason the cash flows from the receivables are impaired through delinquency or default there must be additional support. This support can be through over-collateralisation, letters of credit or repurchase agreements. By underpinning the pool of receivables with one or more of these supports, the investors are guaranteed their cash flows even during times of extreme economic uncertainty.

The amount of credit enhancement is determined by exposing the pool of receivables to various stress tests. The maximum arrears and losses expected during times of hyper-inflation, or in times of severe recession and depression, must be offset by the credit support. Additionally, the liquidity and interest rate sensitivity of the receivables are tested under the same extreme economic conditions. This is to insure that there will be enough cash value in the assets if the trustee or issuer is forced to liquidate the receivables to honour payments to investors. The par value of the ABS minus the worst case environment price, equals the amount of credit enhancement that will be required to receive the investment rating. The higher the rating the more severe the tests.

The issue may use three types of credit enhancement:

(i) over-collateralisation;
(ii) letter of credit;
(iii) repurchase agreement.

Over-collateralisation refers to the amount of receivables placed by the Originator in the ABS that exceeds its par value. This excess serves to cushion the cash flows from any seasonal fluctuations, delinquencies or defaults. The amount of over-collateralisation will vary given the credit risk of the receivables. The Originator recoups the excess value once the ABS matures.

A letter of credit (LOC) is another method often used to support ABSs. The main benefit of the LOC is that it allows the ABS to obtain higher ratings than its issuer. This is accomplished when a highly-rated bank or institution underwrites the LOC, guaranteeing a set percentage of the receivables from arrears and losses.

Repurchase agreements are made with the Originator, who contracts to buy back a set percentage of the receivables at face value. This method still supports

[5]   Standard & Poor's, Credit Review, March 1989, p. 7.

the ABS but does not tie up the Originator's assets, as over-collateralisation does. However, the face value of the repurchase agreement must be shown on the Originator's balance sheet.

The rating agencies practise due diligence when assessing asset backed securities. They only give an opinion on the asset's risk sensitivity based on the information they receive. They do not serve as financial advisers. They continue to monitor the ABS monthly throughout its life and will keep investors informed of any dramatic changes.

UNDERSTANDING THE ABS VALUE AND CASH FLOWS

The minimum value of an asset-backed security is equal to the present value of its net cash flows, or the aggregate face value of its underlying receivables. To prevent over-pricing, one must compare the face value of the receivables with the ABS net present value. For example, suppose there is a pool of receivables valued at a premium and this premium is used to value the security. If all the debtors decide to repay in full the day after the issue is sold, the cash flows would not be able to satisfy the debt on the notes. In this case the total face value of the receivables should have been used. Alternatively, when receivables are sold at a discount the present value method is appropriate.

The following three methods are used to determine present value:

(i) GROSS-TO-GROSS;
(ii) CONSTANT-TO-NET;
(iii) NET-TO-NET.

Applying these three present value methods to the same set of cash flows may yield different results. Therefore it is important to have an understanding of the different methodologies. All these methods assume no pre-payment and use the same payment frequency for the receivables as for the notes:

(i) the GROSS-TO-GROSS method discounts the gross cash flows by the gross rate. The gross rate includes the note rate (coupon rate), the servicing fee and other expenses. This method has a tendency to overstate the note's value;
(ii) the CONSTANT-TO-NET method discounts the gross cash flows, less a static servicing fee and other expenses, by the note rate. This method has a tendency to understate the security's value because it fixes the servicing fee based on the beginning balance of the pool of receivables. Servicing and expenses are normally charged as a percentage, and since this balance is amortising, the expenses are overstated;
(iii) the NET-TO-NET method offers the best approach because it most accurately reflects the true cash flows. This method discounts the net cash

flow (cash flows received by the security holder) and discounts them at the note rate.

A. Certificates for amortising revolving debts (CARDS)

To explore every ABS structure would require reviewing every security issued—a total of 157 as of July 1989. Therefore, selected issues of credit card backed securities, which are referred to as Certificates for Amortising Revolving Debts (CARDS), and auto backed securities, referred to as Certificates for Automobile Receivables (CARS), will be examined. Credit cards represent the largest dollar value in total issued; auto loans are the largest number issued.

CARDS are normally issued paying fixed interest for the first 18 months; they then begin amortising and pay out in a relatively short period. Over the past four years, average monthly repayment rates have ranged from 9.61% for private label cards, which are historically slow payers, to 19.59% for cards like VISA and MASTERCARD. The first issue structured as a sale for regulatory and financial reporting purposes was Bank of America's $300 million 8.20% California Credit Card Trust 1987-A. This paid interest at a fixed rate for the first 18 months, and then fully amortised in the following three months.

Figure 4.

Cash Flows of California Credit Card Trust 1987-A

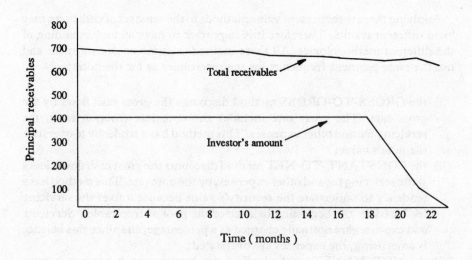

As this graph shows, the over-collateralisation of the CARDS issue serves to cushion fluctuations in the receivables, leaving the investors' cash flows intact. Additionally, the rapid amortisation was expected because of the traditionally high monthly payment rates. Another reason for the quick payout of principal was that the structure of this transaction allocated the cardholder collections on the basis of a fixed percentage rate equal to the investors' proportionate interest in the pool.

SPIEGEL CHARGE ACCOUNT TRUST NO 1

In December 1988 Spiegel Inc, a subsidy of Otto Versand GMBA, securitised its Preferred Charge credit card receivables via the Spiegel Charge Account Trust No 1 (SCAT 1) offering $150 million in investor certificates, yielding a 9.6% annualised monthly rate or a 9.8% bond equivalent yield. This was the first credit card-backed security issued by a German owned company that was underwritten by a German bank. The issue received AAA ratings from both Moody's and S&P.

Spiegel Inc is a retail mail-order merchant that provides open-ended revolving consumer credit to its customers. Spiegel has 61 billing cycles of which 1–16 were included in its first ABS issue. The Spiegel Charge Account Trust No 1 cash flows are supported by over-collateralisation and letters of credit.

(a) Structure

As shown by Figure 5 (page 256), Spiegel Inc sold $190 million worth of credit card receivables to Spiegel Credit Corporation (SCC). This is a special purpose corporation which serves as an intermediary in order to effect a 'true sale' of the receivables. This insulates the receivables from any claims Spiegel Inc's creditors may have against the assets in the event of bankruptcy.

SCC then sells the receivables to the Spiegel Charge Account No 1 credit card Trust for $190 million, which in turn issues $150 million worth of investor certificates to the lead underwriter, Deutsche Bank Capital Corporation (DCBB). The Trust then channels the $150 million cash and a $40 million Seller's Certificate which is sent back through the structure to Spiegel Inc.

Spiegel Inc will continue to service the receivables, passing the cash flows down through the structure to the investors. Any excess servicing income will be paid to a spread account which will fund the cost of Deutsche Bank's 30% Letter of Credit (LOC). This 30% LOC protects the Trust's cash flows from default or delinquent receivables. Given this support, the Trust would have to suffer a $85 million [30% of $150 million plus $40 million equals $85 million] or a 56.67% loss before investors would be affected. Considering Spiegel Inc's historical portfolio performance and servicing capabilities, losses of this magnitude are most unlikely.

Finally, Deutsche Bank issued an additional $20 million service LOC to protect the pool if the servicer went bankrupt. The servicer, Spiegel Inc, accrues collected receivables on a monthly basis and then passes them through the structure to the Trust at the end of the month. If Spiegel Inc goes bankrupt, Deutsche Bank will compensate SCAT 1 to a maximum of $20 million. This ensures a timely and prudent flow of funds to the Trust. If for some reason the servicer exceeds $20 million in its accrual account, the excess must be remitted to the Trust's account within two business days.

Figure 5.

SCAT 1 Structure Diagram

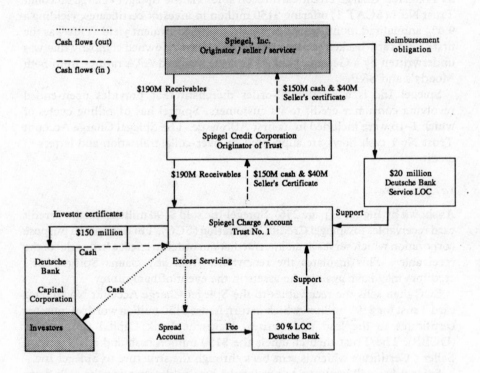

(b) Payments

The Spiegel Charge Account Trust No 1 has a four year maturity with an average life of three and a half years. The payment streams are divided over two periods:

(i) 36 month revolving period;
(ii) 12 month controlled amortisation period.

During the first 36 months SCAT 1 will pay interest only. When the revolving period terminates, the pool will amortise over the next 12 months paying interest and a fixed rate principal reduction of 1/12 per month. Furthermore, Figure 6 shows that the Seller's Certificate serves to cushion the face value of the notes from seasonal fluctuations and interest rate movements. This 26% 'over-collateralisation' subordinated debt reverts to Spiegel Inc following the maturity of the ABS.

Figure 6.

Cash Flows of the Spiegel Charge Account Trust No 1

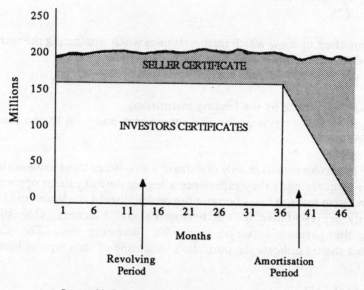

Source: Mr Berry Perhac of DBCC

The beauty of this structure is that Spiegel receives the best of both the financial and tax worlds. Under the provisions of the Statement of Financial Accounting Standards, Spiegel was able to treat this sale as an 'off-balance sheet' transaction. Spiegel converted $150 million of risky receivables into cash at a relatively low cost, dynamically improving its balance sheet complexion. Even though the receivables were treated as a sale for financial accounting purposes, Spiegel Inc was (and still is) able to treat the cash flows as a debt expense under tax accounting rules. This tax saving lowered Spiegel Inc's 'all-in' cost of capital. Moreover, this ABS structure allowed Spiegel Inc, an unrated company, to tap AAA rated funds at 73 basis points over comparable US Treasuries while enjoying secondary tax benefits.

B. Collateralised automobile receivables (CARS)

CARS are backed by self-amortising personal auto loans that are paid monthly with two to seven years maturities. Most loans are at a fixed rate and are secured by a lien on a new car or light truck. Lenders use different methods for calculating interest and have different types of loans.

The three most commonly used accrual methods are:

(i) actuarial method;
(ii) simple interest; and
(iii) rule of 78.

It is important to know which method is used when structuring the security because different methods can affect the ABS payout.

There are two types of auto loans:

(i) direct loans: made by the lending institution;
(ii) indirect loans: originated by the auto dealer and sold to the lending institution.

CARS portfolios consist mainly of indirect loans. When these loans are made on a non-recourse basis they experience a higher default rate as opposed to dealer-recourse loans. This is because the dealer absorbs the losses and is not necessarily representative of the borrower's credit quality. One should consider the portfolio's composition when assessing risk. The CARS prospectus should indicate the portfolio's weighting of each type of loan.

1. FIXED-RATE CARS

In 1984 the failing US automobile industry introduced 'incentive-rate financing'. Through their captive finance subsidiaries, manufacturers offered below market loans to entice buyers. This marketing method has been well received by the US public and the captives now dominate the market. These deep-discounted 'incentive-rate' loans have allowed fixed payment CARS to be issued.

The fixed-payment CARS structure eliminates investors' concerns over pre-payment. This type of structure resembles a corporate bond with a sinking fund and is not directly dependent on pre-payments. The issuer is able to achieve this structure by utilising a guaranteed investment contract which absorbs the pre-paid cash flows. The investment contract guarantees a pre-determined yield for undistributed cash flows. This eliminates reinvestment risk by allowing issuers to park their excessive cash flows with a yield that will support the ABS debt service. To gain a better understanding of this structure we shall review one of Salomon Brothers' CARS issues in detail.

2. SALOMON BROTHERS RECEIVABLES INC, CARS, SERIES 1

Salomon Brothers Receivables Inc, Series 1 (SAL 1) is a AAA rated special purpose company whose assets consist of $442.6 million of collateralised auto receivables purchased from Marine Midland Bank. It issued two notes which Salomon Brothers Inc placed on 17 November 1987. This issue represents the 'pay-through' structure—the same structure that is used when underwriting collateralised mortgage obligations (CMO).

Structure

SAL 1's legal structure and capital flows are shown in Figure 7 (page 260). Marine Midland Bank, NA is a New York bank which purchased and bundled a group of instalment sale contracts from New York State car dealers and then sold them to SAL 1. This indirect, wholly owned subsidiary of Salomon Inc serves as a limited purpose, bankruptcy-remote legal entity, established specifically to issue asset-backed obligations.

SAL 1's notes represent two tranches of senior debt that pay quarterly. Class Y has a coupon of 8.15% with a guaranteed termination date of 15 November 1989, whilst Class A has a coupon of 8.50% with a guaranteed termination date of 15 November 1990. The guaranteed termination dates are attractive to investors because they eliminate maturity uncertainty. The logic for having two tranches is the same as that used when issuing CMOs; varying maturities allow the issuer dynamically to manage cash flow uncertainty resulting from pre-payments.

This transaction was supported by the following three credit enhancements which were issued by the Union Bank of Switzerland:

(i) 8.5% Letter of Credit (LOC);
(ii) 6.85% Guaranteed Investment Contract (GIC); and
(iii) Purchase Agreement.

The 8.5% LOC serves to cushion cash flows from problems with the underlying receivables. If these receivables become delinquent or default, impeding the issuer's ability to pay the note holders, the Trustee—Chemical Bank—will draw on the LOC. This irrevocable letter of credit will support losses to a maximum of $38 million (8.5% of the ABS face value). This LOC cushion should support the receivables, even during harsh economic periods. Delinquencies for the Marine Midland Bank NA auto loan portfolio ranged from 2.38% to 3.39% between 1983 and 1987 with defaults only ranging from 0.53% to 0.59%.

Figure 7.

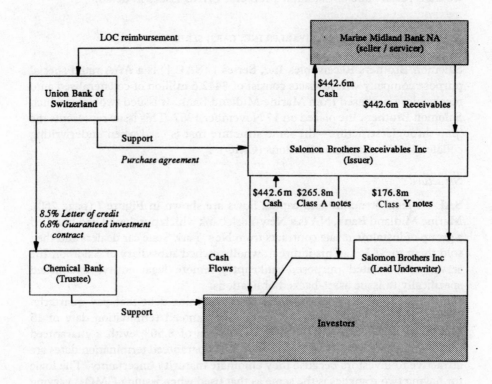

Structure of Salomon Brothers Receivables Inc, Series 1

The 6.85% Guaranteed Investment Contract serves to protect cash flows from reinvestment risk. If interest rates dropped severely, this could affect the yield on intermediate cash flows. For example, let us assume that all the receivables were pre-paid in full the day after the issue is sold and on the same day interest rates dropped to 3%. Three months later when the quarterly payment became due on the note, the issuer would not have enough cash to cover the debt. The Guaranteed Investment Contract significantly reduces this risk.

The Purchase Agreement assures the notes' guaranteed maturity. The underlying receivables are in the form of amortising consumer debt which has pre-payment uncertainty. These receivables can repay at any time or wait the full term of their contracts. If the pool experiences a zero pre-payment rate, then the issuer will not be able to retire the Class Y notes in 1989. Union Bank of Switzerland (UBS), through their repurchase agreement, will buy a substitute Y note in the amount equal to the unpaid balance of the Y notes. If the same problem arises for the Class A notes then UBS will purchase all the remaining receivables. This will enable the issuer to meet its obligations to investors.

To summarise, Marine Midland Bank, NA, which is rated below AA, was able to attain AAA rates via SAL 1. This transaction, which was structured similarly to a CMO, attracted investors because it paid quarterly over a maximum guaranteed life. With a combination of proper credit underpinning, SAL 1 was able to offer two AAA notes that resembled traditional corporate debt.

C. Pre-payment: asset-backed versus mortgage-backed securities

Pre-payment is the most important variable when assessing a US mortgage-backed security (MBS). MBS pre-payment rates exhibit 'negative convexity' with relation to interest rates; that is to say, pre-payment rates increase as interest rates decrease. CARDS and CARS do not suffer negative convexity because of the nature of their underlying securities. Interest rate sensitivity is best shown through the following illustration.

Figure 8.

Pre-payment Rates Sensitivity Based on Interest Rate Movements

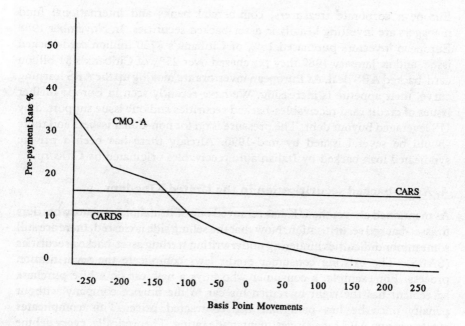

Pre-payment on auto loans is contingent on transfer, cashing out, repossession, loss or death. Effectively, all US auto loans are made with a 'due-on-sale' clause and when the asset is transferred or traded-in the loan must be repaid. This is the primary cause of pre-payment. Cashing out is when the debtor voluntarily repays his loan—a rare occurrence. When a vehicle is repossessed, it is sold and the proceeds are used to retire the debt; losses due to fire, theft or death of the debtor are covered by insurance. Refinancing is usually not economically beneficial for the consumer because auto loan rates are higher on used cars.

Pre-payment sensitivity to revolving credit is not affected by swings in interest rates. Suppliers of revolving consumer credit adjust their rates when there are wide swings in the market. The difference in rates between credit cards is marginal and does not offer any economic incentive for a consumer to pre-pay his debt with another card.

Investors are well aware of the CMO's interest rate sensitivity and are demanding approximately 30 basis points for the additional volatility. The US treasuries rate is considered riskless and serves as a benchmark for investors when pricing risk. A CMO A-tranche risk premium is currently 110 basis points over US treasuries, while ABSs enjoy the narrower margin of 80 basis points.

ASSET-BACKED SECURITISATION IN EUROPE

European corporate treasurers, commercial banks and international fund managers are investing heavily in asset-backed securities. In November 1988 European investors purchased 15% of Citibank's $750 million card-backed issue, and in January 1989 they purchased over 25% of Citibank's $1 billion card-backed ABS deal. As European investors are moving up the ABS learning curve, their appetite is increasing. We have recently seen in Europe further issues of credit card receivables-backed securities and one issue supported by US leveraged buyout debt. The pressure is on for non-dollar issuers and there should be several issued by mid-1990. Already there has been a private syndicated loan backed by Italian auto receivables originated by Citicorp.

A. Asset-backed securitisation in the United Kingdom

As mentioned above, the UK has removed one of its major regulatory barriers to asset-backed securitisation. Now that the selling side is cleared, there are still some minor difficulties hindering underwriting sterling asset-backed securities (SABS). The existing consumer credit laws complicate the securitisation process. For example, a consumer who buys a new car on a hire purchase agreement has the right to return his car to the finance company without penalty once he has paid half the contracted price. This complicates structuring an ABS for an investment grade rating. Theoretically, every debtor could return his car to the originator half paid. The potential losses due to this possibility would appear to make securitisation prohibitively expensive.

Another significant cost is stamp duty. Whenever there is a transfer of assets, the government taxes the value of the transfer at a rate of 1%. There are some exemptions for small transfers but when transacting in hundreds of millions of pounds this tax becomes expensive.

The development of SABS will be limited given the current environment. A thin supply of homogeneous receivables, combined with the previously mentioned UK consumer protection regulations, will limit market penetration. The transfer of receivables is not restricted by English or Scottish law and this is beneficial to SABS market growth. The problem that faces SABS underwriters is not the transferring of assets but what is being transferred. English title law, which dates back centuries, is not conducive to the bundling and transferring of assets. Additionally, UK financial lending methods are splintered and not designed for a secondary market. To find an existing pool of £500 million worth of homogeneous receivables with clear rights of recourse could be a difficult task. The legal restraints, tax costs and standardised financing methods will need to fall in line before sterling asset-backed securitisation can take off.

Medium-term sterling investors prefer floating rate notes over fixed. This could compound the underwriting process because funding fixed-rate debt with floating-rate loans can be dangerous if the margins are thin. If the floating rate 'cost of funds' exceeds the fixed rate 'source of funds', cash flows dwindle and losses are incurred. In the case of credit cards, margins are wide enough to support any short-term swings in interest rates, while long-term movements could be offset by increasing the card rate. Additionally, auto loans could be made on a floating rate, eliminating the floating/fixed rate mis-match.

Given the efficiencies and savings inherent in the securitisation process, SABS should develop as the primary markets are standardised and government restraints are removed. In 1987 sceptics of sterling mortgage-backed securities said that they were a 'fluke' and would never survive in the UK financial environment. As securitisation has established itself in the mortgage market, SABS should also find their niche.

B. Asset-backed securitisation in France (*titrisation*)

After studying the US asset-backed securities market, the French government decided to adopt *titrisation* into its financial markets in the hope that it would stimulate free market growth. The government's purpose for introducing *titrisation* was threefold:

(i) to support the housing finance industry;
(ii) to lower the cost of consumer credit; and
(iii) to give banks an additional means of balance sheet management.

The French government, through an autonomous state agency, *Caisse des*

Dépôts et Consignations (CDC), is taking an active part in developing the securitisation process. While other financial institutions are waiting for the French government to finalise the *titrisation* legislation, CDC, which is given certain legal privileges, has already issued a mortgage-backed security.

The government rightly believes that *titrisation* is an efficient form of intermediation which can help lower the cost of consumer credit. They want to lower consumer credit costs but they do not want to support credit abuse. Therefore, they are allowing only amortising credit to be securitised. This aids the financing of durable goods like cars, but is designed to deter credit card mania.

Finally, *titrisation* offers French banks an effective tool for balance sheet management. French banks need effective ways to improve capital. Currently in France the capital requirement is 5% of assets, but they must have capital backing of 8% by 1992 to be in line with the European Community.

The issues relating to *titrisation* are discussed in much more detail in the following chapter.

CONCLUSION

This chapter provides only a general introduction to non-mortgage securitised debt instruments—a market which deserves continued monitoring, for asset-backed securitisation should continue to show remarkable growth during the new decade. Dr Frank J. Fabozzi, a leading US expert on securitisation, predicts that US securitised debt will surpass government debt during the 1990s.[6]

As capital markets and financing techniques become globalised, ABSs will play a crucial role in corporate financing. Serving as a cost efficient alternative to traditional debt, this method of financing will be adopted in the United Kingdom and the rest of the world. It will be fascinating to see how this method of financing is integrated into the various international capital markets.

---

[6] Fabozzi, Frank J. *The Handbook of Mortgage-Backed Securities*, Probus Publishing, Chicago, Illinois.

Chapter 14

Securitisation in France: Titrisation

Michel Quéré
Freshfields, Paris

INTRODUCTION: THE BACKGROUND

Law n° 88–1201 of 23 December 1988 (the 'Law'), which aims at bringing French law into line with the EEC directive on Undertakings for Collective Investment in Transferable Securities ('UCITS'), introduces a new financing mechanism in France known as *'titrisation'* which is the French translation of the word securitisation (from *titre* = security). The Law has been supplemented by a Decree dated 9 March 1989 (the 'Decree').

Titrisation consists of the transfer by a credit institution of debts to a *Fonds Commun de Créances* (literally: 'common pool of debts') which in turn issues negotiable securities representing the debts which constitute its assets.

The assignment of debts ('*cession de créances*') mechanism is not unknown under French law which offers a choice of several means to achieve it.

First, article 1690 of the French *Code Civil* enables any creditor to assign a debt owed to it. However, in order to make this transfer valid as against third parties, article 1690 provides that the transfer must either be accepted by the debtor in a notarial deed or the debtor must be notified by a '*huissier*' (process server). For commercial reasons this notification process is not welcomed by the transferor and, furthermore, it is impractical and expensive when a pool of debts is assigned which requires the notification of the assignment to all debtors.

The '*délégation*' mechanism, instituted by article 1271 et seq of the French *Code Civil*, avoids the notification process but requires the participation of the debtor in the transfer. Again, if the sale of a pool of receivables is contemplated, recourse to the '*délégation*' is not practical.

The '*créance à ordre*' system was developed but only for debts of a commercial nature. Here, the debt instrument is simply transferred by endorsement in favour of the new creditor or by delivery to the new creditor of the instrument itself made out to the order of the bearer.

More recently, in order to facilitate the granting of credit facilities to businesses, the legislature, by law n° 81–01 of 2 January 1981, known as '*Loi*

Dailly', introduced a simplified '*cession de créances*' mechanism. Under this system, a borrower may issue, for the benefit of a credit institution only, a '*bordereau*' (document) assigning debts owed to it by reason of the carrying out of its professional or commercial activities. The law does not require that the debtor be advised of the assignment, of which it can be notified at any time by the assignee. However, the scope of the law is limited to credit facilities granted to businesses for professional or commercial activities and the debts assigned must also relate to the professional or commercial activities of the assignor.

Thus, none of the existing mechanisms which allow for the assignment of debts could, in practice, turn debts into negotiable instruments. Moreover, a ruling of the '*Comité de la Réglementation Bancaire*' (Banking Regulation Committee) prohibits credit institutions from selling debts to entities which are not credit institutions, thus making it impossible for the banks to refinance credit facilities outside the banking market. The purpose of the Law is to achieve this.

THE PURPOSE OF THE LAW

The Law aims at broadening the sources of financing for banks. It is argued that this would both increase competition and reduce the banks' costs of refinancing. This, in turn, should result in a reduction in the costs of financial intermediation and greater liquidity in the market, which would reduce the costs of borrowing for borrowers. In addition, *titrisation* would enable French banks to improve their capital/liabilities ratios as a result of the removal of loans from their balance sheets. The combined effects of these benefits would improve the competitiveness of the French banks at the EEC level by giving them the legal and financial tools necessary to expand their activities abroad and to meet increased competition.

A. Improvement of capital adequacy ratios

The need to improve French banks' capital adequacy ratios follows a requirement of the Basle Committee Report of July 1988 establishing certain ratios (the 'Cooke' ratios) which will have to be complied with in full form by 31 December 1992. Similar requirements will also be imposed by an EEC directive in the near future.

Under both the Cooke ratios and the EEC directive, the capital/liability ratio of credit institutions must be equal to at least 8%.

The present French requirement is 5% and a survey, as at 30 June 1988, showed that the average ratio for the three 'big' French banks (Banque Nationale de Paris, Crédit Lyonnais and Société Générale) was 6.3% and that for the ten biggest French banks was 6.9%. However, using the same calculation criteria as those of the Cooke ratios, the French banks' ratios would have been around only 5%. In this respect, the introduction of *titrisation* can only facilitate the banks' efforts to comply with the capital adequacy ratios. However, even if *titrisation* improves the banks' ratios, it will not replace the need of French banks for more capital. Therefore, the danger of *titrisation* for French banks is that it will constitute an easy alternative to increasing their capital, which in the future will make them undercapitalised, less competitive and vulnerable to take-over bids.

It should be noted that, for the purposes of calculating the above ratios, both the EEC directive and the Cooke guidelines apply a coefficient to the liabilities which varies according to the type of debt concerned. Thus, under the Cooke guidelines, state debts which are not considered risk bearing are given a nil weighting; loans secured by a mortgage have a 50% weighting only, while consumer loans are weighted at their full principal amount. If concerned to improve their situation with regard to the Cooke ratios, the banks might be inclined to use *titrisation* mainly to clear their balance sheets of certain debts such as consumer credits, which will have a greater leverage effect and could restrict the *titrisation* market to the more risky credit operations. This, in the long-term, might be detrimental to the success of *titrisation* in France.

B. Broadening the banks' sources of financing

French banks at present refinance themselves either through the money market (where they can sell commercial debts or state debts) or on the mortgage loans market (for loans guaranteed by a mortgage).

This latter market, under the control of Crédit Foncier de France, is a market reserved for credit institutions which refinance themselves by issuing promissory notes representing mortgage loans. The debts relating to these loans, however, remain on the balance sheet of the credit institution.

The vast majority of mortgage loans in France are fixed rate loans (although floating rate loans are now developing) and many of them were taken up when inflation rates and interest rates were high. As a result of the fall in interest rates in the last few years, many borrowers have repaid their loans in order to take out more favourable ones or have re-negotiated the applicable rates of interest. The mortgage loans market was severely affected by this, in particular in 1987, following the repayment of a large number of loans. According to the *Association Française des Banques* (French Banks Association), these repayments in 1986–1987 resulted in a loss of approximately 10 billion French Francs to French banks.

Furthermore, the non-banking institutions—which include pension funds, *sociétés de bourse* (stock brokers), insurance companies and UCITS—which had access to this market have progressively been prohibited from investing in the mortgage loans market since 1985.

Titrisation should complete the reform of the refinancing of the residential mortgage loans market carried out in 1985 by allowing the banks to gain access to a new source of long-term refinancing. It is thought that, in this respect, *titrisation* will be more cost effective than the existing refinancing system.

In addition, *titrisation* would transfer the risks of early repayment and non-payment connected with the mortgage loans from the banks to more specialised institutions.

C. Reduction of borrowing costs

The Ministry of the Economy has indicated that *titrisation* offers the possibility of spreading the various costs of banking intermediation which are generally considered to be too high. *Titrisation* should, therefore, improve competition and lead to gains in productivity. This, in turn, should result in a reduction of the borrowing rates—which, according to the Ministry of the Economy officials, could be as much as 1%—which would benefit borrowers. It is also claimed that the greater ease of refinancing by the banks should result in greater availability of credit facilities to borrowers.

However, most consumer organisations, when consulted, were opposed to the project. They were doubtful that, even if *titrisation* results in a reduced cost of funding for the banks, any of the benefit will be passed on to borrowers. In addition, consumers' organisations generally consider that *titrisation* will result in the management of loans and debt collection by an entity which has no relationship with borrowers and will be detrimental to them. It is alleged that borrowers will lose the advantage of the possibility of re-negotiation of the terms of their loans with the lending banks and will lose the benefit of the personal relationships established with the banks. On the evidence of securitisation in other jurisdictions, such as the US and the UK, these fears may be unfounded.

However, the banking community itself appears doubtful as to whether *titrisation* will result in a diminution of borrowing costs for borrowers. During the parliamentary debates, it was alleged that the US experience of mortgage-backed securities which has inspired the French legislation had effectively led to a decrease in funding costs (about 0.55 to 0.65%) but that this had not always reached the level of the borrowers. It was also argued that interest rates on mortgage loans have already reached a low level in France and that a large number of housing loans are directly or indirectly state subsidised, which has made their funding very cheap for lenders, although it is expected that most subsidisation schemes will be radically reformed in the near future.

THE *'FONDS COMMUN DE CRÉANCES'*

The legislature has chosen to create a new entity, the *fonds commun de créances* ('FCC'), the functioning of which is very similar to that of the *'fonds commun de placement'* (more or less equivalent to a UK unit trust) and to simplify the formalities required for the assignment of debts to the FCC. The law also contains provisions aimed at protecting the interests of borrowers, whose debts are transferred and at ensuring the protection of the investors in the FCC. A translation of the relevant provisions of the Law is attached as Appendix A (on page 282) and a translation of the relevant provisions of the Decree is attached as Appendix B (on page 285).

Article 34 of the Law states that 'the FCC is a co-ownership the exclusive object of which is to acquire debts held by credit institutions and the *Caisse des Dépôts et Consignations* in order to issue, in a single issue only, units representing these debts. The FCC does not have legal personality'.

The bill originally prepared by the government provided that the FCC had legal personality. The question of its legal structure was much debated, but it was finally accepted that the FCC did not require legal personality.

According to the Law, the FCC can only acquire debts from credit institutions or from the *Caisse des Dépôts et Consignations*. This is a public body which collects the resources of national public savings institutions, makes long-term loans to public bodies and has a regulatory role in the financial markets. A proposal that each FCC could only acquire debts from one single credit institution was not accepted. The portfolio of debts of the FCC can therefore be acquired from one or from several entities.

The nature and the characteristics of the debts that an FCC can acquire are more fully described in article 8 of the Decree which states that the FCC can only acquire debts whose initial term exceeds two years, to the exclusion of debts for which a provision is made or which present a risk of not being recoverable.

In addition, article 8 of the Decree states that 'the debts acquired are representative of credit operations of the same nature.' This implies some specialisation of FCCs, each of which could only acquire a certain type of debt, such as residential mortgage loans or car loans for instance, but not a mixture of various types of loans. Subject to this, all debts due from the State, public bodies, businesses or individuals, of a civil or commercial nature, could become subject to *titrisation*.

The intention of the legislator is that the FCC is a 'closed' FCC. The issue of units representing the debts acquired by it is made by way of a single issue and the duration of the FCC corresponds to the life of a fixed pool of debts. When those debts are repaid, the FCC itself will disappear. Article 41 of the Law provides that the FCC must be liquidated within the six months following the repayment of the last debt owed to it.

The system chosen aims at ensuring a better protection of investors in the FCC: the debts will be the subject of a single valuation at the time of the issue of the units and no further debt will, in the future, modify the structure of the portfolio (which excludes revolving credit facilities or substitution options from *titrisation*). During the parliamentary debates, it was indicated that it was necessary for the FCCs to remain closed FCCs at least during the time necessary for the creation of a market and to examine the behaviour of the players in this market before authorising FCCs to play a more active role.

Therefore, article 34 of the Law provides that the FCC may not acquire debts after the issue of units. The FCC is not allowed to borrow money or to create a pledge over the debts owed to it and it is not authorised to sell the debts acquired by it, except in the case of its dissolution. However, it is anticipated that the portfolio of debts held by the FCC will generate funds (by way of interest or repayment of principal) which may not be distributed immediately to the unit holders. During the period between the receipt of such funds and their distribution, the FCC is authorised to invest. The Decree indicates the list of the investments that the FCC will be allowed to make and which are considered as non-risk bearing. These are treasury bonds, shares in *SICAVs* or *fonds communs de placement* (French UCITS) (except for *fonds communs de placement à risques* and *fonds communs d'intervention sur le marché à terme*—because of the financial risks which these specific units carry) or securities negotiable on a regulated market (except for units in other FCCs and securities which entitle the holder to subscribe for or acquire share capital in a company—because this might lead to self-ownership of their capital by French companies).

THE SETTING UP AND FUNCTIONING OF THE FCC

Article 37 of the Law provides that the FCC is constituted jointly by a company in charge of its management ('*société de gestion*') and a body ('*dépositaire*') which will act as depositary of the assets of the FCC. Both bodies draw up the '*règlement*' (bye laws) of the FCC, which must be approved by the *Commission des Opérations de Bourse* (French Stock Exchange Commission), after consultation with the *Banque de France*.

The procedure for the establishment of the FCC is similar to that for *SICAVs* and *fonds communs de placement* where, in order to ensure better protection for investors, the role of the *société de gestion* and of the *dépositaire* are clearly separated.

The *société de gestion* takes the decisions relating to the management of the FCC such as the selection of debts to be purchased. The *dépositaire* for its part acts upon the instructions of the *société de gestion*. It recovers the debts to be paid to the FCC and distributes the sums received.

The unit holders do not participate in the setting up of the FCC, which is established solely by the *société de gestion* and the *dépositaire*, and they do not participate in the management of the FCC. They have no right to remove either the *société de gestion* or the *dépositaire*, and there is no organisation of the unit holders as a body or representation of the unit holders vis-à-vis the FCC, the *société de gestion* or the *dépositaire*.

A The *société de gestion*

According to article 40-II of the Law, the *société de gestion* must be a commercial company with the exclusive object of managing FCCs. A *société de gestion* may manage several FCCs. The *arrêté* of 31 July 1989 concerning the rules applicable to the authorisation and the setting up of FCCs (the *Arrêté*) provides that the *société de gestion* must show sufficient guarantees with regard to its organisation, its technical and financial capacities and the experience and repute of its managers. The *Arrêté* further indicates that the *société de gestion* will be deemed to show sufficient financial capacity if its share capital is at least 1.5 million French Francs.

In order to prevent the banks from using an FCC solely as an off-balance sheet vehicle, the *Arrêté* provides that banks or their subsidiaries which sell debts to an FCC can individually or jointly only hold less than a third of the shares in the *société de gestion* of that FCC.

The *société de gestion* represents the FCC vis-à-vis third parties and in legal proceedings. If this provision had not been included in the Law, because the FCC does not have legal personality, it would have been necessary for all unit holders to participate in legal proceedings relating to the assets or the liabilities of the FCC.

The *société de gestion* agrees the terms and conditions of purchase of the portfolio of debts to be acquired by the FCC, draws up its *règlement* (jointly with the *dépositaire*) and, as the case may be, agrees with the selling credit institution(s) or a third party the arrangements for the collection of the debts purchased (article 36).

The *société de gestion* will also decide on the investment of excess funds of the FCC pending their distribution, draw up a six monthly inventory of the assets of the FCC, prepare and publish the periodic information required by the *Commission des Opérations de Bourse* and carry out the liquidation of the FCC.

Neither the Law nor the Decree provides for the possibility of a change in the *société de gestion* during the existence of the FCC. The conditions for the replacement of the *société de gestion* should probably be specified in the *règlement* of each FCC.

B. The *dépositaire*

According to article 40-III of the Law, the *dépositaire* must be a credit institution or an institution approved by the Ministry of the Economy. Unlike the *société de gestion*, the *dépositaire* does not have to be a company ('*société*'). This enables public bodies such as the *Caisse des Dépôts et Consignations* to act as *dépositaire*. In any case, the *dépositaire* must be a credit institution empowered to receive and place funds. Although it is not an express requirement in the Law, the *dépositaire* and the *société de gestion* must be different bodies, as required by the EEC directive on UCITS.

The *dépositaire* must have its registered office in France. Its main duties are the establishment of the *règlement* of the FCC, in conjunction with the *société de gestion*, and to act as depositary for the debts and the cash held by the FCC. In addition, the *dépositaire* is under a duty to ensure the legality of the decisions of the *société de gestion*. The *dépositaire* also controls the bi-annual inventory of the assets of the FCC carried out by the *société de gestion*.

Under article 48 of the Law, the *dépositaire* may request the courts to dismiss the directors of the *société de gestion*. In such a case, a temporary director is nominated by the court until new directors are appointed. If new directors cannot be appointed, the temporary director stays in place until the winding up. It is not clear from the Law whether the reference to the winding up relates to the *société de gestion* or to the FCC. If the Law contemplates the liquidation of the *société de gestion*, it does not indicate what effect this would have on the FCC itself. The Decree, unfortunately, does not define what is meant by winding up in article 48.

Similarly, the Law does not contain any provision concerning the withdrawal or the dismissal of the *dépositaire*. Under the law of 1979 relating to *fonds communs de placement* which was repealed by the Law, the withdrawal of the *dépositaire* resulted in the winding up of the *fonds commun de placement*. The Law is, however, silent on this point and the Decree has not reintroduced the provisions of the law of 1979 in this respect.

C. The role of the *Commission des Opérations de Bourse*

The establishment and the winding up of an FCC is subject to the prior approval of the *Commission des Opérations de Bourse* after consultation with the *Banque de France*, the role of which is to ensure that *titrisation* will not affect French monetary policy by a significant increase of liquidity. In any case, the final decision to authorise the setting up of an FCC lies with the *Commission des Opérations de Bourse*.

The requirement of the *Commission des Opérations de Bourse*'s approval for the liquidation of the FCC may seem rather odd since, in any case, the Law provides that the FCC is to be liquidated after all debts are paid. Consequently, the requirement of article 40-I makes sense only in the case of an early liquidation of the FCC.

Article 35 of the Law states that the *Commission des Opérations de Bourse*'s authorisation of the setting up of an FCC is subject to the preparation of a document (*'document d'évaluation'*) explaining the nature of the units to be issued by the FCC and of the debts which it proposes to acquire, outlining the risks inherent in these debts and the nature and extent of the guarantees relating to the units issued. This document is to be prepared by a rating agency on a list drawn up by the Ministry of the Economy after consultation with the *Commission des Opérations de Bourse*. It must be sent to all unit holders. Article 7 of the Decree states that this document must be prepared prior to the issuing of the units.

A ruling (*'instruction'*) from the *Commission des Opérations de Bourse* relating to FCCs defines more specifically the contents of the application to be submitted to the *Commission des Opérations de Bourse* and the documents which must be remitted by the *société de gestion* in this respect. These include information on the *société de gestion* itself and its shareholders, the *document d'évaluation*, the guarantees offered for the protection of the unit holders, the placing memorandum for the units and the various agreements relating to the setting up and operation of the FCC, such as the agreement relating to the management of the collection of debts assigned to the FCC or the subscription agreement for the units.

The information required by the *Commission des Opérations de Bourse* for itself and for the unit holders is more important in the case of a public placing, both at the time of the setting up of the FCC and during its lifetime. According to the *Arrêté*, a placing of units is considered as private if, inter alia, the units are not traded on the stock exchange and the number of unit holders, which must all be corporate bodies, does not exceed 25 at any time during the life of the FCC. All other forms of placing are considered as public placings. In the case of a public placing, the subscription of the units must be underwritten by a syndicate.

After the *Commission des Opérations de Bourse* has authorised the setting up of the FCC, the *société de gestion* acquires on behalf of the FCC the portfolio of debts described in the documents submitted to the *Commission des Opérations de Bourse* and notifies the *Commission des Opérations de Bourse* of such acquisition. The FCC is deemed established on that date. In the case of a public placing, the placing of the units must then be made within the month following such date.

The *Arrêté* provides that an FCC may issue both units for public placing (defined as type 1 units) and units for private placing (defined as type 2 units). Within the month following the end of the subscription period, the *société de gestion* must apply for the listing on the stock exchange of type 1 units, which must have a nominal value of one million French Francs or less.

The *règlement* established by the *société de gestion* and the *dépositaire* must be approved by the *Commission des Opérations de Bourse* after consultation with the *Banque de France* (article 37). The Law does not contain much guidance regarding the contents of the *règlement*. It simply states that it must indicate how the liquidation surplus, if any, will be distributed and define the accounting period of the FCC which (except for the first period which may be as long as 18 months) may not exceed 12 months. The Decree gives very few details and only states that the *règlement* shall specify how the unit holders are protected against default from the debtors.

Article 39 of the Law provides a penalty of a fine of between 100,000 and 5,000,000 French Francs and six months to two years' imprisonment for the legal or de facto managers of an FCC who place securities without authorisation or who continue such activities despite the withdrawal of the authorisation.

THE UNITS

Article 34 of the Law provides that the units are '*valeurs mobilières*'. Article 1 of the Law defines *valeurs mobilières* as 'securities issued by public or private corporate bodies, transferable by delivery or by entry on a register, which confer identical rights for all categories and which give a right, directly or indirectly, to a certain portion of the share capital of the issuer or a general creditor's right over its assets'. Contrary to the definition in article 1 of the Law, the units are not issued by a corporate body since the FCC does not have legal personality. The Law nevertheless qualifies the units as *valeurs mobilières*, which renders them freely negotiable.

The FCC is considered a risky investment, hence the desire to limit this risky market to corporate and sophisticated private investors. Therefore, it has been decided that the units should have a minimum value of an amount sufficiently high to encourage potential investors to inform themselves of the risks inherent in the proposed investment. The minimum amount of each unit has been determined by the Decree and cannot be less than 10,000 French Francs (which is the minimum required by the Law itself). It is, however, foreseeable that in practice the amount of each unit will be much greater. In addition, article 35 of the Law prohibits door to door selling ('*démarchage*') of FCCs' units.

The units may only be issued after the setting up of the FCC has been authorised by the *Commission des Opérations de Bourse* and it has acquired its portfolio of debts. Unlike other forms of UCITS, the repurchase of units by the FCC is not allowed. This seems perfectly justified in the light of the purpose and the characteristics of the FCC. The units constitute medium to long-term investments. In any case, a unit holder can withdraw from the FCC by selling its unit to a third party.

The FCC units of type 1 are capable of being listed, although (as noted above), the *Arrêté* provides only for a mandatory listing of type 1 units of a nominal value of one million French Francs or less. Such listing will allow the creation of a secondary market in which FCC unit holders could sell their units. A ruling from the *Conseil des Bourses de Valeurs* will have to define how such a secondary market will work and the conditions for the listing of the units on the stock exchange.

The Law provides that the units can have different rights to capital and interest, to allow for the issue by the same FCC of units adapted to the different financial requirements of the various subscribers and the degree of risk that they are willing to undertake.

The Law also provides that *fonds communs de placement* controlled by the selling bank and *SICAVs* managed by persons employed or controlled by the selling bank may not acquire more than 5% of the units in an FCC which will have acquired the debts sold by the bank.

THE TRANSFER OF DEBTS MECHANISM

A. The remittance of a *bordereau*

The legislature recognised that the success of *titrisation* would largely depend on the simplicity and effectiveness of the assignment of debts mechanism. Since the banks are familiar with the mechanism instituted by the law of 2 January 1981 ('*Loi Dailly*'), the adoption of a similar system for *titrisation* was perfectly justified.

Article 34 of the Law provides that the transfer of debts is achieved by the delivery of a document ('*bordereau*').

Article 2 of the Decree states that the *bordereau* shall embody the words '*acte de cession de créances*' and state that the assignment is subject to the provisions of the Law. The *bordereau* shall in addition indicate the assignee of the debts, designate and individualise the debts assigned, and give the name of the debtors, the amount of the debts and their final date of maturity. When the assignment is made by a computerised system allowing for the identification of the debts, the *bordereau* may simply state the means by which the debts can be identified, their number and total amount. The *bordereau* shall also indicate that the assignment shall automatically involve the undertaking from the selling bank to take, upon request of the FCC, any necessary proceedings for safeguarding the security attached to the debts, their release or their enforcement.

According to the Law, the assignment takes effect between the parties and becomes binding on third parties on the date stated on the *bordereau* at the time of its delivery, which also involves the assignment of the security relating to the debts. Therefore, the date on the *bordereau* is of particular importance. Under the system laid down by the law of 2 January 1981, the date of the *bordereau* is affixed by the assignee. No specific formalities are required by the Law or the Decree. If the correctness of the date affixed is challenged, the assignee may prove it by any means.

B. Notification to the debtors

Although the assignment becomes effective upon delivery of the *bordereau*, article 34 provides that the debtors are notified of the assignment by a simple letter. Such notification is not a condition to the validity of the assignment and the Law does not state that such notification needs to be given within a certain period of time. Furthermore, in practice it may be difficult to establish proof of dispatch or receipt of a simple letter. In any case, the notification procedure will involve certain costs, albeit small ones. There may be doubt as to whether and when in practice a notification letter will be sent to the assigned debtors by the FCC.

C. The transfer of security

The Law provides that all security guaranteeing the debts assigned are transferred automatically to the assignee by the delivery of the *bordereau*, although neither the Law nor the Decree require the indication on the *bordereau* of the security, if any, guaranteeing the debts assigned. This raises the question of informing third parties of the transfer of the security, which is further complicated by the absence of legal personality for the FCC, which would require that the security be registered in the name of all the unit holders. In this respect, article 34 of the Law provides that where a specific legislative or regulatory provision requires the identification of the beneficiary as well as for all transactions made on behalf of the unit holders, the name of the FCC can be substituted for that of the unit holders.

For mortgage loans, article 2149 of the *Code Civil* provides that the assignment of mortgages must be registered in the '*Conservation des Hypothèques*' (register of mortgages) in order to be enforceable against third parties. Such registration will involve compliance with certain formalities and will result in increased costs, which will diminish the expected effect of *titrisation* on the reduction of the costs of borrowing. It has been estimated that for a mortgage loan of approximately 500,000 French Francs, the fees paid to the *Conservation des Hypothèques* amounts to about 4,000 French Francs. It is worth noting that in 1976 a new system was developed in France with a view to reducing the formalities and costs involved in connection with the assignment of mortgages. This system involves '*copies exécutoires*', which are like certified copies of notarial deeds and which can be endorsed without having to comply with any legal advertising requirements at the *Conservation des Hypothèques*. It can therefore be anticipated that credit institutions which will use *titrisation* will take advantage of the '*copie exécutoire*' system.

D. The collection of debts

Article 36 of the Law provides that the collection of the assigned debts continues to be undertaken by the assignor, in accordance with the provisions of an agreement entered into with the *société de gestion*. However, the Law provides that recovery can be assumed by another entity if the debtor agrees to it in writing at the time of the transfer of the management of the collection of the debts.

It is not entirely clear what is meant by 'collection' of debts in article 36. For instance, will the mere fact that the payments are to be made into an account with, say, the *dépositaire* be considered as constituting collection? It is not clear from the Law what degree of intervention from the collecting institution will be required for article 36 to apply.

The continuation of the collection of debts from the debtors by the assignor is commercially attractive since it will not result in a disruption of the relationship between the banks and their customers. It was, however, recognised that the transfer of the management of loans and collection of debts by specialised institutions would result in a reduction of the costs of collection which in turn could result in a reduction of borrowing costs. In this respect, it was pointed out that the costs of debt collection by non-specialised institutions could be as high as 5% and that of collection by a specialised institution could reduce these costs to 2 or 3%. However, if a change in the identity of the entity collecting the debts took place, this would ultimately affect the borrower and therefore the Law requires his consent to such a change.

In practice, the collection of the assigned debts will normally be carried out by the assignor. It is likely that the autonomy of the assignor in the management of loans and the collection of debts will be restricted under the agreement entered into by it and the *société de gestion*. This is in the interest of the unit holders. One might therefore be doubtful as to whether a borrower facing financial difficulties could obtain a re-scheduling of its debt or, in the case of a decrease in interest rates, could re-negotiate the terms of his loan under the same conditions if the loan is subject to *titrisation*, notwithstanding that he continues to deal solely with his original lender.

A complication might arise if a debtor refused his consent to the collection of the debts by another entity. The Law does not state whether and how this could have an impact on the earlier assignment of the debt concerned. Presumably, this will be covered in the assignment agreement between the assignor and the *société de gestion*.

THE PROTECTION OF THE UNIT HOLDERS

The question of the guarantees of the debts and the protection of the unit holders was the subject of intensive discussions. The US and the UK experiences served as reference points for these discussions. It was argued that the success of securitisation in the US was largely due to the existence of federal public agencies, whereas the absence of any form of governmental guarantee in the UK restricted the development of the system.

The Law contains a number of provisions aimed at ensuring the protection of the unit holders.

First, as already noted, the FCC is established with the sole purpose of acquiring and managing a single portfolio which is the subject of valuation at the time of transfer of the debts, prior to the subscription of the units. Following this valuation, a notice describing the nature of the portfolio and the risks involved, drawn up by an independent institution, will be distributed to the potential subscribers. The constitution of the FCC is subject to the prior authorisation of the *Commission des Opérations de Bourse* and the *dépositaire* must be an institution approved by the Ministry of the Economy. The *société de gestion* must regularly publish certain information on the FCC. Every six months, an inventory of the debts held by the FCC is to be carried out by the *société de gestion* under the control of the *dépositaire* and the functioning of the FCC is subject to control by a *commissaire aux comptes* (auditor) appointed by the *société de gestion* with the approval of the *Commission des Opérations de Bourse* who must notify the *société de gestion* and the *Commission des Opérations de Bourse* of any irregularities and errors of which he becomes aware in the exercise of his duties. Furthermore, article 40-IV provides that the unit holders are only responsible for the debts of the FCC up to the value of its assets and in proportion to their share, thereby limiting their risk to their initial investment.

In practice, the main risks for the unit holders should be the risk of default from the borrowers and the risk of early repayment of the loans. Article 9 of the Decree states that FCCs must guarantee themselves against the risk of default of the assigned debtors by any of the following ways (or a combination of them):

(i) by obtaining a guarantee from a credit institution or an insurance company, which guarantee shall provide for an immediate payment to the FCC of all sums due to the FCC and unpaid;

(ii) by issuing specific units (*'parts spécifiques'*) which shall exclusively bear the risk of default of the debtors, which *parts spécifiques* shall not be subscribed by individuals or UCITS. Although the Decree does not specify it, it seems logical to consider that these *parts spécifiques* should have a higher return;

(iii) by the transfer to the FCC of a pool of debts for an amount exceeding the amount of units issued by the FCC, the excess constituting a guarantee against the risks of non-payment. In such a case, the risk of default or of early repayment by any debtor is guaranteed by the assignor. If all debts are repaid, it would be normal that the excess payments or at least part of them should be allocated to the assignor. Therefore, the Law provides that the agreement relating to the assignment of debts can include a provision granting the assignor a right over part or all of the liquidation surplus of the FCC.

Article 9 of the Decree also provides that the *règlement* shall specify how the protection of the unit holders is achieved, and that the *Commission des Opérations de Bourse* shall take into account the guarantees the FCC offers to the unit holders when considering the application from the FCC for authorisation.

The cost of such guarantees will decrease the return payable to the unit holders. In addition, neither the Law nor the Decree grant the unit holders any protection against the risk of early repayment, which will vary depending on the type of debts concerned. In France, a risk of early repayment is particularly important when interest rates fall, since the majority of loans are fixed rate loans.

TAX ASPECTS

A. Tax regime of FCCs

FCCs benefit from a neutral tax regime, both on their establishment and on the operations they may carry out.

As a consequence of the absence of legal personality, the contributions made to the FCC do not give rise to any tax.

FCCs are exempt from corporation tax. Moreover, VAT does not apply to the transfer of debts to the FCC or to the various types of remuneration which may be received by the *dépositaire* or the *société de gestion*.

B. Tax regime of the unit holders

It is necessary here to distinguish between individual and corporate unit holders.

1. REGIME FOR INDIVIDUAL UNIT HOLDERS

Taxation of income from FCC units and capital gains realised upon the transfer of such units varies according to whether the units have been issued for a period which is longer or shorter or equal to five years.

(a) *taxation of income*. The recipient may decide to submit his income to progressive income tax (maximum rate of 56.8% in 1988) or to be taxed at a fixed rate (15% plus social charges of 2%) by means of tax withheld at source;

(b) *taxation of capital gains*. Capital gains arising upon the disposal of FCC units issued for five years or less are taxed at 17% on the full amount of the gain.

Liquidation bonuses whenever due may be taxed at source at the rate of 35% (plus social charges amounting to 2%) or taxed at the progressive rate of income tax.

2. TAX REGIME FOR CORPORATE UNIT HOLDERS

(a) *taxation of profits and liquidation bonus*. Profits realised by companies on FCC units are subject to corporation tax at the standard rate, ie 37% for undistributed profits and 42% for distributed profits;

(b) *taxation of capital gains*. Short-term gains realised on the disposal of FCC units held for less than two years are taxed at the standard rate of corporation tax. Long-term gains realised on the sale of units owned for more than two years are taxed at 19%, subject to the allocation by the vendor of the after tax profit in a special balance sheet reserve.

3. TAX REGIME FOR NON-RESIDENT HOLDERS

The tax authorities have indicated that income derived from FCC units when paid abroad or to persons who do not have their tax domicile or head office in France are liable to the withholding tax provided by Article 125 A of the Tax Code. Subject to provisions of double taxation agreements (DTA), the withholding tax applies at the rate of 15%. However, the withholding tax exemptions provided by Articles 125 A III 2è and 3è of the Tax Code apply to interest income received from FCCs when the effective beneficiary of the interest income proves to the debtor that his tax domicile or head office is located outside France. The liquidation bonus would be liable to a 35% withholding tax, subject to the application of DTAs.

Consequently, any interest income received from an FCC by *all* non residents are exempt from any withholding tax. However, in relation to liquidation bonuses only, non-French residents established in countries which have signed DTAs with France may be exempt from the 35% withholding tax, if the relevant DTA provides for such an exemption.

CONCLUSION

The introduction of *titrisation* in France required only a limited number of amendments to the French legal system which already offered several mechanisms allowing for the transfer of debts and underlying guarantees. The mechanism chosen is largely inspired by the '*Loi Dailly*' system instituted in 1981 which is already widely used amongst banks. Their experience in this field should make their adaptation to *titrisation* easy. The main legal obstacle that remains concerns the legal publicity formalities that need to be complied with, particularly in relation to mortgages.

With regard to the Law and the Decree, the main comment that can be made is that the legislature has tried to set down a certain number of principles whilst leaving as much operational flexibility as possible. Hence, the aim of the government to allow various forms of guarantees to be issued and the possibility of creating units carrying different rights. However, as can be seen, many questions remain unanswered.

The Law and the Decree attempt to achieve a balance between the interests and the protection of the unit holders and the development of *titrisation* which requires that the FCC has a substantial freedom in the selection of its debts portfolio.

It is obviously impossible to judge from the text of the Law whether *titrisation* will be successful in France. The government has indicated its intention to have a further debate on *titrisation* in several months time when, with the benefit of experience, if necessary the Law could be amended.

In any case, the success of *titrisation* will depend on the willingness of investors to participate. Their decision to invest in this new market will be based on three criteria: return, security and the liquidity of the market.

The return will depend on the nature of the debts which the banks will subject to *titrisation*. It is generally considered that, at first, the debts likely to be subject to *titrisation* in any volume will be car loans and residential mortgage loans.

As far as security is concerned, the Law and the Decree have attempted to minimise the risks for the investors and to provide sufficient flexibility in the form of the guarantees which can be offered by each FCC to allow potential investors to make their choice as to the return/security ratios they require.

Thirdly, the liquidity factor will depend on the existence of a sufficiently developed and active secondary market, and the level of return and guarantees offered will certainly impact on the development of this market.

At the time of writing it seems as though the trend towards *titrisation* has already started; the first FCC, called CAC-Titrisations, was created just before the end of 1989; it is managed by Eurotitrisation and the *dépositaire* is the *Caisse des Dépots et Consignations*. The guarantees offered to the investors consisted of a first demand guarantee from the *Caisse Autonome de Refinancement* and the *Caisse des Dépôts et Consignations*. The assets of the FCC comprised loans granted by the *Société des Bourses Françaises* to stockbrokers. This deal has received a AAA rating from Moody's. Moreover, other FCCs are expected to be launched in 1990 and certain deals are already fairly well advanced. It is certain that not all transactions will follow the framework established by the Law and the Decree—despite the intentions of the legislature, the degree of structural flexibility in practice is not as great as many of those involved in US or UK securitisations have come to expect. The recent securitisation of automobile receivables originated by Renault points one way forward. Nevertheless, *titrisation* looks set to develop in France as a useful financing alternative for banks and credit institutions.

APPENDIX A

TRANSLATION (FOR INFORMATION PURPOSES ONLY) OF ARTICLES 34 TO 37 AND 40 TO 41 OF THE LAW N° 88–1201 OF 23 DECEMBER 1988

Article 34

The FCC is a co-ownership the exclusive object of which is to acquire debts held by credit institutions or the *Caisse des Dépôts et Consignations* in order to issue, in a single issue only, units representing these debts.

The FCC does not have legal personality. The provisions of the *Code Civil* relating to joint possession do not apply to the FCC. It is also exempt from the provisions of articles 1871 to 1873 of the said *Code*.

It cannot acquire debts after the issue of units, with the exception of debts whose acquisition represents the investment of liquid funds which are to be distributed and acquired in accordance with conditions set out in a decree. The FCC cannot borrow.

Different rights over the capital and the interest can be ascribed to the units.

The units are transferable securities. Holders of them cannot request that the FCC repurchases their units. The minimum amount of each unit issued by an FCC is defined in a decree. It shall not be less than 10,000 French Francs.

The FCC cannot assign the debts which it acquires except in the case of its dissolution in circumstances defined by decree. It cannot use as security the debts which it holds.

The assignment of debts shall be made by the mere delivery of a document the terms of which will be set out in a decree. It will take effect between the parties and will become binding on third parties on the date stated on the document at the time of its delivery. The delivery of the document effects the assignment of the security guaranteeing each debt.

The borrower is informed by ordinary letter.

The assignment agreement may provide for a right over all or part of the liquidation surplus for the benefit of the assignor.

In all cases where a specific legislative or regulatory provision requires the name, first name and address of the beneficiary to be shown as well as for all transactions made on behalf of the unit holders, the name of the FCC can be validly substituted for those of the unit holders.

Article 35

The authorisation of the *Commission des Opérations de Bourse* referred to in Article 40 is subject, in accordance with the provisions of a decree, to the preparation of a document containing an appraisal of the characteristics of the units to be issued by the FCC and of the debts which it proposes to acquire and assessing the risks inherent in these debts. This document shall be prepared by an institution on an approved list drawn up by the Ministry of the Economy after consultation with the *Commission des Opérations de Bourse*. It must then be sent to the unit holders.

Units in the FCC cannot be sold or marketed by door to door selling.

Article 36

The collection of the assigned debts continues to be undertaken by the assignor, in accordance with the provisions of an agreement entered into with the *société de gestion* of the FCC.

However, collection can be assumed by an entity other than the assignor if the debtor agrees to it in writing at the time of the transfer of the management of the collection of the debt.

Article 37

The FCC is constituted jointly by a company in charge of its management ('*société de gestion*') and a corporate body ('*dépositaire*') which will act as a depositary of the assets of the FCC. This company and this corporate body shall draw up bye laws ('*règlement*') for the FCC which must be approved by the *Commission des Opérations de Bourse* after consultation with the *Banque de France*.

A decree will determine the nature and characteristics of the debts that FCCs can acquire and the conditions in which the FCCs should obtain a guarantee against the risks of default of the debtors of the debts which they have been assigned or must obtain a guarantee of those risks from an institution authorised to do so by the Ministry of the Economy. The *règlement* deals with the conditions of allotment of the liquidation surplus.

Article 40

(i) the creation or liquidation of an FCC is subject to the authorisation of the *Commission des Opérations de Bourse* after consultation with the *Banque de France*;

(ii) the *société de gestion* referred to in article 37 must be a commercial company with the exclusive object of managing FCCs. It shall represent the FCC vis-à-vis third parties and for legal proceedings, as claimant and as defendant;

(iii) the *dépositaire* of the assets of the FCC referred to in article 37 must be a credit institution or an institution approved by the Ministry of the Economy. Its registered office must be in France. It acts as depositary for the debts and cash held by the FCC. It ensures the legality of the decisions of the *société de gestion*;

(iv) unit holders are only responsible for the debts of the FCC up to the value of its assets and in proportion to their share in it;

(v) the *règlement* of the FCC deals with the duration of accounting years, which cannot exceed 12 months. However, the first accounting period may be extended to a longer period up to the limit of 18 months.

Within six weeks from the end of each six month period for each accounting period, the *société de gestion* draws up a six monthly inventory of the assets of each FCC it manages, under the control of the *dépositaire*;

(vi) the auditor to the FCC will be appointed by the board of directors, the manager or the management board of the *société de gestion*, for a period of six years, after the approval of the *Commission des Opérations de Bourse*.

The provisions of articles 218 to 222, 230, 231, 233, second and third sub-paragraphs, 234 and 235 of Law n° 66–537 of 24 July 1966 apply to the auditor.

He will notify any irregularities or inaccuracies, which he discovers in the course of his duties, to the directors of the *société de gestion* and to the *Commission des Opérations de Bourse*.

The unit holders shall have the rights of shareholders which are set out in articles 225 and 227 of Law n° 66–537 of 24 July 1966.

Article 41

The *société de gestion* shall carry out the liquidation of the FCC within the six months following the payment of the last debt.

APPENDIX B

TRANSLATION (FOR INFORMATION PURPOSES ONLY) OF ARTICLES 1 TO 9 OF THE DECREE Nº 89–158 OF 9 MARCH 1989

Decree nº 89–158 of 9 March 1989 implementing articles 26 and 34 to 42 of Law nº 88–1201 of 23 December 1988 relating to '*Fonds Communs de Créances*' ('FCC').

Article 1

The percentage referred to in article 26 of the above law shall be 5% of the value of the units issued by the FCC as shown in the latest half yearly report provided for in paragraph V of article 40 of the above law.

The *SICAVs* and *société de gestion* of *fonds communs de placement* shall notify the amount of units held by them in the FCC to the *société de gestion* of the FCC within a period of three weeks from the end of each half-year.

The *société de gestion* for the FCC states in the half-yearly report mentioned in paragraph V of article 40 of the above law the percentage of the units of the FCC held by *organismes de placement collectifs en valeurs mobilières* ('*OPCVMs*').

Article 2

The document referred to in article 34 of the above law contains the following indications:

(i) the title 'deed of assignment of debts';
(ii) reference that the assignment is subject to the provisions of the Law nº 88–1201 of 23 December 1988 relating to *OPCVMs* and creating FCCs;
(iii) the description of the assignee;
(iv) the description and breakdown of the debts assigned, the identification of the debtors, of the total amount of the debts and their maturity dates. When the transfer of the assigned debts is made by way of a computerised process where they can be identified, the document can state only, in addition to the provisions of (i), (ii) and (iii) above, the means by which they are identified and individualised, their number and their total amount;
(v) the reference that the assignment entails that the assignor shall be obliged, at the request of the assignee, to undertake any act necessary to safeguard

the security (for the debts), to effect possible changes to them, to call them, to release them or to obtain their enforcement.

Article 3

The *dépositaire* is in charge of the safekeeping of the instruments incorporating the debts assigned to the FCC.

Article 4

The sum mentioned under the third sub-paragraph of article 34 of the above law can be invested in:

(i) treasury bonds;
(ii) *SICAV* shares or *fonds communs de placement* units with the exception of those referred to in articles 22 and 23 of the above law;
(iii) securities admitted to trading on a regulated market with the exception of FCC units and securities which entitle the holder, directly or indirectly, to subscribe for or acquire the equity of a company.

The *règlement* of the FCC states expressly the rules for the utilisation of these sums.

Article 5

The minimum amount of a unit in a FCC is 10,000 French Francs.

Article 6

If the amount of the residual assets of the FCC is less than 10% of the total amount of the initial issue, the debts held by an FCC may be assigned in one transfer only and for their total amount. The assignment takes place in compliance with the provisions set out in article 2 of this decree.

Article 7

The document referred to in article 35 of the above law is prepared before the issue of the units of the FCC. It is compulsory to issue such a document whatever the nature and characteristics of the debts assigned. This document sets out, inter alia, the characteristics of the debts assigned and of the units issued. It also sets out the nature and extent of the guarantee relating to the units issued.

Article 8

The FCC can acquire only debts with an initial maturity of more than two years and which are not entered on the balance sheet of the assignor as fixed assets and are not bad or disputed debts. The debts acquired must represent credit operations of the same nature.

Article 9

The FCC must protect itself against the risk of default by the debtors of the debts assigned by:

  (i) obtaining a guarantee given by a credit institution or by an enterprise regulated by the insurance code, which in both cases cannot defer payment of moneys due to the FCC;
 (ii) the issue of specific units carrying the risk of default. These specific units cannot be subscribed by *OPCVM*s nor by individuals;
(iii) the assignment to the FCC of an amount of debts greater than the total amount of units issued.

The *règlement* of the FCC expressly sets out the means of guarantee arranged against the risk of default by debtors of the debts assigned.

For the approval of the FCC, the *Commission des Opérations de Bourse* takes into account the guarantees envisaged for the purpose of ensuring the payment of the sums due.

Chapter 15

Towards Securitisation—Trends in the International Financial Markets

John M. Van Deventer
Goldman Sachs International Ltd

Over the course of the past few years, there has been a marked increase in the level of securitisation in the international financial markets. Growth in the Euro-sterling sector has been well chronicled in the earlier chapters of this book, and it is clear that the technology and process of securitisation is proliferating from the US and the UK to a number of other jurisidictions and markets. Indeed, as securitisation was one of the great dynamics of the financial markets in the United States throughout the past decade, today's conventional wisdom holds that the phenomenon will repeat itself in the 1990s in the international markets. Of course, such conventional wisdom must be measured against the particular circumstances of the international markets, and the degree to which factors critical to the growth of securitisation in domestic markets exist or have application on an international scale.

BACKGROUND

The 'internationalisation' of the securitisation phenomenon is premised upon its adaptability to widely different markets, issuers, investors and strategic objectives. Indeed, this is its *raison d'être*—for securitisation, ie the conversion of illiquid assets to marketable securities—is the process by which balance sheet objectives are matched and accommodated to capital markets opportunities. An historical review is illustrative. The technology of securitisation was first deployed by the US government, which by guaranteeing the performance of otherwise illiquid home loans, succeeded in attracting new sources of capital into the housing sector without resort to its own borrowing capacity. The process was subsequently adopted by US thrift institutions, initially to circumvent intra-state banking prohibitions. However, securitisation took on increasing importance to the thrift industry as interest rates de-stabilised, retail deposits disintermediated and credit ratings and access to the capital markets deteriorated. To UK centralised mortgage lenders, securitisation was developed to exploit an arbitrage between retail and wholesale borrowing rates. For well capitalised US insurance companies securitisation was adopted to facilitate diversification into profitable non-core businesses like home lending (as well as to grow core business through cross-marketing synergies) without misapplying policy-holder funds or distorting balance sheets. The same process is now currently underway in the UK insurance sector. For non-financial institutions (eg General Motors, Ford and Sears) securitisation is a tool used to drive retail distribution, as well as to capture retail/financial services synergies. For banks facing Cooke ratio requirements and a deregulated Europe, securitisation offers an important alternative in the critical process of effectively deploying capital. Thus, it is hardly surprising to see well capitalised banks like Citicorp and Barclays in the forefront of their respective markets. A number of the other banks in a number of jurisdictions, including Canada, France, Sweden, New Zealand and Australia, are in the process of initiating asset securitisation programmes.

APPLICATION TO THE BANKING INDUSTRY

Indeed, while the process of securitisation can be adapted to suit any number of situations, the trend is likely to manifest itself most dramatically in the banking sector—and not solely because banks currently hold the bulk of securitisable assets. The new risk based capital standards, the ongoing process of disintermediation, and the accelerating industry-wide consolidation are fundamentally changing the business of banking. Gone are the halcyon days of collecting deposits to make a matched book of loans. Today's equity markets are forcing bank management teams to reconsider and redefine traditional measures of bank profitability. Securitisation will serve as a self-perpetuating catalyst of change within the bank sector as financial intermediaries adjust funding agendas, investment portfolios and business strategies to accommodate increasingly discerning bank equity markets.

Traditionally, the equity markets valued a bank on the basis of whether a positive interest spread was earned—this spread, net of expenses, was then compared to the aggregate capital of the bank. The aggregate return on capital in turn was compared to the performance of other banks, and an individual institution was pronounced weak or strong, and valued accordingly. Little attention was paid to which individual components of a bank's business were profitable and to whether the bank's capital was being optimally deployed. For example, consideration was typically not given as to whether value was added in deposits, or in loan origination—it is quite possible that a particular bank's deposit business could stand on its own, but without cross-subsidisation in the form of below market funds or shared expenses, lending was unprofitable.

Under such circumstances, a bank would be more profitable, on a risk adjusted basis, if it dropped the lending business and instead sold its funds on a risk free basis in the wholesale market, ie by purchasing government obligations. For example, assume a limited amount of capital (2%) invested in plant and equipment—risk adjusted capital required for central government obligations is zero. The net cost of deposits would need to be only 30 bp lower than the equivalent maturity government obligation in order to assure a 15% return on capital. A 15% return on capital would be extremely attractive on a relative basis given that the volatility of returns approaches zero under such circumstances. If, on the other hand, regulators require banks to hold capital at 6% of assets, the net cost of deposits would have to be 90 bp lower than the government obligation to generate the same return on capital. The imposition of regulated (as opposed to market) capital requirements is the reason why highly geared US money market mutual funds investing in Treasury securities have historically competed successfully against banks for retail funds. It also demonstrates why banks have been forced to hold much riskier assets than Treasuries. The equity market demands risk (and return) commensurate with the level of capital deployed.

Today, non-bank competitors provide ready equity/return benchmarks for banking's component businesses. Money market funds, unit trusts and insurance annuity products compete for deposits. Mortgage bankers, centralised lenders, insurance companies and institutional investors compete for loan origination. Mortgage bankers, centralised lenders and non-financial institutions compete for transaction processing. Money management is conducted by mutual funds, money managers and insurance companies (see Table 1 on page 298). Although the process of collecting deposits and making loans was once viewed as a single business, each step in the intermediation process can, and now does, operate on its own. These competitive benchmarks force today's bank to view itself as a collection of businesses. In Table 2 on page 299, the process is broken into four illustrative components: (1) The Depositary which collects funds; (2) Loan Origination which deploys funds collected by the Depositary; (3) Transaction Processing which services assets originated by Loan Origination and/or performs the clearing process; and (4) Money Management which 'buys' money, either from the Depositary or the capital markets, and 'invests' money, either in the bank's own loan production, or in other assets (securities) available in the market.

Given the existence of external competitive equity benchmarks, a bank's commitment to each component business must be appraised by reference to the risks, rewards, and capital required for that specific component business. Separating the business of banking into its component parts allows an evaluation to establish true profitability, accurately allocate expenses, and identify and eliminate cross-subsidisations. Because of the different level of capital required, each component of the traditional banking business has a different level of required profitability. Low risk (low capital) business can be supported by low returns. High risk (high capital) businesses require high returns (see Table 3 on page 300). As the equity markets only pay for value added, engaging in businesses with an appropriate capital gearing relative to more efficient alternative providers will squeeze margins, reduce return on capital, detract capital from more attractive opportunities and accordingly reduce institutional value.

By adopting securitisation technology, a bank can actually separate the lending process into its theoretical components parts: (1) the origination process, (2) the ongoing loan servicing business, and (3) the debt or 'security' representing the funds advanced. These are separate and distinct activities and a bank must commit capital to each accordingly. Indeed, in the United States, each of these various components of the lending process trade as commodities in secondary markets. In particular, the 'security' portion belongs in the securities portfolio, where it is managed or sold depending on its contribution to the securities portfolio business. Money Management's decision to invest (commit capital) in the bank's loan production, as opposed to the various alternatives available in the market place, should be one determined solely upon Money Management's efforts to maximise spread income, and should be made without reference to subsidies to or from other component businesses of the bank. The origination and servicing functions similarly must independently earn a return on allocated capital without reference to, or subsidy by, a presumed securities portfolio role (viz, mortgage bankers). A bank will originate loans in markets where it maintains an advantage. Under opposite circumstances, the bank will forego loan origination and will rely on secondary markets for asset production. Similarly, a bank will keep and compete for or, alternatively, contract out loan servicing. By creating liquidity in the bank's balance sheet, thereby effectively isolating the various components of the lending process, securitisation facilitates a bank's ability to undertake and implement a strategic review of its traditional component businesses.

PORTFOLIO OPTIMISATION

A bank's securities portfolio takes on a new light in this analysis—enabling it to function increasingly as a competitive money management business and an independent profit centre. Traditionally, a bank's securities portfolio served primarily as a liquidity function and as a place to warehouse funds until otherwise profitably deployed. However, with the bank equity market's shift in focus from return on assets to return on capital, optimising returns in the securities portfolio becomes imperative. Effective money management can increase bank earnings dramatically, find hidden capital in the balance sheet, and better insulate an institution from interest rate risk and hostile acquirors.

Take, for example, a bank operating close to maximum leverage and considering new on-balance sheet investments. Prior to introduction of the Cooke ratios, the bank had four basic alternatives. It could either retain profits, raise additional primary capital, dispose of an equal volume of assets, or forego the investment opportunity (see Table 4 on page 301). Increasing retained profits is not often commercially or strategically feasible. Issuing common equity and shrinking the bank's asset size or book of off-balance sheet business are both relatively expensive in terms of their dilutive impact on earnings. By contrast, and in light of the Cooke ratios, rearranging the bank's investment portfolio might provide a very cost efficient way to raise risk-weighted capital ratios.

Assume, for example, the case of a bank that currently holds £10 million in floating rate commercial loans with a net yield (after servicing costs and loan loss provisions) of LIBOR plus 20 bp. The loans have a risk weight of 100% and therefore must be backed with £800,000 in capital, of which £400,000 must be shareholders' equity. Assume that the remaining £9.2 million is financed at LIBOR. This investment generates a gross profit of £140,000. This represents a 17.5% return on capital, and a 35% return on stockholders' equity (see Table 5 on page 302). If, however, the bank sold the loans, the same £800,000 in capital could be used to back a £20 million investment in a sterling floating rate mortgage-backed note with a yield of 32 basis points over LIBOR. In this case, £19.2 million would be financed at LIBOR, and the investment would produce a gross profit of £184,000, for a 23% return on capital and a 46% return on shareholders' equity. The swap generates a 31% increase in the bank's return on equity. Furthermore, the bank would be moving from unsecured commercial loans into AAA rated, highly liquid assets. The results are significantly more dramatic with, for example, US agency mortgage-backed securities. In fact, portfolio adjustments can increase capital ratios and earnings at the same time, thus essentially generating capital at a negative cost (see Table 6 on page 303).

As demonstrated by this example, the opportunity and need for banks to optimise capital through the management of its securities portfolio will impact and accelerate the process of securitisation in a number of ways. In particular, it will create an inherent incentive for financial institutions to securitise assets in order to increase balance sheet liquidity and management capability, to increase fee-related income, to ensure a ready market for loan origination production and to maximise returns on its securities portfolio. The capital markets will increasingly provide a funding source for investments which have an important fee income or cross-subsidy role in a bank's business, but one which cannot be justified on a bank's own balance sheet in terms of return on capital. This will be particularly true as institutions look increasingly to foreign and unfamiliar markets for investment opportunities, where the need to dispose of credit, currency and interest rate risk will become increasingly acute. Through the technology of securitisation, banks will enlist the markets to provide the capital subsidy to those integral and necessary banking functions which otherwise historically have been subsidised by the bank's own balance sheet. This re-ordering of capital within and without the banking sector, an exercise in efficiency, underlies the ongoing disintermediation process.

SOURCING NEW CAPITAL

Of course, the technology of securitisation only serves these ends to the extent that it succeeds in attracting new sources of capital to the particular venture at hand. If new capital is not sourced, the securitisation exercise is essentially frustrated. Witness the early days of the sterling mortgage-backed securities market: great effort and cost was applied, impressive technology was developed and a volume of securities was issued. Unfortunately, the same London-based banks who were funding the centralised lenders on balance sheet were, at first, the exclusive buyers of the securities. Thus ensued a situation where the funding arbitrage underlying the UK securitisation initiative was being realised in large part by the investor rather than the issuer. The situation was reflected in the increasing spread on each successive securitised issue, as well as in the parallel upward shifts in the cost of bank lines to this sector. Securitisation accomplished little other than to develop a complicated and cost intensive alternative (but not cumulatively incremental or cheaper) bank borrowing vehicle. The situation subsequently has been resolved in a significant degree through a combination of aggressive investor education and market responsive structural innovation.

Indeed, today, non-primary market sources of capital underpin the UK mortgage-backed securities market. By segmenting risk and reward according to investor preference, the technology of securitisation attracts otherwise unavailable institutional sources of capital. For example, a US insurance company or Japanese leasing company is an unlikely candidate to take a primary position in the UK residential housing market. Neither party is in an advantaged position relative to the primary market participants to understand and monitor the risks and rewards of such an investment. Yet, once pooled, credit enhanced and engineered into liquid securities with familiar and easily palatable characteristics, such institutional sources of capital can be effectively tapped. Managed mortgage security investment funds have recently been successfully marketed in Japan and Europe to first time investors and represent valuable user-friendly 'primers' to institutional investors who over time are likely to become direct investors in their own right. Meanwhile, securitisation initiatives in non-primary lending markets will provide convenient and readily understandable opportunities for primary market participants to diversify their own securities investment portfolios.

THE SEQUENCE OF EVOLUTION

While virtually all types of assets can and have been securitised, the size and relative homogeneity of consumer loans markets and products facilitates the process. Thus the process of securitisation on an international scale is most likely to be witnessed first, and most dramatically, in the various consumer lending markets. The templates for securitisation initiatives, both from an investor and issuer perspective, are in place and create a natural momentum in these markets. Moreover, in an era of disintermediation of traditional corporate banking functions and increasing multi-national and multi-industry competition for financial services opportunities, the consumer markets, quite simply, are just too large to ignore. For example, the total US mortgage market alone is estimated to be close to $3 trillion; it outstrips the much vaunted US federal government debt by over 40% and represents 45% of total debt outstanding in the United States. Similarly, the UK mortgage market, estimated to be approaching £200 billion, outstrips and has in recent times consistently grown faster than the retrenching government gilt market. The French market stands at FF1.5 trillion, the German market is approaching DM4 billion and the Japanese market is estimated to stand at approximately ¥74.5 trillion. In each of these and other countries, the mortgage market is huge and each has the potential to grow much larger in the face of government sponsored home ownership initiatives. Furthermore, the mortgage relationship is typically thought to be the key to exploiting retail cross-marketing synergies. Not surprisingly, much of the restructuring currently taking place in the European financial services industry has a retail oriented dynamic.

Witness, for instance, the United States. Over $640 billion of the US mortgage market is securitised. Over 35% of mortgages secured by first liens on single residential homes are securitised, and 70% of residential mortgages originated in 1989 have been or will be securitised. In total, over a trillion dollars of mortgage securities have been issued and, in 1989 alone, over $110 billion of mortgage securities were issued. Other consumer oriented markets—in particular, revolving credit cards and automobile loans—are experiencing similar relative magnitudes of growth. While the US, like any market, developed as it did due to factors peculiar to its own experience, the numbers are nonetheless and in any event compelling, and reflect the self-perpetuating character of the disintermediation process in the face of an increasingly capital markets oriented consumer finance system.

The US mortgage industry, a once cosy and predictable business, has changed dramatically during the past ten years. Securitisation has lured new participants into the industry, driving out many of the less efficient. Mortgage lenders now compete for a more sophisticated, cost conscious consumer. A broad array of loan types and other services is now delivered through computerised distribution systems. The secondary mortgage market has become the primary source of mortgage funding, drawing capital from investors across the globe. Consolidation in the primary mortgage market has been rapidly accelerating in a hitherto fragmented market. Mortgage banking firms and thrift institutions have been acquired by such non-traditional mortgage market participants as auto makers, insurance companies, retailers and commercial and foreign banks. These players include Sears, Roebuck & Co, Prudential Insurance Co, General Motors, Ford Motor Company and investment bankers, among others. New mortgage instruments are continuously being created to ensure a link to the capital markets and an ever-expanding mortgage investor base, making mortgages more attractive to invest in and more efficient to trade and hold. Cash flows have been carved up to suit specific types of investors, opening the market to insurance companies, mutual funds, international investors, pension funds, individuals and others. Virtually everything about the mortgage industry, from the way in which a loan is originated to the investor who ultimately funds the loan, has changed throughout this period.

The scenario might well sound familiar, as the same process is seemingly now underway in the UK retail markets. Deregulation and disintermediation has given rise to a host of new players, products and investors. New primary market participants include foreign banks, insurance companies and the new mortgage boutiques. Meanwhile, growing confidence in the long-term viability of the UK secondary market has attracted a number of new secondary participants (both on the issuer and investor sides) and significant corporate strategies premised on such viability have been undertaken. New mortgage products and new security structures are continuously being introduced to exploit primary and secondary market niches and opportunities. As with the US market, the process has a self-perpetuating quality—each new issue, each new issuer and each innovation brings new issuers and new investors into the market. The process is likely to repeat itself in other markets as those markets begin to forfeit their purely domestic character. There have been mortgage securities issued or government sponsored programmes announced in a number of jurisdictions.

TOWARDS AN INTERNATIONAL SECURITISATION MARKET

As witnessed by the historical course of events in the evolution of the secondary markets in the US and the UK, and ultimately of perhaps greatest significance to the development of the international sector, is the fact that the expansionist movement in the secondary markets will not be restricted to traditional participants. Rather, a broad array of multi-national financial institutions and corporates will be increasingly drawn to the secondary markets by the disintermediation of traditional corporate lending opportunities, by consumer oriented cross-marketing economies, by the forecast of growth and strength in various traditional markets, by the need for asset/liability management in increasingly competitive and sophisticated markets and by the critical need for financial institutions to optimise capital.

Of course, one's view of the speed with which changes will occur must be tempered to recognise that the trend towards globalisation in the financial markets may face its greatest and most stubborn challenge and, if ultimately successful, cause the most profound change in the various consumer lending markets. In Europe, as is the case in the United States and in Japan and elsewhere, it is this sector of the financial markets that is most deeply embedded in idiosyncrasies peculiar to a particular culture's tradition of property possession and ownership. The rites of personal property ownership are, or at least have been, an inherently domestic phenomenon. Understanding the nuances of a foreign market can be difficult; attempting to transfer technology, to develop homogeneity of product and process and to achieve economies of scale can be daunting. Furthermore, mortgage markets in many jurisdictions have tended to be characterised by rigid regulatory systems which, while ratified to foster home ownership, have had a secondary but very pronounced if unintended effect of inhibiting competition external to the regulatory scheme. Thus, as exemplified by today's German Pfandbriefe banks, by the British building societies of five years ago, and by the US thrift industry throught the post war era until the mid 1970s, retail markets have been characterised by closed, cartel-type competitive environments. Even in newly deregulated markets, inertia may prevent easy accessibility to certain markets. As anyone who has been involved in a securitisation project knows too well, the process is never an easy one—and the 'vanilla' transaction remains elusive. By its nature, securitisation involves innovation. By definition, innovation implies time and cost. Not surprisingly and in large part for this very reason, the US securitisation new issuance market is increasingly characterised by frequent and efficient users.

Nonetheless, the once insular domestic markets are indeed turning global, in a number of manifestations and in response to a number of market forces. In Europe, for instance, the spectre of aggressive new competitors in the various domestic markets has driven home the need for traditional participants to develop an appropriate response to the new reality. It is clear that financial institutions and, indeed, corporates, will need to realign businesses not only to exploit opportunities in new markets, but also to protect current market volumes and advantages. The restructuring is well underway, but not nearly complete. Institutions which are able to adapt to exploit new realities and opportunities in an expanding international marketplace will flourish at home and abroad, insulated from shifting competitive dynamics in deregulated domestic markets. Institutions which fail to exploit new opportunities will find their traditional lines of business increasingly threatened by aggressive, sophisticated and multi-faceted supra-national financial institutions with overwhelming capital resources, analytical tools and marketing strengths. To witness this phenomenon, one need only look at the example of the haves and have-nots that have emerged in the post-deregulation environment in the United States and the identical process which is now underway in the UK. To survive and thrive, institutions will need to achieve asset generation and, concurrently, funding capabilities beyond their own borders and beyond their traditional lines of business. The process of debating and implementing strategies is well underway. Not surprisingly, the strongest and best managed of these institutions are approaching the issue opportunistically rather than defensively, ie looking for opportunities to expand across borders even as their own borders become exposed. The speed with which the inertia of an entrenched domestic market ultimately can be overcome in the wake of deregulation is evident in the breakdown of the once but now defunct British building society cartel over the course of the past few years and the recent emergence to dominance of nationwide mortgage lenders in the once highly fragmented US market.

CONCLUSION

The collective impact of trends in the financial services markets, trends which are being pushed to the forefront by such events as the unified Europe initiative, the capital convergence standards and the globalisation of the financial markets generally, will be several and, to a degree, potentially countermanding: a broadened appeal and understanding of securitised assets across a significantly expanded and international investor base, a broader array of securitised investment alternatives and opportunities, a shift in yield relationships among these alternatives and an increased focus on direct investment opportunities across domestic borders. The trend towards securitisation is neither surprising nor aberrant—but rather is consistent with the natural evolution of a mature and increasingly sophisticated international capital market. Nor is it difficult to anticipate acceleration of the process in anticipation of certain pending events, including, in particular, the unified Europe initiative and implementation of the Cooke ratio capital standards. Both are scheduled to be operational by 1992, both are already having a visible impact in the financial markets. Thus, while actual deal flow in the international securitisation sector has been and continues to be preceded by a much higher volume of dialogue, the trend is grounded upon firm footing and will persist and quicken against a backdrop of intensified global competition and consolidation in the financial services markets and the increasingly immediate need for capital and the efficient deployment of capital throughout the global banking sector. Securitisation is not a panacea and does not have universal application. It is, however, a useful tool for large and frequent users who can efficiently harness its technology; in this sense, the application of securitisation will closely track the trend towards consolidation in the financial services industries, as in turn it catalyses and hastens the process.

Table 1

Each of a Bank's Traditional Businesses Has A Number of Competitors in Today's Marketplace

Business	Competitors
Deposit Gathering	Money Market Funds Unit Trusts Insurance Products
Lending	Mortgage Bankers Centralised Lenders Insurance Companies Travel and Entertainment Cards Retailers Finance Companies Capital Markets
Money Management	Mutual Funds Money Markets Insurance Companies
Transaction Processing	Mortgage Bankers Clearing Houses Specialised Processors

Table 2

Banking is Comprised of Several Component Businesses

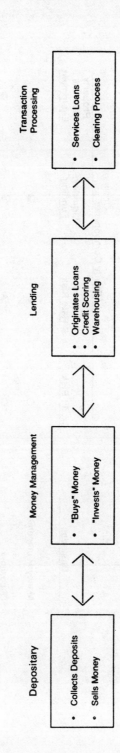

Depositary

- Collects Deposits
- Sells Money

Money Management

- "Buys" Money
- "Invests" Money

Lending

- Originates Loans
- Credit Scoring
- Warehousing

Transaction Processing

- Services Loans
- Clearing Process

Goldman Sachs

Table 3

Each Component of the Banking Business Has Its Own Equity Requirement

	Equity Components			
Business	Credit Risk	Interest Rate Risk	Liquidity/Funding	Property Plant & Equipment
Money Management	Low	High	Medium	Low
Depository	Low	Medium	Medium	High
Loan Origination	High	Medium	Medium	Medium
Transaction Processing	Low	Medium	Low	High

○ Low   ◑ Medium   ● High

Table 4

Capital Raising Alternatives

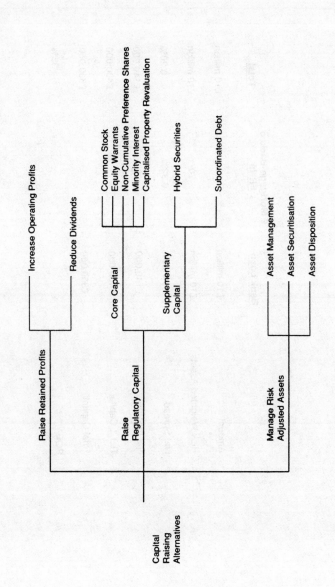

Goldman Sachs

Table 5

Current Portfolio

	Bank Loan	£ Mortgage-Backed FRNs	Total
Amount	£10 million	£0	£10 million
Risk Weighted Assets	£10 million	£0	£10 million
Net Spread	0.20%	0.32%	0.20%
Net Income	£140,000	£0	£140,000
Tier 1 Capital	£400,000	-	£400,000
Total Capital	£800,000	-	£800,000
ROE			35%

Table 6

"Optimised" Portfolio

Trade: Sell High Risk, Low Return Assets
        Buy Low Risk, High Return Assets

Example:	Bank Loan	£ Mortgage-Backed FRNs	Total
Amount	- £10 million	+ £20 million	£20 million
Risk Weighted Assets	- £10 million	+ £10 million	£10 million
Net Spread	0.20%	0.32%	0.32%
After-Tax Income	£0	£184,000	£184,000
ROE			46%

Appendix 1

Summary Terms of Outstanding Sterling Floating Rate Collateralised Issues

Issue Date	Issuer Issue amount £m	Rating *1	Initial Margin *2	Stated Final maturity (Av. life) (years) *3	Step-up Margin *2	Call Option *4	Front-end Fees %	Further Advances	Substitution	Prepayment Mechanism	Credit support: Principal	Credit support: Interest	Listing
1985 Feb	MINI 1 50	-/-	0.375	Feb 2010 (NS)	n/a	No Max. From Feb 1990	0.35	n/a	100% to Feb 1987; limited to Feb 1992	Drawing by lot—Issuer can purchase/cancel	Bank of America 5% Protection Fund	Protection Fund allows interim claims	Lux
1987 Mar	NHL 1 50	AAA/-	0.20	Sep 2013 (NS)	n/a	£10m From issue date	0.50	£7.5m to maturity date	n/a	Pro-rata—Issuer can purchase/cancel	Sun Alliance 10% insurance	Financial Security Assurance	Lon
Mar	TMC 1 200	AA/-	0.25	Sep 2014 (NS)	n/a	£20m From Mar 1992	0.50	n/a	n/a	Pro-rata—Issuer can purchase/cancel	Sun Alliance insurance §	Salomon	Lon
Jul	HMC 1 150	AAA/-	0.25	Jul 2017 (7.1)	0.50 from Jun 1997 or when principal falls below £30m	£30m or From Jun 1992 *	0.60	£11.25m to Jun 1997	£15m to Jun 1990	Drawing by lot—Issuer can purchase/cancel	Sun Alliance 5% insurance. Issuer's capital of £5.5m	Issuer's capital of £5.5m	Lux
Aug	TMC 2 100	AA/-	0.375	Nov 2014 (NS)	0.50 from Aug 1997	£10m From Aug 1992	0.50	n/a	n/a	Pro-rata—Issuer can purchase/cancel	Eagle Star insurance § Reinsured by Trade Indemnity	Salomon	Lux
Oct	NHL 2 A Notes 100	AAA/-	0.275	Oct 2014 (NS)	0.50 from Oct 1994	£10m or From Oct 1994	0.60	n/a	n/a	Pro-rata—Issuer can purchase/cancel	£11m B notes	Contingency Fund from NHL. Deferral of Interest on B Notes	Lux

Date	Issue	Rating	Margin	Maturity	Margin	Amount/From		Amount	n/a	Redemption	Insurance	Placing	
Oct	TMC 3 100	AA/–	0.375	Apr 2015 (NS)	0.50 from Oct 1997	£10m From Oct 1992	0.40	n/a	n/a	Pro-rata—Issuer can purchase/cancel	Eagle Star 5.75% insurance Reinsured by Trade Indemnity	Salomon	Lux
Nov	TMC 4 100	AA/–	0.375	May 2015 (NS)	0.50 from Nov 1997	£10m From Nov 1992	0.40	n/a	n/a	Pro-rata—Issuer can purchase/cancel	Eagle Star insurance § Reinsured by Trade Indemnity	Salomon	Lux
Nov	NHL 3 A Notes 100	AAA/–	0.25	Nov 2014 (NS)	0.50 from Nov 1994	£10m or From Nov 1994	0.60	n/a	n/a	Pro-rata—Issuer can purchase/cancel	£10.5m B Notes	Contingency Fund from NHL. Deferral of Interest on B Notes	Lux
Dec	DOMUS 1 100	A+°/A1	0.35	Dec 2014 (NS)	0.50 from Dec 1997	£10m from Dec 1992 or no max from Dec 1997	0.50	£10m to maturity date	n/a	Drawing by lot—Issuer can purchase cancel	Sun Alliance 10% insurance	Union Bank of Switzerland	Lux
1988 Feb	HMC 2 A Notes 175	AAA/–	0.35	Feb 2015 (6.4)	0.50 from Feb 1998	No Max. From Feb 1993	0.60	£24m to Feb 1998	n/a	Drawing by lot—Issuer can purchase cancel	£14m B Notes	Deferral of Interest on B Notes	Lux
Mar	MFC 1 A-1 Notes 175	AA/Aa1	0.425	Mar 2020 (NS)	0.50 from Mar 1998	No Max. From Mar 1993	0.50	£30m to maturity date	n/a	Drawing by lot—Issuer can purchase cancel	£25m A-2 Notes. Eagle Star 100% insurance	Pool policy allows interim claims. Deferral of Interest on A-2 Notes	Lux
Apr	TMC 5 125	AAA/–	0.35	Sep 2015 (NS)	0.50 from Mar 1998	£25m From Jun 1993	0.50	n/a	n/a	Pro-rata—Issuer can purchase/cancel	Eagle Star insurance.§ Reinsured by Pohjola Finance	Salomon—Backed by Pool Policy	Lux
Apr	TMC 6 100	AAA/–	0.325	Oct 2015 (NS)	0.50 from Apr 1998	£10m From Apr 1993	0.55	n/a	n/a	Pro-rata—Issuer can purchase/cancel	Eagle Star insurance.§ Reinsured by Pohjola Finance	Salomon—Backed by Pool Policy	Lux

BARINGS

Appendix 1—*continued*

Issue Date	Issuer Issue amount £m	Rating *1	Initial Margin *2	Stated Final maturity (Av. life years) *3	Step-up Margin *2	Call Option *4	Front-end Fees % *4	Further Advances	Substitution	Prepayment Mechanism	Credit support: Principal	Interest	Listing
May	RPS 1 200	AAA/-	0.35	May 2018 (7.0)	0.50 from May 1998 **	£20m or From May 1993	0.60	n/a	100% to May 1991	Drawing by lot—Issuer can purchase/cancel	Eagle Star 10.25% insurance. Reinsured by Pohjola Finance and Skandia	Commerzbank	Lux
Jun	TMC 7 100	AAA/-	0.325	Nov 2015 (NS)	0.50 from Aug 1998	£10m From Aug 1993	0.50	n/a	n/a	Pro-rata—Issuer can purchase/cancel	Eagle Star insurance. § Reinsured by Pohjola Finance	Salomon—Backed by Pool Policy	Lux
Jul	HMC 3 A Notes 150	AAA/-	0.325	Jul 2015 (6.7)	0.50 from Jul 1998	No Max. From Jul 1993	0.375	£20m to Jul 1998	n/a	Drawing by lot—Issuer can purchase/cancel	£11.5m B Notes	Deferral of Interest on B Notes	Lux
Jul	TMC 8 100	AAA/-	0.325	Dec 2018 (NS)	0.50 from Sep 1998	£10m From Sep 1993	0.50	n/a	100% to Jun 1991	Drawing by lot—Issuer can purchase/cancel	Eagle Star insurance. § Reinsured by Pohjola Finance	Salomon—Backed by Pool Policy	Lux
Jul	MAES 1 200	AAA/-	0.325	Jul 2018 (7.0)	0.50 from Oct 1998	No Max. From Oct 1993	0.45	n/a	100% to Jul 1991 *ff*	Drawing by lot—Issuer can purchase/cancel	Eagle Star 10% insurance. Reinsured by Hansa	Morgan	Lux
Jul	RPS 2 200	AAA/-	0.325	Jul 2018 (7.0)	0.50 from Jul 1998 **	£20m or from Jul 1993	0.50	n/a	100% to Jul 1991	Drawing by lot—Issuer can purchase/cancel	Eagle Star 10.25% insurance. Reinsured by Hansa	Commerzbank	Lux
Aug	MFC 2 B-1 Notes 115	AAA/Aa2	0.325	Aug 2023 (7.0)	0.50 from Aug 1998	No Max. From Aug 1993	0.45	£18.9m to maturity date	100% to Aug 1991	Drawing by lot—Issuer can purchase/cancel	£11m B-2 Notes. Eagle Star 100% insurance	Pool policy allows interim claims. Deferral of Interest on B-2 Notes	Lux

	Issue	Rating		Maturity					Redemption	Subordination/Insurance	Guarantor/Bank	Listing
Sep	EF 1 135	AAA/ -	0.30	Sep 2015 (NS)	0.50 from Sep 1998	£27m or 0.40 from Dec 1993	n/a	n/a	Pro-rata—Issuer can purchase/cancel	Eagle Star insurance. § Reinsured by Hansa	Westdeutsche Landesbank	Lux
Sep	TMC 9 200	AAA/ -	0.325	Feb 2019 (NS)	0.50 from Nov 1998	£20m From Nov 1993 0.45	n/a	100% to Aug 1991 *ff*	Drawing by lot—Issuer can purchase/cancel	Eagle Star insurance. § Reinsured by Pohjola Finance	Salomon—Backed by Pool Policy	Lux
Oct	TMC 10 200	AAA/ -	0.30	Mar 2019 (NS)	0.50 from Dec 1998	£20m From Dec 1993 0.50	n/a	100% to Sep 1991	Drawing by lot—Issuer can purchase/cancel	Eagle Star insurance. § Reinsured by Pohjola Finance	Salomon—Backed by Pool Policy	Lux
Oct	NHL 4 A Notes 100	AAA/Aaa	0.275	Oct 2015 (NS)	0.50 from Oct 1998	£10m or From Oct 1993 0.40	n/a	n/a	Pro-rata—Issuer can purchase/cancel	£10.75m B Notes	Contingency Fund from NHL. Deferral of Interest on B Notes	Lux
Oct	MFC 3 C-1 Notes 120	AAA/Aaa	0.30	Oct 2023 (NS)	0.50 from Oct 1998	No Max. From Oct 1993 0.275	£20.1m to maturity date	100% to Oct 1991	Drawing by lot—Issuer can purchase/cancel	£14.2m C-2 Notes. Eagle Star 100% insurance	Pool policy allows interim claims. Deferral of Interest on C-2 Notes	Lux
Nov	MS 1 A Notes 200	AAA/ -	0.30	Oct 2023 (7.5)	0.50 from Oct 1998	No Max. From Oct 1993 0.325	No Max. to Oct 1991	100% §§§ to Oct 1991 *ff*	Drawing by lot—Issuer can purchase/cancel	£20m B Notes. Eagle Star 100% insurance	Sumitomo Bank. Deferral of Interest on B Notes	Lux
Dec	TMC 11 °°° 500	AAA/Aaa	0.275	Mar 2020 (7.2)	0.50 from Mar 1999	£50m From Mar 1994 0.40	n/a	100% to Mar 1992	Drawing by lot—Issuer can purchase/cancel	Eagle Star insurance. § Reinsured by Pohjola Finance and Hansa	Salomon—Backed by Pool Policy	Lux
1989 Mar	SRF 1 A Notes 150	AAA/ -	0.20	Mar 2021 (7.9)	0.50 from Mar 1999	No Max. From Mar 1994 0.325	£20m to Mar 1992	No max. 100% to Mar 1992	Drawing by lot—Issuer can purchase/cancel	£20m B Notes	Deferral of Interest on B Notes	Lux
Jun	MAES 2 300 ****	AAA/ -	0.15	May 2017 (2.1)	0.50 from Aug 1993	No Max. From May 1993 0.15	n/a	n/a	Pro-rata—Issuer can purchase/cancel	Eagle Star 10% insurance. Reinsured by Hansa	Morgan	Lux

BARINGS

Appendix 1—*continued*

Issue Date	Issuer Issue amount £m	Rating *1	Initial Margin *2	Stated Final maturity (Av. life) (years) *3	Step-up Margin *2	Call Option *4	Front-end Fees %	Further Advances	Substitution	Prepayment Mechanism	Credit support: Principal	Interest	Listing
Jun	GMF 175	AAA/ Aaa	0.20	Jun 2019 (6.2)	0.50 from Jun 1999 ***	£17.5m From Jun 1992	0.125	n/a	100% to Jun 1992	Pro-rata— Issuer can purchase/ cancel	Sun Alliance 10% insurance	Morgan	Lon
Jun	CMS 1 A1 Notes 110	AAA/ Aaa	0.10	Jun 1992 (1.5)	0.40 from Jun 1992	No Max. From Jun 1992	0.125	n/a	n/a				
	A2 Notes 65	AAA/ Aaa	0.1875	Mar 1996 (4.8)	0.50 from Jun 1997	No Max. From Jun 1997	0.20	n/a	n/a	Pro-rata— Issuer can purchase/ cancel	£14.7m B Notes	Contingency Fund from NHL. Deferral of Interest on B Notes	Lux
	A3 Notes 35	AAA/ Aaa	0.20	Sep 1996 (7.5)	0.50 from Jun 1999	£31.5m or From Jun 1999	0.30	n/a	n/a				
Jun	TMCP Tranche No. 1 250	AAA/ Aaa	0.18	Aug 2030 (7.2)	0.50 from May 1999	£25m From May 1994	0.25	n/a	100% to May 1992	Drawing by lot—Issuer can purchase/ cancel	Eagle Star insurance. § Reinsured by Hansa	Salomon— Backed by Pool Policy	Lon
Aug	HMC 4 A Notes 150	AAA/ -	0.18	Aug 2021 (8.8)	0.50 from Aug 1999	No Max. From Aug 1992	0.19	£18.8m to Aug 2004	100% to Aug 1994	Drawing by lot—Issuer can purchase/ cancel	£9m B Notes	Deferral of Interest on B Notes	Lux
Sep	CMS 2 A Notes 250	AAA/ Aaa	0.18	Sep 2026 (4.2)	0.50 from Sep 1999	£25m or From Sep 1994	0.15	n/a	n/a	Pro-rata— Issuer can purchase/ cancel	£22m B Notes §§	Contingency Fund from NHL. Deferral of Interest on B Notes	
Sep	MS 2 150 f	AAA/ —	0.18	Sep 2028 (6.4)	0.50 from Sep 1999	No. Max. From Sep 1994	0.15	No Max. Subject to amortisation	100% to Maturity Date§§§§	Drawing by lot—Issuer can purchase/ cancel	Eagle Star insurance. 100% Reinsured by Hanover Re. 10%	Barclays	Lux

BARINGS

		*1	*2	*3		*4					§		
Sep	TMC P1 Tranche No. 2 250	AAA/—	0.18	Jul 2029 (7.2)	0.50 from Jul 1999	£25m From Jul 1994 OR No. Max. From Jul 1999	0.27	n/a	100% to Jul 1992	Drawing by lot—Issuer can purchase/cancel	Sun Alliance & Royal Insurance§	Salomon—Backed by Pool Policy	Lon
Dec	TMC P3 Tranche No. 4 (A) 100	—/Aaa	0.18	Oct 2029 (1.52)	0.50 from Oct 1993	£25m ☐☐ from Oct 1994 or No Max. from Oct 1999	0.13	n/a	n/a	Drawing by lot—Issuer can purchase/cancel	Sun Alliance & Royal Insurance§	Salomon—Backed by Pool Policy	Lon
	Tranche No. 4 (B) 150	—/Aaa	0.25	Oct 2029 (6.52)	0.50 from Oct 1999	£25m ☐☐ from Oct 1994 or No Max. from Oct 1999	0.30	n/a	n/a	Drawing by lot—Issuer can purchase/cancel	Sun Alliance & Royal Insurance§	Salomon—Backed by Pool Policy	Lon
Dec	TCM 1 175	AAA/—	0.25	Jan 2029 (8.5)	0.50 from Jan 2000	No Max. from Jan 1995	0.45	£50m to Jan 2000	100% to Jan 1995	Drawing by lot—Issuer can purchase/cancel	Sun Alliance 8.25% insurance	Barclays	Lux

*1   Standard & Poor's Corporation/Moody's Investors Service Inc.
*2   %p.a. over 3 Month £ LIBOR, payable quarterly
*3   Issuer's average life assumption at launch (assuming call when interest margin steps up)
*4   Maximum permissible amount outstanding at first call date (if applicable) and/or first call date
n/a   Not applicable
(NS)   Not stated in prospectus
☐☐   Substitution allowed providing mortgage balance does not exceed scheduled amount during year: (Y/E Feb—Max. Bal.): 1988—£47m; 1989—£42m; 1990—£36m; 1991—£30m; 1992—£25m.
☐   Issuer's option to call Tranche 4 is dependent upon the outstanding mortgages within whole pool.
*   Partial optional redemption by issuer after call option date
**   Step up date will be triggered earlier if pool balance falls below £20m
***   Step up margin may apply if mortgage balance should fall below £17.5m
****   Issuer has option to issue further notes up to a maximum of £200m in principal over issue term
§   % Pool coverage not public information
§§   Subject to confirmation
§§§   Can substitute mortgages at any time if borrower switches into fixed-rate product
§§§§   Controlled amortisation of 2.5% per quarter until maturity.
eo   As from Sep 1989 this issue was downgraded from A+ to A− by S&P and from Aa3 to A1 by Moody's (Oct. 89)
∞   Stated final maturity for all notes is June 2016
∞∞∞∞   4 tranches totalling £500m. Initial interest period for tranches 2 and 3 were two months and one month respectively, reverting to three months thereafter. Fungible from 31 March, 1989
f   Issuer has option to issue further notes up to a maximum of £100m in principal with one year of closing date
ff   Issuer has announced that substitution facility may not be utilized on future interest payment dates

Appendix 1—*continued*

Issue date	Issuer / Issue amount £m	Rating *1	Coupon *2	Issue price %	Front end fees %	Final maturity	Yield *3	Launch spread *4	Mandatory redemption	Optional redemption	Listing
1988 Nov	HMC 101 / 100	AAA/-	11 1/8	102 1/4	1.875	Nov 1993	10.523	83	If interest rate swap is terminated by either party.	If any tax is imposed on the Notes.	Lux
1989 Mar	HMC 102 / 100	AAA/-	11	101 3/4	1.875	Mar 1994	10.532	75	If interest rate swap is terminated by either party.	If any tax is imposed on the Notes.	Lux

*1 Standard & Poor's Corporation/Moody's Investors Service Inc.
*2 %Payable annually
*3 %Yield (annual) at launch based upon issue price less full fees
*4 Semi-annual spread based on yield over applicable 5 year gilt in bps

Issuer	Full name	Originator	Administrator
CMS 1	Collateralised Mortgage Securities (No 1) PLC	National Home Loans Corporation plc	National Home Loans Corporation plc
CMS 2	Collateralised Mortgage Securities (No 2) PLC		
DOMUS 1	Domus Mortgage Finance No. 1 plc	Chemical Bank & Chemical Bank Home Loans Ltd ('CBHL')	BNP Mortgages Limited (Known as CBHL until Aug. 1988)
EF 1	Exclusive Finance No. 1 PLC	United Dominions Trust Limited ('UDT')—indirect wholly owned subsidiary of TSB Group PLC	Mortgage Express Limited—a wholly owned subsidiary of UDT
GMF	Gracechurch Mortgage Finance PLC	Barclays Direct Mortgage Service—operational department within Barclays Bank PLC	Barclays Bank PLC
HMC 1	HMC Mortgage Notes 1 PLC	Household Mortgage Corporation PLC	Household Mortgage Corporation PLC
HMC 2	HMC Mortgage Notes 2 PLC		
HMC 3	HMC Mortgage Notes 3 PLC		
HMC 4	HMC Mortgage Notes 4 PLC		
HMC 101	HMC Mortgage Notes 101 PLC		
HMC 102	HMC Mortgage Notes 102 PLC		
MAES 1	MAES Funding No. 1 PLC	Canadian Imperial Bank of Commerce & CIBC Mortgages plc	CIBC Mortgages plc
MAES 2	MAES Funding No. 2 PLC		

BARINGS

Code	Issuer		
MFC 1 MFC 2 MFC 3	Mortgage Funding Corporation No. 1 PLC Mortgage Funding Corporation No. 2 PLC Mortgage Funding Corporation No. 3 PLC	Allied Dunbar Mortgage Trust Limited Abbey Life Funding Limited	Mortgage Systems Limited
MINI 1	Mortgage Intermediary Note Issuer (No. 1)—Amsterdam BV	BankAmerica Finance Limited ('BAFIN')	Bank of Ireland Home Mortgages Limited—(known as BAFIN until Mar. 1987)
MS 1 MS 2	Mortgage Securities (No. 1) PLC Mortgage Securities (No 2) PLC	First Mortgage Securities Treasury Limited Treasury Limited	First Mortgage Securities Treasury Holdings Limited Treasury Holdings Limited
NHL 1 NHL 2 NHL 3 NHL 4	NHL First Funding Corporation PLC NHL Second Funding Corporation PLC NHL Third Funding Corporation PLC NHL Fourth Funding Corporation PLC	National Home Loans Corporation plc	National Home Loans Corporation plc
RPS 1 RPS 2	Residential Property Securities No. 1 PLC Residential Property Securities No. 2 PLC	Bank of Ireland Home Mortgages Limited —(known as BAFIN until Mar. 1987)	Bank of Ireland Home Mortgages Limited —(Known as BAFIN until Mar. 1987)
SRF 1	SRF Mortgage Notes 1 PLC	Allied Dunbar Mortgages Limited & HMC High Equity PLC	HMC plc/HMC Services Limited
TCM 1	Temple Court Mortgages (No 1) PLC	Legal & General Mortgage Services Limited	Temple Court Originations subcontracted to TMC Portfolio Services Limited
TMC 1 TMC 2 TMC 3 TMC 4 TMC 5 TMC 6 TMC 7 TMC 8 TMC 9 TMC 10 TMC 11 TMCP TMC P1 TMC P3	TMC Mortgage Securities No. 1 PLC TMC Mortgage Securities No. 2 PLC TMC Mortgage Securities No. 3 PLC TMC Mortgage Securities No. 4 PLC TMC Mortgage Securities No. 5 PLC TMC Mortgage Securities No. 6 PLC TMC Mortgage Securities No. 7 PLC TMC Mortgage Securities No. 8 PLC TMC Mortgage Securities No. 9 PLC TMC Mortgage Securities No. 10 PLC TMC Mortgage Securities No. 11 PLC TMC P.I.M.B.S. PLC TMC P.I.M.B.S. First Financing PLC TMC P.I.M.B.S. Third Financing PLC	The Mortgage Corporation Limited	The Mortgage Corporation Limited

Appendix 2

Bank of England Notice to Institutions Authorised under the Banking Act 1987

LOAN TRANSFERS AND SECURITISATION
(BSD/1989/1   FEBRUARY 1989)

Introduction

1. This notice sets out the Bank's supervisory policy on the treatment of loan transfers involving banks. It draws on the legal analysis contained in the consultative paper 'Loan Transfers and Securitisation' published by the Bank of England in December 1987, which is reproduced as an annex to this notice.

Coverage

2. The notice covers both the sale of single loans and the packaging, securitisation and sale of loan pools. It also covers the transfer of risk under sub-participation agreements. Although most references in the notice are to sales of loans, the policy in principle also applies to sales of other forms of assets, and to the transfer of risks under contingent items such as letters of credit and acceptance credits. It also covers the transfer of undrawn commitments.

Implementation

3. The policy set out in this notice has immediate effect, but will not be applied to past sales or packaging schemes which are 'grandfathered'.

Aims of the policy

4. The Bank's principal policy objectives are to ensure that:

(i) loan sales and packaging achieve their intended effect of passing rights and obligations from the seller to the buyer;

(ii) all the parties to the transaction fully understand the responsibilities and risks they have assumed or retained; and

(iii) any material risks to buyers or sellers are properly treated in the Bank's supervision of banks.

Methods of transfer

5. The Bank considers that the method of transfer of a loan can have an important bearing on the risks assumed by buyer and seller. An assessment of the implications of different methods under English law appears in the Annex.

6. The cleanest transfer of risk is achieved by *novation*, where the existing loan is cancelled and a new agreement substituted, which transfers all the seller's rights and obligations to the buyer. A legal or equitable *assignment*, if properly structured, can also achieve an effective transfer of the seller's rights and the remedies available to him to enforce those rights. But the seller retains any outstanding obligations (for example, to advance further funds), while the buyer's rights may be impaired by any rights of set-off that exist between the borrower and the seller. Where the assignment is silent (ie the borrower is not notified), there may be additional risks for both buyer and seller—for the buyer because the absence of notice to the borrower removes some legal protection he would otherwise have; and for the seller, because as lender of record he will remain subject to requests to reschedule or renegotiate. The third most common technique, *sub-participation*, does not transfer any rights, remedies or obligations from seller to buyer, but is an entirely separate non-recourse funding arrangement, under which the buyer places funds with the seller in exchange for acquiring a beneficial interest in the underlying loan, but the loan itself is not transferred. In this case, the buyer assumes an exposure to the borrower, but is also at risk to the seller, because he has lent to him and because he relies on him to pass through funds received from the borrower.

Supervisory treatment

7. The Bank will apply the following treatment to a loan (or a part of a loan) transferred using the above methods, subject to the further conditions specified in paragraphs 8 and 14 below:

(i) a transfer through novation will be regarded as a clean transfer. The loan will therefore be excluded from the seller's risk asset ratio and included in the buyer's;

(ii) a transfer through an assignment duly notified to the borrower will be regarded as a clean transfer, provided that the buyer has taken reasonable precautions to ensure that his rights under the transfer are not impaired by an intervening right; for example, a right of set-off between seller and borrower. A minimum requirement should be a warranty from the seller that no such right of set-off exists;

(iii) a transfer through a silent assignment will usually be regarded as a clean transfer. However the seller must recognise that as he remains the lender of record he will be the focal point for pressure from the borrower to reschedule or renegotiate the terms of the loan, or advance further funds. The volume of loans to individual borrowers sold on a silent assignment basis needs to be subject to appropriate internal controls. Silent assignments may also pose additional risks for buyers (see paragraph 17 of the Annex), and these need to be kept under careful review. If it is not satisfied on these points the Bank may disregard a transfer of a loan through a silent assignment in calculating the risk asset ratio of the seller;

(iv) a loan sub-participation, while not transferring in a legal sense the rights of the original lender, aims to have the same economic effect. Where a loan is funded in whole or in part via a sub-participation, the Bank will recognise the transfer of credit risk by excluding it (or the relevant part) from the original lender's risk asset ratio, and including it in the sub-participant's as a claim on the underlying borrower. The sub-participant should normally, as a matter of best practice, acquire a charge over the underlying assets. The Bank may require justification where this has not been done;

(v) where banks transfer undrawn commitments to lend (or part of them), the commitment (or part) will be excluded from the selling bank's risk asset ratio only when the transfer is either by novation, or by an assignment accompanied by formal acknowledgement from the borrower of a transfer of obligations from the seller to the buyer. A transfer by means of silent assignment or sub-participation will not lead to the exclusion of the commitment from the selling bank's risk asset ratio. Instead it will be treated as a transfer of the seller's exposure from the potential borrower to the buyer. The buyer's assumption of a commitment (or part) will be included in its risk asset ratio as a claim on the borrower, irrespective of the method of transfer used.

8. The above policy in relation to the method of transfer will be applied provided that the following conditions are satisfied:

A. In the case of the transfer of a single loan (or part of a loan)

(i) the transfer does not contravene the terms and conditions of the underlying loan agreement and all the necessary consents have been obtained;

(ii) the seller has no residual beneficial interest in the principal amount of the loan (or that part which has been transferred) and the buyer has no formal recourse to the seller for losses;

(iii) the seller has no obligation[1] to repurchase the loan,[2] or any part of it, at any time (although he may retain an option to do so provided the loan remains fully-performing);

(iv) the seller can demonstrate, to the satisfaction of the Bank, that it has given notice to the buyer that it is under no obligation to repurchase the loan[2] nor support any losses suffered by the buyer and that the buyer has acknowledged the absence of obligation;

(v) the documented terms of the transfer are such that, if the loan is rescheduled or renegotiated, the buyer and not the seller would be subject to the rescheduled or renegotiated terms;

(vi) where payments are routed through the seller, he is under no obligation to remit funds to the buyer unless and until they are received from the borrower. Payments voluntarily made by the seller to the buyer in anticipation of payments from the borrower must be made on terms under which they can be recovered from the buyer if the borrower fails to perform.

B. Packaging schemes[3]

9. The process of packaging loans together and selling them as a block or pool can compound risks which are often negligible when a single loan is transferred. For example a seller—or originator—of a pool of loans is more at risk from his misrepresentation as to their quality than if only one of those loans is involved.

10. Sellers—or originators—of loans who continue to administer (or 'service') them as a securitised portfolio in order to maintain borrower relationships or to earn fees can also run explicit operational risks. Their continued identification with the loans can mean that their commercial reputation is committed and a completely clean break is not achieved. The Bank is concerned that banks in this position may come under pressure to support losses incurred by the investors/buyers and may be inclined to do so in order to protect their name.

11. These operational and 'moral' risks will be present where a bank originates and/or services a portfolio of loans whether they were ever on its balance sheet or not. They apply both to vehicle and pool participation schemes.

12. In the past the risks associated with loan administration have not warranted

---

[1] Except where arising from warranties given in respect of the loan at the time of its transfer, provided that these are not in respect of the future credit-worthiness of the borrower.
[2] Not applicable to sub-participations.
[3] Schemes involving the 'packaging' of a single loan or commitment are not covered by this part of the notice.

special treatment (see the Measurement of Capital paper, paragraphs 30–32) as the capital required to cover credit risk helps to protect a bank against other risks as well. This would no longer be the case, however, where functions have been unbundled so that the credit risk lies with a third party.

13. The Bank believes that the risks from close association with a securitisation scheme can assume material proportions. The arrangements controlling the association should be carefully assessed and monitored, and subject to internal audit. These may be included in the scope of the reports on records and systems which reporting accountants will prepare each year for management and the Bank (see policy notice BSD/1987/2). The Bank will take into account any significant operational risks not related to balance sheet items when setting a bank's minimum permissible (or 'trigger') risk asset ratio. In exceptional cases it may wish to apply an explicit capital requirement against this sort of risk.

14. In addition to conditions (i) to (vi) in paragraph 8, the Bank will require the following conditions to be met by a bank acting as servicing agent[4] of loan packaging schemes, in order to ensure that its role is not seen as being more than acting as an agent.

(vii) the Bank will expect the servicing agent to have evidence available in its records that its auditors and legal advisers are satisfied that the terms of the scheme protect it from any liability to investors in the scheme, save where it is proved to have been negligent;

(viii) the servicing agent must be able to demonstrate that it has taken all reasonable precautions to ensure that it is not obliged nor will feel impelled to support any losses suffered by the scheme or investors in it. Any offering circular should contain a highly visible, unequivocal statement that the servicing agent does not stand behind the issue or the vehicle and will not make good any losses in the portfolio;

(ix) the servicing agent (or any other group entity covered by the Bank's consolidated supervision of a group of which the servicing agent is a part) may not own any share capital in any company used as a vehicle for the scheme; nor in any other form hold a proprietary interest in or control over that company either directly or indirectly. For this purpose 'share capital' includes all classes of ordinary and preference share capital;

(x) the Board of a company used as a vehicle for a scheme must be independent of the servicing agent, although the latter may have one director representing it;

(xi) the name of a company used as the vehicle for a scheme must not include the name of the servicing agent or imply any connection with it;

---

[4] The Bank would expect to be consulted when a bank proposes to act jointly with one or more other administrators.

(xii) the servicing agent must not bear any of the recurring expenses of the scheme. However, the agent may make a one-off contribution to enhance the credit worthiness of a vehicle. It may also lend on a long term subordinated basis to the vehicle provided that the loan is only repayable following winding up of the scheme. Any transactions under these headings must be undertaken at the initiation of the scheme and disclosed in any offering circular. They will be deducted from capital for capital adequacy purposes;

(xiii) the servicing agent may not intentionally bear any losses arising from the effect of interest rate changes on the scheme. However, the agent may enter into interest rate swap agreements at market prices with the vehicle. There should be provision for unintended temporary losses arising from normal administrative delays in changing mortgage rates to be recovered by the servicing agent as soon as possible;

(xiv) a servicing agent may not fund a vehicle or scheme (except within the terms of condition xii above) and in particular may not provide temporary finance to a scheme to cover cash shortfalls arising from delayed payments or non-performance of loans which it administers;

(xv) a servicing agent may not retain an option to repurchase (or refinance) loans except where the loan portfolio has fallen to less than 10% of its maximum value and the option extends only to fully-performing loans.

15. If any of the above conditions is not satisfied, the assets administered by the servicing agent will be consolidated with its balance sheet for risk asset ratio purposes.

Banking Supervision Division
Bank of England

February 1989

Annex

METHODS OF TRANSFER

1. This annex contains a brief review of the position under English law in relation to the disposal of loan assets. The Bank wishes to stress that:

(i) except where indicated, this annex deals only with the position under English law; the position in other jurisdictions may differ;
(ii) the annex does not consider the tax position of transfers, in particular stamp duty and stamp duty reserve tax;[1]
(iii) the legal position is complex and reliance should not be placed on this annex; where appropriate, independent legal advice should be taken.

2. The annex does not cover the transfer of any security which may support a transferred loan. It is nevertheless important that buyers should ensure that they acquire the full benefit of any security.

Transfer methods

3. Strictly speaking, loans cannot be 'sold' in the same straightforward way as tangible assets (eg cars, equipment etc); a technical but important point. There are, however, three basic methods of transferring the rights and/or the obligations under a loan—novation, assignment and participation—and, throughout this annex, the shorthand 'seller' and buyer' is used: 'seller' referring to a bank which is disposing of an asset, by whatever means; and 'buyer' referring to the new lender, transferee, assignee or participant.

Assignment

4. In general, a lender *may assign his rights* under a loan agreement to a third party; ie his rights to interest and principal.

5. A loan agreement may, however, impose restrictions on assignability and it is likely that, if they were breached, the buyer would gain no direct rights against the borrower and may have difficulty in enforcing the assignment against the seller.

6. It is also uncertain whether a buyer can take an assignment of the benefit of certain typical clauses in a loan agreement; eg a provision for grossing-up or for payment of increased costs. Such obligations of the borrower may be construed

---

[1]   Although not considered here, the tax position could be of relevance, for example to the attempt by a buyer to enforce a loan. If the transfer has failed to be stamped when it should have been, the buyer may be unable to enforce the loan in the Courts.

as personal to the original lender and, as such, unassignable. Even if this is not the case and the loan agreement extends the relevant clauses to assignees of the original lender, it is arguable that an assignee cannot obtain greater rights than those of the original seller; ie that the buyer cannot claim the benefit of, say, a grossing-up clause or an increased costs clause save in circumstances, and to the extent that, the original lender could have claimed the benefit of such clauses.

7. More significantly in the supervisory context, a lending bank may *not 'assign' its obligations* under a loan (or any other) agreement, since these can be transferred only with the consent of all other parties (including the borrower). In order to get over this, an 'assignee' of obligations (as well as rights) will sometimes undertake to meet the assignor's obligations as a condition of the assignment. But this does not actually release the assignor from those obligations to the borrower (or any other parties to the loan agreement), it merely reduces the risks arising out of them.

8. A seller/assignor therefore remains liable to the borrower in respect of any unperformed obligations under the original loan agreement. So that, for example, the undrawn part of a facility may not be transferred by assignment. Similarly, assignment can be an imperfect means of selling multicurrency loans, where the primary lender has continuing obligations throughout the term of the loan to switch its currency in certain circumstances.

9. Even where a loan is fully drawn down and the original lender has no outstanding obligations to the borrower, the original lender may still have obligations to other parties (eg in a syndicated loan, to indemnify the agent and/ or to share recoveries with the other lenders). These obligations will remain on the original lender notwithstanding an assignment. The buyer may agree to be liable to indemnify the seller in respect of such liabilities and may (although this is less clear) be liable directly to the other parties on the basis that the buyer is not entitled to take the benefit of a contract without the burdens.

10. Subject to any provisions to the contrary, assignments are made (and taken) subject to equities. An assignee's rights may therefore be subject to, for example, any rights of set-off which the borrower may have against the assignor, whether arising out of the loan agreement itself, any associated transactions or any other transactions entered into prior to the borrower receiving notice of the assignment. An assignee's claim on the borrower would be impaired by any such rights of set-off.

Types of assignment

11. Assignments for the purpose of disposing of assets may fall into two basic legal categories:

(i) statutory (or legal) assignments, transferring both legal and beneficial title;
(ii) equitable assignments, transferring 'only' beneficial title.

(a) Statutory assignment

12. A statutory assignment will 'pass and transfer' from the seller to the buyer all the legal rights to principal and interest and, in most circumstances, all the legal remedies available against the borrower to ensure discharge of the debt. That is, the buyer acquires the full *legal and beneficial* interest in the loan and is accordingly able (for instance) to sue the borrower directly without having to join the seller/assignor.

13. In order to be a statutory assignment, a transfer must satisfy the conditions of s 136 of the Law of Property Act 1925 (see the Appendix to this Annex for the relevant part of s 136). In particular, it must:

(i) be *in writing* and signed by the seller;
(ii) be absolute—that is, unconditional and not merely by way of security;
(iii) cover the *whole* of the loan;
(iv) be completed by *notice in writing to the borrower* (and any other obligors, eg a guarantor).

(b) Equitable assignment

14. An equitable assignment, by contrast, transfers only beneficial *not* legal rights. In consequence a buyer may not be able to proceed directly against a borrower. Instead, the seller must be joined in any action. This is purely procedural; the seller is not liable for the debt.

15. An 'equitable assignment' includes an assignment which fails to satisfy one of the s 136 conditions. An assignment will therefore be equitable where inter alia:

(i) part only of a loan is assigned—for example, where a loan is split between a group of buyers; or
(ii) it is not in writing; or
(iii) written notice is not given to the borrower (eg for 'commercial reasons').

16. As to (iii), where the borrower is not notified of the transfer, although the assignment is valid as between the seller and the buyer, the seller remains the lender of record, the lender in the mind of the borrower and repayments will be made by the borrower to the seller (who can give a good discharge).

17. Moreover, *notice (written or oral) secures some important protections for the buyer.* For example:

 (i) if notice is given, the borrower must make payments to the assignee/buyer (unless directed otherwise); without notice, the assignee/buyer has to give credit to the borrower for any payments to the assignor/seller made in ignorance of the assignment;

 (ii) notice gives the assignee/buyer some protection against intervening equities (in particular those independent of the agreement assigned); without notice, further equities and, in particular, rights of set off, may arise between the borrower and the assignor/seller: this could happen with major corporates which have an active trading relationship with the selling bank—Bank A assigns to Bank B a loan to Corporate X but without notice; Corporate X subsequently places money with Bank A; Corporate X may be able to set-off the two amounts if Bank A does not repay;

(iii) notice prevents the assignor/seller and borrower from varying the underlying contract;

(iv) where there are successive assignments of the same loan, the priority of the assignee/buyer can be determined by the order in which *written* notice was given to the borrower; notice may therefore protect a buyer against subsequent (accidental or dishonest) assignments.

18. It would accordingly seem to be good practice to give written notice and, if practicable, to obtain confirmation from the borrower that:

 (i) there is agreement on the amount of the debt;
 (ii) the borrower has no notice of any other assignment;
(iii) the borrower has no right of set-off against the assignor;
(iv) the contract between the borrower and assignor/seller has not been varied (for example by a side letter).

19. It should be noted that an equitable assignment of a legal interest in a loan (ie of a legal chose in action) creates an equitable interest in the debt (or an equitable chose in action). Any on-sale by way of a further equitable assignment is therefore an equitable transfer of an equitable chose in action, and is in consequence subject to different provisions from the original sale (in particular s 53(1)(c) of the Law of Property Act 1925 might apply, in which case the assignment would have to be in writing and signed by the assignor).

Novation

20. The cleanest way of selling a loan and the *only* way of effectively transferring both rights and *obligations* is novation. This entails cancelling the original rights and obligations, and substituting new ones in their place, although the only substantive difference is the identity of the lender. The buyer steps into the shoes of the original lender/seller who ceases to have any *obligations* to the borrower.

21. The technique can be somewhat cumbersome, however, as the consent of *all* the parties to the original loan is needed; ie, the borrower, any other lenders and possibly even the guarantor in the case of a syndicated facility. Steps have been taken to overcome this—see 'Transferable loan facilities' below (paras 31 to 33).

22. Novation avoids the difficulties of assignment in relation to 'transfer' of obligations and whether the buyer can be entitled to greater rights than the original lender/seller. However, difficulties may arise in particular in relation to secured loans, priorities, consents and questions as to the value given by the buyer (eg to avoid problems in relation to preferences and invalidation of floating charges under the Insolvency Act 1986).

Sub-participation

23. Unlike 'novation' and 'assignment', the terms 'participation' and 'sub-participation' are not terms of art as a matter of English law. Rather, they are market expressions applied to the 'sale' of a loan by way of a back-to-back non-recourse funding arrangement: the buyer deposits a sum of money (equal to the whole or part of the underlying loan) with the seller on terms under which the moneys are repayable (and interest is payable) if and only if the seller receives payments of principal (and interest) from the underlying borrower, and subject to a maximum of the amount received. (This is sometimes called a funded sub-participation or a sub-loan.)

24. The sub-participation, as customarily documented, is a separate legal agreement from the underlying loan, creating a debtor-creditor relationship between buyer and seller. The buyer does not (or at least is not intended to) acquire any legal or beneficial interest in the underlying loan, nor any contractual relationship with the ultimate borrower. In consequence, in contrast to novations and assignments, the buyer does not have any direct recourse to the borrower and is not able to exercise any of the seller's rights against the borrower. Nor can the buyer benefit from any of the other provisions of the underlying loan contract (such as grossing-up in the event of the imposition of withholding tax). The buyer's rights are against the seller and he can benefit only from the provisions of the sub-participation agreement.

(a) Types of participation agreements

25. Some banks use standard documentation for sub-participations. A *medium term agreement* may be used for individual loans and may be drawn widely so as to cover simple bank loans, syndicated credits, guaranteed loans, multicurrency loans, and loan facilities which are wholly or partly drawn.

26. A *'short-term master participation agreement'* may be used for a series of

short-term loans made under a rollover facility. Technically, each loan is repaid at the end of each interest period, notwithstanding the fact that a new loan is immediately and (in practice) automatically advanced, often without an actual movement of funds. The commercial effect can be equivalent to interest period stripping—as the buyer purchases the interest earned on a short term loan. Such sub-participation agreements tend to be drafted to cover all participations during the life of the facility.

(b) Double credit risk for buyer

27. An important feature of many sub-loans is the double jeopardy of the buyer; that is, that the buyer has a credit exposure to both the seller and the underlying borrower. Say Bank A makes a loan to Corporate X which it 'sells' to Bank B by way of sub-loan. If Corporate X fails and the liquidator recovers 50p in the £, Bank B gets 50p in the £.

28. If Bank A fails and the liquidator pays out 1p in the £, Bank B has a contingent claim in the liquidation. If the Corporate X loan is repaid in full, Bank B still gets only 1p in the £. If Corporate X also fails and nothing is recovered, Bank B gets nothing.

29. A possible remedy for buying Bank B is for its sub-loan to be secured by way of mortgage or charge over Bank A's loan to Corporate X. But banks appear to be reluctant to grant such charges, perhaps in part because they may need to be registered with the Registrar of Companies.

Risk participations

30. Risk participations are used for the undrawn part of a loan facility. Basically, the participant undertakes to fund any drawings on the facility by way of a non-recourse sub-loan. Risk participation is accordingly a commitment (i) to finance the lending bank and (ii) to take on the credit exposure to the borrower.

Transferable loan facilities

31. Many loans are now structured to ease transfer. Essentially, the borrower (and other parties to the loan) agree in advance that the loan—or parts of a loan—may be transferred freely or subject to conditions. The transfer is generally executed between the buyer and seller but with some registration procedure involving an agent bank. Buyers are able to make subsequent transfers and thus the transferable loan facility ('TLF') should help to increase the liquidity of the underlying asset.

32. There are three basic varieties of TLF: the Transferable Loan Certificate ('TLC'), which is based on *novation*; the Transferable Loan Instrument ('TLI'), which is based on legal assignment and the use of debentures (and thus can only be used where a loan is fully drawn); and the *Transferable Participation Certificate* ('TPC'), which combines TLC 'technology' with sub-participation.

33. The TPC is designed in part to avoid multi-tiered sub-participations: ie a sub-participant 'on-selling' the loan to another sub-participant so that in effect Bank 3 is funding Bank 2 which is funding Bank 1 which holds the underlying loan. The use of the TPC should enable Bank 3 to step cleanly into the shoes of Bank 2 and thus to have a direct contractual relationship with Bank 1.

Other legal issues affecting transfers

34. Whatever the method, transfers are complex legal transactions needing great care and professional advice. For example, as already noted, successive equitable assignments may be subject to slightly different conditions.

(a) Local law

35. In addition, it is important that all parties to a sale should recognise that, although the novation, assignment or sub-participation may be made under English law, the effectiveness of the transfer may depend on the laws of other countries. The following can all be relevant:

   (i) the law governing the underlying debt;
  (ii) the law of the place of incorporation or residence of the borrower or any guarantor;
 (iii) the law to which the buyer or sub-participant is subject;
 (iv) the law of the place where the debt is to be paid;
  (v) the law applicable to any other parties to the loan—eg the law of incorporation of the agent bank;
 (vi) the law of the place(s) in which any secondary market operates.

36. On the whole, novation and assignment are more likely than sub-participation to be affected by local law considerations.

37. Issues which may arise include:

  (i) *priorities* may be forfeited in some jurisdictions if the transfer is by way of novation;
 (ii) *consents and notices* may be necessary to make the transfer fully effective; eg exchange control consents may need replacing if transfer is by novation or assignment;

(iii) *formalities* may need to be observed; this can be particularly important when the borrower is from a civil law country—for example, in France notice of assignment may need to be served by a 'huissier';

(iv) *withholding tax* may arise in relation to the buyer.

(b) Bankers' duty of confidentiality

38. The simple issue here is that, if a seller discloses to a buyer information about the borrower which was provided in connection with the loan, the seller may have breached its duty of confidentiality to the borrower unless the borrower has consented (in the loan agreement or otherwise) to such disclosure. In consequence, sellers have to exercise great care. Since this may have the effect of limiting the information available to buyers, it could help to ensure that buyers make their own independent credit assessment, which is very important as a matter of general prudence.

Appendix to the Annex

LAW OF PROPERTY ACT 1925

The following is the text of the relevant part of s 136 of the 1925 Act:

'136(1) Any absolute assignment by writing under the hand of the assignor (not purporting to be by way of charge only) of any debt or other legal thing in action, of which express notice in writing has been given to the debtor, trustee or other person from whom the assignor would have been entitled to claim such debt or thing in action, is effectual in law (subject to equities having priority over the right of the assignee) to pass and transfer from the date of such notice—

(a) the legal right to such debt or thing in action;
(b) all legal and other remedies for the same; and
(c) the power to give a good discharge for the same without the concurrence of the assignor.'

Appendix 3

Transfer of Mortgages

STATEMENT OF PRACTICE

1. The lender will not transfer a mortgage of residential property to a body outside its company group without the consent of the borrower obtained in accordance with this Statement.

2. The lender will not rely solely on any consent to the transfer of a mortgage which is contained in legal documents, unless the lender drew to the borrower's attention in the mortgage application form or by other means, before the mortgage was completed, the possibility that the mortgage might be transferred.

3. The lender may seek the borrower's *general* consent to transfer of his mortgage. For new mortgages, this will be done before the mortgage is completed. For existing mortgages on which general consent has not previously been given this will be done by individual approaches to the existing borrowers concerned, giving them a reasonable opportunity to decline to give their consent. Any transfer made under a borrower's general consent will be carried out in a way which does not cause the borrower to lose his entitlement to mortgage interest tax relief at source (MIRAS); and it will be to a body which also adheres to this Statement of Practice on the transfer of mortgages.

4. Notwithstanding any general consent which the borrower may have given, the lender will seek the borrower's *specific* consent to any transfer under which the lender would cease to:

(i) exercise whatever discretion in the setting of the mortgage interest rate is allowed under the mortgage; *or*
(ii) determine the conduct of relations with borrowers whose mortgage payments are seriously in arrear;

unless the special conditions set out in note 2 below are met.

5. Before seeking either specific or general consent from the borrower, the lender will provide sufficient information as will enable the borrower to make an informed decision as set out in the Appendix.

Notes

1. This Statement of Practice is not intended to prevent:

  (i) transfers of mortgages *within* the lender's company group;

 (ii) the employment of an agent to manage the mortgages, so long as control of decisions on the two key matters referred to in paragraph 4 are kept in the hands of the original lender; or

(iii) transfers connected with the making of further advances to the borrower; or

(iv) the transfer of a mortgage in a way which departs from this Statement of Practice, if the lender claims to face serious business difficulties.

2. Transfers may proceed under a *general* consent if:

 (i) there is an agreement under which the original lender continues to conduct arrears cases as the agent of the transferee, and the agreement specifies that the transferee's policy on handling arrears will be identical to that of the original lender; and

(ii) the agreement also specifies that the transferee's policy in exercising any discretion in setting of mortgage interest rates will be identical to that of the original lender.

Appendix

INFORMATION TO BORROWERS

General consents

When seeking the borrower's *general* consent to the transfer of his mortgage, as described in paragraph 3 of the Statement of Practice, the lender will provide a clear explanation of the implications of the transfer of the mortgage for the borrower.

Where there is to be or may be an arrangement under which the original lender will service the mortgage as an agent of any transferee, this explanation will confirm that the transferee's policy on the handling of arrears and setting of mortgage interest rates will be the same as the original lender's, and that the original lender will handle arrears as its agent. It will also specify a minimum length of time for which any agency agreement will be effective (subject to the satisfactory performance of the agent).

Specific consents

When seeking the borrower's *specific* consent to the transfer of his mortgage, as described in paragraph 4 of the Statement of Practice, the lender will provide the borrower with the following information:

 (i) the name and address of the intended transferee, and of any holding company, if applicable;
 (ii) a description of the intended transferee and of his business, including details of how long he has been in operation, and of his experience in the management of mortgages;
 (iii) an explanation of the arrangements which will apply for the setting of the mortgage interest rate and for making normal repayments if the transfer takes place.

In addition it is recommended that lenders should include with this information a statement of the intended transferee's policy in dealing with cases of arrears and default. This may, of necessity, have to be couched in general terms, and may contain a statement to the effect that cases have to be considered in the light of their individual circumstances.

Index